A HISTORY OF GRIMSBY

UNIVERSITY OF HULL PUBLICATIONS

A HISTORY OF
GRIMSBY

Edward Gillett

Published for the UNIVERSITY OF HULL *by the*
OXFORD UNIVERSITY PRESS
LONDON   NEW YORK   TORONTO
1970

Oxford University Press, Ely House, London W. 1

GLASGOW NEW YORK TORONTO MELBOURNE WELLINGTON
CAPE TOWN SALISBURY IBADAN NAIROBI DAR ES SALAAM LUSAKA ADDIS ABABA
BOMBAY CALCUTTA MADRAS KARACHI LAHORE DACCA
KUALA LUMPUR HONG KONG TOKYO

© *University of Hull 1970*

DA
690
G85
G54
1970

*Printed in Great Britain by
Butler & Tanner Ltd., Frome and London*

Preface and Acknowledgments

More than thirty years ago, as a research student, I was directed by Dr. F. W. Brooks to look at the Grimsby archives and was greatly impressed with their range and with the need for a history of the town which would take them into account. Other duties prevented me from doing anything about this until 1952 when I was appointed honorary archivist to Grimsby Corporation. The prospect of producing a history seemed remote until a few years ago when it became clear that some co-operation between the Corporation and the Publications Committee of the University of Hull might be possible for this purpose. This present work is partly the result of such co-operation for which I am most deeply grateful to both bodies. I owe a great deal also to the help and advice received from friends and colleagues, among whom I must especially name Dr. F. W. Brooks, Dr. Philip Larkin, University Librarian and Secretary to the Publications Committee, Mr. L. W. Heeler and Mr. F. W. Ward, successively Town Clerks of Grimsby, Mr. E. H. Trevitt, Borough Librarian, Mrs. J. Varley, Lincolnshire County Archivist, Dr. L. Hotson, Mr. P. J. Shaw, Mrs. Dorothy Owen, Dr. Gordon Jackson, Mr. T. H. Storey, Mr. F. Walsham and Mr. E. Caborn; and to the late Miss L. Greenfield and the late Rev. A. C. Sinclair. I am particularly grateful to Mr. A. M. Gibbon and Mr. T. H. Storey for reading the proofs. Mr. D. Waite made the maps.

The notes at the end of each chapter, indicated by numbered references in the text, consist exclusively of lists of sources.

E. G.

Grimsby
December 1969

Contents

	Preface and Acknowledgments	v
	Key to Abbreviations	ix
I	The Site and Origins of the Borough	1
II	The Haven and Foreign Trade	19
III	Medieval Fishing and Coastal Trade	31
IV	Piracy, Magnates and Decline	48
V	Monks, Friars, Nuns and Churches	69
VI	The Reformation and the Gentry	86
VII	The Town in the Sixteenth Century	98
VIII	Holles, the Haven and the Civil War	120
IX	Restoration and Electioneering	133
X	The Parliamentary Borough 1688–1782	144
XI	Returning Prosperity	155
XII	The French War and the Growth of the Town	169
XIII	The Last Days of Corruption	193
XIV	The New Corporation and the Docks	212
XV	The Arrival of the Smacks	228
XVI	Police and Public Order	236
XVII	Smacks, Apprentices and Owners	247
XVIII	The County Borough	276
	Postscript: the Twentieth Century	291
	Statistical tables:	
	1. Population and Fishing	301
	2. Apprentices imprisoned	302
	3. Grimsby shipping 1814–1960	303
	Appendixes:	
	I. Early Parliamentary History	304
	II. The Grammar School	308
	Index	309

Illustrations

facing page

1. Post-mill, Cartergate, on the town side of the route taken a few years later by the line to New Holland 16
2. St. James's Church before restoration, from the west end, with its eighteenth-century aisle windows and the old town hall and market place on the extreme right 80
3. Old town hall and market place from roof of the Corn Exchange, c. 1860. This town hall, an eighteenth-century brick structure, including a gaol, stood on the site of the fourteenth-century timber-framed hall 148
4. Norwegian ice-barques in dock at Grimsby at the time of the 1897 Jubilee 230
5. An early steam trawler, the *Median*, with the bridge and wheel-house aft 272

Maps
(*at end*)

Grimsby and Medieval Lincolnshire
Medieval Grimsby
Grimsby in 1625
Grimsby in 1840
The Growth of Grimsby
Grimsby and the Docks 1960

Key to Abbreviations

In the notes on sources, the following abbreviations have been used.

1. *Manuscript sources*

Those in the Public Record Office have the prefix PRO and those in the Lincolnshire Archives Office the prefix LAO. All other manuscript sources are in the Grimsby archives, as follows:

Chamberlains—Chamberlains rolls and draft accounts.
CB (Misc.)—Miscellaneous and fragmentary court books.
CRG—Court Rolls.
Court Leet—16th-century court leet verdicts and by-laws.
Extent—Bailiffs extent books, 1491 and 1547.
Fines—Final Concords.
GCB—Court Books.
Letters—Letters described in HMC as 'Royal and other letters'.
LBH—Minutes of the Local Board of Health.
MB—Minute Book, Council and General Purposes.
MB(WC)—Minute Book, Watch Committee.
MB(SA)—Minute Book, Urban Sanitary Authority.
Ordinances—Ordinances of 1498 and temp. Elizabeth.
SP—Sessions Papers.
... to Moore—Correspondence of Arthur Moore.
TC—Tennyson Correspondence.
Turnpike—Minute Book of the Grimsby-Wold Newton Turnpike.

2. *Printed sources*

APC—Acts of the Privy Council (new series).
CCR—Calendar of Close Rolls.
CPR—Calendar of Patent Rolls.
CSPD—Calendar of State Papers (Domestic).
CJ—Commons Journals.
CMD—Report of a committee to inquire into and report whether any and what legislation is desirable with a view to placing the relations between owners, masters and crews of fishing vessels on a more satisfactory basis ... Cmd. 3432, 1883.
Election Minutes—House of Commons: Great Grimsby Election Committee, Minutes of Evidence ... ordered to be printed 22nd April 1793.
HMC—Reports of the Historical Manuscripts Commission. Where not otherwise stated the reference is to 14th Report, Appendix, part viii.

Key to Abbreviations

HCP—House of Commons Papers, No. 377 (1893), Minutes of Evidence.
G. Gaz.—*Grimsby Gazette*.
G. News—*Grimsby News*.
G. Obs.—*Grimsby Observer*.
LAAS—Reports of the Lincolnshire Architectural and Archaeological Society.
LPHVIII—Letters and Papers, Foreign and Domestic, of the Reign of Henry VIII.
LNQ—Lincolnshire Notes and Queries.
LRS—Lincoln Record Society.
LRSM—Lincoln, Rutland and Stamford Mercury.
Rot. Hund.—*Rotuli Hundredorum*, Record Commissioners, 1831.
VCH—The Victoria History of the County of Lincoln, Vol. II.

The above are descriptions of abbreviations, not of all sources used. Other sources are given their full title in the notes at the end of each chapter, and in these notes nothing other than information as to sources is given.

I

The Site and Origins of the Borough

At the end of the middle ages Grimsby lay on a flat, low-lying peninsula, extending northwards to the tidal waters of the haven and hemmed in by salt marshes on the east and west sides which extended as far south as the Salt Ings on the west, where the Grimsby Town Cricket Club now has its ground, and on the east side of the peninsula to an area between the abbey and Weelsby, of which the People's Park now forms part. The town was connected with the rest of Lincolnshire by a single road running north and south, which is now Bargate. Near the nunnery, where the College of Technology now stands, the road was flanked by ditches and willows, with the chapel of St. Andrew, formerly served by a hermit, a little further north. Then, as now, the road split into three branches, which had perhaps originated as separate pathways to the haven from an early settlement near the corn fields.[1]

The buildings of the town began at this junction of roads, and the streets extended as far as the two branches of the haven in a pattern not materially different from that of the present except in a few places where it was altered by the railway in 1847–8. The older branch of the haven formed the eastern boundary of the built-up area and was crossed by Simwhite-bridge, where the River-head now is, and a little further south by Holm Bridge. Certainly the latter, and probably both bridges, were of timber. The northern boundary of the built-up area was formed by the West Haven. Probably there had always been a stream there, but this part of the haven was constructed in the fourteenth century. It was crossed by the Stone-bridge in Flottergate, and a little further to the east by Carterbrigge, which ceased to exist in the sixteenth or seventeenth century. Between these two bridges the stream was called Burncreek, and was probably a good source of fresh water, since no one was allowed to wash clothes in it.[2]

Though much of the street pattern survives, the church of St. James is the only architectural survival from these times. But the sites of other buildings are known, and something of their appearance may be conjectured. At the west side of Cartergate, near the present level-crossing, was the Franciscan Friary. The Augustinian priory lay between the West Haven, Flottergate and Sanctuary Lane, near the Stone-bridge. Beyond the Stone-bridge, the Burgh-dike crossed Flottergate. By the end of the middle ages it was known only as a common sewer, but its name, and the fact that it can also be traced on the south side of the town, show that it was probably the defensive ditch inside which the earliest settlement had been made near the haven.[3]

A stone cross stood in the market place near the prior of Ormsby's house and the town hall. The town hall stood in the market place. The burgesses already had a common hall in 1286 when they joined with other Lincolnshire people to petition the pope for the canonisation of Robert Grosseteste, assembling in their hall for this purpose. It was still in use in 1391, two years after the decision had been made to build a new town hall and gaol. Dunghills must have been heaped against the walls of the old hall, since they had to be removed when the foundations were dug for the new one, which was completed by 1395. It was a timber-framed structure, open to the market on the ground floor, with the hall above. The walls were partly of mud tempered with sand and plaster, and partly of brick from Beverley, and the roof was of tiles, also brought from Beverley by boat. In course of time the spaces under the hall came to be filled with stalls, shops and a dwelling house, occupied in 1507 by the town clerk. On rare occasions the town hall was called the Guildhall (*Guyhalda*), but the guilds were of little importance and the use of the name was infrequent.[4]

There were few secular buildings as solid as the town hall. Most were thatched with reeds gathered from the marshes, and were of post-and-truss construction. When John Bayous dismantled his house at a site called *Pogrounde* in 1452 another man came and stole the timbers. He can hardly have carted them away, since normally carts were not used inside the town. He must literally have carried the house away; and it was not at all unusual for a house to be taken down and re-erected on a different site. But there were some substantial buildings. There were tiles on Isabel atte Wode's house in 1391, because she complained that they were damaged by ball games, and in 1369 William de Grymesby ordered 8,000 slate-tiles from Knottingley for a roof of approximately 40 feet by 80 feet. These cannot have been typical houses. Most were comparatively flimsy structures, and there was much open space inside the town, though in some parts the frontages were so crowded that there were complaints of the water from the roof of one house dripping on to the next.[5]

The Site and Origins of the Borough 3

Brick had been used in the town as early as the fourteenth century. By the end of the fifteenth century part of the Rayner-Chantry house was of brick, brick chimneys were being added to older houses, and one or two inhabitants were bricklayers. For a structure of any importance, however, timber was still the basic material, though trees of suitable growth were becoming rare within a reasonable distance. Two water mills were constructed on the West Haven in 1424–5, and temporary dams were made at the Stone-bridge and Carterbrigge. All the larger timber for this work came from Balne near Doncaster, where the master carpenter and others rode to view it before it was bought. It was loaded into three keels and came to Grimsby through Snaith and along the Aire and Ouse, a journey of sixty miles or more. When timber was needed to repair a mill it came along the Ancholme from Broughton and travelled at least thirty miles.[6]

When the new mills were made on either side of the West Haven they were linked by a new bridge called Milnebrigge which probably took the place of the old Carterbrigge. The lessee of the mill was allowed to erect bars at the bridge and keep them locked except for those who needed to come through with their carts, though at most times the use of carts inside the town was severely restricted in order to protect the pavement. The pavement was not, of course, the footway but the metalled portion of the road. The marshy site of the town made it necessary in almost every year to spend a certain amount on road repairs. The chamberlains of 1421–2, for example, spent 42s. 6d. on paving in various places, and in some years an exceptional effort was made and a committee elected to assist the chamberlains with road repairs. This was expenditure met out of borough funds, and there were also occasional windfalls from wills as in 1465 when Agnes Burton left £6 for the roads. But, as a general rule, the roads were reserved for horses and foot passengers. William Graynesby was fined 40s. in 1423 for breaking the pavement by bringing a cart shod with iron on to it many times. The offence was serious and the fine heavy in proportion. An ordinance of 1476 re-stated the ancient custom. Each year the chamberlains were to make the bars according to custom, and especially at the Stone-bridge. At the south end of the town, if any cart came to the bars at Bryghowe* it was to be unloaded and the corn carried on horseback to the haven. Carts removing household goods could pass through the bars, but none with merchandise.

* These were probably near the junction of Bargate and Brighowgate where St. Mary's cross then stood.

At the Stone-bridge the bars could be opened only for those living north of the West Haven to bring corn, hay or thatch for their households. This amounted to a virtual exclusion of wheeled traffic from the town, but the state of the roads was always less than perfect. Encroachments by dunghills were constantly being presented and in 1501 the state of the highway in Deansgate was such that the servants of Alexander del See thought that they could dig two large pits for the repair of walls and leave them unfilled without this attracting unfavourable attention.[7]

The corn fields lay at the south end of the town and contained some 640 acres, of which 40 acres were still remembered to have been part of the king's demesne before the borough gained possession of the manor in the thirteenth century. The abbey had the largest holding, of 220 acres, Henry Grimsby had 100 acres, the Nuns 72 acres and Peter del See 80 acres. There were also seven holdings of more than five acres, and twelve of less than five acres. Both in the town and in the fields, much property was in the hands of outsiders. Some were nobles, such as the Earl of Westmorland, Lord Scrope and Lord Willoughby, Sir Richard Tunstall and Sir Martin del See. There were proprietors of lesser status who belonged to Patrington, Wrawby, Healing and no doubt others who cannot now be identified: and in addition to the religious houses of Grimsby itself, the nunnery of Orford (in Binbrook), the abbeys of Thornton, Newsham, Humberstone and Revesby, and the priories of Alvingham, Sixhills, Bullington, Newstead, Ormsby and Worksop held burgage tenements. Very often the town had the appearance of being a little self-governing republic, cut off from the rest of the world except for its trade. This pattern of land ownership alone shows that the borough had never been an island entire of itself, and never would be.[8]

And even now, five centuries or more after it first came into existence, the borough bore traces of its origin in a wider settlement group, or soke. The mayor and burgesses were still lords of a small manor at Swallow, though they were in danger of losing it through the encroachments of the Tailboys family. They had shown their sense of their predicament by refusing to admit a tenant to lands in the manor until he swore that he would never convey them to any gentleman. They had a manor at Bradley too, and here they were endangered by Lord Wells, though it would be the plebeian Wrights who would ultimately wrest it from them. And at Clee they still held their third manor, which they were never to lose entirely.

The Site and Origins of the Borough

But they were now near to losing everything which had once caused the town to flourish. Their independence, each year more and more limited by county magnates and justices of peace, was little more than nominal. The mayor might parade with the two silver maces carried before him,* and on occasion he could be a tyrant to his fellow burgesses. Against the great and wealthy, and against the misdoings of their servitors, he was usually powerless. The stocks, the pillory and the ducking stool† served only for the correction of much humbler people. Emot Marshall for leaving her master's service was put in the stocks, Katherine Wilson, a shipman's wife, was put in the pillory on a cart and drawn round the town as a common scold, a humble successor of the woman whom the burgesses had unjustly put in the tumbril in 1200 and for which they were fined ten marks by the king's itinerant justices. Elizabeth Brown was given a week to leave the town for keeping a brothel, and such expulsions, usually of women, were not uncommon. Perhaps these petty offenders seem more important than they really were, because occasionally the court rolls report their actual words and in a sense we almost hear them. One woman called another 'hure' and another produced the tantalising variant 'freshore'. A weaver, zealous for the closed shop, said to his neighbour 'John Brown, if thou work in Grimsby I shall break thee head across', and the previous night a man broke the doors and windows of a house in St. Marykirk lane, crying out 'Without thou let me in to lie with thee, I will break an arm or a leg of thee.'[9]

To deal with such outbreaks there were the bailiffs, the constables and the petty constables who formed the town watch. In 1404 there had been three petty constables for Brighowgate and Wellowgate, one for Deansgate, three for the market, one for Baxtergate, two for North St. Marygate and two for the district near the West Haven called *Somertymyng*. They performed their duties irregularly and ineffectively, though not without some danger. One night in 1434 the two men serving as the town watch tried to arrest Robert Tevelby, who drew a dagger and shot an arrow at them. They pursued him to a house near the haven and shot at him. It is hard to know what importance to attach to petty affrays of this kind. Certainly they were constantly being presented by the chamberlains. The fines were a source of

---

* Though re-made, they are still in use. They were bought in 1394–5, the larger from the executors of Richard Misen, a former mayor, for 23s. 4d., and the smaller from Roger del Dale, a former common sergeant, for 18s.

† This was at a place called *Cukstolpitt* in the market.

revenue, and it is more likely that the town, in the days of its decline, was losing no opportunity of adding to its depleted revenues than that violence was actually increasing. Nevertheless, after a long life, it often seemed that the borough was on the point of extinction; but it was to be saved by the perquisites of electioneering until the time came for it to be transformed by the docks, the railway and the fishing industry.[10]

The continuous history of Grimsby begins with the Scandinavian settlement, perhaps as early as 866 when the Danes attacked York. Writing about the middle of the twelfth century Gaimar mentions Grimsby in connection with this campaign.* The *Heimskringla*, on the other hand, makes no mention of the place, which it regards as part of Northumbria, until Eric Bloodaxe's conquest in 939. At this point, however, Snorri Sturluson also refers to the events of 866, adding that many place names in Northumbria, such as Grimsby, are Norwegian. The convergence of these two accounts seems to suggest 866 as the earliest ascertainable date in the history of the town.[11]

As yet, however, it may be premature to speak of a town. The earliest Scandinavian settlers valued Grimsby for its haven, a tidal creek off the Humber fed by springs of fresh water. In the early days of the borough, the inhabitants knew that their ancestors had come from the other side of the North Sea. Grim appeared on their earliest seal, and they apparently believed that he was buried in the town which he had founded. The stories which were current about Grim as early as the twelfth century cannot be taken as historical, though they probably contain a good deal of mutilated history. Gaimar knew them, and his version is that Gunter, King of Denmark, was slain in battle by King Arthur, Arthur being in the story, incidentally, because Gaimar knew the Anglo-Saxon Chronicle and could not find anywhere else to fit Havelock in as King of England. Havelock, he says, was Gunter's son, and on the death of Gunter, Grim fled with him to England. His ship was so damaged that he could only use its timbers for making a house. In his new home he lived by selling fish and salt. Havelock, under the name of Cuheran, was a cook in the service of a king named Edelsie at Lincoln, and was by him married to the true heiress Argentille, whom Edelsie wished to disinherit. Learning of his royal birth at Grimsby, Havelock crossed the sea and conquered Denmark, and then returned to take England from Edelsie.[12]

* 'More than twenty thousand went on foot. . . . At Grimsby they passed the Humber. . . . All went to York.'

The Site and Origins of the Borough

We also have, from the early part of the thirteenth century, the *Lai d'Haveloc*, which somewhat amplifies the local details. Here also Grim lived by fishing and by selling salt. He first gave the place its name. No one lived at the haven until he built the first house, from the wreckage of his ship, but soon he was joined by peasants from the surrounding country, and a town with a market grew up. In the late thirteenth-century English 'Lay of Havelok the Dane' we seem to be dealing with an independent and possibly more ancient tradition. Havelock is enough of a Christian to vow that he will found a house of black monks at Grimsby but still enough of a pagan to burn churches and strangle monks and nuns. His wife's name is now Goldeburgh, as it is on the ancient Grimsby seal also.[13]

In all this there seem to be shadows of real history. The centre of the fields of Grimsby lay half a mile south of the haven, and until the nineteenth century all the houses were near the haven rather than the fields. This is what we should expect if settlers coming from the sea and attracted by the possibilities of the haven were joined by peasants, as the *Lai* says, who were already settled in the district. There is nothing improbable in the story that Grim was a fugitive from Denmark, and although antiquaries are justly suspicious of houses said to be built from ship's timbers, Grim's house built from wreckage is no more incredible than the house at Ravenserod which was certainly built in this way. And the earliest inhabitants would be expected to trade in salt since little if any can have been produced in Holderness, while Grimsby lay towards the northern extremity of the Lincolnshire coastal salt industry.[14]

In Domesday Book Grimsby appears as shared between Drogo de Beureure, Ralf de Mortemer and the Bishop of Bayeux. The principal holding was that of the bishop. He had the customs and the ferry, rendering 40s. This holding, which appears to have included the haven had been worth £12 in 1066 and was now worth £30. The increased value may merely reflect the profit of a new toll taken by Losoard, obviously on behalf of the bishop.* On the sokeland of the manor, in Grimsby and in the adjacent hamlets of Clee, Itterby and Thrunscoe there were 55 sokemen and one villein Drogo de Beurere held no more than one bovate with four villeins, in Grimsby, as part of his manor of Weelsby. Ralph de Mortemer's holding was split between Grimsby and Swallow, six miles away on the Wolds. There was a church and a priest, more probably at Swallow than at Grimsby, since the church

---

* Losoard was the Bishop's man at Hemswell, Tealby and Rigsby.

of the former at the present day includes pre-Conquest work and the church of the latter does not. His mill, rendering 4s., could be the haven mill, and the ferry rendering 5s. was certainly at Grimsby. There was land for four and a half teams, most of which with Ralf's two teams in demesne, eleven villeins and ten bordars we may tentatively assign to Grimsby, and seven sokemen, most probably belonging to Grimsby.[15]

What the Bishop of Bayeux held at Grimsby had formerly been held by Rayner the Deacon who had fled overseas, and before him by Eiric, the only pre-Conquest landholder at Grimsby whose name is known with certainty. Turgot, who became Prior of Durham and Bishop of St. Andrews, was another fugitive, probably contemporary with Rayner, who reached Norway through Grimsby. He escaped by bribing the guards at Lincoln castle and hid himself in a Norwegian ship in the haven, at Grimsby, which happened to be carrying the Conqueror's ambassadors to Norway. He was pursued to Grimsby but not found when the ship was searched. When he came out of hiding, when the ship was at sea, the ambassadors demanded that he should be returned to England, but he reached the court of Olaf Haraldson in safety.[16]

This is one of several contexts in which post-Conquest Lincolnshire appears as a kind of remoter suburb of Norway. When a house of Augustinian canons was founded at Grimsby in the early twelfth century its dedication was to St. Olaf, King of Norway, as well as to St. Augustine. The Abbot of Grimsby, an Englishman, accompanied Stephen, the legate of Alexander III, to Norway and was able to draw his attention, on the homeward voyage, to the ability of St. Cuthbert to stop storms in the North Sea. A seal of the abbey was found on the coast of Norway in 1911.* In the *Orkneyingers Saga* Kali, at the age of fifteen, came with merchants from Bergen to Grimsby, where he met many men from Scotland, Norway and the Orkneys. They remained for five weeks with their ships drawn up on the mud of the haven.

> Weeks of grimmest walking five
> Have we waded through the mud;
> In mid-Grimsby where we were
> Was no want of mud and mire.

Among others he met Gillichrist who claimed that he was the son of Magnus Barefoot,† with kinsmen in Ireland.[17]

* The seal was placed in the Riksarkivet, Oslo.
† For Lincolnshire connections of Magnus Barefoot, Ordericus Vitalis, *Historia Ecclesiastica*, Book IX, Chapter VIII.

At the beginning of the twelfth century Grimsby already had more than one church. Henry I about the year 1114 granted the churches of Grimsby, which Osbert the sheriff had held, to Robert Bloet, Bishop of Lincoln. It seems safe to assume that these were the two parish churches of St. James and St. Mary, and that they already existed at the period of the episode described in the *Orkneyingers Saga*.

The Norwegian trade of Grimsby is mentioned in a charter of Henry II in favour of the citizens of Lincoln. All Norwegians coming to Grimsby or other ports of Lincolnshire were to pay their toll at Lincoln. Significantly, Grimsby is the only port actually named in this context. In 1162–3 William de Grimesbi was in Norway with a ship provided for that purpose, to buy hawks and gerfalcons* for the king. William de Bradela went with him.[18]

Apart from aids and tallages, Grimsby was now worth £111 a year to the crown. In 1158–9 Ralph, son of Drogo, accounted for £111 of the farm of Grimsby. This was called the new farm, but since the tithe of Grimsby with which Henry I endowed Wellow Abbey was £11, the farm was probably £111 about the year 1130. Half or more of the farm was probably accounted for by land in the soke of Grimsby, and some of the men who were assessed in 1167–8 for the aid to marry the king's daughter probably belonged to the soke rather than to the town. Alan of Laceby, assessed at 20s., was one of these, and Bernard Corveser's aid was two marks. The others who are named were each assessed at 20s. Three of them, Agemund, Orm and Grimkel, had Scandinavian names. The one other who is named was Berenger Ruffus. The lesser men of Grimsby were assessed collectively at two marks. The others were obviously the rich men of the town, and another was Brenting of Grimsby who in 1175–6 owed ten marks for licence to agree with David the merchant.[19]

In 1194 Grimsby, though without any charter, was sufficiently established as a borough for Roger de Lacy to make the Grimsby customs the basis of the liberties of his own borough of Pontefract. The customs of Grimsby are described in detail in the Pontefract charter and throw some light on the state of the former in the late twelfth century. There was almost complete freedom to buy and sell land, and the owner of any part of a toft had the same liberties as one who owned a whole toft. There is a reference to those who had built several houses on their tofts and let them to others—a clear indication of the growth of population and presumably of trade also. The burgesses had their

* Large falcons able to take herons.

own court, and except in pleas of the crown, could not be forced to go to any other court. They seem to have been allowed to select their own reeve each year, provided they were willing to pay the sheriff as much as the highest bidder. In the proceedings of their court, there was great insistence on absolute verbal exactness, and a burgess could so easily fail in his plea by unnecessarily adding to what he should say that we can see why in 1201 they were anxious to free themselves from *miskenning*—the liability to fail in any action through the most trivial verbal slip. A provision to the effect that any burgess should be free to take corn by sea or land wherever he wishes may mean that this was the most important commodity exported from Grimsby.

The burgesses of Grimsby appear as witnesses to a late Henry II charter. In 1198 Grimsby is called a borough and since Caistor, in the same context, is also called a borough, the Exchequer was obviously using the term somewhat loosely. Both, in fact, were part of their sokes,* each of which had fairly extensive autonomy. In both the king was in the habit of making grants to his servants. In 1175-6 William de Colevill was granted land worth £20 a year in the soke of Grimsby, and Haket of Rideford also had £20 a year in the soke. This latter became the Rideford manor at Irby-on-Humber, and Irby is heard of no more in connection with the soke, though the Grimsby manor at Swallow, the next village to the west, still survived in Tudor times. Royal grants progressively attenuated the soke, and increasingly Grimsby came to mean the town and its haven.[20]

In 1200 Ralph of Bradley received £80 to provide materials for a castle for the king at Grimsby. Work was in fact started but no trace of a castle has ever been discovered and all that can be determined as to its position is that it was on land which later belonged to the Templars. A royal castle would have been a serious threat to the customary liberties of the soke. In 1201 the men of Grimsby bought a charter of liberties. At Michaelmas 1201 they gave sixty marks and a palfrey so that they could enjoy the same liberties as the men of Northampton; and Ralph of Bradley gave forty marks, and a palfrey, to be freed of all responsibility for the castle. The work was abandoned and in 1215 Robert of Bassingburn, now the tenant of these lands in Grimsby formerly held by Ralph of Bradley gave twenty-eight marks for all the stone and lime intended for the king's castle at Grimsby. The relation between the castle and the first charter would thus seem to be obvious.[21]

* This Pipe Roll also refers to the customs of Scartho, which was part of the Grimsby soke.

The Site and Origins of the Borough

In the early part of 1201 John and his court were within easy reach of Grimsby. In January they were at Lincoln, Stow, Louth, Beverley, Immingham and Driffield. In February they were in Yorkshire. In January, with the court at Immingham, the nuns of Grimsby received a grant of the 27s. which they had been accustomed to render for their lands. The first charter of the borough was issued on 11 March 1201 at Nottingham, and on 15 March 1201 the burgesses received a second charter, issued at Geddington, granting them a fair of fifteen days to commence on 25 May each year. The first charter gave the burgesses the same liberties as those of Northampton in regard to pleas of the crown and the internal affairs of the borough. No burgess, unless he was a moneyer or a minister was to be impleaded outside the borough except in matters affecting land not inside the borough. There was to be no judicial duel, no *murdrum** fine, no scotales.† The men of Grimsby were to enjoy freedom from toll and lastage throughout the kingdom except in London. They were to have their court weekly, in which there was to be no *miskenning*, to hear pleas concerning all debts for which pledges had been given in Grimsby. The reeve could take distraints if any burgess was forced to pay toll.

The charter did not withdraw the borough from the sheriff's jurisdiction, nor allow the men to farm the town themselves. In 1207 they gave sixty marks and a palfrey to have their town in fee-farm‡ and for the first time accounted for the farm themselves for a whole year. (In 1160–1 they had accounted for the farm for one quarter.) They paid £70 6s. 4d., which was considerably less than the full farm. But they did not, in fact, farm the whole of the soke. Ralph of Bradley had land worth 60s. a year, the nuns land of 17s. a year, Geoffrey de Nevill land of £20 a year in Laceby and Geoffrey de Ver land of £20 a year in Scartho.[22]

The manor of Grimsby had usually been separate from the town and the soke and so continued even after the burgesses began to account directly for their farm. In 1160–1 the sheriff accounted for 103s. 8d. for the restocking of the manor and 23s. 7d. for work on the mill. The 1201 charter did not give the manor to the borough. In 1203 Walter of Laceby and William of Cotes gave £18 to have the farm of the toll

---

* *Murdrum:* a fine on the whole wapentake for any dead body found and not proved to be English.

† *Scot-ale:* an ale-drinking festival at which all had to be present and pay a contribution to the reeve or bailiff.

‡ If the town had been granted to them in fee-farm they would have enjoyed their privileges permanently so long as they paid the fee-farm rent.

and the mills of Grimsby with the soke for £50 a year. The men of Grimsby were to be free to come and go with their merchandise according to ancient custom, so plainly something more than merely the farm of the mills and manor was involved. Sometimes the burgesses were allowed to farm the demesne. In 1212–3, for instance, they were to be allowed to take their crops when the demesne was granted in fee-farm to Robert of Bassingburn. In 1217 the manor of Grimsby was granted to Robert de Vallibus to maintain himself in the king's service. The charter of 1227, which granted the borough in fee-farm to the men of the town merged the demesne and the manor in the borough and there were no further grants separating them.[23]

Though Grimsby did not even approach genuine independence before 1227, the charters purchased from John reinforced the traditional privileges derived from the soke. When in 1202 William the baker of Grimsby was appealed before the justices of assize at Lincoln, and did not come, the case was respited on account of the liberty of Grimsby. In 1218 we hear for the first time of a mayor. The men of Grimsby were ordered to have Baldwin, son of Robert of Grimsby as their mayor. At the Lincoln eyre of 1219 he was found not to have disseised Gilbert of his free tenement at Scartho. This was one of several Grimsby cases heard in 1219, but in 1226 the justices itinerant were ordered to go to Grimsby to hold assizes.[24]

In the civil war at the end of the reign of John William of Wagen', Reiner the merchant, Reginald of Kanondic' and Godfrey, son of Thoye were taken as hostages but were released in 1216 when the men of Grimsby made fine with two palfreys and £100. John was never in Grimsby until the very end of his reign though in 1203 his hunt was transported from Knaresborough to Grimsby. On 3 October 1216 he issued letters patent at Grimsby giving safe conduct to two ships which had arrived from Norway. With John dead, Grimsby was granted by Prince Louis in November 1216 to William of Huntingfield until he should have land elsewhere to the annual value of £100. The grant never took effect, and on the defeat of the barons, William went for a time on crusade.[25]

In 1206 the burgesses were to have had their town in fee-farm, to enjoy those liberties which they had formerly had, to be answerable to the sheriff only for pleas of the crown, and to have all this embodied in a charter, which they never received. It was not until June 1227 that they obtained a charter granting the town in fee-farm at a rent of £111 per year. They never, in practice, seem to have paid the full sum, the

The Site and Origins of the Borough 13

value of lands in the soke at Laceby, Bradley, Little Cotes and Scartho not actually held by the borough being deducted from the rent. A third charter, in 1256, in effect recognised the permanent cession of most of the lands in the soke by reducing the fee-farm rent to £50 per year. The burgesses were heavily in arrears with their payments in 1268 and had not paid off all the arrears by 1272. Philip, a former mayor, was committed to the Fleet but released on payment of 40s. fine.[26]

These financial embarrassments, unlike those which were to recur in the fifteenth century, were not the result of actual poverty but rather of local disturbances arising from the war at the end of the reign of Henry III. Geoffrey, son of Ralph of Bradley, was with Baldwin Wake at the sack of Lincoln. Sir Richard de Vilers was also a rebel, and his manor of Little Cotes was seized by Sir Robert de Neville. In 1267 Ralph of Bradley himself killed Ralph Wolway of Grimsby, and various depredations were said to have been committed against the men of Grimsby both in the town and elsewhere. It seems likely that about this time the burgesses contemplated defending their town with a wall. There is no trace of a wall, and no mention of one in the borough archives which, however, do not commence until a century later; but the Burgh-dike appears in many scattered references of the fourteenth, fifteenth and sixteenth centuries, and was no doubt originally constructed as a defence for the inner, built-up part of the town.[27]

If in fact the borough required no more than a ditch for its defence, it was nevertheless throughout the middle ages deeply implicated in violence and coercion, which usually happened at sea, or elsewhere at a considerable distance from the town, so that it was pointless to rely on fixed defences. As we shall see, much heavier reliance had to be placed on the cultivation of correct relations with those who were in a position to harm the town. But violence was always in the background. In 1228 the Bishop-elect of Orkney was killed at Grimsby and Abraham le Mariner had letters of safe-conduct to sail to London with the longship in which the Bishop had come to Grimsby. In the same year William of Briggeho (a Grimsby name), was hanged at York because he was involved in piracy, off Sandwich, against a ship owned by William Belemund. The fact that both the pirate and the shipowner belonged to Grimsby, and that the goods were afterwards sold there, suggests a considerable degree of local anarchy.[28]

Nevertheless the community of interest among the burgesses was strong enough to make it exceptional for royal intervention to be sought in local disputes. Gilbert Reyner complained in 1286 that he had been assaulted by William, John and Philip Fraunk; but they had already been bound to keep the peace and were members of a family with estates at Brigsley and elsewhere in the county as well as enjoying a dominant position in the town.[29]

The jurors whose verdict is given in the Hundred Rolls do not complain of violence by their fellow townsmen. It was something which they could settle among themselves. They do complain of violence by their more powerful neighbours. Philip de Gurneys, bailiff of Hugh de Neville at Laceby, arrested a cart belonging to William, son of Benedict, with 3,000 herrings. They were left to rot and William was imprisoned for a day and a night without food or water. The Neville's soon ceased to be lords of the manor in Laceby which had formed part of the soke. When the jurors gave their verdict, Sir Walter de la Linde held the manor. His steward, John Malet, also imprisoned Grimsby men and left their herrings to rot. His men, and the men of Gilbert of Little Cotes impeded men going from Grimsby to the haven of the Freshney, and took toll from them. Two men from North Thoresby assaulted Alan of Kirton in Grimsby market place, and through fear of the Earl of Lincoln and his bailiff the town could do nothing. For two years his bailiff at North Thoresby distrained goods passing to and from Grimsby. He also came to Waltham and seized the cart of Henry Ayer of Grimsby, in which his wife and his maid were travelling, and kept the cart and two horses until Henry Ayer and other burgesses redeemed them for ten marks. These were no doubt merely petty interferences with trade and traffic. An opportunity rarely arose for the borough to make a specific complaint with any hope of success. Instead, it was forced to accommodate itself to an environment in which many people were much more powerful than a small medieval borough.[30]

The Knights Templars gave the Grimsby jurors particular cause for complaint in that they were both feudal magnates and spiritual persons with a substantial holding inside the borough. In 1185 they held one toft of the gift of William son of Ralf, and another of the gift of Ralf son of Dru. Some time in the middle of the thirteenth century, Alan le Aumener, also called Alan of Bassingburn, granted them land in Grimsby to the value of £4 15s. 0½d. per year, and by virtue of this grant they claimed a right to hold a court in the borough, to have the burgesses grind their corn exclusively at their windmill, and to demand mortuary dues from their tenants. They obtained papal letters citing

The Site and Origins of the Borough

the burgesses before their courts of Gloucester and Northumbria, against the royal prohibition. Soon the aggrieved burgesses were to see the disappearance of these enemies with the dissolution of the Templars, a dissolution which in Grimsby was so complete that all trace of their lands in the borough has disappeared, since here, in contradistinction to what happened in most of Lincolnshire, their lands were not transferred to the Hospitallers.[31]

Much of the Grimsby verdict in the Hundred Rolls concerns the trade and customs of the town, but to see this in its context we must go back to the beginning of the century. The relative importance of Grimsby can be judged from the duty of one-fifteenth charged in 1203-4 on the trade of the south and east coast ports. Grimsby paid £91, Boston £780, Lynn £651, London £836, Southampton £712 and Hull £344. Grimsby was thus a long way behind the leading ports, but ahead of Hedon, Scarborough, Yarmouth, Colchester and twenty-one other ports, including Immingham, Barton and Selby. There is no means of knowing which were the most important commodities in the Grimsby trade. Wine was imported, since in 1206 seven merchants paid heavy fines for selling wine illegally, and in 1228 some of this was certainly being imported from Spain. Timber was imported from Norway. In 1230 there were ten Norwegian ships in the port with timber. Two years previously the King of Norway had sent falcons and gerfalcons to Henry III with two clerical envoys, who were then licensed to take up to four hundred quarters of corn from Grimsby. There was oil and tar in the ship taken by pirates off Sandwich. The mayor and bailiffs of Grimsby were in the list of those who in 1228 were ordered to arrest goods of the men of Ghent. In 1230 a ship of Gravelines was arrested in the haven, and three German ships were similarly arrested in 1242. In 1203 the men of Grimsby paid five marks for the right to trade in dyed cloth as they had done in the time of Henry II.[32]

In 1201 the inhabitants of the town included a tanner, a mason, a weaver, a dyer, a thatcher, a smith and a miller. Their names are known simply because they had been tenants of those tofts which John confirmed to the Abbey, and it cannot be ascertained how many more there were. Obviously there were shipowners and mariners also. Three of them, William, son of Bode, Robert Boleman and Peter le Cogger took their ships from Portsmouth to St. Malo in the king's service in 1230.[33]

By the middle of the century there were disputes between the rich men and the poor concerning merchandise. The charter which was issued to compose these differences in 1258 remained a fundamental part of the law of the borough for five centuries. It was confirmed by a patent of Richard II in 1391, again by Henry VI in 1439, and yet again by Henry VIII in 1510. Attempts were made as late as the nineteenth century to enforce trading customs derived from this grant of 1258. The two things which stand out most clearly are that fish was the most important article of trade and that there was a strong egalitarian element in the trading customs highly unfavourable to the richer merchants. All herrings, fish and other merchandise were to be sold openly and in daylight, and any burgess present at the sale of the merchandise could claim a share in it. No more than one third of any cargo could be reserved for a burgess who had contracted with the shipper. The rest must be available for communal purchase. If French or Flemish fishermen reserved their catch for a particular burgess, he must make it available for sale to all his fellow burgesses. Otherwise it would be seized by the bailiffs on behalf of the community for the king's use, and the offending burgess would be enforced to pay a toll to the bailiffs of twelve pence for each last of herrings and the same for each hundred mullet.* All free men of the country present at the landing of herring or other fish or victuals should be free to buy, a provision which would seem to have been inconsistent with the special privilege accorded to burgesses.† No inhabitant of Grimsby was to send a boat to meet an incoming ship to effect a reservation of merchandise, under penalty of half a mark. All these provisions were primarily about fish caught in the open sea. In addition, no fish caught in the Humber was to be sold in boats or houses or anywhere except in the market, the penalty for offenders being a fine of half a mark or seven days in the stocks. The only other commodity named in the charter was corn, which no baker was to buy before the first hour. All debts were to be paid promptly. A creditor could inform the bailiffs who would then order the debtor to pay within three tides if he had bought fish, or within three days if he had bought corn or other merchandise. If he defaulted, the bailiffs must pay from the

* This is probably the origin of the 'commune lucrum' or 'common profit' which appears in later chamberlains' accounts.
† 1257 and 1258 were years of famine. The Louth Park Chronicler recorded that excessive rain at harvest time destroyed the crops. In the south there were cases of poisoning, probably because of rye tainted by ergot. Matthew Paris believed there was a plot by foreigners to poison all the nobles of England. (Annales Monastici (Rolls Series) 205, 208, 211, Matthew Paris, Chronica Majora V, 707.)

1. Post-mill, Cartergate, on the town side of the route taken a few years later by the line to New Holland

The Site and Origins of the Borough

common fund, and take twice the amount owed from the debtor. If a burgess owed any debt outside Grimsby and distraint was taken, in order to enforce payment, from another burgess, the bailiffs should order the burgess who owed the original debt to go and obtain release of the goods, where they had been distrained, by discharging his debt.[34]

These last two clauses were obviously intended to encourage merchants to trade in the borough by guaranteeing payment of their debts, and it seems likely that they were part of the primitive customs of the town. Nevertheless, the borough archives contain no evidence that this communal responsibility was ever enforced after the mid-fourteenth century, and since there are no court rolls earlier than that period, it is impossible to confirm that it was ever enforced. But the other customs, or modifications of them were enforced even in the seventeenth century. Whether they would be enforced or not depended on whether the richer or the poorer burgesses controlled the town, and the first we hear of offences against the charter by the rich men is in the Hundred Rolls verdicts.

The Grimsby jurors simply said that the borough had a charter of Henry III concerning merchandise and that it was being abused to the damage and confusion of the town and the countryside. Eleven men, five of whom were dead, were then named as principal offenders. The jurors of Bradley wapentake, in which Grimsby was situated, named eight men, four of whom, including William Fraunk, were not named by the Grimsby jurors. 'They have used their liberties concerning merchandise at their haven of Grimsby otherwise than they ought in that they do not allow the poor men of Grimsby to share with them in buying and selling according to the liberties granted to them.'[35]

William Fraunk was one of those who were found to have taken wool out of the kingdom without licence during the dispute with the Count of Flanders; but he took no more than four sacks, and the quantities reported as illegally exported from Grimsby were small by comparison with those in other parts of the county. A merchant of Cologne shipped fifty sacks with the king's licence, but the geographical position of Grimsby was not very favourable for the collection of wool, and the enforcement of the 1258 charter may have discouraged the accumulation* of capital.[36]

---

* In this connection it may be noted that in 1239 John de Ponte owed five marks to Samuel the Jew of Grimsby and the Exchequer of the Jews was to see that this was repaid at the rate of one mark a year. In the twelfth century there was another Grimsby Jew, Nehemiah.

NOTES

1. PRO, MPB, 14; GCB, 96v.
2. Chamberlains 18 Ric. II; CRG, 19 Hen. VII, 12 Oct.
3. GCB I, 180v.
4. CRG (3), 4 Hen. IV, 13 March; GCB I, 164v; LAAS (1915), 26; CRG, 14 Ric. II, Chamberlains 14 Ric. II, 7 Edw. IV; GCB, 126v, 166v, 354v.
5. CRG, 6 Hen. IV, 14 Ric. II, 43 Edw. III; CRG (4), 5 Hen. IV and (12), 12 Hen. VI.
6. GCB I, f. 95; Chamberlains 1424-5.
7. CRG, 26 Hen. VI, 19 April; GCB I, f. 9; CRG (2), 2 Hen. VI, 12 Oct.; GCB I, f. 41v; CRG, 15 Hen. VII, 7 April and 2 Hen. VII, 19 April; 17 Hen. VII, 22 April.
8. 1491 Extent in Grimsby Archives.
9. Chamberlains 18 Ric. II; GCB I, 60v; CRG, 24 Hen. VI, 15 and 16 Nov.; 3 Hen. VI, 25 Jan.; 33 Hen. VI, 29 May; 22 Edw. IV, 15 June; 7 Hen. VII.
10. CRG (17), 5 Hen. IV, 30 Oct.; 12 Hen. VI, June.
11. Gaimar, 'Estoire des Engleis', Rolls Series, 112. *Heimskringla* (Everyman Edition) I, 86.
12. LAO Glebe Terriers. Grimsby 1634. Bell, *Le Lai d'Haveloc and Gaimar's Haveloc Episode* (Manchester U.P. 1925), 78.
13. 'The Lay of Havelock the Dane', ed. Skeat, Early English Text Society. LRS XXII, 269.
14. J. R. Boyle, *Lost Towns of the Humber*. Inquisition taken at Grimsby 8 Sept. 1290.
15. LRS, 'Domesday Book and Lindsey Survey', 4/70, 71; 30/14; 36/1; 70/14.
16. Ibid., 70/13; Symeon of Durham, 'Historia Regum', Rolls Series, II, 202.
17. Reginald of Durham (Surtees Society) I, 108-9. 'Saga Book of the Viking Club' VIII, Part 2, 147. 'Orkneyingers Saga', Rolls Series, 62.
18. LRS, 'Registrum Antiquissimum' I, 43. Calendar of Charter Rolls II, 7. Pipe Roll Society VI, 28, 66.
19. Ibid., I, 64; XII, 60; Ibid., 22 Hen. II, 112.
20. F. M. Stenton, *Danelaw Charters*, 200. Pipe Roll Society, 10 Ric. I, 24 Hen. II, 7.
21. Pipe Roll Society, 2 John (Michaelmas 1200); 3 John (Michaelmas 1201); 8 John (Michaelmas 1206); Rotuli Chartarum, 177; Pipe Roll Society, 16 John, 154.
22. Pipe Roll Society, 8 John (Michaelmas 1206); Pipe Roll Society IV, 15.
23. Pipe Roll Society, 5 John (Michaelmas 1203). Madox, *Firma Burgi*, 251.
24. LRS XXII, 828. Selden Society LIII, 106, 30, 208, 417. *Rotuli Litterarum Clausarum* II, 141.
25. *Rotuli Litterarum Patentium* I, 168, 1866. British Museum, Harleian Charters, 43, 1377. Selden Society LIII, 495.
26. *Rotuli de Oblatis et Finibus*, 338. Grimsby Archives, 1227 charter; ibid., 1256 charter. Madox, *Firma Burgi*, 159, 184.
27. Calendar of Inquisitions (Misc.) I, 313, 799, 282. CRG, 10 Hen. VI, 4 Feb. 1432; CRG, 12 Hen. VI, 13 April 1434.
28. CPR (Hen. III) II, 197, I, 20, 23.
29. CPR (Edw. I) II, 206.
30. *Rot. Hund.*, 243a, 290a, 291. 292b.
31. B. A. Lees, *Records of the Templars in England in the Twelfth Century*, 115. *Rot. Hund.*, 290a. Grimsby Archives, 1491 Extent.
32. A. L. Poole, *Domesday Book to Magna Carta*, 96; Pipe Roll Society, 18 John; CCR (Hen. III) I, 71, 367, 80, 49, 366; CCR (Hen. III) IV, 433.
33. *Rotuli Chartarum*, 411; CPR (Hen. III) II, 156.
34. Calendar of Charter Rolls II, 14 and *Inspeximus* in Grimsby Archives, Patent of 15 Ric. II; HMC, 238.
35. *Rot. Hund.*, 263b, 291b.
36. *Rot. Hund.*, 293b; CCR (Hen. III), 159.

II

The Haven and Foreign Trade

The trade of Grimsby with Lincolnshire was of necessity largely confined to places accessible along the Humber, the Trent and the Witham. In 1196 the men of Lincoln paid 20s. and one falcon for licence to come to an agreement in a dispute about toll with the men of Grimsby. Herrings may very well have been taken to Lincoln by road, and the verdict given in the Hundred Rolls seems to concern this kind of trade. As mayor of Lincoln William Holgate had unjustly taken the horses of Grimsby men. But most of the other complaints about tolls on traffic from Grimsby relate to places on the Trent. Toll was unjustly taken at Torksey and at Nottingham. Robert of Dunham, as bailiff of William de Valence, took stallage at Gainsborough, and there was a similar exaction by Roger Lestrange at Kinnard's Ferry, which is now Owston Ferry. At East Stockwith the men of the Earl of Cornwall forced Grimsby ships to come to land, and took from them herrings, money and other valuables.[1]

The town could not have existed without this waterborne trade, and this, as well as more distant enterprises, depended on a harbour which had suited longships in the days of the Scandinavian settlement but which was much less suitable for ships of deeper draught. The haven, now largely obliterated by the construction of docks and the culverting of open water courses in the town, was fed by springs rising near the Humber estuary, and in the early middle ages was tidal to points now more than a mile from high-water mark. The course of the haven was roughly north to south. The navigable portion terminated at the present-day River-head in Victoria Street, but formerly had stretched several hundred yards further south along the eastern edge of the town. In 1201 the canons of Wellow had a water mill on the old haven outside their cemetery, which lay at the east end of the present-day Abbey Road. As it was then called the old haven it had presumably already ceased to be frequented by shipping, though the complex of roads which existed in that region to the south of the River-head shows its importance in the earliest history of the town. The course of the haven lay entirely inside the town, but there was also the haven of the

Freshney only a short distance beyond the boundary. At this time the Freshney entered the Humber without any diversion through the town. As long as the soke was a reality the burgesses were free to enjoy whatever accommodation it offered, since it lay inside the soke; but now the bulk of the soke had gone, and the burgesses found their jurisdiction largely confined to the borough. As the draught of ships increased, and as the low-water mark receded, it was necessary to do something about the only haven over which they could exercise authority.[2]

It is significant that the grants of tolls to Grimsby by Henry III in 1255 and 1261 were for amending the port as well as for paving and enclosing the town. In 1280 quayage was granted for three years. In the same year complaint was made to the king that the haven was so filled with mud and sand that ships could not use it. Inquiry was made whether it would be to the damage of anyone if the Freshney were diverted to flow into the haven. The jurors found that the site of the mill of William of Apeltrefeud (this was later known as the Haven Mill) would be affected. Sir Walter de la Lynde would lose the 2s. a year which he had been receiving from those who dried their nets on his land, and with three others would lose two and a half acres of pasture. If the new course of the Freshney was through Milnewell Creek, the men of Little Coates would need a bridge for cattle and carts to cross into a common of 200 acres. Unless the channel was well dug and with strong sluices, there would be tidal flooding at Great and Little Coates and Laceby. Plainly this means that the haven was completely filled by spring tides and that the burgesses were really complaining about the obstruction of the haven at neap tides. This is further borne out by the jurors' finding that the new channel would be 2,800 feet long, with a breadth of 240 feet, which must mean the breadth at the highest tides.[3]

Grimsby was compelled to wait another sixty years before anything drastic could be done, though nothing indicates the decay of trade in that period. The condition of the haven was something of a disadvantage in view of the competition which was now being felt from the new port and borough of Ravenserod which stood on Spurn point when Spurn and the Holderness coast were a mile or more to the east of their present position. As the anchorage at Ravenserod cannot have offered safety comparable with that of Grimsby, the complaints which the men of Grimsby made about the infringements of their privileges by those of Ravenserod must really have arisen from more liberal trading practices in the new port.[4]

The condition of the haven cannot have been as bad as a literal interpretation of the Grimsby complaints made it appear to be. In 1296–7, for example, 436 quarters of corn were sent out of Grimsby to Edward I's forces in Flanders in two ships, both named *Blythe*, and both belonging to Grimsby shipowners, Robert son of Alan of Grainthorpe and Peter Duraunt. In 1301 Grimsby was required to send a ship to join the king's forces at Berwick. The *Godyere* of Grimsby was one of the ships which in 1303 carried the tools and bolts for assembling a prefabricated bridge across the Forth during Edwards I's campaign in Scotland in that year.[5]

This is not the picture of a decaying port. Towards the middle of the fourteenth century the competition of Ravenserod was no longer feared and some of its inhabitants migrated to Grimsby. One of these was John of Cotes with his plot in Wellowgate and another was John atte See who gave land to the Grimsby Austin Friars in 1315. The diversion of the Freshney was still something to be desired, perhaps as much because it would put an end to a haven outside the jurisdiction of the borough as because of the good which it might do to the Grimsby haven. Another petition to this end was made in 1329, apparently without result. In 1335 the burgesses for the first time hinted that the haven was so obstructed that unless drastic measures were taken they might be unable to pay their fee-farm rent, a hint which they could safely give as the farm was no longer received directly by the crown. They petitioned to be allowed to appropriate the king's waste places in the town. In April 1341 they finally received a grant of the wastes and marshes, but they had already excavated a dock on the northern edge of the town. This, later known as the West Haven, is the only part of the medieval harbour which is still substantially intact. The wording of the 1341 verdict is equivocal, but there seems little doubt that the West Haven was constructed at this time. There are frequent references to it in court rolls. The piece of common pasture called 'Somertymyng' (which obviously means summer meadow) was cut by the new dock and most of the southern portion filled up by building, called 'Newbyggyng', with the increase in prosperity which the completed project brought about.[6]

With the fourteenth century, it is possible to examine in greater detail the voyages of Grimsby shipping overseas, and the places from which foreign shipping entered the haven. In 1310 William Toller was engaged in the Baltic trade. One of his ships, carrying corn to England from East Prussia, was wrecked in the port of Malestronde in Norway.

William Barel, the master of the ship, came to an agreement with the king's bailiff for the removal and safe keeping of the cargo, but ignoring this, the bailiff seized the cargo and imprisoned the crew for a year and a half. Geoffrey le Taverner of Grimsby carried a letter from Edward II to the King of Norway setting forth these facts, but was himself thrown into prison. Another ship of William Toller, laden with cloth from East Prussia was captured near the town of Westfale by Evel the Yonge, Arnald his brother and other pirates. It was found impossible to obtain restitution, the Archbishop of Cologne, the lord of the town, simply asserting that the malefactors were not to be found, though many burgesses of Grimsby saw them there. The sheriff of Norfolk and Suffolk was therefore commanded to seize goods of the men of Westfale to the value of £300 in order to obtain satisfaction for William Toller. In 1312 Robert Norton of Grimsby was one of the English merchants whose goods were seized at Stralsund in retaliation for the burning of a ship of Stralsund at Berwick on Tweed.[7]

From the very nature of medieval records, we hear more of the casualties suffered in the overseas trade of the town than of the successful voyages, which must have been much more usual. One man, at any rate, prospered and owned property in Dantzig. He was Robert Godebarne, concerning whom the mayor, and other burgesses sent a letter to Dantzig at the instigation of George Percy of Hull. In 1362 Godebarne had been a burgess of Grimsby. He was dead before 14 March 1391 when Percy was arraigned in the borough court charged with having fraudulently represented that he was heir to the whole of Godebarne's lands and goods in Dantzig. In addition he was charged with adding names of Grimsby burgesses not originally written in the letter testimonial issued on his behalf. He entered into a bond to the effect that before Michaelmas he would produce a letter of the Dantzig authorities testifying that the letter which he had taken to them was properly authenticated under the mayoral seal. He also demanded that his accuser should come forward and make his charge publicly. Accordingly, four days later, Walter Godebarne brought an action against him for fraud in that he had falsely represented himself to be the heir of Robert Godebarne who had died at Dantzig in Prussia, and so had sold his tenements and goods to the value of two hundred marks. Percy then changed the grounds of his defence, denying the competence of the court to adjudicate concerning matters transacted in Prussia.[8]

Percy seems to have had no doubt about his ability to go to Dantzig

The Haven and Foreign Trade 23

and return within six months, since he gave a bond for £40 that he would do so. There was a similar case in the borough court in November 1394 which also suggests a fairly frequent traffic between the Humber and East Prussia. Margaret, widow and executrix of Robert Tolson sued Robert Steresman for a debt of 25s. owed to her late husband. Steresman did not deny the debt, but said that he had made a contract with Tolson, which affected the debt, when they were in Dantzig at midsummer. The widow then agreed to modify her claim if he could produce in court John Rysom, John Sheldon and other yeomen (*valetti*) said to have been present at the making of the new contract.

John Mote of London hired John Clyens in Grimsby, at Easter 1445, to be master of a ship for a voyage from Grimsby to East Prussia, and back to the Orwell. Clyens broke his contract and Mote unsuccessfully sued him in the borough court, claiming £40 damages.[9]

Grimsby was not large enough to attract Hanseatic merchants in any numbers. Their connection with the town was often accidental and involuntary. In 1387 the mayor arrested a ship of Bremen which had reached Grimsby through an error of navigation when bound for Lynn. The pretext for the mayor's action was that the ship and merchandise were enemy goods, but the merchants were able to show that they were not enemies and had been trading with Lynn for five years. In 1434 Grimsby men were said to be implicated in piracy, along with men of Hull, against the *Marie Knyght* of Dantzig and another called *Cogship of Campe*. A jury empanelled at Grimsby found, not surprisingly that Henry Clyderow and other men of Grimsby had not taken part in the capture of any ship of Dantzig.[10]

Yet Baltic merchandise and men of German origin were well known in Grimsby. Amy Helyng claimed, in August 1392, that Peter Gotson came to her house and forcibly removed six 'firsparres'. In 1463 Richard Hall claimed six pounds of hemp from Robert Waltham, or an equal quantity of merchandise of Prussia. 'Dutchmen', often connected with the Hanse, frequently appear in the court rolls. Lutkyn Bernston 'de Hans' in 1437 sued Henry Johnson, Dutchman, in the borough court for a debt owed for herrings, and a crossbow, for taking twenty-two bowstaves, eight barrels of herrings and eight barrels of eels from his ship, and for breach of an agreement to pilot the ship to Lynn. There was a separate action between them, which went in favour of Lutkyn Bernston, concerning a pipe of red wine, a hogshead of white Gascon wine of the previous year's vintage and a bar of Bay salt.

c

Thomas Johnson, Dutchman, in 1461 sued Gelys Flawndour, a Fleming, for a debt of 20s. Antony Antonyson, merchant, of a ship called *Maryknyght*, and Hugh Cornelesson whom he sued for debt also appear to have been Germans. Hans Speryng, sued in 1431 by John Rasyn because he failed to deliver certain toys (*instrumenta joci*) called 'Joly Walte and Malkyng' was probably yet another German, perhaps domiciled in the town. The Dutchman said to have absconded from the service of John Dene (mayor in 1444, 1447 and 1452, coroner in 1450, 1451, 1459–63) also looks rather like a resident alien. Reginald Petir, a German (*Tutonicus*) who in 1491 paid a fine of 40s. to be made a burgess must have been either a resident, which seems unlikely since his name never again appears in the records, or a regular trader.[11]

Grimsby trade with the Low Countries, in spite of the absence of any notable trade in wool, figures more prominently than that with Germany and the Baltic. In 1355 the mayor and bailiffs arrested a small boat belonging to certain Flemings, laden with uncustomed wool. The collectors of customs at Hull were ordered to go to Grimsby to value and dispose of the boat and the wool, and to reward the mayor and bailiffs with a quarter of the proceeds. In retaliation, the Flemish owner, William Hert, procured the arrest at Lescluses of the ship of Ralph Utterby of Grimsby. Utterby then got his ship released by giving a bond for £20 with John Scardeburgh and John Tirwhit as sureties that he would either return with his ship or produce letters from the King of England testifying that the arrest of the wool was lawful. On the passage back to England, Utterby's ship was captured in the North Sea by the king's enemies. He was thus unable to return with the king's letters at the date specified, and Scardeburgh was made to forfeit £10 under the bond.[12]

But, as will be seen more fully when we consider the borough customs affecting the herring trade, peaceable intercourse with Flemings was much more usual. In 1434 Thomas Copeman, of Zeeland, had an action in the borough court against Thomas Lyster for breach of contract. In the previous year Henry Simondson was hired at Grimsby to pilot the *Christopher* of Yarmouth to Flanders, and afterwards sued the owners, John Candeler of Marham and William Snory for his wages. A jury awarded him 16s. 8d. William Wele, in 1375, brought an action against William Emanson for trespasses commited by one man from Blakeney and two Flemings who were under Emanson's 'hostage'. In 1400 William Wele was himself host for certain Flemings, along with William Duffeld who put their ships on the mud shore against the Freshney and also in the haven at 'Somertymyngs' at 'Fulsemerk'. The ships were afterwards dug out in such a manner as to obstruct navigation, so that Wele and Duffeld were fined 33s. 4d. Hugh Edon, in 1469, sought to have enrolled before the mayor his agreement under which he undertook to buy white and red herrings, tar and pitch, madder, oak planks, flax, iron, fruit and nuts, wax, pots and pans and glass from Peter Florenson, of Norwyk in Holland.[13]

From the rarity of reference in the borough archives, trade with France, except through Calais, was of smaller importance. In 1395 there was an action between Richard Barbour and Robert Burton arising from their joint purchase at Bordeaux of red wine to the value of £10, and other dealings in wine at Hull and Grimsby to a total of forty marks. John Takell hired Robert Spenser to be master of the *Margrite* for a voyage to the Bay of Biscay, and kept him waiting in Grimsby for fourteen weeks. John Edon and Henry Johnson had gone still further, since actions in which they were involved in 1424 had to be adjourned until their return from Castille. An action for debt in 1441 arose out of a loan of 33s. 4d. made by John Hampton to John Pye in Normandy. An apothecary and a merchant, on behalf of the society of the merchants of Vannes in Brittany, renounced any claim which they might have against William Richardson of Messingham or any other merchant of Grimsby by reason of the purchase of goods stolen from the merchants of Vannes. This looks much less like ordinary trade than like the piracy which we shall see was an outstanding feature of Grimsby seafaring in the fifteenth century. John Gascoigne, described as a Frenchman, was made a burgess in 1510 for a fine of 20s., with Christopher Ayscough esq., as his surety. And there can be no doubt about the nationality of Peryn Franchman who was sued for debt at Grimsby in 1432 by Robert Baynthorp of the Bail of Lincoln.[14]

Calais appears in connection with Grimsby fairly frequently. In the court roll for May 1390, with a marginal entry 'Copy of a certain letter on behalf of the commonalty sent to Calais for the removal of anchorage' there is enrolled a letter sent under the common seal by the mayor, bailiffs and burgesses of Grimsby to the mayor and bailiffs of Calais and to other ministers there, requesting that by virtue of their charter privileges, Grimsby burgesses should no longer be required to pay anchorage tolls at Calais. This obviously implies that Grimsby ships were often at Calais. William Wele, in 1390, brought an action under the Statute of Labourers against Matthew Hewson, alleging that he had hired Hewson for four years and that Hewson deserted from the ship in which he should have sailed to Calais under John Pog. In 1369 Roger atte More claimed £3 which Walter Stalyngburgh owed him for his share in a ship. Stalyngburgh acknowledged that he had agreed to buy a share, but claimed that the money was payable only when the ship returned from Calais, and she had not yet been there. Walter Westeby of Grimsby, merchant of the Staple of Calais, in 1444 had a tenement with a cellar in Watergate-strete at Calais. John Sheryffe (mayor in 1459 and 1470, coroner in 1468) was also a merchant of the Staple. The chamberlains in 1459 charged him with having broken the common ordinance by secretly buying herrings from a ship of Calais and afterwards conveying the rest of the merchandise outside the liberty. He was probably justified in his belief that his interest in the town was strong enough to enable him to ignore the terms of the 1258 charter, since a few months later he became mayor. His will, made in 1477, provided for his burial in the church of St. Mary at Calais and mentioned his land at Bradley and his Grimsby property in St. Mary-gate and Brighowgate.[15]

Berwick on Tweed and Scotland were probably of greater importance to Grimsby than was Calais. Men with sufficient capital to engage in the wool trade, of which Calais was the focus, were rare in Grimsby. At Berwick and north of the border there was usually a demand for the surplus corn of the Grimsby district, and in Grimsby there was a ready market for Scottish fish, including salmon, a traffic which was of sufficient importance to attract London fishmongers. Again, the smallness of Grimsby, and the absence of collectors of customs actually belonging to the port, was probably a particular attraction to Scots doubtful of whether trade with England was prohibited or possible at any particular time.[16]

Much of the Scots trade was for the supply of English forces in Scotland and the effects of warfare are much more visible in this trade than in any other in which Grimsby ships and merchants were engaged. In 1368 William Jonesson of Aberdeen, with merchandise from Lescluses, was forced by stress of whether to put into Grimsby. The mayor and bailiffs, in spite of the truce with Scotland, arrested the ship. Under the terms of the truce, ships of either nation could take refuge from storm or buy victuals in the ports of the other. The men of Grimsby maintained that Jonesson had not been driven in by storms, but that he really came to trade and tried to sell a pipe of wine brought ashore. The cargo also included woad, salt and peas, and money and silver to the value of £10. In spite of the fact that Jonesson resisted arrest, the mayor and bailiffs were ordered to restore his goods in accordance with the truce.[17]

In this instance the Grimsby men seem to have shown marked hostility to the Scots. Yet in other instances, Scots who had no reason to expect amity in England came to Grimsby apparently in the expectation that they would be safe there, or could overcome whatever force the local authorities were able to bring against them. In September 1377 there was an order to arrest five Scottish ships which had touched at Grimsby on their way to Scotland, with armour and provisions. These were probably the ships of John Mercer, who, having done acts of violence against English ships in the Channel, had come to Grimsby. He was arrested and brought before the King's Council. He had probably been unaware that one Grimsby man, Walter Wele, had good reason to hate him, since he had just lost a ship and goods valued at £200 to the Scots, the crew being killed. He petitioned in Parliament for compensation to be awarded to him from goods of the Scots lately arrested at Hull and Grimsby.[18]

Grimsby and Saltfleet Haven were among the places from which the export of corn to Scotland was prohibited in March 1386. William Helmesdale, or Elmesale as he was more usually called, loaded a ship at Grimsby with two hundred quarters of malt for export to Scotland, through the agency of a Scots friar. Ignoring the arrest by the mayor, he took the ship away by night, but was subsequently able to show that he had the authority of John Neville of Raby, one of the Wardens of the Marches to bring the malt to Scotland in part payment of the ransom of Ralph, Lord Greystoke who was a prisoner. Yet at the same time all Scots ships touching at Grimsby, Hull, York and Wells, were being arrested and all their goods, save for wool, delivered to Henry Percy, Earl of Northumberland, also a Warden of the Marches.[19]

Safe conducts were often thought necessary for trade with Scotland. William Edon, in October 1447, claimed 5s. from John Pye for his voyage to Scotland. Pye in his turn sued Thomas Somerby for breach of contract to sail to Aberdeen in the *Mary* of Boston. Pye was probably interested in fish. Somerby counter-claimed against him, alleging that Pye had represented that he held a safe conduct for Somerby's ship with twelve mariners and a cabin boy, whereas the document was actually for six mariner's and two merchants. In 1499 two Scots merchants, Andrew Maillyng and Andrew Swan produced a safe conduct from Henry VII for a ship or ships of 100 tons, with two masters, sixteen mariners, three cabin boys and all things necessary for defence.[20]

Any Scot could find himself in danger. Sir John Pygot, in 1441, alleged that John Byrde had assaulted Margaret, servant of himself and of his wife Elizabeth, taking articles from her to the value of £20. Byrde simply made the defence that she was a Scot and that he took her prisoner. Sir John Pygot was forced to abandon his action. It is not surprising that Agnes Clapam, another Scot, hired John Person for 4s. to escort her from Lincoln to Grimsby. She failed to pay him the 4s. which he claimed as his wages. Matthew Clerk, a Scot, was presented in the borough court, in 1451, for an assault on Richard Walton. John Almer, a chaplain, in 1448 assaulted John Vailans, a Scots priest, and Philip his clerk.[21]

This petty violence was not important in itself, but it does signify the fairly regular presence of Scots in Grimsby. Similar testimony can be derived from the case of Margaret Wykeham who called Stephen Palmer a thief and his wife, Ellen 'Scotyshmanhore', saying that a Scot had given her a knife as payment. Trade with Scotland was a usual feature of the medieval economy of Grimsby. The borough court rolls regularly record such cases as that of Robert Redburne who claimed 40d. from Simon Randeby for the freight of malt to Scotland, and of William Elmesale who sued John Fraunceys for 20s. which he owed him for his passage from Scotland in the ship of which John Shildon was the master. Shildon, incidentally, appears to have been one of those who was at Dantzig in 1394.[22]

In 1504 Andrew Wodd of Leith refused to accept payment in English money, saying it was but 'oaff'. John Hattlyff told him that he must accept it as money current in England, but as a Scots merchant and mariner Wodd said that he would not accept it even from the King of England himself.[23]

Fish, and especially salmon and herrings, were the main Scots commodities which interested Grimsby merchants. John Newport esq., several times mayor and member of parliament, in partnership with John Bramley, engaged John Williamson of South Shields, formerly of Hartlepool, to convey two or more lasts of salmon and two lasts of herrings in barrels, from Berwick to the quay at Newcastle. He delivered them outside the quay, so that they were forfeited, some time about August 1448, though it was not until 1465 that they found an opportunity of starting an action against him at Grimsby. In 1474 a fine of 40s. was imposed on Richard Bikeryng, one of the four quartermen, because he took two hundred fish from a Scots ship at the haven before the arrival of the ship had been reported to the mayor, contrary to the charter of merchandise, which was, of course, the 1258 charter.[24]

In the course of this trade, however, the charter of merchandise could be ignored if the merchants engaged in it were of sufficient standing. Hugh Edon was mayor five times, and coroner fourteen times, between 1454 and 1487. In 1469 he was able to have a bond enrolled in the mayor's court according to which Andrew Brayle and Andrew Crammy, both of Edinburgh, would at their next coming to Grimsby offer the whole of their merchandise to him and to his partners, Del See, Empryngham and Bele, at a lower price than they would offer it to anyone else. This was the means of compromising an action which the partners had started against Crammy and Brayle for their failure to deliver, according to contract, two thousand salt-fish, called mud-fish 'wel set and swete' at £10 per thousand, a last of salmon, 'full pakked, rede and swete' at 16s. per barrel, a last of oil at 12s. per barrel and six 'weye' of salt at 12s. per 'weye'. As additional compensation for breach of contract they also agreed to give a barrel of salmon and twelve couple of salt-fish. They were probably regular traders to Grimsby. In October of the same year they were back again when they were sued by Thomas Totehill and James Jervays for non-delivery of twelve 'wey' of salt at 12s. 6d. per wey.

NOTES

1. Pipe Roll Society, Chanceller's Roll, Richard I, 372; *Rot. Hund.*, 293b.
2. *Rotuli Chartarum*, 311; Calendar of Charter Rolls, II, 14.
3. CPR (Hen. III) IV, 96; V, 39; Dugdale: Draining and Imbanking, 147.
4. G. de Boer, Institute of British Geographers Transactions and Papers 1964, 71-81; Boyle, op. cit.
5. LRS XXVI, 184-9; CPR (Edw. I) III, 583; Brown, Colvin and Taylor, 'The King's Works' I, 416-7.
6. Grimsby Archives, Final Concords, 3, 1344. CPR (Edw. II) II, 294. Dugdale, loc. cit. CPR (Edw. III) III, 200; V, 17; Calendar of Inquisitions (Miscellaneous) II, 1759. Grimsby Archives, 1491 Extent.
7. CCR (Edw. II) I, 325, 349, 361, 451.
8. CRG, 14 Ric. II; Catalogue of Ancient Deeds III, C3706; CRG, 15 Ric. II.
9. CRG, 18 Ric. II; 24 Hen. VI, 21 April.
10. CCR (Ric. II) III, 225; CPR (Hen. VI) II, 357; CRG, 13 Hen. VI, 21 Sept.

11. CRG, 16 Ric. II, 17 August, 2 Edw. IV, 14 Feb.; LRS LVI, 68 (203); CRG, 15 Hen. VI, 16a; 1–2 Edw. IV, 2 Nov., 2 Edw. IV, 25 Sept. 1463; CRG, 10 Hen. VI, 3 Sept.; 29 Hen. VI, 9 Dec. 1450; GCB I, f. 43v.
12. CCR (Edw. III) X, 248.
13. CRG (14), 13 Hen. VI, 19 Jan.; CRG (13), 12 Hen. VI, 20 Oct.; CRG, 49 Edw. III; CRG, 2 Hen. IV, Oct.; GCB I, f. 3b.
14. CRG, 18 Ric. II, 16 March; CRG (2), 4 Hen. IV, 19 Dec.; CRG (4), 2 Hen. VI, 22 Feb.; (6), 2 Hen. VI, 20 June; CRG (21), 20–1 Hen. VI, 15 Nov.; CPR (1476–85), 831; GCB I, f. 91.
15. CRG, 13 Ric. II, 17 May; CCR (Edw. III) X, 291; CRG, 14 Ric. II; (3), 42 Edw. III; CCR (Hen. V) IV, 323; CRG (46), 37 Hen. VI, 30 Jan.; GCB I, f. 353.
16. Calendar of Inquisitions (Miscellaneous) I, 1739; CPR (Edw. II) I, 282; CPR (Edw. I) III, 227, 325; CPR (Edw. III) II, 552.
17. CCR (Edw. III) XII, 319.
18. CCR (Ric. II) I, 291, 320.
19. CCR (Ric. II) III, 413; II, 297; III, 487. CRG (38), 26 Hen. VI, 25 and 27 Oct. GCB I, f. 356.
20. CRG (21), 20–1 Hen. VI, 22 Nov.; 25 Hen. VI, 15 Dec.; (42), 30 Hen. VI: 27 Hen. VI, 25 Nov.; 9 Hen. VII.
21. CRG 14 Edw. IV; 3 Ric. II; (1a), 2 Hen. IV, Dec.
22. HMC, 272.
23. CRG, 8 Edw. IV, 16 March. GCB I, f. 62v.
24. CRG 5 Edw. IV, 24 Sept., 31 Oct.

III

Medieval Fishing and Coastal Trade

Fish was not merely important in connection with the trade between Scotland and the medieval borough. It predominated in most aspects of the Grimsby economy. The position of the town at the mouth of the Humber made it possible for herrings to be landed in good condition, and the proximity of so many local salt workings made it relatively economic to cure herrings and other fish, an advantage to the town probably somewhat diminished as the importation of foreign salt became more common. From the earliest times, the salt and fish trades seem to have been connected.

Court rolls and chamberlains rolls, until the sixteenth century, constantly refer to fish and fishing. In 1399 the borough spent 12s. for a thousand herrings and 6s. on six salt-fish sent to John Skipwith, the sheriff, at Cawthorpe. A 'butte', a 'kelyng' and a skate were also sent to him, and there was a similar gift of fish to the justices of peace at the Caistor Lent sessions. The tolls which the borough levied on fish yielded a substantial profit to the town. In 1390 an ordinance was passed that henceforth the bailiffs should take from each ship two codlings for each quarter of a hundred landed but should not take 'kelyngs'.* A toll was also levied on buyers of fish. In 1392-3 it amounted to 42s. 11d. and was apparently in respect of herrings only. In 1394-5 the collectors accounted for £12 5s. for fish and herrings sold at the haven. In 1402-3 the chamberlains accounted for £6 14s. 3d. including toll on forty lasts and 3,000 herrings landed between 4 October and 1 November at the rate of 3s. 4d. per last of the old custom (*de verteri consuetudine*) and toll on a much smaller quantity of fish landed during Lent. The toll in 1421-2 had sunk to 19s. 11d. for fresh herrings and other fish at the haven, and in 1424-5 to 19s. 6d. for herrings, 'buttes'† and skate. This decline probably reflects a less stringent attitude to tolls rather than an actual decline in trade, though it may be noted that as late as 1454 the bailiffs, by then the most financially straitened of the borough officers, tried to claim a toll of 2s. 4d. for 700 fish, which seems a high rate.[1]

* A kelyng was a large cod. The hundred was probably the long hundred of 120.
† Buttes were large flat fish (c.f. halibut, turbot).

Much of the fish landed at the haven was not caught by local fishermen. About 1190–6 the canons of Wellow were adjudged to pay to the canons of Bridlington ten marks for tithes which they wrongfully took, presumably at Grimsby, from Filey fishermen. In 1455 John Williamson, mariner, of Scarborough, had a leadline distrained, and forcibly resisted the distraint, for refusing to pay toll on red and white herrings and salt-fish. Allecok of Tetney, in October 1389, was allowed to sell herrings in the town on Saturday, in the morning and for domestic consumption only, and in contravention of the charter continued to sell them in the afternoon. There was, in fact, a constant conflict between fish merchants and the fishermen who landed their catch at Grimsby on the one hand, and the borough officers on the other, who were trying to maintain those local customs which were most to their advantage. In 1381 Simon Elynson bought four lasts of herring from a Scarborough ship before they had been officially viewed by the four quartermen. He was fined 40s. William Elmesale was charged with similarly buying eight lasts of herrings from a Scarborough ship, but was found to have done so lawfully, in the presence of the quartermen. William Paule bought four lasts from Thomas Bla, of Saltfleet Haven, about the same time, the sale being made in his house and upon his bench, contrary to the charter. It was therefore ordered that the herrings, valued at sixteen marks, should be seized and declared forfeit. Three lasts had been put in William Burton's house to be dried. The mayor, accompanied by the coroners, chamberlains and others went to this house and sought to view the fish, but William Burton locked the door against them, as did William Elmesale, who had taken one last for drying.[2]

Though the fishermen who brought their catches to Grimsby were strangers to the town, and in some measure at the mercy of local customs, they could on occasion appeal successfully to a universally accepted code. John Pog, for instance, in 1392 claimed that he could prove his case against the defendant, Thomas Lytherpole, by waging his law. Lytherpole answered 'that it is the usage in England that all fishermen are treated alike in profit and in loss and he should not be allowed to wage his law'. It was Lytherpole who won in this case. The local custom might be against him, but the town could not afford to alienate visiting shipmasters. Pog had been his host and had lent him his boat and otherwise assisted him to sell his catch. Lytherpole was unable to make a satisfactory sale, and then claimed that it was Pog's duty to provide him with salt to preserve his fish. The salt, according to Pog, was duly provided, and Lytherpole left his host without any reasonable cause.

A host could come into conflict with the borough by serving his alien guest too well. In September 1435 the chamberlains charged John Haven with causing herrings to be sold at too high a price. He was host to a Fleming who was selling herrings in the market at eight a penny. Haven came and told him not to sell more than six a penny, and tried to remove the herrings to his house when the mayor ordered them to be sold at the lower price. Similarly Thomas Pye spoke, as host, to a Fleming, who immediately put up the price of herring and mackerel: and Thomas Lyster secretly bought herrings at night from a Fleming in the sea-haven.[3,4]

The curing of herrings and their shipment to inland buyers was a constant feature in the life of the town. Those most active in the trade were usually the leading figures in the borough. In 1468 Richard Manfeld, William Est and John Cok were charged with the unlawful shipment of fish. Each had been mayor at least once. Contrary to the charter of merchandise, instead of using the common staith, they had dispatched 300 salt-fish, three barrels of herrings and two barrels of haddocks from the haven. John Cotes, mayor in 1378, sent 3,000 red herrings to Robert Bullington to be hung and dried in his house. On the day agreed for delivery of the cured herrings, Martinmas 1394, Bullington refused to give them up.[5]

At the town hall, in December 1390, John Hesilden hired Robert Perch to go to York for him with a letter to Robert Otteway and receive 15s. 4d. payable there for herrings supplied by Hesilden, and Robert's father, William Perch promised that the son would faithfully perform his task. But, instead, he not only failed to bring Hesilden his money but also committed such robberies (*latrocinia*) and other enormities at York that Hesilden's credit there was gravely damaged. He brought an action against the father in the Grimsby borough court and recovered the 15s. 4d. but was unable to show that his credit had suffered. Gilbert Smith, in 1393, sued Roger Megson of Burringham, for breach of an agreement to carry nine and a half lasts (probably about nineteen tons) of Smith's herrings to Dunham on Trent. The next day William Elmesale sued Megson for failure to carry nine lasts and one 'mays' of red herrings to Dunham. These are instances of herrings carried inland by water transport. Smaller quantities were also transported by road, though for much shorter distances. William Hosier, for example, sued John Doget for 18s. which he owed him since 1400 for herrings sent to Caistor. The significance of this local trade is also shown by the attitude of the justices of the peace. In 1385, sitting at Caistor, they found that William Patrington, of Grimsby, had forestalled four lasts of fresh herrings at Grimsby so that none of the country could be served. Twelve years later William Patrington was on the point of being outlawed in the King's Bench in proceedings arising from this offence. He also forestalled, with Robert Bolyngton and John atte Hall, the catch of twenty herring boats, amounting to 100 lasts, so that the men of the country could not buy their food. Robert and John Bolyngton one night in Grimsby Haven took ten lasts* of fresh herrings from a ship with their boats, so that men from Ludborough and other places in Lindsey could not buy herrings for their households. This interest of the county justices in the Grimsby fish trade was no doubt one of the principal reasons for the desire of the borough, never fully realised, to be exempted from their jurisdiction. The regulation of the trade by the justices was seen as a totally different thing from regulations made by borough ordinances, under the 1258 charter. In the former case it was to be expected that the needs of the consumer would be a significant factor. In the latter case, it was only the trading interests of the smaller as against the bigger merchants which were taken into account, and the household consumer, except perhaps in the town, was hardly considered at all.[6]

The trade at Grimsby nevertheless remained sufficiently attractive for a number of London fishmongers to take an interest in it. They are known mainly from scattered references in the court rolls to disputes in which they became involved while in Grimsby, but enough survives to give us some idea of how they were involved. John Pye appears to have been the one with the strongest connection, probably because he was a Londoner and a member of a local family. In 1447 he assaulted Thomas Somerby of Boston in Somerby's ship. Thomas Somerby was joined by Sir Robert Willoughby in his purely commercial litigation against Pye, and the parties agreed to submit to arbitration. The Pye family first appear in the records with the bond which John Pye of Grimsby, mariner, gave in 1424 to the rector of Scartho. Thomas Pye of Grimsby, merchant, was pardoned in 1428 for his outlawry, on surrendering to answer for a debt of £4 13s. 4d. owed to John Bury of London, fishmonger. In 1458 John Pye of London, fishmonger, summoned William Gabded in the borough court to account for the money which he had received as agent for the sale of between seventy

---

* A last was about 12,000 herrings, or 12 barrels of other fish.

and eighty barrels of salmon. He produced four sureties from Clee who were bound in 100 marks that they would produce Gabded to answer John Pye and William Grymesby, esq., Gabded seems to have been able to meet the claims against him. In November 1468 William Broune of London, fishmonger, assaulted John Laxton with a dagger and a year later Laxton had an action against him for debt. In 1473 Sir Robert Constable of Flamborough was awarded judgment against Thomas Norton, of London, fishmonger, for a debt of £8 6s. 8d., Norton having failed to appear within forty days of being summoned. Four men were appointed to value such goods as he had left in Grimsby, which were found to consist of seven barrels of oil and stockfish.[7]

Grimsby men were quite clearly much more involved with the trade in fish rather than in fishing at sea. No other conclusion is possible when one considers the rarity, with one important exception, in the borough records of references to fishing voyages by contrast with the relative frequency of those to other kinds of shipping. William Holm, in 1403, in the North Sea sold nets to William Brygham of Stallingborough, for 2s. Peter Curtays was owner of a vessel of which Haune Phelipson was master and John Howeson supplied ale, bacon and other victuals for a fishing voyage in the North Sea. It is quite possible that Curtays belonged to Clee, where the family was long established, rather than to Grimsby. Other references to fishing are on the whole more likely to refer to fish-traps than to deep-sea fishing.[8]

Between 1424 and 1449, however, there are references to fishing voyages to Iceland. John Bacon of Grimsby demanded in September 1424 that Richard Burton of Clee should return the leather apron which he had taken to Iceland. Geoffrey Haynson was in Iceland in July 1431 when Henry Laceby's action against him had to be adjourned for this reason. John Walker owed Robert Dawson 20d. for 'styrrage' to Iceland in 1423 or earlier. There were probably Icelanders occasionally in Grimsby, such as the Deryke Islandman who assaulted John Nicholas by punching him, and Nicholas Orknayman may very well have arrived in the same ship. William Smith owed William More 12d. for herring fishing with him in Lent, 1432, and at the beginning of Lent had received a sailing-stone, a primitive compass, from John Edon, for a voyage to Iceland. He was to have returned the sailing-stone and 3s. 4d. for its hire on his return to England. Edon claimed that he was offering to return a different and inferior sailing-stone. The same William Smith in 1449 sued William Est for 5s. 6d. which he owed him for his hire in Iceland and was himself sued by Richard Manfeld.

Manfeld had delivered £6 worth of salt in Grimsby which he was to take to Iceland for fishing and he was either to return it to Manfeld or give him salt-fish of the same value, which he failed to do. Edon, who lent the compass, Est, who had hired William Smith, and Manfeld, who provided him with salt, all occupied the office of mayor once at least between 1428 and 1450. Others were less identified with the control of borough affairs. Nothing more is known of Thomas Wodehouse who in 1451 sent two ships, the *Mary*, and the *James*, to Iceland and owed John Bayous, a Grimsby man; six marks for the king's custom. He was probably a stranger, as Bayous was unable to sue him until 1454. There was a similar difficulty with the claim of John Schepyng against William Brightwell of Cromer. It was not until 1435 that he was able to sue him for the 22s. of his wages which he had agreed to pay him six years previously for a voyage from Grimsby to Iceland.[9]

Some of the references in the borough records relating to fishing may indicate, as others certainly do, the practice of fishing from nets permanently attached to stakes in the Humber. William Hosier demanded from John Bacon the return of three lines lost in fishing. Since Bacon was interested in the Iceland fishery, these were probably lines used in fishing at sea. In other cases, however, deep-sea fishing probably does not come into the picture at all. In July 1392 a man from Clee was sued by the bailiffs for non-payment of his toll on fish, and in 1402 Hugh Brigg was charged with evading toll on bait carried through the town for fishermen of Clee. In each of these cases we may be dealing with men who were using nets fixed to stakes, since this was certainly done at Clee. John Urchanhede and Agnes his wife started Chancery proceedings against John Empryngham who wrongfully kept possession of three acres of meadow and a fishing place in Clee which should have descended to Agnes from her grandfather, Simon White. The jurors of Clee manor in 1434 presented that Richard Fulneby had acquired certain 'fysshegarthes' in the Humber by right of his wife. These were east of the Grimsby Haven. Others were near the entrance of the haven, or to the west of it. The chamberlains for 1402–3 received 8*d*. from two fishermen for spreadage of nets in the marsh, which seems to imply that they were drying nets taken in from one of these fish-garths. They were also called net-stands. Robert Baumburgh in 1450 was granted a lease for life, paying 6*d*. rent per year, of 'Blakman Netstonde', which took its name from the beacon called Blakeman at the entrance to the haven. About ten years later the borough gave a lease of the same net-stand, in the water of the

Humber, to Matthew Cok. The men of the manor of Clee claimed rights of wrock and waif as far as another fishery called 'Fauconernetstond'.[10]

Fishing from stakes could be a danger to navigation. A court roll of 1455 contains a copy of the verdict of a jury at Barton which dealt with dangers arising from stakes in the Humber and the Trent. Walter Duffeld was put in the town gaol and only released when his brother gave a bond for 100s. when it had been found in 1389 that he had encroached upon the Humber bank near west side of the haven with a fish-garth (*gardino piscatorio*). It had originally belonged to Thomas Berneston and over a period of twenty years Duffeld had moved it 300 fathoms.[11]

Newcastle coal was second only to fish in its importance in the life of the town. There was a constant traffic with the north-east coast, and men from Newcastle and Northumberland were often in Grimsby, as when John Couper of Newcastle one Sunday night assaulted the bailiffs in the performance of their office and threatened them with a poleaxe.[12]

It is quite clear that coal was brought to Grimsby from Newcastle and corn sent to Newcastle from the haven. Laurence Crak in June 1390 had four and a half quarters of corn and malt in a boat in the haven to be taken on board his ship, almost certainly for Newcastle, and not only refused to pay $2\frac{1}{4}d$. toll to the bailiffs but also made rescue when they arrested his boat. In 1437 William Thomesson of Newcastle, master of the *Mary*, loaded in the haven sixty quarters of corn for William Norton and eight quarters of barley for John Lytster, both also of Newcastle. The market was particularly good that year. Thomas Lytster was charged with engrossing corn and having three chambers for storing it. James Swyner of York, owner of the *Katerine* took on board ninety quarters of barley, peas and beans supplied by Grimsby men for shipment to Newcastle. In all seven men, including the Abbot of Wellow and John Wryght of Croxby had over 200 quarters of corn stored in various places in the town until it could be sent to Newcastle.[13]

Coal is one of the commodities most frequently mentioned in litigation at Grimsby, and until the sixteenth century there is no evidence that it was shipped from anywhere other than Newcastle. John Wright in 1474 was charged with selling sea coal in his house for 3d. a measure and then putting the price up to 4d. He claimed, successfully, that the custom of the borough did not apply to a sale made in his own house.

John Carter, in April 1379, was alleged to have stolen coal from William Elmesale to the value of five marks, probably from the ship from which Richard Magson stole a quarter of corn. Earlier in the same year Elmesale had a dispute with William Watkinson of Fulstow Marsh (now Marsh Chapel) about the carriage of coal from Grimsby to York and other goods from York to Grimsby. Elmesale's case was that Watkinson's keel went to York with only half the quantity of coal which could have been carried, and returned with insufficient merchandise. Watkinson's defence was that he took all the coal that was ready for him and that Elmesale's agent at York would supply him with no more goods than he brought. Thomas Day, one of the jurors, was challenged by the defendant on the grounds that as master of Elmesale's ship he could not be impartial. The bailiffs ordered the challenged juror to swear, but he refused and was fined for contempt. The rest of the jury gave a verdict for the plaintiff, not for the 20s. which he claimed but for 40d.[14]

Thomas Funteney lost a ship, the *Mary*, at Newcastle laden with coal in November 1390 through the negligence, he alleged, of Adam Hayton, the purser, who stayed on shore for a week after the coal was on board, without victualling the ship so that to avoid starvation the crew deserted. It was therefore through his negligence that the *Mary* grounded on 'Haukesnesse'. Earlier in the year the ship had been at Hull with wine, of which the purser sold one tun, for which the owner now summoned him to account. Robert Broune of Selby, in 1370, was owner of two shares in the *Mary*, presumably another *Mary*, and Thomas Ingson owned the third share. They also were jointly interested in the *Rodeship* which was at Newcastle for coal. A certain John Thorntonhous owed 6s. 8d. for his deliverance from prison at Newcastle. William Smith, interested also in Iceland and the herring fishery, failed to pay 5s. on behalf of Richard Manfeld to William Bakon at Newcastle.[15]

Grimsby was occasionally a port of call for ships between Newcastle and the south. Henry Smith of York, 'Wlman', and William Mayhew of Colchester engaged John Skynner of Shotley, Sussex, to be master of their ship, *Katerin*, to sail from Colchester to Newcastle. Storms in the North Sea in February 1424 forced the ship to shelter in the Humber, and the master brought her into Grimsby for repairs. Coal was occasionally transhipped from Grimsby to Colchester. In 1431 Henry Stalyngburgh was arrested at Colchester when he was in Henry Laceby's ship with coal. Generally speaking, however, Grimsby coastal

Medieval Fishing and Coastal Trade

trade was with the north, and some of the links with northern ports may have arisen in consequence of Grimsby ships putting in on voyages to and from Newcastle.[16]

The links with the north were strong enough to leave some evidence of an actual movement of population. Of the burgesses recorded in the fifteenth century, there are twelve with surnames derived from the northern counties,* as against forty-one derived from Lincolnshire place-names and fifteen from place-names of the East and West Ridings of Yorkshire. Some individuals can be identified. Andrew Bell, of North Shields, yeoman, became a Grimsby burgess in 1490, and Cuthbert Witton, admitted as burgess in 1485, was more probably from the north than from Lincolnshire. Occasionally it was necessary for a north-countryman to prove that he was English. Thomas Lytster in 1434 had to give a bond for £5 to be forfeited if he did not produce letters testimonial to the mayor showing the English birth of his servant, Robert Richmond, alleged to be a Scot. In 1492 the clerk of the court recorded that Thomas and Alexander Nicholson said that they were born at Doddington in Glendale and at Chatton, Northumberland. In 1455 Hugh Edon as mayor supplied letters testimonial for Robert Dauson to the effect that he was a liege of the King of England, and as son of John Dauson was baptised at Easington, County Durham. The Edon's themselves were probably from the north.[17]

There is also some evidence of migration from Grimsby to the north. John Hedely, mariner, formerly of Grimsby belonged to Whitby in 1487 when Stephen Newdyke paid £3 19s. to him on behalf of Alexander del See. William Bridde was hired in 1392 to work as a fuller at Newcastle for a year at a wage of 18d. per week without food, and half a mark for 'oversilver'. Robert Dauson, mariner, of Newcastle, formerly of Grimsby, owed five marks to William Smyth in 1457. He may have been the Robert Dauson for whom the mayor provided letters testimonial. Richard Manfeld, a former mayor, but outlawed at the time of his death died at Hartlepool in 1482-3.[18]

There was some trade with the East Riding and the Yorkshire coast towns, somewhat limited by the fact that they had little to offer which could not be obtained in Lincolnshire. Thomas Warde of Sewerby, fisher, was outlawed, and subsequently pardoned, in 1441, in the action brought against him by William Fosse of Grimsby, who also impleaded men of Flamborough, Withernsea and Hornsea Beck, most of

* Pelton, Edon, Ogle, Gaunce, Manfield, Copeland, Whittington, Whitworth, Witton, Seamer, Tyndale and Lilburn.

D

whom were seamen of one kind or another. The Humber towns, and especially Hull, figure very much more prominently in Grimsby trade. The ferry to Hull was in constant use. In 1398 William Wele and John Mumby complained that John Pogge, as mayor, was hindering them in their enjoyment of the ferry, under threats of imprisonment and confiscation. From time immemorial the men of Grimsby had enjoyed the right to have a ship or boat to ferry passengers, corn and other merchandise across the Humber. Wele and Mumby petitioned the crown, and the mayor was ordered to impose upon them no restriction not used in times past. This was in all probability a quarrel about the ferry monopoly claimed by the borough which leased to others the right to ply across the Humber. The dangers of the passage may be reflected in the case of Joan Barowe. In June 1475 she went down on her knees and prayed that Agnes Carter and the whole boatload should be drowned in the Humber before they reached Hull. By the end of the century the rent for the ferry had declined to 6s. 8d. a year, which reflects the decline of Grimsby trade which, as we shall see, was visible in most of its aspects in the latter part of the fifteenth century. The ferryman was to report all suspect persons or goods to the mayor. A burgess and his servants paid 1d. for the journey to Hull, and 12d. per ton for goods. The fare for a non-burgess was 2d. and 18d. per ton. The decline in the value of the ferry may also be attributable to the failure of the town to maintain its privileges against such magnates as Sir John Neville. Walter Laceby complained in 1450 that he had hired the ferry from the bailiffs and that Edward Taillour, shipman, took payment for the ferry from various people. Taillour, significantly, had the backing of Sir John Neville.[19]

All the available evidence points to a good deal of trade with Hull, though considerably less than with Newcastle. Hull was a rival and much more important port, and could supply nothing comparable with Tyne-side coal. Nevertheless, intercourse with Hull was frequent. Without it, there would have been no need for a ferry. There was certainly some migration between the two towns. Apart from common surnames which provide no basis for a judgment, there were in the fifteenth century at Hull burgesses named Fountenay, Northiby, Shireff, Douce, Auncell, Gabdede, Odlyn and Haynson, names which were common in Grimsby. No Grimsby burgess is recorded as coming from Hull, but Robert Beverley who became a burgess at Hull in 1424-5, was of Grimsby; and the Simon and John Grymesby, mayors of Hull, presumably were descended from a family derived from

Grimsby. William Amyas, hired at Hull, deserted from the ship of Walter atte Bryg. Simon Est, of Hull, in 1463, said in the Grimsby court that he bought a boat for 20s. paid by the hands of the Prior of the Hull Charterhouse. Hugh Edon bought a hogshead of white wine at Hull and complained in June 1449 that Edward Taillour stole some of it when bringing it to Grimsby. William Gisburgh in 1459 owed William Horme of Hull for twenty-six tons of plaster and John Neutone for his labour in sailing from Beverley to Grimsby. Robert Pye of Grimsby was jointly concerned with William Burton of Hull in a venture which ended in the borough court with their claim to £26 from two shipmasters from the Netherlands, John Lowe of 'Westerscowe' and John Simondson of 'Brwshawen'.[20]

Quite apart from Hull, much Grimsby trade followed the Humber and the rivers flowing into it. Timber for a new mill was bought in 1469–70 at Broughton and carried by water, in the same way in which seventy years earlier tiles had been brought from Beverley for the new town hall. It is not clear how John Porter of Grimsby came to incur the debt for which Robert Hedon, Master of the Hospital of Saint Giles at Beverley sued him in the bailiffs' court, but it seems likely that the churchwardens of Saint James, Hedon were able to sue Robert Wadworth of Tealby because the business of both parties brought them to Grimsby often enough to make this the easiest way of attempting to recover the debt. The same is true of the action of William Croftes and John Broun of Paull who, with John Aunger, their vicar, were involved in a dispute with John Kaa about his failure to sail in their ship.[21]

The trade in turf for fuel also followed the Humber. Turf could be dug in the Grimsby marshes, but the commons were too valuable to risk damaging them in this way. Turf was also obtainable, but does not seem to have been obtained from the villages of the Lindsey coastal marsh. From the twelfth century onwards it was turf of the 'west country', as the Doncaster–Goole–Howden area was known in Lincolnshire, which was the usual source of fuel. In the single village of Swinefleet seven Lincolnshire religious houses, Wellow among them, had rights of turbary. We find William Elmesale trading in turf as well as in coal and herrings. In 1375 he began an action against Thomas Pigott who in the previous year had undertaken, in the river Ouse at Hook, by his servant, Robert Steresman, to deliver turves to the value of two marks. William Hosier bought between two and three thousand turves from William Brekesikell who warranted that those inside would be as good as those outside, which they were not. Wood, both for timber and for fuel, came from the same district. John Whitley, for example, in January 1499, came before the mayor to record that in partnership with the wife of Robert Swalowe he had bought a keel-load of wood and kids from John Adam of the west country. By doing this he was able to avail himself of the privilege enjoyed by all burgesses of paying no toll on wood brought for their own fuel which they did not intend to retail. It was no doubt as a result of this river trade that William Turpyn of Fishlake became a burgess, with his five sons, in 1474, with a view more probably to evading toll than to living in Grimsby.[22]

This trade was not exclusively in fuel. Peter Hobson sold coal to William Baron of Swinefleet. Robert Broune of Selby sold ox-hides at Grimsby, and in 1371 John Pervant stole thirty-six of them. Thomas Bate of Wakefield was a debtor of John Rysum of Grimsby, and Grimsby ships were among those which in 1442 were said to be hindered by the bridge over the Aire at Snaith which, following a petition in Parliament, was to be provided with a lifting span four feet in width to be raised by any shipmaster so that he could pass through with his mast.[23]

London, and indeed the whole area south of the Wash, were much less significant in Grimsby coastal trace than the counties north of the Trent. Except for fishmongers, Londoners rarely appear in the medieval records, and other indications of trade with the south are equally scanty. John Pog, in 1392 charged Richard Storour with enticing his servant, against the statute and with negligence in looking after a boat in the Orwell, so that it was sunk and the oars and other things in it lost. In the previous year John Huker of Hastings, whose ship was arrested for a debt claimed by Peter Askeby, broke arrest and left his mainpernor,* Robert Burton, to the mercy of the court. Geoffrey Pedde, one of the more prominent burgesses of the time, was distrained at Hastings, about 1395, for pavage tolls taken at Grimsby from a burgess of the Cinque Ports (*Fipportes*) and was given 5s. 6d. by the chamberlains in compensation, Gilbert Smith at the same receiving 8s. 4d. for his goods similarly distrained at Scarborough. Gilbert New of Sandwich was in Grimsby in November 1401, when he assaulted John Barn of Hedon. Richard Manfeld said that his ship, *Michael*, was unlawfully taken to Sandwich on 4 August 1454. The next year John Rolynson of Plymouth was charged by the chamberlains with assaulting William Cok with

* The person who gave 'mainprise' for him, that is, who acted as his surety.

an iron shovel. John Mason of Erith, owner of the *Thomas* of London was in Grimsby with his ship when he died in 1407.[24]

It seems likely that trade with the south was mainly in the agricultural surplus of north-east Lincolnshire. This would explain the presence at London in 1350 of the *Godyere*, belonging to William Bakestere of Grimsby, whose crew resisted the king's searchers so that the ship would have been declared forfeited to the crown but for the fact that the owner succeeded in proving that he was not on board at the time. William Edon, with interests in most aspects of Grimsby sea-borne trade is seen as interested in trade with London in the action which he brought in 1468 against Peter Hobson for damage sustained by twenty quarters of peas and beans in Hobson's ship, the *Peter*, which he had warranted to be tight and dry and able to sail from Grimsby to London. Robert Burton of Grimsby and William Elmesale, both outlawed in 1380, were indebted to London citizens whose surnames denoted their Lincolnshire origin and who are likely to have been their partners in this trade.[25]

The wool trade at Grimsby was purely local. The occasional glimpses which we are afforded of an export trade are really of unsuccessful attempts at smuggling wool out of a port which it was hoped would be sufficiently obscure for that purpose. In 1454 Stephen Jonson in the *James* of Hull loaded fifty-one sacks of wool and fleeces at Grimsby for export to Zeeland. The ship was arrested by the deputy customers and he put up a violent resistance. The next year John Shireff, who was, of course, a merchant of the Staple, John Ladyman and Richard Scott were bound over to produce a certificate of the delivery of 1,378 fleeces. Wool unlawfully exported in 1338 through Grimsby consisted of ten stones from Waltham, twenty-one stones from Hatcliffe, twenty-four stones from Waith and three stones from Brigsley, which indicates both the relative unimportance of the trade and the nature of the area for which the town could serve as a market for wool. The quantities of wool reaching Grimsby were nearly always quite small. The note in the court roll on 8 July 1435 is an exception. The bailiffs were to remember that there were ten sarplers and 3,400 fleeces in a keel of Thomas Molde on 12 June and twenty sarplers in the same keel on 17 June. Obviously there was no question of this wool going abroad directly from Grimsby. The chamberlains of 1402-3 received only 12*d*. for three carts used in the transport of wool, though no doubt rather more wool than this would come into the town, since there is every reason to suppose that pack-animals were used much more extensively than carts. Occasionally wool was brought in from the other side of the Humber. Thomas Kelk, Rector of Great Cotes, in 1472 undertook to deliver six stones of Lindsey wool to Thomas Duffield and defrauded him by substituting inferior wool from Holderness.[26]

There is some evidence of shipbuilding at Grimsby. In a proof of age in 1359 John Toynton remembered that he had begun to build the ship called *Maundelayn* on 29 June 1338, finished her about 21 September and launched her on the Humber at Grimsby on 9 October. Walter Swanland, in 1375 hired John Barowe to sail in his ship the *James*, apparently as ship's carpenter. When Barowe was required to come and help with the repair of the ship he refused, and she was lost for lack of a rudder. There was probably a local shortage of shipwrights at that particular time. Robert Redburne complained a few days later that he had hired a certain William, formerly servant of Robert Lenne, as a carpenter to work on his ship until the repairs were completed. John Jakeson came by night and enticed him away, so that he had to hire another carpenter for 30*d.* per week. Shipwrights occasionally appear on the court rolls, such as the Robert Grene who was defendant in an action brought against him by Robert atte Milne in 1378. It is not until 1502, however, that we find a burgess, Richard Maclay, identified as a shipwright.[27]

Frequently we find ships owned on a share basis. Hugh and William Duffeld were owners of a cog and a dock at Grimsby in 1469, the word dock, of course, being used in its original sense of the hollow in the mud where the ship could lie at low water. Hugh atte Brig joined the crew of William Holme's ship at Christmas 1390 on the understanding that he should have a single share of the profit but left on 2 February and remained on shore for three tides, so that the master lost his profit. Quite often ships sailing from the haven are found not to belong to anyone in Grimsby but to an owner from the adjacent parish of Clee, such as Thomas Smyth, whose cog was arrested in 1420 at the suit of Robert Gardiner of Hull.[28]

Grimsby, like any other port, from time to time found its ships pressed for the king's service at sea. In 1322, by petition in Parliament, the burgesses of Grimsby, along with those of Ravenserod, were discharged from making provision for the king's land forces since they were obliged to find two ships for his service at sea. An unnamed ship of Thomas Haynson, the *Godyer*, and the *Blithe* were arrested in June 1343 for the war with France. Walter Stalyngburgh hired John Holand on 2 February 1369 to serve in his crew for a year, and Holand deserted on 20 July when the ship was in the service of the king. Holand apparently found it prudent to keep out of the way after deserting, since the case against him was not heard until November 1370. Grimsby and Barton were jointly required to provide a balinger (a ship, probably without forecastle, derived from the whale-ship) in February 1379. Robert Emanson refused to pay the two marks he was required to contribute for the cost of this vessel. The bailiffs, finding no goods outside his house on which to distrain, placed a seal on his house, which he broke. In June 1387 the mayor was required to forbid all shipping to leave the haven and to see that ships were armed to defend themselves against attack. The town had to provide a balinger once more in 1401, and in 1412 men were impressed for a barge to be sent to sea for the defence of Scarborough and Grimsby.[29]

The king's service may have made little difference to the mariners employed in it, however unprofitable it may have been to shipowners, since their ordinary life was a kind of warfare at sea. Ships had to be in a state of defence and could expect to be attacked by almost anyone. Nicholas Palmer of Beverley said in 1394 that he had been attacked at night by Matthew Campe, an alien, and his ship sunk in the Humber, but this was probably no more than an accidental collision, since both parties consented to arbitration. Richard Misen had his ship attacked off Flamborough Head, and a member of the crew removed, but William Flering, the alien whom he accused, was able to prove that at that time, 14 September, he had been in harbour with his ship at Scarborough. John Pye was a pledge for Thomas Kirkby's ransom. He tried to recover it from him in the borough court, but Kirkby said that it was not claimable for another two days. John Shireff and William Glasyner, in 1475, compromised their differences about a ship which sailed to the north country and was captured. Enemies at sea were not necessarily aliens. John Selby alleged that it was Walter Skott who attacked his ship with arrows off Saltfleet Haven in June 1365. Skott said that he was not in England at the time, and succeeded in waging his law. What he really proved was that he was outside the jurisdiction of the court, and his reliance on such a defence implies that he was guilty of piracy. There was certainly no question of his being an alien. Again, on 10 March 1432, Brian Curtis, of Clee, and his crew, were captured by his enemies at sea—not aliens but simply personal enemies of Curtis. Each prisoner was ransomed for six marks 3s. 4d. Since Curtis could not pay, William Raven and the rest of the crew paid for him.[30]

Ships sailing out of Grimsby were armed for defence. This would seem to be the likeliest explanation of how two chaplains, Thomas Ripon and John Godfray got hold of the gun which they fired one night in 1378, to the great alarm of the town, then probably hearing gunfire for the first time. More usually, ships were defended with bows and arrows. John Shildon's ship, for example, was supplied with two dozen arrows by Walter Staynton in 1423. Ships so armed were capable not simply of defending themselves. They were quite capable of attacking others if the opportunity offered, and there is good reason for supposing that in the fifteenth century a number of Grimsby men were active as pirates. In their earlier accounts of Grim he was a Danish prince, or a fisherman. In their later accounts, at a time when they were identifying a fifteenth-century effigy of a knight as Grim, he had become a pirate. The piratical activities of some fifteenth-century knights no doubt had some connection with the changing image of the town's now legendary founder.[31]

NOTES

1. CRG, 6 Hen. IV, 21 July, 16 Dec.; 16 Ric. II, 8 Oct.; (14), 13 Hen. IV, 23 Nov.; Chamberlains 18 Ric. II; 13 Ric. II, 15 May; Mayor's account roll 1392-3; Chamberlains 4 Hen. IV, 9 Hen. V and 3 Hen. VI: CRG, 32 Hen. VI, 19 Feb.
2. Farrer 'Early Yorkshire Charters' II, 467; CRG, 33 Hen. VI, 4 Feb.; 13 Ric. II, 26; LRS LVI, 37 (96); CRG, 5 Ric. II.
3. CRG, 16 Ric. II; (15), 13-14 Hen. VI, 12 Sept.
4. CRG (10), 10-11 Hen. VI, 8 Sept.; (12), 12 Hen. VI, 26 Aug.
5. CRG, 8 Edw. IV, 13 March; 18 Ric. II, 6 April; (44), 33 Hen. VI, 17 Dec.
6. CRG, 14 Ric. II, Dec.; 17 Ric. II, 19 and 20 Dec.; 6 Hen. IV, 20 Feb.; LRS LVI, 29 (70, 71), 30 (75), 65 (192).
7. CRG, 26 Hen. VI, 18 and 21 Dec.; CPR (Hen. VI) I, 505; HMC, 258; CRG, 36 Hen. VI, 16, 26 and 30 June, 11 July; 37 Hen. VI, 20 April; 8 Edw. IV, *post* 27 Nov.; 9 Edw. IV, 3 Dec.; 12 Edw. IV, 15 May and 9 Feb.
8. CRG (4), 5 Hen. VI, 20 Dec.; 18 Ric. II, 13 Nov.
9. CRG, 3 Hen. VI, 4 Sept.; (10), 9 Hen. VI, 10 July; (4), 2 Hen. VI: 25 Hen. VI, 14 Oct., 19 April; 10 Hen. VI, 26 May, 12 Aug.; (39), 27 Hen. VI, 7 and 26 Jan.; (43), 32 Hen. VI, 19 Feb.; (15), 13-14 Hen. VI, 25 March.
10. CRG, 10 Hen. VI, 9 Jan.; (2), 15 Ric. II; (2), 4 Hen. IV; PRO, C1/17/219; CRG, 12 Hen. VI, 31 March; Chamberlains 4 Hen. IV: CRG, 28 Hen. VI, 19 July; 1-2 Edw. IV; (21), 20-1 Hen. VI, 4 April.
11. CRG, 33 Hen. VI, 16 April; 13 Ric. II.
12. CRG, 8 Edw. IV, 25 Oct.; 26 Hen. VI, 10 July; (40), 28 Hen. VI, 7 Aug.; (15), 13 Hen. VI, 19 April; (15), 13 Hen. VI, 29 Aug.
13. CRG, 15 Ric. II; (16a), 15 Hen. VI, 12, 19 and 30 March, 6 April; 14 Edw. IV, 25 Jan.; Misc. CB, 2-3 Ric. III, 16 Aug.
14. CRG, 14 Edw. IV; 2 Ric. II; 15 Ric. II.
15. CRG, 15 Ric. II, 5 March; 3 Ric. II; 2 Edw. IV, 22 June and 4 March; 27 Hen. VI, 19 Jan.

Medieval Fishing and Coastal Trade 47

16. CRG (1), 1 Hen. VI, 30 May; (9), 9 Hen. VI, 29 May; (42), 32 Hen. VI, 30 May; 14 Ric. II.
17. GCB I, f. 34, f. 22v; CRG, 13 Hen. VI, 22 Dec.; 7 Hen. VII, *post* 28 May; GCB I, f. 116v.
18. CRG, 17 Ric. II, 16 Oct.; (45), 36 Hen. VI, 2 Nov.; HMC, 258.
19. CPR (Hen. VI) III, 463; CCR (Ric. II) VI, 277; CRG, 3 Hen. IV: (3), 4 Hen. IV, 13 Feb.; 15 Edw. IV, *post* 29 April; Ordinances, lines 96–8; CRG (40). 28 Hen. VI, 9 Feb.
20. CRG, 45 Edw. III; 2 Ric. II; 2 Edw. IV, 25 April; (39), 27 Hen. VI, 25 June; CPR (Henry IV) I, 498; HMC, 258; CRG, 37 Hen. VI, 2 March; (3), 2 Hen. VI; 6 Hen. IV, 30 April.
21. Chamberlains 9 Edw. IV: CRG (9), 9 Hen. VI, 12 June; CRG, 9 Hen. VII: 28 Hen. VI, 27 July.
22. John of Gaunt's Register (Camden Society) II, 1221; CRG, 49 Edw. III; 16 Ric. II, 6 Aug.; 14 Hen. VII, Jan.; GCB I, 36v; 18v.
23. CRG, 14 Edw. IV, 28 July; 45 Edw. III: CPR (Henry IV) II, 77; *Rotuli Parliamentorum* V, 44a.
24. CRG, 15 Ric. II; (4), 14 Ric. II; Chamberlains 1395; CRG, 3 Hen. IV, 21 Nov.; 32 Hen. VI, 7 Aug.; (44), 33 Hen. VI, 8 July; HMC, 269.
25. CCR (Edw. III) VIII, 217; CRG, Edw. IV, 5 July; Calendar of Inquisitions (Miscellaneous) IV, 291.
26. CRG (43), 32 Hen. VI, 23 May; Calendar of Inquisitions (Miscellaneous) III, 1628; CRG, 13–14 Hen. VI, 8 July; Chamberlains 4 Hen. IV; CRG, 12 Edw. IV, 10 Sept.
27. Calendar of Inquisitions X, 427–8; CRG, 49 Edw. III; (1), 2 Ric. II; GCB I, f. 80.
28. CRG, 8 Edw. IV, 25 Jan.; (3), 14 Ric. II, 7 Jan.; 8 Hen. V, 3 April.
29. *Rotuli Parliamentorum* I, 405a; CCR (Edw. III) VI, 13; CRG, 44 Edw. III; CCR (Ric. II) I, 333; CRG (1), 2 Ric. II; CCR (Ric. II) III, 327; CCR (Hen. IV) I, 418; CPR (Hen. IV) IV, 477.
30. CRG, 18 Ric. II, 21 Oct.; 21 Hen. VI, 2 May; 14 Ric. II; GCB I, f. 13v; CRG, 44 Edw. III; (10), Hen. VI, 13 May.
31. CRG (1), 2 Ric. II; (3), 2 Hen. VI, 25 Oct.

IV

Piracy, Magnates and Decline

A small port at the mouth of the Humber was admirably suited for piracy. The Humber was not simply the route to Hull but also a refuge for storm-bound ships engaged in coastal trade. In later times we frequently hear of pirates and privateers in the Humber mouth in time of war. The Star Chamber heard the case of the *Jesus* of Dantzig, captured in 1525 off Grimsby, in the mouth of the Humber, by French pirates from Boulogne, and taken to Whitby, where the Abbot of Whitby was among those who bought the cargo. A town actually situated in the Humber mouth could hardly be better from the point of view of pirates themselves. They never had to sail far to pick up a prize. They did not have far to run, if the intended victim turned out to be too strong, and as the prevailing winds gave them the weather-gauge, they could choose their moment to attack. Then, if they were successful, Grimsby was small enough to make it possible to dispose of the looted merchandise without undesirable publicity.[1]

In 1405 two men of Brill in Holland were sailing to Scarborough with herrings when their ship was captured, by men apparently from the Cinque Ports, and taken to Grimsby where it and the herrings were sold. The captors were to be brought before the King and Council. About the middle of the fifteenth century—the date is uncertain—John Beaumont was at sea in a ship of Dordrecht which was captured by a balinger of which William Scott of Winchelsea was the master, and John Lambert of Scarborough and William Brabroke, fishmonger, of London, the owners. The ship was taken into Grimsby, where the captured goods were sold. The customers and comptroller at Hull sent on to Grimsby a copy of a letter of Henry VII forbidding all lieges to buy from or sell to those Danish pirates who plundered French, Spanish and Portuguese ships and frequented English ports and creeks.[2]

This shows Grimsby as a place useful to pirates belonging elsewhere. Much more significantly, the borough records show that there were Grimsby ships capable of offensive action, including piracy. In 1432 Roger Graynesby and John Edon, both ex-mayors, John Pye and seven others agreed to submit to arbitration the disputes which had arisen among them after their ships had recaptured from the French the *James* and the *Mary* of Lynn. Alan Tomlynson, in 1452, claimed that Nicholas Lourance owed him 20s. for the ransom of a Frenchman, Peter Calmount, and four marks for his board and lodging for thirty-two weeks. Lourance, and to a somewhat smaller degree Tomlynson, were both associated with Sir John Neville, who at that time came near to having control over the town.[3]

In 1449 Marcus van Calon and other merchants of Bruges complained that their ships had been pillaged by servants of Sir John Neville as they were sailing to Lynn. Nicholas Lourance was a servant of Sir John Neville. Thomas Goland, in 1451, was prosecuted under the Statute of Labourers by William Harrop, another of Neville's servants, for failure to sail in the ship of Sir John Neville 'in war at sea wherever God shall dispose'. In the previous year Goland had also deserted from Harrop's balinger, which can hardly have been a merchant ship. Robert Peresson took gunpowder from a ship of Sir John Neville. Thomas Pykeryng deserted from a barge of Sir John Neville in 1450. John Cogwryght of Hull assaulted Adam, servant of Sir John Neville, with a dagger, and Adam a few days later assaulted the mayor with an axe. Neville's ship, the *Scott*, was attached at the suit of John Neuport esquire in 1448. William Edon was prosecuted by Hugh Edon for taking a boat of Sir John Neville. In 1454, the latest date at which we have any record of Neville's shipping interests, he had a barrel of flour stolen from his ship, the *Katerin*.[4]

Sir John Neville, then, had ships at Grimsby between 1448 and 1456. His servants are known to have committed piracy, and some of their activities in Grimsby suggest piracy more than any kind of maritime trade. They may also have been, and probably were, ordinary shipmen interested in trade and fishing. His claim that William Long, master of the *Margaret* of London had taken an anchor from his ship sounds very much like the usual kind of dispute between one master and another. His claim to £12 from Thomas Hesilden, made in association with John Bunde, a Newcastle merchant could have arisen out of a purely commercial venture; but it could also have been a case of maintenance in the fifteenth-century sense of the word. We may suspect maintenance also in his suit against Thomas Yonge for taking his boat in the haven, where it was in the keeping of William Edon, to Hull. But a Grimsby jury could on occasion find against him. They found that Yonge had not taken the boat, and that he had not broken the arm of John Grome, servant of John Raven of Winthorpe.[5]

William Harop, at a time when he appears to have been master of a ship of Sir John Neville equipped for war, had a claim against Thomas Shirref of Berwick for a share in the ransom of prisoners. William Smyth, who is not known to have any link with Neville, in 1458 claimed from Michael Peresson £5 for his ransom, a claim which in the end he had to bring in the name of two others, as he had been outlawed for the last ten years. Harop's position in the town was altered as soon as his master ceased to have a ship at Grimsby. Hugh Edon, almost Neville's *alter ego*, brought actions for debt against Harop in 1459.[6]

Other men of the same standing as Neville took the same kind of interest in shipping. In 1451 Thomas Swage lost the fourth share, which he had just bought, in the *Katerin*, late of Barton when the ship was claimed by a certain Clarell Paskall on behalf of Lord Roos, his master. Thomas Swage, also alleged that John Strange had violently seized his ship and caused him to be cited in the Admiralty. Nicholas Lourance, known as a servant of Sir John Neville, was also connected with a barge of Lord Tailboys, of which Thomas Williamson was the master. John Neuport, a knight of the shire and five times mayor, also appears to have had his ship. Richard Shipman, at any rate, was his servant, and John Wright took him away on his ship.

On balance, the town lost more by piracy than it gained. The disposal of captured goods was no doubt a profitable business to those fortunate enough to have a share in it. Henry VII commanded the customers of Hull, who sent a copy on to Grimsby, to see that there was no intercourse with Danish pirates who plundered ships of France, Spain and Portugal. But in the long run warfare at sea could only be harmful to a small and not very prosperous port. When, about 1480, the burgesses petitioned the Earl of Westmorland for a permanent reduction of their fee-farm rent, in representing to him the plight of the borough they named the misfortunes of war first in the list of causes of its decline. There was no land warfare within many miles of Grimsby, though perhaps some of the affrays of the gentry in and around the town looked to them like war. They must have been thinking of war at sea. On the other side of the Humber Paull Holme tower illustrates the general insecurity of the estuary in the later middle ages. The townsmen, for their security, had to rely on a policy of coming to the help of the victor. The borough survived, with its privileges technically immune. For shipping, it was quite another matter.[7]

Next in the causes of their decline, the burgesses named the obstruc-

Piracy, Magnates and Decline

tion of the haven. This came near to being a permanent feature of the town's history. For the next three centuries the haven was becoming less navigable all the time. When Holles began to compile notes for his history in the decade before the Civil War, and when local men began to take an interest in their records at the end of the eighteenth century, the silting of the haven was the only cause which they could see for the decay of the town. Yet it was far from being the sole cause. The disappearance of the longship and its replacement by the cog or roundship had made it necessary to excavate the West Haven in the fourteenth century. The further increase in the size of ships would in any case have made the haven less suitable than it once had been, and the recession of high-water mark made things worse. What is not explained is why the town did practically nothing about it. The fact that there was tidal flooding inside the town even in the sixteenth century shows that the case was not hopeless.[8]

The entrance to the haven was marked by a beacon or sea-mark called Blakeman. It had stood in the time of King John, and in 1258 was granted to the Grimsby nuns. Among the causes of dispute in 1307 between the abbot and the Austin Friars, whose house was near the haven, was the practice which the friars had developed of reading the Gospel and administering the sacraments to sailors. Drowned bodies taken from the water called the haven of Seynt Mariebrigge were buried in the parish church of St. Mary which was probably more closely connected with the shipping interest than St. James, since it was in St. Mary's that the mariner's guild had its altar. The guild was responsible for a votive ship which was ceremonially taken round the town every Plough Monday.[9]

From time to time orders were given to remove ships, presumably derelicts, from the haven. In 1390, for example. John Helyng was given twelve weeks to remove his ship, under penalty of half a mark. In 1429 Thomas Smyth dug a ditch and threw earth into the West Haven. The ordinances forbade mariners to cast ballast in the haven, and they were allowed to take ballast from the green 'swarth' only under the supervision of the common sergeant. In 1416 the burgesses assembled in the hall agreed that they must do something to improve the haven and make ordinances both for the haven and for the marsh. Money was to be raised in the abbot's parish, by which they meant Wellow, in which they expected to get £36, as well as in the rest of the town. Whatever they did may have been negated by the construction of two water mills, in 1424, at the far end of the West Haven. A dam was constructed, which was broken by the ship of Walter Manby and William Gaunce, against a new bridge of timber, which was later replaced by the Stone-bridge.

William Smithson deserted from Gilbert Holme's ship, of which Haune Phelipson was master, by jumping ashore near the Freshney, because he feared the master's threatening words. This was in 1393, the latest date at which we hear of the mouth of the Freshney used as a haven. In the haven proper no arrests could be made for any action in the borough court. The case against Richard Manfeld, whatever it may have been, was dismissed in 1447 because he was unjustly arrested in the haven with his ship afloat, contrary to the custom of the town. Four common measures were kept at the haven for discharging lime, coal, corn and other merchandise, the penalty for the use of any other measure being 2d. for a burgess and 4d. for any other. An ordinance was passed in 1465 exempting from toll all victuals brought to the haven, but this only affected market boats, since 'aliens and great fishers' were excepted. Tolls on keels and boats amounted in 1469–70 to no more than 10d. for the ringage of certain boats and 6s. for landage from twelve keels.[10]

Andrew Bell, a burgess who had recently come from the North Shields to settle in the town appeared in the borough court and declared that in March 1492 Barton Hundesworth, mariner, maliciously landed from his ship and cast the moorings loose, so that the ship floated away on the ebb-tide and was wrecked by grounding across the haven.[11]

The fee-farm rent played such a significant part in the medieval decline of the borough, that it will be appropriate to say something about its history here. It became part of the dower of Queen Eleanor in 1275, and of Queen Margaret's dower in 1305. In 1319 it was granted to Edmund of Woodstock, Earl of Kent, the youngest son of Queen Margaret and Edward I, and from him through Joan, Duchess of York who died in 1434 it descended to Ralph Neville, second Earl of Westmorland.

In 1461 the town was ordered to pay the earl £50 yearly and the arrears, but from about that time, though there was no formal reduction of the rent, he was satisfied with £30 each year, and the influence over the borough which the threat of demanding the full amount could always give him. He wrote from Raby Castle in 1452 notifying the mayor and bailiffs that he had granted John Neuport, esquire, an annual pension of ten marks out of the fee-farm rent, and very significantly, Neuport was mayor seven times between 1457 and 1476, including three consecutive years. The third earl, who succeeded in 1484, two years later granted a pension of five marks a year, charged on the rent, to Sir Thomas FitzWilliam of Mablethorpe, Recorder of London. In 1491 he granted the fee-farm rent of Grimsby to Ralph, Lord Neville, his eldest son, and Edith, Ralph's wife. On the death of Ralph, the rent remained with Edith as part of her jointure, and when she married Sir Thomas Darcy, the town paid it to him each year.

The town was anxious to have the rent drastically reduced and in 1464 managed to get a letter under the signet requesting the earl to be content with £10 yearly, in view of the impoverishment of the town. The letter which this prompted the earl to send from Brancepeth cannot have been at all comforting. He would grant no permanent reduction. For this year, he would abate £10. Beyond that, what he would do would depend on the behaviour of his well-beloved friends the mayor and bailiffs. In practice, he made this reduction every year and 'put in respite' a further £10, the effect of which was that the town accumulated a debt of £10 yearly, of which he could at any time demand the repayment. On occasion, he would remind his well-beloved friends that they must deserve the continuance of his favour, and they seem to have deserved it as long as he lived. On his death, they suddenly found themselves less deserving. In 1483, the year before he died, they sold eighty ash trees growing in the Spital Garths for the great necessity and welfare of the town in petitioning the king, the earl and his counsel. By 1487, they had decided to surrender the borough into the king's hand and lose their privileges if the earl demanded more than £26 13s. 4d. Two years later, the mayor and twenty-four burgesses subscribed to a similar resolution to surrender the borough if the earl should demand more than £30, and in all probability, for a while they made the same resolution annually. On the face of it, the burgesses were afraid of having to pay £50 a year instead of £30. It hardly seems likely that the town was by then so poor that it would be forced to abandon its privileges if the higher sum were demanded; and this, in fact, is not what they were afraid of. What they really feared was that the accumulated debt of several hundred pounds might be demanded of them. The threat was always there.[12]

Naturally the burgesses did not simply screw up their courage to surrender the borough rather than try to meet supposedly impossible financial burdens. They made their plight known both to the Earl of Westmorland and to the Crown, and the archives include copies both of their petition to the earl and of a letter under the signet. The petition stressed the poverty of the town. There had once been over a thousand households, and two hundred years ago inquests had found that the town was worth £69 yearly to the king. Now there were not even a dozen substantial men to uphold three parish churches, two houses of friars, the abbey and the Nuns' Priory. The burden of the fee-farm rent had been the greatest cause of their present poverty. Although the earl annually forgave them £20 of the rest, the rest was more than they could pay and was the ruin of the bailiffs whose duty it was to pay it, and people were afraid to come and live in Grimsby. They therefore prayed that the earl would grant to them, under his great seal, a permanent reduction to £20 yearly.[13]

The royal letter to Westmorland also stressed the poverty of the town and the burden of the fee-farm rent. A commission was to be appointed to survey the town and to determine its capacity to pay. The earl, if he wished, could send his counsel to sit with the commissioners, and he was reminded that if the burgesses became so desperate as actually to surrender the borough the annuity which had descended to him from Edmund of Woodstock would lapse permanently. Sir William Tirwhit and John Heneage were duly appointed commissioners and on 9 January 1492 found that on the assessment of the fee-farm rent made in 1286 and its apportionment to individual tenants in Grimsby and the manors of Clee, Bradley and Swallow, the town could now pay no more than £27 12s. 6d. each year.[14]

Apparently Westmorland was not at first to be contented with anything less than £30. One of his counsel wrote after a visit from some of the inhabitants urging him to see that the town was provided with an Exchequer acquittance for the farm; that is to say, that he should receive the smaller sum but cause the Exchequer to issue a receipt for £50.* He and his son must have done so, since for several years the town had no further trouble on this account. Sir Thomas Darcy proved less indulgent. The mayor, with three others, was sent to intercede with him for the arrears of £100 which he was claiming and to persuade him to compound as the Earl of Westmorland had done for forty years. It was hoped that he would accept the arbitration of Master Simeon, Dean of the King's Chapel. If he would not, the king should be petitioned; and if, in spite of everything, the mayor and his three colleagues should find themselves committed to prison on account of the arrears, all the burgesses would share the cost of obtaining

* This letter may have been addressed to Ralph, Lord Neville, and not to his father, the third earl.

Piracy, Magnates and Decline 55

their release.[15] By 1508 Darcy seems to have been willing to cancel the arrears and to be content with £30 a year.[16]

The town had been in real difficulty, but it would be a mistake to see this as a proof of dire poverty. No doubt the townsmen were poorer than they had once been. But the fee-farm rent was collected in a manner which had become quite archaic. In 1286 the town had been surveyed and each house or plot of land assessed for its individual apportionment of the fee-farm rent. If anyone failed to pay, or if a house became derelict, the two annually elected bailiffs had to meet the deficiency out of their own resources. In the course of the fifteenth century it became more and more difficult each year to find two men who would serve as bailiffs. Every expedient was tried short of the reform of the borough constitution which would have solved the problem. The borough never relieved them of the responsibility of securing an acquittance at the Exchequer, and each bailiff was personally responsible to the borough for any failure in this respect. No effort was made to re-assess the property in the town, and very little was done to strengthen the bailiffs' authority to deal with defaulters.

In 1467 Peter del See and William Duffeld, bailiffs of the preceding year, were committed to gaol by the mayor for the king's rent. Peter del See was released on finding security for payment of his share of £20, but William Duffeld remained in the town gaol. This danger of imprisonment for debt was something which every bailiff had to face, though there were times when the town was willing to help the bailiffs.[17]

Richard Dowson, on entering upon his term of office in 1472 was assured that if he discharged his responsibilities, the borough would fully indemnify him at the end of the year. He was to collect the profits and revenues of the town and account for them every Saturday, pay 40s. to William Est which the town owed him and hold a court when necessary. He would have no responsibility for the watch, unless he wished, but he must attend the assizes at Lincoln and twice appear before the justices at their Caistor sessions. In practice the liability of any individual bailiff was usually limited but the borough would rarely be satisfied with less than about £3 from him and both the outgoing bailiffs in 1498 were required to give bonds for £20 that each of them would indemnify the mayor and burgesses in respect of £15 of the king's rent.[18]

Indeed, at the best of times, the office was burdensome. As late as 1510 the mayor's court acknowledged that each year the bailiffs had 'great labour and business and great loss of their goods', so that men

E

were afraid to dwell in the town in case they should be elected to that office. Every year two men, it was said, were ruined by being elected to it. The evidence does not wholly support this claim. Most of the bailiffs in the second half of the fifteenth century were elected immediately on being admitted as burgesses. The fine, usually of 40s., which a new burgess had to pay, was usually remitted in these cases. Between 1492 and 1500 eleven out of fourteen bailiffs were newly admitted burgesses treated in this way. The full fine was never taken when a new burgess was made a bailiff, but in some cases instead of the fine being wholly cancelled, it was reduced, but the small reductions granted would hardly seem to be adequate compensation for the ruin which a bailiff was supposed to incur.[19]

A good many burgesses were exempted from election to the bailiffship. John Bayous was exempted for four years in 1447 as was Robert Whittington two years later. Sometimes a burgess was exempted from office during the period in which he was paying the instalments of his fine. Many, not specifically exempted, were never made bailiff. Patronage may have counted for something. Nicholas Lourance, no longer representing Sir John Neville in borough litigation, nor described as his servant, was bailiff in 1463-4. William Lytster was granted a charter exempting him from all offices for life for a fine of six marks, and William Smyth, in 1446 gave five marks in return for an exemption from the bailiffship sealed with the common seal.[20] The bailiffs of 1491-2 were relieved of most of their responsibilities for seven months by seven of the more senior burgesses, each of whom served for a month at a time. This was an exceptional expedient, undertaken at a time when the burgesses were contemplating the surrender of the borough as the only way out of their difficulties.[21]

The bailiffs did, of course, have other official responsibilities. They had a sergeant, such as William Hunt, who was hired for the year 1464-5 for 26s. 8d. and a gown. They had to pay him themselves each year and provide him with the same sort of gown as the mayor's sergeant. They were to receive escheats and felons' goods, appear before the justices of gaol delivery, and before the justices of peace with a panel of burgesses. In 1389 the bailiffs had to account to the borough for a ship from Wilgrippe, sunk in the haven and afterwards salvaged with eleven and a half marks in gold and silver. They were to obey the mayor, and James Cope and Robert Colby in 1459 had to give a bond for 100s. that they would do so. They held their court, probably at most times through a deputy such as Robert Constable who in 1474 sued one of the bailiffs of 1467–8 for arrears due to him. Even after leaving office, they could be sued by a disgruntled litigant for debts awarded in their court but not actually recovered. This happened, for example, to the bailiffs of 1449 two months after their term expired, and after a similar interval to the bailiffs of 1501. But their main concern was always the collection of the fee-farm rent. They might be assaulted, as the bailiffs of 1369 were, in the course of collecting the king's rent. On the other hand they could enter any tenement and take distraint for rent not paid, though sometimes the distraint could be taken with less trouble, as when Henry Layceby and Richard Waltham arrested timber on the highway in Brighowgate. All too often their duties were still incomplete when the time came for them to leave office. It was not until March 1451 that the bailiffs elected in 1447 and 1448 respectively were able to produce their Exchequer acquittances in the borough court, after which most of their troubles were presumably over, though as late as November 1451 the bailiffs of 1447–8 were suing William Markham for rent, toll, a fine and costs arising from writs.[22]

From the point of view of their fellow-townsmen, the only necessity for bailiffs arose from their responsibility for the king's rent. So long as this was collected, no more was really needed from them. Already in 1477 it was recognised that a bailiff need not be an inhabitant. What he must always be was a man with a freehold which would guarantee his ability to discharge his financial obligations, and if he was allowed to find a substitute to serve for him, care must be taken to see that he too had a freehold. A mariner could exempt himself for a yearly fine of 4*d.*, but in theory at any rate, every man with a freehold should take his turn. As the possession was the important qualification, in the late fifteenth and early sixteenth centuries, non-resident freeholders were often made bailiffs. Since they did not actually serve but simply bore the monetary burden, women also were occasionally elected. Isabel Beverley was elected bailiff, probably in 1511, and in compensation it was granted to her in 1512 that if she should marry, her husband should be exempt. And it was felt that a bailiff's widow should be specially privileged, as, for instance, was Joan Tailour, whose second husband became exempt because her first husband had taken his turn as bailiff.[23]

Because of its inability to solve the problem of the fee-farm rent, the borough could never dispense with the favour of noble patrons or ignore the constant shifts of power within the county in the turbulent Lancastrian era. Sir John Neville was able to practice piracy not simply because Grimsby was highly suitable for it, but also because he was brother of Ralph Neville, second Earl of Westmorland. In 1451 the late bailiffs owed £32 not to Westmorland, but to Sir John Neville. A man so powerful as Neville could not be ignored. John Newport esq., was his pensioner with a pension of ten marks yearly out of the fee-farm rent, granted in 1452. Again and again from 1459 to 1464 Neville appeared as a plaintiff in the borough court, usually with Hugh Edon, five times mayor, or Nicholas Lourance acting in his name. William Est, arrested for making rescue in 1450, was released pending the coming of Sir John Neville. In 1454 the deputy customers were willing to refer their case against Stephen Jonson for shipping uncustomed wool to Neville's arbitration. There was also a Ralph Neville, who appears briefly in an action against the abbot in 1460 and is not heard of again.[24]

The gentry, rarely heard of in the fourteenth-century borough court, become more and more predominant in the course of the fifteenth century. Sir William Skipwith was awarded 16s. against Thomas Germthorp in 1379. The verdict was not necessarily arrived at on the merits of the case. In 1387 he took forty-eight men at arms and archers to rob Adam Wyot, a clerk, at Grimoldby. In 1392 he violently deprived Lady Sibyl Darcy of her dower in Manby, and no one dared act for her at the assizes for fear of his malice; nor was his behaviour any better when he was sheriff in 1397. Indeed the appearance of the county gentry and magnates in the borough court can never safely be regarded merely as a matter of law. The background of violence, actual or potential, rarely appears. But it is immediately visible when we view them in relation to the life of the county, and Grimsby jurors were not ignorant of what might happen to them. When the borough is found acting against the gentry there is always an explanation of such apparently irrational conduct. A court roll in 1399 for example, shows a servant of Sir Henry Ridford of Irby as bound to keep the peace. It was not the mayor, however, who bound him but the county justices. Already at this date Ridford had received two pardons for killing men in Lincolnshire. He was himself a justice of the peace, a knight of the shire, and a Speaker of the House of Commons. When he was a commissioner of array in 1390 it was agreed by all the burgesses that he should be presented with a pipe of white wine for making the array—impressing troops—within the liberty. This was the prudent, the only possible way of dealing with him. If his servants offended against the peace, the justices might be strong enough to deal with them. Grimsby certainly was not.[25]

Occasionally we can see clearly the complex inter-relations between the gentry with whom the borough had dealings. Sir Thomas Cumberworth* of Somerby was not only one of the county justices when he had William Duffeld arrested at Grimsby in 1435 but also, as his will shows, a follower of Ralph, Lord Cromwell. Lords Cromwell, Willoughby and Welles, as feoffees, brought an action against John Empryngham in 1428. Two of the other feoffees, Fosse and Graynesby, were certainly Grimsby men. They, no doubt, were the real instigators of the action, and their noble patrons would guarantee a successful outcome; and when Lord Welles went to Ireland in 1438, one of those who went in his retinue was John Kendelby of Grimsby.[26]

Unfortunately for the town, the gentry sometimes carried their feuds into Grimsby. Roland Newton esq., of Grimsby, in 1454 was bound to keep the peace against Thomas Barnardeston, presumably of Great Cotes, and to appear before the king and his council. Godfrey Hilton, who complained that Patrick Langdale of Waltham and a dozen or more assaulted him in his house at Beelsby, himself came to Grimsby, armed as if for war with swords, bows and jacks of defence, and with other unknown evildoers, assaulted James Seymour, intending to kill him. John Thornton of Little Coates came to Grimsby in 1442 and in warlike array assaulted Richard Ashby, saying 'Come to judgment and I will save thee harmless'; and nothing could be done about it because John Tailboys sent a letter from Stallingborough, removing the case to the jurisdiction of the county justices. Thornton was not a safe man to quarrel with. Sixteen years later the bailiffs had the custody of his goods when he was indicted for killing Thomas Jackson.[27]

Members of the Tailboys family frequently brought actions in the Grimsby court. Walter Tailboys, Lord of Kyme, John Tailboys esq. and the parson of Ashby sued John Shildon for debt in 1443, a glaring case of maintenance, since the real plaintiff was the parson of Ashby. John Tailboys in 1454 was awarded £10 against Robert Nundy of Brocklesby, and in the same year, along with Christopher Conyers of Hornby in the North Riding, brought actions against the parson of Irby and John Cok of Grimsby. Robert Tailboys, possibly the son of the self-styled Earl of Kyme, made an affray on Thomas Duffeld in 1475.[28]

If the great men of the county had been at peace with one another, borough diplomacy would have been fairly simple. Their enmities

* Formerly custodian of Charles, Duke of Orleans.

made it exceedingly complex. Broadly speaking, the borough did the bidding of the Tailboys family, whatever it might be; yet, with exceptions, the Tailboys were enemies of Lord Cromwell, and he too must be obeyed. In 1454, for example, the bailiffs obeyed a warrant from Cromwell to deliver Robert Gylett to Philip Foster. The prisoner was described as a servant, and his fate may have been like that of the servant of Sir William Tailboys seized by armed men at Boston and held in Tattershall Castle until Lords Willoughby, Welles and Cromwell could hold a court to hang him. On this occasion Tailboys was able to appeal for the help of John, Viscount Beaumont; and in other connections, Beaumont could give his commands to Grimsby and expect them to be obeyed. When, at his request, Ralph Chaundeler was made a burgess in 1449, the names of all who agreed to this were carefully recorded. They knew they were giving hostages to fortune.[29]

We have already seen that Hugh Edon owed his special position in the town to the patronage of the Earl of Westmorland. John Neuport was a bird of the same feather, but whereas Edon was primarily a merchant, Neuport, with some interest in shipping, was really a minor squire. It is uncertain whether he is the same man as the John Newport of Riby, sheriff of Lincolnshire in 1445 and a knight of the shire in 1450. He certainly was the Newporte, described as a squire, of Little Coates, who in 1465 was able so to intimidate the burgesses that John Shireff, duly elected as mayor, dared not take office. The opposition to him on this occasion was headed by the coroners, Hugh Edon and John Cok; and there was a party in the borough favourable to him, of which the leading members were William Est and Richard Manfeld, both merchants and shipowners.[30]

By the fifteenth century the court books occasionally recorded polls for the election of burgesses to represent the borough in Parliament. There was nothing democratic about such a process of election. As often as not the choice of members really lay with one of the magnates who dominated the affairs of the town. Polls seem to have been no more than a way of recording which burgesses followed which magnate. On one well-known occasion the Earl of Westmorland simply wrote from Brancepeth telling the mayor to send the writs to him so that he could return two of his counsel and save the borough the cost of their wages. Richard Fulnaby* was of the party of Sir John Neville. He was mayor in 1439; though he apparently never served in any

---

* He was noted as a disturber of the peace in 1454 when he defied the mayor's proclamation against carrying arms and refused to give up his staff to the sergeant.

inferior office he was elected to Parliament in 1427, 1441 and 1442, when he was also a retainer of Lord Roos and of Tailboys of Kyme. John, Viscount Beaumont was able to secure the election of his servant, Ralph Chandeler, in 1449 simply by making his desires known to the mayor. Chandeler was returned again in 1453 with John Langholm of Louth and Conisholme, yet another follower of the Tailboys family.[31]

From the middle of the century the influence of Sir Thomas Burgh of Gainsborough, a son-in-law of Lord Roos, was felt very strongly. In 1466 he appointed Thomas Moigne and John Neuport, esquires, to arbitrate a dispute about cottages in Grimsby, and himself occasionally acted as arbitrator. John Saynton, an officer of the Duchy of Lancaster, a member of a family established at Santon near Scunthorpe, and twice a member for Lincoln, was admitted burgess in 1462 as the servant of John Burgh esq. Votes were cast for him in an election of 1463, and he was one of the burgesses returned in 1485 and 1487. His servants made an affray in the town in 1480 when he was recorder. Richard More, a Grimsby merchant, had been fined 100s. in 1450 for making rescue from the sergeant and disfranchised in 1481 for defying the mayor; but in 1483 he was returned as one of the borough members at the instance of Sir Thomas Burgh and the Duke of Gloucester.[32]

In 1469 Thomas Broghton, then mayor and formerly a burgess in Parliament, twice rode to Sir Thomas Burgh on the town's business. The following year Burgh, a leading Yorkist, had his house at Gainsborough destroyed by Richard, Lord Welles, in the Lancastrian rising of 1470, but he survived this and all other crises, as did his local protégés, the Missendens. Bernard Missenden esq., had an annual pension of 13s. 4d. from Sir Thomas, paid by the town, and was, admitted a burgess in 1473 with his seven sons. They were violent and difficult neighbours. John and Robert Missenden, in 1481, probably during the annual feast at the Hospital of St. Mary Magdalen, assaulted one of the chamberlains, along with their followers from Laceby and Aylesby. They were armed with swords, bows, shields and lances and the mayor was quite unable to arrest them. Two of the Missenden servants in 1499 assaulted William Vicars, one of the coroners, with swords and shields; and in 1491 it seems to have been the violence of the Missenden family which forced the burgesses to swear on the massbook with a crucifix never to seek maintenance by the gentry in their disputes and to support the mayor with their weapons if necessary.[33]

The only Grimsby man of the same rank as the Neuports, the Fulnaby's and the like who were elected to represent the borough was

William Grimsby, styled Sir William. He was returned in 1449 and in 1472–5. There had been a family of this name in the town since the fourteenth century. The estate,* second only to that of the Abbey, amounted to a hundred acres, and he held other land in Clee and at Howden. He succeeded his father John in 1449, and his son, Henry, held his lands in Clee by 1492. He was Treasurer of the Chamber and held various offices under Henry VI. He fought as a Lancastrian at Wakefield and Towton, and his lands were then granted to the John Ferriby *alias* Agas who became a burgess in 1455 and represented the borough in Parliament in 1467–8. William Grimsby was reported to have died of black jaundice in the Marshalsea in 1462, but he was actually in France with Queen Margaret as a herald and may have been knighted by her. He may have accompanied her to Scotland. Henry the Minstrel,† who wrote about this time, refers to a pursuivant called Grimsby, of great stature, and noted for his travels. He was also reported to have been executed after Tewkesbury, but in fact he was pardoned in 1471, his attainder was reversed in 1472 and by 1474 was back in Grimsby.[34]

The uncomfortable pressure which the gentry exerted on the borough in the fifteenth century inspired the burgesses to draw up what can only be described as a written constitution. In 1491 they swore that without fear they would support the mayor in defence of their chartered liberties, if necessary with armed force. They would have no one as mayor or bailiff except such as would be profitable to the town and its good government, elected by a majority of votes of the burgesses. Differences between burgesses were to be settled by arbitration, and they were to seek no maintenance except that of the mayor, to whom they would immediately report all offences by John Missenden, or by any other gentleman or yeoman. They bound themselves under oath to keep these articles secret, but within a year William Glasyner, an ex-mayor and one who had sworn to uphold these articles, had gone to William Lilburn, gentleman, and suggested that he should reconcile himself with Missenden, 'and if so he and ye be friends and lovers, he sets little by the mayor and other his burgesses of Grimsby'. This contempt went unpunished. Manifestly it was of little use to expect written ordinances to keep out the gentry; but a much

* His lands in Grimsby included the farm called Lathegarthes. In the seventeenth century we begin to hear of Grimsby Farm, which may have been the local seat of this family. Its site is now occupied by the house belonging to the Children's Department called the *Cedars*.

† Mr. M. P. McDiarmid of the University of Aberdeen put me on to this.

more exhaustive set was drawn up and sworn to in 1498, and these seem to have been of sufficient force in the internal affairs of the town to require some revision about the middle of the reign of Elizabeth.*35

The burgesses were at the centre of the system described in these ordinances. Even in the fourteenth century many householders had been non-burgesses, and there were complaints that there were many living in the town, carrying on crafts and trades, who were well able to be burgesses, but refused to have themselves enrolled, and so escaped heavy burdens by payment of a fine every year to the bailiffs. In 1390 the mayor forbade two men to trade or to exercise their crafts as if they were burgesses unless they had themselves made burgesses, and one of them, Peter Gotson, answered that they would remain within the liberty whatever the mayor might try to do, and would not become burgesses. The confirmation, obtained in 1391, of the 1258 letters patent, seems to have been a tactical move in the war between burgesses and non-burgesses, intended to prevent the latter from enjoying the trading privileges of the former. The practice was forbidden, but continued to flourish. In 1392 a list was compiled of various persons who paid fines as regrators and takers of excessive profits 'against the lord king's statute and the liberty and ancient ordinances and customs of the town of Grimsby'. They were probably non-burgesses, paying fines for the privilege of carrying on their occupations. There were four regrators, one of whom had sold geese and pigeons retail, and two who had forestalled peas and beans; but there were also six bakers, fifty-four brewers, mostly men, three butchers, four shoemakers, seven shearmen, a carpenter, two slaters, four thatchers and ten weavers.[36]

In 1450 there were seventy burgesses, and forty-eight in 1491. Any man or woman could, in the 1498 ordinances, buy his freedom of the borough for 20s., but a man who married the daughter or widow of a burgess† could have his freedom‡ for 6s. 8d. New burgesses could only be admitted at a court consisting of at least one borough officer and a majority of the twenty-four senior burgesses. An apprentice to a burgess could also gain his freedom for 34d. on the completion of his indentures so long as they were properly recorded. No one could enjoy burgess privileges unless he had land in the town worth 2s. a year.[37]

* The Elizabethan revision exists only in an undated draught. In HMC the date of the 1498 ordinances is incorrectly given as 1435.

† In 1498 this rule applied to widows only in those cases where their husband had already served as bailiff.

‡ As regards daughters, the rule applied in 1389.

As soon as a man became a burgess, he was liable to be elected to any office, unless an exemption was granted to him, but he gained freedom from market tolls and from tolls on carts and could enjoy the privilege of taking his share of the fish which could only be sold at the haven under the supervision of the quartermen who were elected each year. Other merchandise was divided into four portions by the quartermen and the burgesses cast lots for their shares. In the case of fish, at any rate, they were apparently to buy only for the needs of their household, since they could not re-sell without licence from the mayor or the quartermen. In the Elizabethan revision of the ordinances it was apparently intended that the quartermen themselves should buy fish, acting as agents for the others, who were then under an obligation to take up their shares, or be fined. It was also intended that no merchant coming to the haven could sell his goods except through the quartermen until he had waited forty days. Clearly the borough felt that the legality of these customs derived from the letters patent of 1258 which had regulated the trade of the town in a famine year; and they obtained confirmations in 1391, 1439, 1510 and probably 1555 and 1562. To have the benefit of these customs was regarded as a valuable privilege, occasionally granted to various Lincolnshire gentry in the fifteenth and sixteenth centuries; but they must also rank as a factor in the economic decline of the town. A burgess with sufficient influence could no doubt put a very loose interpretation on the 1258 rules; but where they were interpreted strictly, as they seem to have been on occasion, they hindered any large-scale trade in herrings. It could happen that if a merchant made a good bargain with a herring fisher, he could take no more than a third of it himself. If he made a bad bargain, he was left to bear the loss. These restrictive customs did not apply to trade with English fishing vessels which paid a toll of one fish in thirty and were then free to sell to anyone. Smaller craft could be free of toll for 4d. a year.[38]

Each September the burgesses elected* the mayor, and a panel of twenty-four of them, drawn up by the chamberlains, then elected the chamberlains, coroners, constables, auditors and the common sergeant.

* In the Elizabethan revision of the ordinances it was specified that 'every burgess shall give his voice freely without plotting beforehand'. By the fifteenth century, at any rate, the burgesses were severely restricted in the choice of a mayor to at most three candidates, none of whom could be freely nominated by an ordinary burgess. The mayor and his council of twelve selected three burgesses as candidates. The mayor and the 'house', which probably meant the common councilmen, then eliminated one of the three. The mayoral election was then held in the church, and any burgess voting for anyone other than the existing mayor or the two candidates made himself liable to a penalty of 6s. 8d. A letter under the signet of Henry VII gave additional sanction to this procedure.

Apart from drawing up this panel of senior burgesses, the chamberlains presented all affrays and shedding of blood and looked after the finances of the town. They also, in 1462, kept a banner with the king's arms, another bearing the arms of Grimsby, and the keys of the common chest in St. Mary's church. By the sixteenth century there were twelve aldermen and twelve common councilmen. The aldermen had already existed in the fifteenth century, when they were first described as the mayor's secret council. Twice a year, with this council, the mayor made his circuit of the town to see that houses were kept in repair and that highways, boundaries and watercourses were maintained. All burgesses attended him with their weapons at the leper hospital on the feast of St. Mary Magdalen, and elsewhere on St. Bartholomew's day; and on Plough Monday they were required 'to go with the ship and be with the mayor and go with him in his circuit about the town and fields and not depart from him without licence'. This ceased after the Reformation, and the aldermen and common councilmen then simply attended the mayor and bailiffs from his house to morning and evening service on the principal feasts.

The mayor could order the arrest of any person committing an offence in his presence, and any alderman could do so in the absence of the mayor. With a strong mayor, the power attached to his office was almost unlimited, but defiance of the mayoral authority was as common as its arbitrary exercise. John Astyn, in 1389, cried out rebelliously, that he and others would not be ruled by the mayor but only by his fellows and equals, and in 1469 William Edon, at his tavern, said that the mayor abused his power and that he intended to put him down from his bench. To assist him, the mayor had a sergeant who was to eat and be maintained in the mayor's household, have a fee of 20s. a year, with a livery gown, and 'be an able manner of person of nurture'. Some of the sixteenth-century sergeants were in fact attorneys.[39]

The mayor had a discretionary power to mitigate penalties imposed on those who broke the peace by drawing a sword or a knife. Anyone who urged the mayor to pardon an offender against the peace made himself liable to the same penalty. In all cases the penalty for a burgess was only half the penalty which could be exacted from other persons. For non-payment of a fine or an offence against the ordinances the mayor could command a burgess to remain in the common-hall. This was a kind of mitigated imprisonment, of which the fourteenth-century court rolls show instances. If he left the hall without licence he lost his position as a burgess. While he was in the hall, he could not have visitors to drink or revel with him, but he could have visits from his family and servants provided that the sergeant was present.

All matters of any importance were transacted in the borough court.* All burgesses had to attend at Easter and Michaelmas, but at other times only those required had to be there. In the court, no one could assist either party in a case except as his attorney, a function not yet requiring any legal qualification. Everyone knew the customs of the borough, and almost any burgess was in a position to act as an attorney, though the rules forbade him to act for a 'foreigner' against a burgess. Plaintiffs, if they wished, could appear at the bar themselves, or put their complaint in writing.†⁴⁰

Arrests in civil actions were frequent, but there were days when no such arrest could be made, and it was then safe for debtors to go abroad, and for strangers liable to be sued to enter the town without fear of the consequences. These days were the Wednesday market day, from Saturday sunrise until Sunday afternoon, the period of the two annual fairs, from the morning of Good Friday to the afternoon of the next Thursday, and from the time when the noon bell was rung on Christmas Eve until the 'plough-ship' had been led about the town on Plough Monday. No arrest could be made in the house of a burgess without his consent, or in any other houses unless the door stood open. If the appearance of a defendant in court could not be secured by his arrest or the taking of distraints, he could be outlawed and perhaps contrive to live for long periods in this condition, since the 1498 ordinances stipulated that each year the mayor and his twelve burgesses should fine all outlawed men living in the town.‡⁴¹

Just how many inhabitants there were is not easy to establish. It is perfectly clear that Grimsby was a small town growing poorer. If that had not been the case, the problem of collecting the fee-farm rent would have been solved more easily. The rental showed that the town outside the fields consisted of 646 tofts, but only 468 of them were in the built-up part of the town. If all the tofts were built on in the late thirteenth century when the rental was first drawn up, there may have been a maximum of 2,000 inhabitants; but when it was revised in 1491 many of the tofts had no buildings on them and the population may

---

* Women were sometimes recorded as present as burgesses at a borough court. Alice Constable and two other women burgesses were among those who in 1482 agreed to re-admit Thomas Williamson to his freedom.

† No court could be held on the Wednesday market day except a court of piepowder for strangers coming to the market.

‡ Richard Manfield's goods escheated to the crown when he died an outlaw in 1481.

very well have been less than a thousand, and declining. A century later the vicar said he had 500 communicants and there were no nonconformists. Presumably the population was then well under a thousand, and the town would appear to have been smaller than some Lincolnshire villages such as Haxey or Crowle.

NOTES

1. Yorkshire Archaeological and Topographical Journal II, 248-51.
2. CPR (Hen. IV) III, 150; PRO, C1 17/95 and 95B; HMC, 244-5.
3. CRG, 10 Hen. VI, 11 Jan.: (42), 30 Hen. VI, 20 May.
4. CPR (Hen. VI) V, 316; CRG, 32 Hen. VI, 1 April; (41), 29 Hen. VI, 7 June; 28 Hen. VI, 1 Oct.; (41), 29 Hen. VI, 8 July; (40), 28 Hen. VI, 3 Oct., 7 Oct. and 13 Jan.; CRG, 26 Hen. VI, 6 March; (42), 30 Hen. VI, 2 May; 32 Hen. VI, 1 Aug.
5. CRG (40), 28 Hen. VI, 10 Oct. and 9 Jan.; 33 Hen. VI, 10 July.
6. CRG (42), 30 Hen. VI, 14 March; 27 Hen. VI, 9 Nov.; 36 Hen. VI, 12 and 17 May; 38 Hen. VI, 23 Oct.
7. CRG, 33 Hen. VI, 10 April; 25 Hen. VI, 24 Oct. and 20 July; HMC, 244, 269.
8. Calendar of Charter Rolls II, 14; F. Roth, 'English Austin Friars' II, 163; Calendar of Inquisitions (Miscellaneous) III, 351; Ordinances, lines 54 and 61.
9. CRG, 13 Ric. II, 15 May; (1), 7 Hen. VI, 26 July; Ordinances, lines 45-6; CRG (3), 4-5 Hen. V; Chamberlains 3 Hen. VI.
10. 16 Ric. II, 2 May; CRG, 25 Hen. VI, 12 Sept.; 3 Hen. VI, 18 Oct.; GCB I, f. 36; Chamberlains 9 Edw. IV.
11. CRG, 7 Hen. VII.
12. CCR (Hen. III) VI, 483; Calendar of Charter Rolls II, 192; CPR (Edw. I) IV, 369; Calendar of Charter Rolls III, 416; GCB I, 80v, 354v; Catalogue of Ancient Deeds IV, A7485; CCR (Hen. VII) I, 1192; GCB I, 70v, 71; HMC, 251; GCB I, 46v; HMC, 270; GCB I, f. 32, 122v; HMC, 268.
13. HMC, 269-70.
14. HMC, 247; 1491 Extent in Grimsby Archives.
15. HMC, 252; GCB I, f. 73v.
16. Bailiffs' Acquittance, 23 Hen. VII.
17. CRG (15), 13 Hen. VI, 14 April and 11 June; GCB I, f. 10v; CRG, 12 Edw. IV: 37 Hen. VI, 15 Jan.; GCB I, f. 51v.
18. GCB I, f. 17, f. 45v, f. 22, f. 31v, f. 72.
19. GCB I, f. 147; HMC, 270; CRG, 12 Edw. IV, 13 Oct.; 15 Edw. IV, 10 Aug.
20. CRG, 25 Hen. VI, 7 Feb.; 28 Hen. VI, 14 Oct.
21. CRG, 3 Edw. IV, 4 Oct.; (17), 15 Hen. VI, 10 April; 25 Hen. VI, 10 Oct.; 7 Hen. VII, 8 June.
22. GCB I, f. 35; Ordinances, line 72; CRG, 13 Ric. II; 37 Hen. VII, 16 June; 14 Edw. IV, 5 April; 29 Hen. VI, Dec.; 18 Hen. VII, 18 Jan.; 44 Edw. III; Ordinances, lines 37-8; CRG, 10 Hen. VI, 5 Oct.; 29 Hen. VI, 23 March; 30 Hen. VI, 13 Nov.; 9 Edw. IV, 23 Nov.
23. GCB I, f. 42; Ordinances, line 79; GCB I, f. 23, f. 77v, f. 80v, f. 152.
24. DNB xl, 277; CRG, 30 Hen. VI, 25 Nov.; GCB I, f. 354v; CRG, 28 Hen. VI, 27 July; (43), 32 Hen. VI, 23 May; 33 Hen. VI, 22 April; 38 Hen. VI, 9 June and 12 Aug.
25. CRG, 2 Ric. II; Selden Society: *Select Cases in Chancery*, numbers 24-6; CRG, 1 Hen. IV, 7 Dec.; 13 Ric. II.
26. CRG, 6 Hen. IV, 6 May; (13c), 8 Hen. IV 20 Nov.; 13-14 Hen. VI, 14 April;

A. Gibbons, *Early Lincoln Wills*, 174; CRG (13B), 6 Hen. VI, 10 Feb.; CPR (Hen. VI) III, 156; CRG, 25 Hen. VI, 16 Jan. and 13 July.

27. CCR (Hen. VI) VI, 31; PRO, C1/6/60; CRG, 27 Hen. VI, Jan.; 21 Hen. VI, 10 Sept.; 37 Hen. VI, 9 Nov.
28. CRG, 21 Hen. VI, 20 July; 33 Hen. VI, 7 Dec.; DNB xlviii, 433; CRG, 33 Hen. VI, 13 March and 29 July; 14–15 Edw. IV; 32 Hen. VI.
29. *Paston letters* I, 96–8; CRG, 27 Hen. VI, 6 Feb.
30. *History of Parliament (Biographies)*; PRO, C1/31/339.
31. HMC, 252; *History of Parliament (Biographies)*; HMC, 250; CRG, 27 Hen. VI, 6 Feb.
32. GCB I, f. 37, 25; Hill, *Medieval Lincoln*, 279; GCB I, f. 6v, 30v, 49v; CRG, 20–1 Edw. IV, Dec.; HMC, 258; PRO, C1/17/219; CRG, 28 Hen. VI, 4 July; CRG, 20 Edw. IV, Feb.; GCB I, 27v.
33. Chamberlains 1469; GCB I, 17v; CRG, 20–1 Edw. IV; 15 Hen. VII, Sept.; HMC, 252.
34. *History of Parliament (Biographies)*; 1491 Extent in Grimsby Archives; CRG, 28 Hen. VI; 7 Hen. VII, April; 33 Hen. VI, 1 July; Scottish Text Society, *Schir William Wallace* VII, 297 sequ; CRG, 14 Edw. IV, 14 May.
35. HMC, 241–3; GCB I, f. 58v; Ordinances, temp. Eliz.
36. Ordinances, 1498; CPR, Ric. II, 18 Nov. 1383; CRG, 13 Ric. II, Jan.; 16 Ric. II, 8 Oct.
37. CRG, 13 Ric. II.
38. Ordinances, 1498; HMC, 238–9.
39. GCB I, f. 287.
40. GCB I, f. 26, 223v.
41. GCB I, f. 11; Mary Bateson, *British Borough Customs* (Selden Society).

V

Monks, Friars, Nuns and Churches

The Augustinian abbey of Saint Olaf and Saint Augustine of Wellow was founded between 1128 and 1132 by Henry I. Though it was not among the earliest Lincolnshire foundations, it was nevertheless for a few years the only autonomous religious house in the north of the country. Thornton was not founded until 1138, and until then the only monks to be found within a day's journey of Grimsby were the handful at Winghale (in South Kelsey), colonists from Sées in Normandy, at Covenham, where the monks were dependants of St. Carileph, Le Mans and Burwell, a cell of La Sauve Majeure near Bordeaux.[1]

The dedication, and the fact that the abbot went to Norway with the papal legate, would seem to show that the abbey was less Norman than Anglo-Scandinavian in its earliest days. Apart from this, and a few names of abbots, there is no indication of who the monks were in the days when the monastery was growing, building its church and cloister and possibly reclaiming land on the south side of the town, and adding to its endowments. By the end of the twelfth century the monastery, in addition to Wellow, had 33½ tofts in Grimsby. Ranulph, Earl of Chester, gave the churches of Tetney, Clee and Huttoft, with land at Tetney and Humberstone; Geoffrey Trussebut the church of Riby, and Gilbert de Turribus the church of Cabourn. There was also a turbary of twenty acres at Swinefleet, in the West Riding, perhaps already the principal source of the fuel used in Grimsby. Henry I's original endowment consisted of the tithe of the manors of Grimsby and Laceby. In the history of the abbey this was a perennial source of conflict. The bailiffs of Grimsby in 1239 were commanded by Henry III to pay to the abbot the £11 which was the tithe of the farm of Grimsby and also the tithe of the mill of Kaldehall, which belonged to the manor. The bailiffs were caught up in the conflict between the abbot and the rector of St. Mary's, who was claiming the tithe of the mills of Grimsby for himself, and they had decided to withhold payment to the abbot until the rival claims were adjudicated.[2]

The abbey, with only about one-fifth of the revenue of Thornton, was never a wealthy one. Indeed in 1228 the monks had licence from the king to preach and solicit alms for repairs anywhere in his dominions. In 1316 Ralph Skirbeck, a mayor of Grimsby, gave 3½ bovates of land with 3½ acres of woodland and 27s. in rents in Clee, Holme, Weelsby and Bradley, and about the same time Wellow added very materially to its local estates by acquiring the manor of Weelsby from the Cistercians of Meaux near Hull, but only in consideration of a substantial rent.[3]

In 1305 the abbot made a tithing agreement with Walter Well and Walter, son of Richard Storme of Itterby in the parish of St. Saviour of Clee—a parish of which there is no mention elsewhere. They undertook to mark as belonging to the abbot every fifteenth fish which they caught at sea, or in the Humber, with cords, lines or nets. If they sold their catch in some other port, the abbot was to have a fifteenth of the value, and the same proportion of the value of those 'fish' which they would not commonly catch, namely congers, salmon, porpoises or turtles. If it was seriously contemplated that they might ever catch a turtle, they were obviously going far out into the Atlantic.[4]

By 1372 the abbey had lapsed into a deplorable state of misrule and immorality. While John Utterby was abbot he had misappropriated £208 received for wool and tithes. Along with William Northcotes, who had been cellarer for twenty years without rendering accounts, he conducted a private trade in corn, and charged his losses to the abbey. Three chaplains offered to maintain the abbey and its services with nine canons out of revenues from the manor and parsonage of Riby alone, leaving all the rest to the abbot and his friends, and four Grimsby burgesses were prepared to farm Riby for £40 a year. The abbot, however, leased it to a chaplain, Ralph Kirmington of Brocklesby, for eleven years for a single fine of £200.

Some of the economic difficulties of the abbey were simply a consequence of the general decline of population and prosperity after the Black Death. At Lathegarthes, in Grimsby, there had once been two ploughs. Now there was one. At Weelsby there had been four and there were now two. At Clee there had been a single plough and now there was none. The manor of Holme was almost waste, and at Holme, Swallow, Cabourne, Thorganby and Riby there were eight ploughs fewer than formerly. Again, the fact that there were five corrodiers* in the monastery was not wholly to the discredit of the house, since this abuse was almost universal, and in any case the abbot was from time to

* Persons who had given land or money in return for a corrody or guaranteed maintenance in the monastery for life.

time required to admit royal pensioners with their families. But two of the corrodies were held by Joan atte Routhe and William her son, a child of four.

Joan, in fact, was the principal cause of scandal and was deeply implicated in the misgovernment of the abbey. She was nicknamed 'Fetys Jonet'. She had a chamber in Canonbig, near the abbey gate, repaired with timber and reeds belonging to the monastery; but she also slept in the abbey. The abbot, with Thomas Stallingborough, a canon, and William Northcotes, the cellarer, did not sing mass or get up for the night-time services, but remained in bed with Joan, and Alice, her servant. They and Joan kept the abbey seal, in spite of the bishop's prohibition. They used it to give her the reversion of property in Canonbig. Though for the past twenty years there had been no distribution of alms to beggars at Grimsby, the abbot and Joan atte Routhe lived on capons, sucking pigs, geese, pigeons, wine and the best ale in the town.

The cellarer was as evil as the abbot. In 1356 he had been sent to the papal court in a suit with the vicar of Clee regarding his church. Instead of prosecuting this business, he used the opportunity to acquire the manor of Thorganby for himself and to become a papal chaplain. With £80 borrowed from Sir Walter Goxhill, William went on a pilgrimage to Jericho with Joan atte See. He had so abused his office that the good canons would rather face ruin by his going overseas once more than have him remain. He had acquired a manor at Saxby and given it to Joan atte See, and jointly owned with her 400 sheep and much other livestock. He was as spiteful as he was greedy. Because Richard, who was then abbot, would not appoint him to any office on his return from Jericho, he reminded the Exchequer that the £80 originally borrowed from Sir Walter Goxhill and now with interest amounting to £120, was now a debt due to the crown since Sir Walter had forfeited his goods by rebellion in living overseas, contrary to a royal prohibition. He fomented law-suits with the townsmen, causing great hatred between the abbey and the town, where he liberally entertained his friends.

There were, of course, canons of Wellow who kept their vows, notably William Nutell and William and Robert Utterby, who had jointly proposed to maintain the abbey out of the revenues accruing from Riby. The two Utterbys were physically assaulted because of their stand for virtue. The abbot, Joan and their party falsely accused William of having false keys and using them to steal conventual property. When, by the bishop's commands, he was at Humberstone abbey, the abbot of Wellow with Thomas Stallingborough and an outlaw named Eudo Loutheholm attacked him with swords and knives, and stripped him. Robert Utterby came to Wellow, also by command of the bishop. As he lay in his bed in the dormitory the abbot came with his friends and servants, including his brother, Richard, and Walter Weelsby called 'Northcotesman', and attacked him with such fury that he was lucky to escape with his life.[5]

The abbot was deposed for his misdeeds, and there is nothing to show that the abbey ever sank to this level of degradation again. From the point of view of the town, however, the moral character of the monks was less important than the fact that there was constant rivalry and overlapping between the jurisdiction and privileges of the abbot and those of the borough. If business was transacted in Wellow, there was great difficulty in bringing an action in the borough court as when Richard Barton, in 1370, was able to avoid paying for three tunics and two pairs of hose because the agreement had been made in Wellow. Yet the borough court in practice frequently heard cases in which either the plaintiff or the defendant belonged to Wellow, or, as it was more often called, the liberty of Canonbig. Occasionally the abbot's liberty was called the parish of St. Augustine of Wellow. Though the abbot did fealty for his lands in the borough court and was prepared to sue there if necessary, he normally refused to be sued. John Breton tried to recover a debt of 6s. 8d. from the abbot in the bailiffs' court in 1463, and the abbot declared that the abbey had a grant from Edward IV and his royal ancestors that the abbey should not be sued except in the Common Bench or the King's Bench. But if the abbot overstepped his liberties, the town reacted immediately. Thomas Grefe, the abbot's bailiff, in 1404 arrested Thomas Waterleder at Isabel atte Wode's inn in the market, for a debt owed to Henry Glover of Wellowgate, and took him into the abbot's liberty. For this gross contempt the bailiff was imprisoned in the new borough gaol, until he paid a fine of 40d.[6]

In the middle of the fifteenth century disputes with the abbey were especially bitter. On 26 January 1450 thirty-six burgesses met in the common hall and resolved that with all their goods and chattels they would await judgment in the quarrel and various other matters pending between the town and the abbey. Nothing was recorded of the nature of the quarrel, but the names of the thirty-six, as well as of sixteen absentees, were all noted, with the small sums which each was to subscribe immediately for the common cause. The next day Robert

Stilling, one of the abbot's servants, broke the common bars and 'stolpes'. In April 1451 the mayor and burgesses elected twelve of their number to represent them in the matters at issue between the town and the abbot. In October the late bailiffs sued Henry Sutton, the abbot, and John Aylesby, one of the canons, with William Studfall and Robert Fox, presumably for arrears of the fee-farm rent. The new bailiffs ordered the common sergeant to arrest John Aylesby and the two laymen, but all three violently resisted. It was no doubt in consequence of this disturbance that the mayor received a royal letter commanding him to cease from troubling the abbot 'and always keep our peace against the said abbot and his brethren and servants, and in especial against the said John Aylesby, so that he may safely ride and go for the profit of the said place, as his duty is, and not to be perturbed nor letted by you to sue unto us for the weal of the said church as ye will answer unto us at your peril'. In December 1451 eighteen burgesses involved in the dispute appeared before Henry Hawley, a county justice and a member of a family holding land at Clee, and in 1453 he was appointed to arbitrate the dispute jointly with Thomas Moigne, also of Clee and a former burgess in Parliament, or with John Portington.[7]

Whatever the results of this arbitration, eight years later relations again became very strained. The abbot was moved to comment in a sermon on the venality of Grimsby jurors. News of what he said came to the ears of the mayor and bailiffs, and they caused a memorandum to be entered on the court roll: 'To hold in mind that the abbot of Wellow in the feast of St. Lucy Virgin last past openly declared and said in his sermon that divers of the jurors of Grimsby was hired and took wages to pass contrary against their conscience the which he declared openly to great slander to the town and great rebuke to the king's court there holden.' The immediate occasion for so much ill-feeling may have been that a few weeks earlier John Forman, probably an officer of the abbey, entered the liberty of Grimsby and arrested Joan Beel.[8]

A frequent cause of the dispute was the liability of the abbot's tenants, as well as the rest of the townsmen, to pay knights'-pence, a term which apparently covered the wages of the two burgesses sent to the House of Commons as well as the contribution made by the town towards the expenses of the knights of the shire. A matter of principle was involved, and the borough thought it worth while to spend freely in presents to the sheriff and in lawsuits to maintain its rights. In the financial year 1424–5, the abbot's tenants paid 15s. $5\frac{1}{2}d.$ out of the whole sum of £7 13s. 9½d. without any resort to law. This was less than one-eighth of the total paid by the town for knights'-pence in Parliament, but slightly more than an eighth of the wages of the borough members. Clearly, for the time being, the town had won its case.⁹

Always, however, the great cause of conflict was the rivalry between the abbot's jurisdiction and that of the town; and when the town, in an attempt to compose other differences, ceded land to the abbot in 1471, it was careful to specify that although this land was no longer under the civil jurisdiction of the borough court it was not added to that of Wellow. The agreement, to endure for eighty years, was made by the arbitration of Robert Sheffield—probably the Robert Sheffield of Butterwick who represented the borough of Bedwin in the Parliament of 1467–8. The town was no longer to be required to pay the £11 a year to the abbey, the tithe of the farm of the borough which had formed part of the original endowment. The abbey, for its part, was no longer to pay to the bailiffs each year the £3 13s. 11½d. which represented the contribution towards the fee-farm rent paid in respect of the land and houses in Grimsby which belonged to the abbey. The marsh called Wulfoo, extending southwards from Holme Bridge to the corn field, of which a third had belonged to the town, was to be held by the abbey in severalty, that is, in such a manner that all common rights ceased. The abbey in the same way was also to have land in the East Marsh amounting to six acres and a rood, the water and waste ground east of the haven up to the sea-dyke of Wulfoo, and waste land on the west side of the haven from Holme Bridge, where the railway now crosses Doughty Road, to the sea-dyke 'gote' in Wellowstoke-lane, a point in Abbey Road immediately east of Garden Street. The abbey could erect a water-mill in this waste, and did so, but neither the officers of the abbey nor those of the town could make any arrests for civil actions in any of the ground newly ceded. The fact that this might create a sanctuary for debtors was less important to either party than the need to prevent the other from extending its jurisdiction. A bridle path was to be kept open for the town along the west bank of the haven from the sea-dyke 'gote' to the abbey water-mill, which was near where Wintringham Road now joins Ainslie Street. The abbey was also to have the fishery which extended eastwards along the Humber bank from the haven which Matthew Cok had held, and to enclose a plot sixty-four feet square for drying nets.¹⁰

The abbey made other additions to its estates in the fifteenth century. About 1450 John Dene and six other Grimsby men, acting as feoffees, conveyed to the abbey the land in the marsh east and south of the abbey up to Weelsby formerly held by Sir William Weelsby. In 1427, by petition in Parliament, and on payment of £10, the abbey was licensed to appropriate the vicarage of Clee. On the death of Thomas Luffe, the last vicar, Richard Fleming, as bishop of Lincoln, sanctioned this appropriation in 1431, allowing the canons of Wellow to appoint a secular priest, whom they could dismiss at any time, to serve the cure; and a papal mandate confirmed this. This meant an increase of £26 in the yearly income of the house; and as if to emphasise the subordination of the curate, the abbot almost immediately brought an action for trespass against him in the borough court.[11]

The Augustinian nunnery of St. Leonard, founded before 1184 on a site now occupied by the College of Technology, was always in some way subordinate to the abbey of Wellow. In the last phase of their history the nuns were still doing washing for Wellow and in their early days, in 1232 and in 1303 and 1310, canons of Wellow were appointed as wardens of the nunnery. In 1296 the nuns were licensed to beg because of their poverty, and for the same reason in 1394 were exempted from payment of a subsidy. But St. Leonard's priory was no poorer than other houses of nuns. The nuns at one time held a turbary at Swinefleet adjacent to that of the abbey. They held the advowson of the church of Little Coates and the tithes of East Ravendale. In 1258 they were granted the tolls paid by the mariners and fishermen for the beacon called Blakeman at the haven. The extent of the town taken in 1491 recorded that they held five bovates, each of $10\frac{1}{2}$ acres, in the fields of Grimsby, with $22\frac{1}{2}$ acres and a croft. At the dissolution they were said to have 82 acres of arable land and 66 acres of pasture, with a rent of £1 from a windmill.[12]

In 1392 the prioress had 180 sheep which William Milner drove with his dog from the Milncroft to the Bourdyke. At Martinmas she had 282 sheep which John Stallingborough, a shepherd, undertook to tend for a year. When she complained that he failed to account for thirty-six of them, he said that at 'barlytyme' they were stolen, or had strayed in the fields. When in 1406 a fire destroyed the church, cloister, dormitory and most of the other buildings, deeds were lost relating to property and rents in Grimsby, Scartho, Cleethorpes, Weelsby and in seventeen other places. There is no other record of any property belonging to the priory in most of them, and it seems likely that the deeds simply related to the life interest of individual nuns in various plots of land.[13]

There was nothing to bring the nuns into the same sort of conflict with the town as we find in the case of the abbey. Nevertheless the prioress appeared very frequently, both as plaintiff and defendant, in actions in the borough court; usually for small debts due for such articles as fish and coal. The nuns were not particularly prone to go to law. They were simply involved in the life of the town, and frequent minor litigation was part of the social structure. On one occasion at any rate the religious status of the nuns proved a considerable advantage. William Lynton, in 1417, assaulted the prioress, Beatrice, and her servants. She was able to insist that he should kneel to ask her pardon, and swear publicly upon a book that he would not repeat his offence.[14]

Simon Scopwick, a hermit, lived in 1342 in the hermitage of St. Andrew next to the priory. The nuns had their own graveyard where a papal indult of 1390 gave them the right to bury their own servants and others who might desire burial there. Thomas Heengham, the nuns' priest, at the nearby Spital House, attacked John Petypas and his wife in 1394 with a knife. In 1508 they had at least two servants, since one of them, Robert Tharhald, attacked another, Robert Craxton, at the priory, and drew blood.[15]

Removal of stone after the dissolution was so extensive that excavation of the site has revealed no trace of the church except a single voussoir with dog-tooth ornament. The prioress in 1462 arranged that William Glasyner of Louth should make three windows with a crucifixion in the centre, Thomas Smith on the right, and his father on the left. Presumably they were the donors. She provided Glasyner with a quantity of glass worth 3s. 8d., but he failed to produce the windows.[16]

Next in order of foundation were the Grimsby Grey Friars or Franciscans. The house already existed in 1240 when Henry III gave them twenty oaks from the forest of Sherwood, and in 1313 they planned to make an underground conduit for water to the friary from Holm, a project which involved tunnelling under the haven or the laying of pipes across its bed. The site of the Grey Friars was west of St. James's church, on the north-west side of Cartergate, near the level crossing called Friargate, a place-name of no greater antiquity than the railway itself.[17]

The ideal of poverty did not save the Franciscans from actions in the borough court. Robert Waltham, their warden, in 1446 even brought an action for trespass against Richard Bridlington, one of the friars. Joan, their cook, wife of Robert Green, was named in 1463 as a common scold. A Franciscan of about the same period claimed that he could not be sued in any court.[18]

Steward, bailiffs, and all the court [he wrote], please it you to be informed as the laws and king's statutes ordain before this time that none abbot, monk, friar, nor canon, nor none continual obedientiary ought not nor may not to answer to no temporal action commenced against him without his abbot, prior or warden of his convent licence or else by licence of the conservator of their order; and also I may not minister no manner of goods without special licence of my lord of Lincoln; and forasmuch as divers actions are counselled against me I ought not to answer unto you without leave of my sovereign and conservator of mine order, standing as conventual friar and obedientiary.

It was no doubt the recollection of an earlier conflict with ecclesiastical authority which caused the bailiffs to preserve this letter. There was a tradition, recorded by Gervaise Holles, that in 1307 the mayor and burgesses had been excommunicated for hanging a clerk, Richard Nottingham, for theft. In fact the sentence of excommunication pronounced by the abbot of Wellow at the bishop's command, and openly proclaimed in Lincoln cathedral, had been incurred merely for wrongfully bringing him before a secular court; but the conflict was troublesome and was long remembered. Again, in 1389, William Elmeshale, a leading burgess of the time, was excommunicated for contumacy by the abbot of Westminster, and had to appeal to the pope in order to avoid imprisonment for remaining obdurate. Though a burgess might suffer by coming up against the authority of church courts, the borough court usually had no difficulty in upholding its authority in secular matters against the courts spiritual. In 1417 Thomas Aland was fined for taking proceedings in a church court against H. Cotes in a matter not pertaining to a will or to matrimony; and William Beatniffe complained that John Hammond had tried to use canon law in order to upset an award of arbitrators. When necessary, the borough recognised a case as lying outside its jurisdiction and pertaining to canon law, as when John Ingle, a shoemaker, was nonsuited in 1492 because his complaint belonged to canon law.[19]

The house of Austin friars at Grimsby was founded in 1293 when William Fraunk gave the site. Within the next thirty years William Dudale, John atte See of Ravenserod, William Tollere, William Brocklesby and Simon Grimsby made grants of land adjacent to the original house. The site lay between the present-day West Haven and Sanctuary Lane.[20]

The canons of Wellow saw the Austin friars as serious rivals and induced Oliver Sutton, Bishop of Lincoln, to put an interdict on their house within a few months of its foundation. The immediate occasion for the dispute was their failure to pay an annual rent of 6*d*. to the church of St. James for a certain croft. No less a person than the provincial prior of the order came to Grimsby in 1300 to visit Wellow and examine, along with the prior of the Grimsby Austin Friars, the deed on which the abbot, as impropriator of the church, based his claim that the friars should pay this rent. They finally agreed to pay in 1307, and the bishop, John Dalderby, removed the interdict; but the fact that they also agreed to much more reveals the real nature of the dispute. The missionary function of the canons of Wellow had been discarded and the friars had stolen their popularity. They had been preaching to sailors in the haven, and they agreed that they would no longer do this, or read the gospels to them, receive offerings from them, or take the sacrament to the sick. They would never take tithes, or anything due to the church. They would not absolve excommunicated persons, nor hear confessions, except in accordance with canon law and in so far as was allowed by the special privileges granted by the pope. At the greater feasts, they would not allow parishioners to attend matins or vespers in their church, and except at Easter and Pentecost, at those times when mass was celebrated in St. James's, there would be no mass in their church. When high mass was being celebrated in St. James's, they would not preach in their own church or in the streets or public places. Parishioners could, however, be buried in their cemetary, but except for the second mass, which could be in the friars' church, offerings and masses for the dead belonged to the church of St. James.[21]

It is clear that they were highly popular as preachers and confessors, and right up to the dissolution, the frequency of minor bequests of money in wills attests a kind of continuing popularity. Yet in 1339, eighty-three men of Grimsby, led by Thomas Skirbeck, and including a butcher and a tailor, attacked Walter Beelsby, the prior, and Simon Grimsby and John Keelby, two of his brethren. Clearly they were not universally popular. In 1352, when the bishop was at Scartho, he appointed Nicholas Fotherby, an Austin friar of Grimsby, as confessor and penitentiary save in reserved cases. Probably he would have few penitents among the townsmen of that time.[22]

The little that is known of the later history of the Augustinians at Grimsby shows them as being as much involved in lay affairs as the other religious. In 1458 there was a dispute among the friars which was profoundly discreditable. William Gedney, the provincial prior of the order, and Robert Northiby, one of the friars, appeared before the bailiffs to claim the repayment of 5*s*. 10*d*. lent to John Frieston, the prior, and Thomas Newland, who was to succeed him. They not only denied that there was any debt, but also asserted that Northiby was an outlaw, indicted for felony, and consequently incapable of bringing any action. Thomas Bordcleaver, a friar, but perhaps not an Augustinian, was arrested for various offences committed at night, by John Page, one of the bailiffs, and attacked him with a 'twohandstaff'. John Gray, bachelor and Austin friar, in 1481 made an affray with William Hesywode. It was no doubt in this troublesome period of their history that the Augustinians found it necessary to obtain a royal letter commanding the mayor and burgesses to cease from molesting them by riotous attacks, and by indicting various friars without any reasonable cause.[23]

The friars and the nuns enjoyed the same rights of sanctuary as the parish churches. Indeed the popularity of the Austin friars in this connection seems to have given Sanctuary Lane its name. If it was more popular than other sanctuaries, the reason would appear to be that its proximity to the haven made escape easy. In 1341 Geoffrey, son of William, a thief, fled to the church of St. James and a few days later abjured the realm; and Christiana Lodesham, actually taken for stealing three pecks of malt, was allowed to abjure the town. In 1349 William Dumpin of Stallingborough killed John Kay of Laceby at Grimsby with a knife, not found but valued at a penny. He took sanctuary in St. Leonard's priory, abjured the realm, and set off for Dover.[24]

In an age of perpetual litigation the right of sanctuary was used even more by defendants in civil actions than by criminals, frequently in order to avoid imprisonment for debt. Peter Ferriby of Barton, in 1393, owed William Sothiby, also of Barton, for ten quarters of barley. The parties were given leave by the borough court to confer, and the debtor took advantage of the adjournment to flee to the Greyfriars. In 1521 the action of Peter Bell, a mariner, against John Cranshaw, a tailor, failed because the defendant had been attached in the liberty of the Austin friars. An ordinance was made in 1464 forbidding arrests and attachments in churches and churchyards. When John Hansherd, the common sergeant, was required in 1532 to destroy a dog which had killed a ewe, he was nevertheless not required to pay the fine usually imposed on an unsuccessful litigant, because he had been attached in the church, contrary to the ordinance. And although it does not appear that any Grimsby fugitive ever reached Beverley, where the right of sanctuary was for as long as a man cared to remain there, its reputation was well known, and in 1520 Robert Read was found to have slandered William

Toll by telling him, in the presence of the mayor, that he ought to walk to Beverley and seek sanctuary—plainly, it would seem, something which no man of good character would need to do.[25]

The hospital of St. Mary Magdalene, often called the 'spital house', also enjoyed a doubtful reputation. Frequently, when a new keeper or warden, usually a layman, was installed by the borough, he was required to undertake not to keep a brothel there, and not to give hospitality to suspect persons for more than a night without letting the mayor know. Presumably there was a close correlation between an evil life and the skin diseases which in medieval England were wrongly regarded as leprosy.

The hospital, on the south side of the town and on the west side of Bargate, already existed in the thirteenth century. In 1389 it was ordered that John Pervant should produce before the mayor the bell belonging to the leper hospital which his wife had given to the abbey. There was a chapel there, to which the bell belonged. John Mumby, the keeper of the hospital in 1500, was ordered on the mayor's circuit to see to the cutting of eight ash trees to repair the roof and walls of the chapel and house, which must, therefore, have been at least in part a timber-framed structure, as most of the houses in the town were. The ash trees grew at the hospital. Eighty of them were sold for £3 6s. 8d. in 1483 to help to meet the great expenses of the borough regarding the Earl of Westmorland, and as soon as possible the town would spend five marks on the hospital. When a new keeper or warden was admitted, it was usually specified that he should be allowed to fell timber for repairs.[26]

The warden was required to receive lepers resorting to the hospital, but their reception was not automatic. Walter Sloothby was summoned to show what right he had to be in the leper hospital, and it is to be presumed that he had not been properly admitted. John Russell, on the other hand, with Cecily, his wife, sought to be admitted to the hospital of St. Mary Magdalene, and was sworn. Yet known lepers were simply expelled from the town. In January 1447 a jury found that Ann Litster and Margaret her daughter were infected with leprosy. The bailiffs, under a penalty of 40s. were to see that they were no longer in the town by Shrove Tuesday. The next year John Broughton, on being found infected with leprosy, was ordered to remove himself. This leaves a suspicion that while some people with skin diseases were regarded as really lepers, which they were not, other people were called lepers simply because they enjoyed the privilege of living at the

2. St. James's Church before restoration, from the west end, with its eighteenth-century aisle windows and the old town hall and market place on the extreme right

hospital. Margaret More, called a leper, brought an action for trespass against John Yooke, a hermit, and she appeared personally in court; and every year, on the feast of St. Mary Magdalene, the mayor and burgesses went to the hospital for games of wrestling, and the keeper had to provide four gallons of ale.[27]

For the warden, the hospital was a source of profit. Stephen Crofts farmed it for six months in 1447 for 6s. 8d. More usually, the office was held for life. The warden swore to maintain good government, receive lepers, arrange the annual feast and provide six cartloads of gravel each year to repair the road between the hospital and the bars. It was then his privilege to hold the hospital with its land in the fields as long as he wished. When Alexander Stirling, with Marion, his wife, were admitted to keep the hospital, they were also required to provide a priest for the sick twice weekly, or once at least. William Tomlinson of Scartho, a plumber and their immediate predecessor, was admitted in 1510 to keep the hospital for one year as a bede-house; but when the mayor tried to end his tenancy, he produced letters, purporting to be sealed by the mayor, before the king and council, showing that the office had been granted to him for life. The mayor was commanded not to deprive him without reasonable cause shown to the king and his council.[28]

Although people sometimes spoke of the parish of St. Augustine of Wellow, the town was divided between the parishes of St. James and St. Mary. Two-thirds of the town and fields were in the parish of St. James, and the rest in St. Mary's. The boundaries cannot now be reconstructed, but on rogation days the clerk of St. Mary's rang handbells round the fields and the churchyard. One boundary mark was St. Mary's cross at a corner of Brighowgate. Robert Hill threatened the bailiff there with a knife when he was trying to arrest him in accordance with the mayor's proclamation against those who wandered at night or loitered suspiciously at street corners. Part of the haven known as the haven of St. Marybrigg lay inside St. Mary's parish, and corpses found there were buried in St. Mary's churchyard.[29]

The church had entirely disappeared before Holles in the seventeenth century recorded the misfortunes which he believed had come to the families of those who demolished it. It lay between Victoria Street and the three streets still called St. Marygate. Holles said that its tower served as a sea-mark, but there may have been two towers since the churchwarden's account for 1411-12 mentions the south bell-tower. It was necessary to fix iron hooks to the wall to suspend the bell-ropes so that boys would not be able to swing on them. There was a western chapel, a vestry, the choir, a south porch, a rood-loft and an Easter sepulchre. Elizabeth Pelton left 6s. 8d. for painting the image of St. Michael and the Easter sepulchre, but these may very well have been in St. James's. St. Mary's was roofed with lead, and there were at least three bells, and a clock broken by the ringers. There was a thatched work-shed in the churchyard, kept locked so that ladders could not be taken out without permission. The thatch had been damaged in a gale, and a cart knocked down part of the church-yard wall.[30]

Receipts from collections in the church were mediocre, and the sums spent on candles and vestments unimpressive. Twelve houses and small parcels of ground belonged to the church fabric in various parts of the town. The repairs accounted for show that they were timber-framed with walls of mud and stud. Some were thatched, some tiled, and one had a barrel on the roof as the louvre or smoke-vent from a central fire-place.[31] All this was in 1411–12.

In 1451 William Sigge, the rector, leased his benefice to a chaplain, Robert Pye, for three years. The lease was recorded by the archdeacon, but the rector made his complaint about breach of contract to the borough court. Frequently the rector was an absentee and a pluralist. The rector of greatest local distinction was Edmund Grimsby, probably of the same family as the fifteenth-century herald and member of Parliament. By 1333, as well as being king's clerk and parson of St. Mary's, he was also a canon of Beverley, Southwell and Salisbury. He founded the Rayner chantry in the church of St. James and died in 1355 at the papal court of Avignon.[32]

The churchwarden in 1411–12 was John Elmsale, a chaplain. In his year of office, at the Archbishop's visitation, the date of the patronal festival of the church was altered to coincide with that of St. James's. Both churchwardens in 1454, John Dean and William East, were connected with shipping, and so was Hugh Edon who was churchwarden in 1480. St. Mary's would seem to have been the mariners' church and to have declined as the haven silted and the shipping interest declined. The mariners' guild had its altar there.* In 1507 they were ordered to make a ship to stand in the church of St. Mary before the light belonging to the plough, and all the burgesses were to contribute 20s. within a year. All the other known guilds, however, were in St. James's, which must have figured more significantly in the lives of the townsmen.[33]

Though the church of St. James has, in detail, been much altered by restoration, externally it preserves much of the appearance which it

* As late as 1571 Alexander Coulston owed 6s. 8d. to the plough-ship.

must have had in the later part of the fourteenth century. The west door of the nave with its late Norman arch, and brick which could be Roman in the wall above, antedates the first charter, and the nave arcade, with the clerestory which seems also to echo a triforium, belongs to the first half of the thirteenth century. From the beginning the plan, for a small town, was grandiose, with eight turrets at the angles of the nave, choir and transepts, and it is easy to see how, in post-monastic times, the parishioners came to believe that this had once been the abbey church.

But it was nothing of the kind. The abbot was the impropriator. He took the great tithes and selected the vicar for the bishop's approval; but legally his interest went no further. In the first century of its existence the church may have been served by a stipendiary priest whose employment could be ended whenever the abbot chose. The first perpetual vicar, David, a chaplain, was appointed *circa* 1220 when Hugh of Welles was bishop. His income was derived from a third of all offerings, 6s. a year from the abbey, half an acre of land, and tithes of cows, calves, sheep, wool, flax, geese, hens and eggs. Taken literally, this would mean that those burgesses who were not farmers were tithe-exempt. In fact they were not, and tithe disputes during the episcopate of Robert Sutton seem to reflect an attempt to ensure that trade and shipping as well as agriculture should pay tithe. The benefice was valued at ten marks a year, which means it was a little better than average, and the vicar was also required to provide for a deacon and a second priest.[34]

In 1344 Edmund Grimsby founded the chantry of Holy Trinity, known as the Rayner chantry, in St. James's, with the endowment of one priest to celebrate perpetually for the souls of Edmund and members of his family. Chaplains were to be appointed by the mayor and twelve of the better and more discreet burgesses. The borough exercised a general supervision over the property of the chantry, and the situation of the priest's house seems to have been the origin of Chantry Lane. Robert Watson, who was the chantry priest in 1530, was licensed by the mayor and burgesses to go away for two years to study at Oxford or Cambridge, on condition that he found a substitute to serve in his absence.[35]

The present tower and crossing were erected, at any rate in part, at the expense of John Ingson in 1355. William Wele received a licence from the bishop in 1395 to build a charnel house under the chapel of St. Mary and All Saints against the north aisle; but two years later the church was in need of repair and the pope granted an indulgence for all those visiting it on seven feast days and giving alms for the fabric.[36]

Some ecclesiastical matters in the borough court rolls may relate to any of the churches in the town. In 1462, for example, there is reference to a painted cloth before the altar of St. Ann, with no indication of where the altar was. But for the most part St. James's* figures much more prominently than St. Mary's, and must have been the principal church. In 1432 we hear of the alderman of the Ascension Guild, in 1459 of the alderman and two wardens of the guild of St. Mary in St. James's, and in 1486 of the alderman of the Trinity Guild. Peter Mason, a former mayor, who died in 1535, wished to be buried in the north aisle of St. James's, 'before Our Lady of Pity', and left small sums to the guilds of the Trinity, the Ascension and St. George. He was also alderman of the guild called 'of Holy John of Bower' which may have had its altar in St. James's, and the guild hall, often called St. John a Bower house, was on the south bank of the West Haven.[37]

Though both churches were sanctuaries business was transacted in them. Neither church was free from crime or violence. Robert Hunmanby, a chaplain, was outlawed in 1381 for stealing 30s. from a chest in St. James's belonging to another chaplain, William Benningholm. William Walranson, formerly a servant of Walran, the rector of Cawthorpe, and John Hosier, did penance standing in white sheets at an angle of the wall of St. Mary's. John Locksmith and his servant came to see the spectacle, and the penitents assaulted them. In 1415 Nicholas Forbet, a clerk, stole a silver chalice and a paten, worth 100s., in the keeping of Thomas Burgh, one of the churchwardens of St. James's. One Sunday in 1460 John Bayous assaulted William Hatcliffe in St. James's, and in 1462 John Tomlinson attacked Walter Laceby in St. Mary's churchyard.[38]

At the end of the fourteenth century the chamberlains were paying the clerks of St. James's 4s. for ringing prime and curfew, with 3d. for ringing in winter. By 1505 there was also a clock, and it was the duty of John Russell, the bellman, to look after it and to ring prime and curfew.[39]

NOTES

1. CPR (Hen. IV) I, 202; VCH, 238.
2. Camden Society: *John of Gaunt's Register* II, 1221; Farrer Early Yorkshire Charters II, 467–8.

---

* In 1459 there was a guild of St. Mary's in St. James's church.

Monks, Friars, Nuns and Churches 85

3. CPR (Edw. II) II, 477; Calendar of Inquisitions (Miscellaneous) III, 838.
4. GCB I, f. 349.
5. Calendar of Inquisitions (Miscellaneous) III, 850; Calendar of Papal Letters III, 595.
6. CRG, 44 Edw. III; 14 Edw. IV, 20 May; 7 Hen. VII, 26 Feb.; 2 Edw. IV, 6 Oct.; 6 Hen. IV, 25 Nov.
7. CRG (40), 28 Hen. VI, 26 Jan.; 29 Hen. VI, 21 April; 30 Hen. VI, 9 Oct.; HMC, 243; CRG, 30 Hen. VI, 21 Dec.; CCR (Hen. VI) V, 328.
8. CRG, 1–2 Edw. IV, 15 Dec. and 9 Oct.; 2 Edw. IV, 2 Feb.
9. Mayor's account roll, 1392; Chamberlains 9 Hen. V and 3 Hen. VI.
10. HMC, 258; GCB I, f. 72v.
11. CPR (1427), 464; Ibid. (1438), 297; GCB I, f. 96; CRG, 10 Hen. VI, 25 Aug.
12. LRS, *Visitations of Religious Houses;* LAO, Dalderby Memoranda, 178v; VCH, 161–3; Calendar of Charter Rolls II, 14; Dugdale, *Monasticon* IV, 546–7.
13. CRG, 15 Ric. II, 17 Ric. II, 24 Nov.; CPR (1405-8), 193.
14. CRG (3), 4–5 Hen. V, 13 Oct.
15. CPR (1340–3), 507; Calendar of Papal Letters IV, 324; CRG, 18 Ric. II, 9 Nov.; CRG, 24 Hen. VII.
16. CRG, 3 Edw. IV, 26 June.
17. VCH, 219; 1491 Extent in Grimsby Archives.
18. CRG, 2 Edw. IV, Aug.; (15), 13–14 Hen. VI; Letters 3.
19. LAO, Dalderby Memoranda, 112v; LNQ I, 43; CCR (1389–92), 85; CRG (3), 4–5 Hen. V, Nov.; (40), 28 Hen. VI, 4 Nov.; (41), 29 Hen. VI, 1 March and 3 July; 7 Hen. VII, May.
20. F. Roth, *English Austin Friars* II, 116, 155, 183, 208, 283, 306.
21. Ibid., 134, 163.
22. Ibid., 322; VCH, 218.
23. LAO, Register VIII, 28; CRG (4), 5 Hen. IV, Nov.; Roth, op. cit., 711; CRG, 24 Hen. VI, 3 Nov.; (46), 37 Hen. VI, 14 Nov.; 12 and 21 Edw. IV; HMC, 243.
24. Grimsby Archives, Coroners' Roll.
25. CRG, 16 Ric. II, 29 April; CB (Misc.), 12 Hen. VIII, 25 Sept.; GCB I, f. 354v; CB (Misc.), 23 Hen. VII, Jan.–March; CB (Misc.), 12 Hen. VIII, 18 May.
26. CRG, 13 Ric. II, 19 Oct.; CRG, 15 Hen. VII, 7 April; GCB I, f. 46v, 38v; VCH, 234.
27. CRG, 2 Hen. IV: (40), 28 Hen. VI, 9 Feb.; 25 Hen. VI, 17 Jan.; 27 Hen. VI, 17 Dec.; (47), 38 Hen. VI, 29 Oct.; GCB I, f. 41.
28. CRG, 25 Hen. VI, 18 April; GCB I, f. 37v, 38v, 60, 169, 147v; HMC, 248.
29. CRG, 2 Hen. IV, 19 April; Calendar of Inquisitions (Miscellaneous) III, 351.
30. Grimsby Archives, Churchwarden's Account; LAAS VI, Part I, 30; CRG, 36 Hen. VI, 25 Dec.
31. CRG, 3 Ric. II; GCB, 62 v.
32. CRG, 33 Hen. VI, 23 Feb.; Calendar of Papal Letters II, 372, 387, 407; III, 542.
33. CRG, 32 Hen. VI, 16 May; HMC, 258; CB (Misc.), 23 Hen. VII, Jan.; LAO, Inventories 50/58.
34. LRS, *Register of Hugh de Welles* III, 58.
35. GCB, 74v–75v, 265v.
36. LAO, Register XII, 444; Calendar of Papal Letters V, 277.
37. CRG, 1–2 Edw. IV, 13 July; (10), 10 Hen. VI, 31 May; 37 Hen. VI, 12 April; CB (Misc.), 1 Hen. VII, 8 May; LAO/LCC, 9 Jan. 1534–5.
38. CRG (1), 3–4 Hen. IV: LRS LVI, 155, 235; LAO, Register XV, 143v, CRG (40), 28 Hen. VI, 17 Aug.; CRG (21), 20–1 Hen. VI, April.
39. Chamberlains 18 Ric. II; GCB I, 84v.

VI

The Reformation and the Gentry

Archbishop Whitgift related to his biographer, Sir George Paul, how his uncle, the last abbot of Wellow, had often told him that the end of the old order was near. This story may well be apocryphal. The abbot, however, took the precaution in January 1535 of leasing the manor of Holme, reserving to himself the right to build a chamber above the parlour in the manor house which he could occupy himself if he wished. As the rent was only 40s. a year, he probably took a substantial fine. If the abbot was gifted with as much foresight as his nephew believed, we may see some of the incidents affecting the relations between the religious and the town as signs of the coming Reformation; but as we have seen, there always had been friction of one kind or another.[1]

In 1507-8 the mayor and burgesses passed an ordinance that no corn or malt was to be carried 'within this franchise' to any mill except to the common mill. If this was strictly enforced, since Wellow could not be reached except through some part of the franchise, this would be to the great detriment of the abbey mill. In January 1509 Thomas Mechelson officially informed the mayor 'that my lord of Wellow should call the mayor and his brethren false harlots and said he should handle them as false extortioners'. In 1514-15 the abbot was fined for an affray made by the abbey within the liberty of the town and in 1520 the miller of Wellow had come into the town and carried a quantity of corn away from Robert Bell's house 'contrary to an act made of ancient time that no miller of Wellow shall lead no corn'.[2]

By 1521 the borough was sufficiently aware of its grievances to draw up a list of articles against the abbot. The mill figured among them. It was said to stop the course of water in places where it should come to the haven. The abbot, contrary to an agreement, was refusing to pay bustages, which would later have been called rates or assessments, and knight's-pence. The officers of Wellowgate took a suspected felon who had fled from the town, imprisoned him and locked him in the stocks, and then let him go without trial. Harry Smith took a young man from the town into Wellowgate, where he took him to the hall and locked him in the stocks, to the hurt and prejudice of the borough. Worse still, in March, Robert Wright, a canon of Wellow, forged a deed at the house of a burgess, Robert Richardson *alias* Roper, and persuaded William Hatcliffe, who was 'distempered' to seal it.[3]

When there was a shortage of corn, the canons and friars came in for their share of blame. Richard Durham, prior of the Austin friars, had dealings in corn which in 1521 involved him in a dispute with Nicholas Draper, a burgess, about malt bought at Caistor. In December 1523 he was presented for forestalling the market by buying corn while the sacks were still on the horses' backs, and an ordinance was then made that no corn should be sold in the market until the sacks were set down, and the horses led away. In March 1528 the warden of the Greyfriars, in the house of Thomas North, glover, received 7s. 4d. for a quarter of beans from a Stallingborough man just as Richard Empringham was about to buy them for 6s. 8d. Five days later, Thomas Lincoln, a canon of Wellow, lay in wait in Bargate to meet men bringing corn to the market, and offered £8 for a load of beans.[4,5]

And among the burgesses there was always a party, sometimes even a majority, which enjoyed the favour of the abbot. One of these was John Horncliffe, who became a burgess and alderman in 1532. He probably came from Holderness as he had lands there and was related to Philip Miffin, an attorney with interests in Hedon as well as in Grimsby. When he died in 1534-5 he made bequests for masses at Market Rasen, and for gilding the rood at Hedon. He was to be buried in St. James's in front of the image of St. Erasmus. He left his one-third share in the ship *Christopher* of Grimsby to his son Robert, one of the more active rebels of 1536. The interest of the family, closely linked with that of the abbot, accounts for the part which the son played in the rebellion. The abbot was to have John Horncliffe's best horse. One son, John, was a canon of Wellow, and was to have £5 a year for eight years from the Holderness lands to study, with the abbot's licence, at Oxford or Cambridge. Robert, the other son, was a tenant of the abbey at Holme and Wellow and John, the father, two years after he became an alderman, had a thirty-year lease of the abbey manor at Swallow, paying a rent of twenty-one quarters of barley a year.[6]

When Gerard Uflett, a gentleman, took the lease of the manor of Holme, he undertook to maintain the hall and kitchen of the manor-house, and to allow the two priests or canons celebrating in the chapel to occupy the great parlour.* When the abbey was surrendered in 1536 there were eleven canons. Its annual value was £95, and the bells, with the roof lead, were worth £202. More than half the revenue came from Grimsby, Wellow, Holme and Weelsby, and from the churches of Clee and Grimsby. Thomas Moigne, the steward of Weelsby, was put to death for his part in the Pilgrimage of Grace, but Anthony Missenden, the chief steward, and Hugh Grantham, the auditor, both members of families of some importance, were not implicated, nor were William Dixon, bailiff of Humberstone, and John Blacke, bailiff of the abbey lands in Grimsby, North Thoresby and Waltham.[7]

Though the Pilgrimage of Grace began at Louth, Cromwell believed that the rebels had got their guns from Grimsby; and several of the leading townsmen were with the insurgents. Two days before the first outbreak, William Morland, formerly a monk of Louth Park was at Grimsby. His nominal business was to deliver capacities to former canons of Wellow, that is, documents entitling them to seek preferment as secular priests. His real purpose, or so the crown thought, was to foment rebellion. He admitted that he had dined at Grimsby but would say no more of his host than that he was a tall man with a tall wife, living in a street with a name which he could not remember. There were other visitors, including a shipman from Hull, who told them how, at Hull, the people had sold all the church plate and jewels and used the money to pave the town. He suggested that the same course should be followed at Grimsby since the town was very foul. In any case, if they did not sell their plate, it was likely to be confiscated. The tall man answered that the chancellor of the diocese was coming on Tuesday for a visitation, and they did not intend to receive him favourably. They were never, as it happened, to have the chance of facing him. The Horncastle rebels killed him before he could get to Grimsby.[8]

Guy Kyme of Louth, afterwards executed, came to Grimsby as soon as the rebellion started. He had been sent, he said, by the justices, about the removal to Lincoln castle of men who were suspected to be the pirates who had taken a ship of Faversham, but the honest men of Grimsby preferred to be responsible for them themselves. Through him or someone else from Louth the news of the rising was conveyed to Grimsby. The commons turned out with their arms and equipment, and Leonard Curtis rode to the gate of the Austin friars and threatened

* On the map of 1625 there is a building marked with a cross, near the present-day Holme Hill school, which may have been the chapel.

The Reformation and the Gentry

to have the place set on fire if the prior did not join them the next day. He was let in to speak personally with the prior. Under Richard Thimolby, eighty men set out to join Sir John Thimolby, his brother.[9]

Anthony Curtis of Clee and Grimsby, a cousin of Leonard, and related also to Robert Aske, the leader of the much more formidable rebellion in Yorkshire, was active among the Holderness insurgents. The Duke of Suffolk believed that Anthony Curtis, with Robert Horncliffe, were the people who had first made Aske swear allegiance to the rebels in Lincolnshire. Horncliffe brought a letter to the rebels of Hull from those of Lincolnshire, signed by one of the Empringham's of Grimsby, to say that Lincolnshire had now returned to its allegiance. At Hull this letter was denounced as a forgery, and Horncliffe, with Anthony Curtis and William his servant, were thrown into prison. In the middle of November they escaped and came to Suffolk at Barton, but their troubles were not over. Suffolk, hoping they might still be executed, sought to have their lands granted to him. Curtis, he said, had an estate worth forty marks a year and Horncliffe one of twenty marks. To prove his loyalty, Curtis offered to go and kill Aske, and denied that he ever administered the oath to him. No advantage seems to have been taken of this offer, which perhaps was not to Horncliffe's taste. At any rate, by January 1537 both were at liberty in Grimsby when Curtis made an affray on Horncliffe and drew his blood. Both were on the list of rebels to be executed at Lincoln on 6 March, but their inclusion must surely have been a formality, and both were found to come within the terms of the pardon.[10]

By 17 November 1536 part of Suffolk's forces lay in Grimsby. The king's ships were with guns at the haven. The failure of the rebellion at first made no difference to Leonard Curtis. He was on a Grimsby jury in January 1537, but by 20 June he had found it prudent to go overseas, and his action for debt long pending against John Bays was adjourned until his return. He did return, however, and was mayor in 1539–40. His widow married Thomas Portington of Castlethorpe, a grandson of John Aske.[11]

So the Grimsby rebels seem to have had no difficulty in making their peace with the authorities, helped by the good advice of Philip Miffin of Hedon, gentleman. He was already a burgess, and in January 1537 was declared to be a special friend of the borough and was exempted from all office. He was one of those who had tried to defend Hull against the rebels, and knew how the rebellion was going in the north. When the question arose whether the fee-farm rent should be sent to Brancepeth castle in spite of the insurrection in the north it was Miffin who correctly advised the town to pay. The town acted on his advice, sent the money, and rewarded Miffin by granting him a piece of ground on the east side of the haven called Baily Close.[12] Miffin had been busy in Grimsby affairs since 1512 and was no doubt well known.[13,14]

Anthony Curtis, the most prominent and most equivocal of the Grimsby rebels, like his cousin Robert Aske, was a lawyer of Gray's Inn. He was son and heir of Brian Curtis, inheriting an estate in Clee which had once belonged to Henry Grimsby, the manor of Holme Hill, and lands in Cleethorpes, Weelsby and Humberstone. He survived the rebellion for another twenty years, his son, Thomas, succeeding him in 1556. Horncliffe, who seems to have become his enemy, was made a burgess in 1537, and was dead before April 1542 when Jane, his widow, delivered £30 of his goods to her brother, James Dynewell, clerk. Dynewell was probably an uncle of the future Archbishop Whitgift. Except for Horncliffe, and perhaps the Curtis's, none of the known rebels held much land from the abbey. Henry Whitgift, the father of the Archbishop was an abbey tenant, and so was John Bellowe, who was at the beginning of his career. So, indeed, were others who were either neutral in 1536, or active in the dissolution of the Grimsby religious houses.[15]

Thomas Hatcliffe esq., was receiver and bailiff of the estates of Wellow Abbey from Michaelmas 1535. Sir Thomas Heneage, later gentleman of the bedchamber, had a grant of the manor of Barton on Humber in 1536 on the attainder of Henry Norris, and in March 1537 Hatcliffe got a lease of certain abbey lands. In 1544 Heneage paid £14 14s. to the crown and gave up his manor of Barton in exchange for the crown interest in Hatcliffe's lease, and the lands leased to Hatcliffe were to come to Heneage and his heirs when the lease ended. So, in 1558, Heneage finally obtained the lands of the abbey in Wellow, Clee (excluding the rectory), Weelsby and Scartho, a wood of $19\frac{1}{2}$ acres called Bradley Wood, and the advowson of St. James. Robert Whitgift, the last abbot, had his pension of £16 a year, but the pensions of the other monks never seem to have been paid.[16]

As late as April 1538, William Young of Grimsby, a priest, left 10s. for the two observants of the Grimsby Grey Friars to sing a trental of masses, with 6s. 8d. to Dame Joan Rose of the Nunnery, and 8d. to each nun and the prioress. The Nunnery was dissolved in 1539. John Freeman dissolved the Grey Friars, where there were still friars, in October

1538. The lead and bells, worth £80, he delivered to Mr. William Hatcliffe. The Austin friars were dissolved at the same time. John Bellow bought the site of the Grey friars in 1543. The site of the Austin friars was temporarily entrusted to the mayor and aldermen, and they tried to get a grant of it to store guns and other things needed for defence as it lay conveniently close to the sea; but in 1546 it was sold to Augustine Porter and John Bellow. In the same year Porter and Bellow received a grant of the Nunnery.[17]

A few of the ex-religious remained in Grimsby. Robert Lindley, Vicar of St. James's, had a pension of £3 for the cure of Wellow and must have been some kind of clerk under the abbot. John Jordan, formerly a nun of Sempringham, lived in Grimsby with her husband, Robert Dobinson, a summoner. Margaret Ridsdale, formerly the Prioress of St. Leonards, had a pension of £4 a year. Three of the nuns had 30s. a year, and one other a pension of 33s. 4d. With their death, the last traces of monasticism disappeared from the town. Soon men forgot where the abbey church had been. They began to grow superstitious about it, and told how 'there was plainly seen a great sheet of fire to come out of Holderness over the Humber, and to light up on the Abbey House, as they called it, which burnt it all down to the bare ground, with the men in it, and all the corn stacks and buildings upon it'. And because the town had become less prosperous when these stories were told, the fire at the abbey, which actually happened in 1623, was seen as the visitation of divine justice, and the poverty of the town was the penalty of sacrilege.[18]

But the town had not yet sunk too deep into poverty, and some of its inhabitants grew rich out of the proceeds of the Dissolution. Of these the most notable was John Bellow, M.P. for Grimsby, with John Constable in 1554 and in 1559 with Mr. Harrington, and four times mayor. He was probably the son of a Stallingborough husbandman, who died in 1538, leaving Philip Miffin as the supervisor of his will. John Bellow in 1534 had a life-patent from the abbot to act as his attorney in the King's Bench, with a pension of 10s. a year secured on land at Tetney. He also had a lease of the abbey land at Swinefleet. By then he was a servant of Thomas Cromwell and in 1536 was caught by the Louth rebels at Legbourne Priory. Christopher Ayscough, gentleman usher, reported to Cromwell that Bellow had been baited to death by dogs with a bull-skin tied to his neck, an atrocity so spectacular that news got as far as Vienna. A few days later, however, he had come safely to Lincoln. For the next year or so he remained

Cromwell's servant, delivering beans for his household at Stepney, and farming both Legbourne and the dissolved Priory of Newstead on Ancholme. From 1542 to 1547 he farmed the new park at Thornton College, fencing it for the king, and it was probably about this time that his marriage to Ursula Appleyard, niece of the last Abbot of Thornton, took place. He bought the site of the Grimsby Grey Friars, the abbey manors of Holme and Swallow, and the tithes of Clee, and leased Newstead Priory, which subsequently became his residence. By 1543, however, he was living in Grimsby, bought a toft which had belonged to Alvingham Priory, and owned land in the Little Field which had once belonged to the Grey Friars. By the time he had become mayor of Grimsby for the first time, his career had been sufficiently varied to render it prudent for him to obtain a general pardon (not extending to treason), and in that year he was Escheator in Lincolnshire and a Commissioner of Sewers, as well as Justice of Peace in Lindsey, Kesteven and the East Riding. He further signalised his rise to affluence by vesting his estate at Holme, Clee and Grimsby in feoffees.[19]

Bellow was clearly one of those who did not need to read Machiavelli to know how to comport himself. He simply got on, making enemies, and possibly some friends. His knowledge of the world no doubt helped the town to obtain a grant of the Rayner Chantry estate to endow the grammar school, and the frequency with which he held office sufficiently indicates how powerful a new man of moderate estate could become in a small and not very prosperous borough. He over-reached himself in 1558 when he had to obtain a pardon for abetting his son, Sylvester, in breaking into the vicarage of Cadney and harbouring a horse-thief from Beverley.

To Sir Gervase Holles (1547-1627) the corporation of Grimsby seemed to be mostly 'mean and mechanic fellows'. There were exceptions to this rule, sometimes numerous, but for much of the sixteenth century this would seem to have been their true character. Peter Mason, when he was mayor in 1513-14, was allowed to have his mace borne before him by his son, Michael, but was allowed to do without the mace when he went to his tanyard. When the great inquest fined him for defaults in the exercise of his craft during his mayoralty, he called them 'a meinie of false harlots'. He was supported by another tanner, Philip Hamby, and together they urged the great inquest to be wise what they did, for if they punished men as they were wont to do, they would cause many to run forth of the town.[20]

Their quarrels were petty and unceasing. In 1516 another tanner, Richard Horseman, abused Thomas Sheriff, the town clerk, in St. James's church, calling him a false knave and accusing him of tampering with a record of the borough court. The bailiffs' sergeant was found to have packed a jury, given evidence for the plaintiff, and forced the jury to give a false verdict, When another jury returned an unpleasing verdict one of the chamberlains, and John Hodson, another tanner, called them false harlots and said they were all foresworn. Thomas Brigg slandered the mayor, saying that he could neither get nor take money as the said mayor was always ready to pluck and take it from him by extortion. John Hatcliffe, in 1540, displayed a kind of class consciousness when he said to the mayor's lieutenant, Richard Empringham, 'Turd in thy teeth, I am as good a man as thou but for thy goods!'[21]

Yet the evidence of these quarrels does not wholly support the view that those involved in them were mere mechanics. Richard Empringham was a gentleman and a landowner. When Leonard Curtis was mayor, John Kingston slanderously declared that three pieces of salt turbot which he was selling in the market were unwholesome. Perhaps they were. But the seller of fish came of a family of gentlemen and his widow married into a more ancient family; and John Kingston, in 1543, had a commission to raise men for the war with Scotland and acquired an estate of 1,700 acres in Grimsby, Bradley and other north Lincolnshire villages.* It was not unusual for burgesses to own land in the county. John Ancell had land at N. Somercotes, Christopher Atkirke at Barnoldby, John Kelsey (of Lathegarths) at Elkington, Richard Alenson at Ashby and William Talbot at Tealby. What was unusual in Kingston's case was the size of his estate. His son, a noted duellist, became gentleman of the horse to the Earl of Rutland before he settled down in Grimsby to commit adultery with the town clerk's wife; and Kingston's daughter married a son of Sir William Skipwith of S. Ormsby.[22]

Some of the county gentry were owners of property in Grimsby. In the 1580's these included Richard Thimolby, son of Sir Richard Thimolby of Irnham, Sir Robert Tyrwhitt, George Heneage esq., Lionel Skipwith esq., Francis Missenden esq., William Heneage esq., William Bard and Hugh Griffin, gentlemen. At the same time there were persons of the same class resident in the town. They were possibly

---

* He was also interested in shipping. In 1540 at Somercotes he bought a boat and an anchor from John Scarlett, master of the *Anne* of Calais.

landless younger sons living on annuities and attracted to Grimsby by the market and the cheapness of provisions. They included Leonard Cracroft and Thomas Hatcliffe, esquires, and William Kirton, William Pormort, Christopher Wentworth and John Sutcliffe, gentlemen. Some were certainly poor. William Palmer, gentleman, was worth only £8 12s. when he died in 1573. Others were better endowed. Solomon Sutcliffe, who became alderman in 1598, had a brother who was Dean of Exeter and a son who was a courtier of James I.[23]

Whether as residents or proprietors, the gentry connected with Grimsby were not mere spectators in the affairs of the borough. Sir Christopher Ayscough of Ashby was mayor in 1511 and 1533. His cousin, Sir William Ayscough of Stallingborough, was admitted as burgess for his good offices to the town. When Richard Day, a cooper, refused to remake the common measures in a manner which he believed was intended to defraud countrymen, he appears to have appealed to Sir William who wrote a stern letter to the mayor.

> Ye are very extreme against my servant in that thing which is right for the common weal of your town and the country both. I must needs see that my servant have right, and the better for this my writing, or else ye shall cause me to put the matter to further knowledge, which I should be sorry to do, as knoweth Our Lord, who preserve you.*[24]

Possibly resentment against such interference as this was a motive which caused the burgesses to try to limit the election of gentlemen as mayor. In the presence of Richard Thimolby, the mayor and himself a gentleman, and of thirty-six other humbler burgesses, it was resolved that no non-resident was to be elected mayor and that anyone urging the contrary should be disfranchised. Nevertheless, on thirty-six occasions in the sixteenth century the mayor was an esquire or a gentleman related to landed families and on seventeen other occasions the surnames of the mayors suggest similar connections.[25]

There was a party which felt strongly that the borough was safest when it was in the hands of gentlemen. In 1541 Richard Thimolby

---

* Sir William was father for the martyr Ann Ayscough. She married Thomas Kyme who held eighty acres of arable land, divided into three farms in the manor of Clee, in right of his wife, of the mayor and burgesses. Sir William Ayscough also had three perches of arable at Horley Hills in the same manor. A Robert Ayscough, gentleman, appears in the court records of 1536 as assaulted by Mr. Bellingham, and Richard Ayscough of Grimsby, gentleman, in 1576 left £40 for the education of his nephew Francis, if the estate would stand it.

The Reformation and the Gentry

with two other gentlemen were appointed to make regulations for the keeping of good order. In 1564 George Hustwaite, one of the bailiffs, said before the mayor that he prayed God that the putting of Mr. Empringham into the hall and other stout doings were not a further trouble to the town. On Twelfth Night he said to George Lusom, the town clerk, that it would be a good deed and very necessary that the borough should be ordered by the wise justices of the county and the liberty clean taken away. When the mayor ordered him to the bar to answer for his contempt, he was rebellious. He was supported by Mr. Richard Thimolby, whom the mayor then called a ruffian, and Thimolby then boldly threatened to be revenged on him if he could find him outside the liberty, and Mr. John Thimolby and Mr. Edward Skipwith then added their threats. The town clerk, a few days later, said, 'There are no more honest men in this town but rake-hells, except only Mr. Mayor and Mr. Empringham.'[26]

In 1553 Francis Ayscough wrote from S. Kelsey to Sir William Cecil to suggest that the church of St. Mary at Grimsby should be demolished. Cecil could have the lead, and he himself would like the timber and the stone. The town, 'in great ruin and decay and nothing so populous as it hath been', did not need two churches, and the rector was an absentee. St. Mary's survived a few more years, and the two parishes were consolidated in 1586. In the next generation, Gervase Holles believed that great misfortune had come to all the families which had sacrilegiously used the stones of the demolished church.[27]

Some Grimsby families certainly resisted the Elizabethan settlement of the church. Michael Empringham, alderman, and twenty-four others were named in 1564 as persistent absentees from church, and in the following year twenty-one persons were named as illegally absenting themselves from church to go wild-fowling. After the Northern Rebellion, Robert Morton, who had been in Rome for three years, was under suspicion of sending messages to Thomas Westworth at Grimsby. In 1565 Thomas Lewsham, a servant of Sir Charles Danby, came to Grimsby with information about secret masses in Yorkshire and was examined by Sir Richard Thimolby and Tristram Tyrwhitt.[28]

Where the sympathy of particular individuals lay is sometimes difficult to decide. In November 1584 Mark Holt* then living at Grimsby, was denounced as a Jesuit by Sylvester Bellowe. He was also believed to have torn up the Queen's proclamation against papal bulls

---

* There was actually a Jesuit named William Holt who had been active in Scotland and became rector of the English College at Rome.

and seditious books. He was bound over to appear when required, residing in the meantime at the parsonage of Everingham in Yorkshire. He made his escape, and John Hatcliffe, as mayor, was held responsible. But Sylvester Bellowe, his accuser, and son of the eminently Protestant John Bellowe, was himself suspected to be a recusant. In 1577 there was an information against him for unlawfully bringing crosses into the country for his daughters, and in 1586 Sir William Pelham called him a company-keeper with papists; but Pelham was trying to force him to sell the manors of Cadney and Howsham.[29]

The position of the Pormorts was less ambiguous. George Pormort, formerly of Gray's Inn, and mayor in 1565 married a Bleasby of Bleasby. Their second son, Thomas, studied at Rheims and Rome and was sent as a seminary priest on the English mission. He was arrested in 1591 and executed in St. Paul's churchyard on 20 February 1592.*[30]

NOTES

1. PRO, SC, 26 Hen. VIII, 2006, mem. 53-57v.
2. GCB I, f. 311, 360v.
3. CB (Misc.), 13 Hen. VIII, Oct.; CB (Misc.), 12 Hen. VIII, 8 April.
4. CB (Misc.), 13 Hen. VIII, 18 May; CB (Misc.), 15 Hen. VIII, 8 Dec.; CB (Misc.), 19 Hen. VIII, 31 March, 19 Dec.
5. GCB I, f. 160v; CB (Misc.), 15 Hen. VIII, 26 June.
6. GCB I, f. 253; LAO/LCC, 1535-7, 3; PRO, SC, 26 Hen. VIII, 2006, mem. 53-57v.
7. VCH: *Valor Ecclesiasticus*, IV, 67-8.
8. LPH VIII (1537), 177, 481.
9. Ibid., 593; 828, xii.
10. LPH VIII XII, Part I, 70, viii; XI, 996, 1103; XII, Part I, 581, 591.
11. CB (Misc.), 28-9 Hen. VIII, 30 Jan., 26 June, 15 Jan.
12. GCB I, f. 258v, 262v.
13. GCB I, f. 151, 159, 163.
14. GCB I, f. 96v, 168v, 175, 175v, 180, 179, 222.
15. CB (Misc.), 28 Hen. VIII, 4 April; Court Leet, 3 and 4 Philip and Mary; GCB I, f. 266v; CB (Misc.), 37 Hen. VIII, 17 Sept.
16. LPH VIII, XIX, Part I, 2610 (78), 98); XI, 489; LRS, LIII, 57.
17. LAO/LCC, 1538-40, 54; VCH, 219; LPHVIII, XVIII, 413, 567.
18. LRS LIII, 147, 107, 46; Surtees Society: *Diary of Abraham de la Pryme*, 154; LAO, Heneage, Wellow Rental, 1622, 1624, 1625.
19. GCB, 289v, 291v; LAO/LCC, 1538-40, 221; LPHVIIIXI, 585, 828; XIV, Part II, 341; NS, XVII, 57; CPR (Edw. VI) I, 200, 212, 78; IV, 432; CPR (Philip and Mary) IV, 58-9.
20. Camden Society, NS, LV, 197; GCB I, f. 168; CB (Misc.), 5 Hen. VIII, 8 and 13 Nov.

---

* John Spencer, a Jesuit (1601-71) who also used the name Vincent Hatcliffe was born in Lincolnshire and was probably the Vincent, son of George Hatcliffe, gentleman, baptised in St. James's 31 August 1600. A John Spencer had been baptised there 22 October 1566.

The Reformation and the Gentry 97

21. CB (Misc.), 8 Hen. VIII, Dec., 12 May; 23 Hen. VIII, 20 June; CB (1539-48), Sept. 1540.
22. Ibid., 18 Feb. 1540; Camden Society, NS, LV, 214; CB (1539-48), Nov. 18 1540; LAO/LCC, 1506, 27; 1546; 1557 iii, 61; LAO, Inventories, 8/207, 50/55.
23. Maddison, *Lincolnshire Pedigrees*, 958; Court Leet, Easter, 1582, Easter 1587; LAO, Inventories, 54/210; GCB I, f. 321v; Maddison, op. cit., 939.
24. Ibid., 60; GCB I, f. 94, 154v; CB (Misc.), 16 Hen. VIII, 16 June; CB (Misc.), 28 Hen. VIII, 4 April and 32 Hen. VIII: CB (Misc.), 27 Hen. VIII, 11 Jan.; LAO/LCC, 1576, 2.
25. GCB l, f. 175v, 209v.
26. GCB I, 267; HMC, 280; CB (1562-75), f. 37.
27. HMC *Salisbury* I, 109; HMC, 295.
28. CB (1562-75), f. 36v; HMC *Salisbury* II, 191-2; Strype, *Annals* I, Part II, 196.
29. DNB xxvii, 208; APC, NS, XIV, 37; HMC, 282; CSPD (1547-80), 578; CSPD (1581-90), 305.
30. R. Challoner, *Memoirs of Missionary Priests*, 186; DNB liii, 358.

VII

The Town in the Sixteenth Century

In the course of the sixteenth century the haven continued to deteriorate, but up to the middle of the century, at any rate, trade in coal and corn played a significant part in the economy of the town, and for villages up to fifteen or twenty miles distance, as at Walesby, where a road was called Grimsbygate, Grimsby Haven was the obvious outlet. The silting of its course, by some attributed to the water mills, took place so gradually that it never seems to have caused alarm, and efforts to prevent it were only of the most modest kind. In 1519 thirty-eight men promised donations up to a total of £12 2s. 4d. for a pair of cloughs to amend the haven. They were built at Simwhite-bridge, and each year a man was paid 4s. to look after them. The next year four men were elected to look to the haven and the burgesses promised to carry out their recommendations, but if they ever made any it was not thought necessary to record them. There were people at Newcastle, however, for whom the state of the haven was of some concern as affecting the coal trade, and in 1537 Michael Mason, an alderman and son of one of those elected to look to the haven in 1519, came back from Newcastle with the money he had received towards the improvement of the haven.[1]

Ordinances affecting the use of the haven were made each year at the Easter and Michaelmas courts, but few of them involved any corporate expenditure. Ships or boats could still come as far as the present-day River-head, sometimes damaging Simwhite-bridge. The mayor in 1514 agreed to forgo part of his pension as a contribution towards the repair of the bridge and orders were regularly made that no vessel should use it as a mooring. There were common staithes or jetties at the haven and near the bridge, and orders were made that timber landed from ships should not be left lying there. Great timbers for Ashby-cum-Fenby church were brought to the haven in a keel by Robert Wright of Waltham in 1522. Orders were frequently repeated that butchers and fishmongers should not throw their refuse into the West Haven near the stone bridge above the water-mill, or anywhere except on a falling tide, and that clothes and tripe were not to be washed within thirty feet of the water-mill. These, however, were not so much measures for the preservation of the haven as public health regulations. Much of the town's water came out of the West Haven.[2]

Without the trade in coal and corn—we hear much less of the fish trade than in the fifteenth century—the town would have been of little significance. The larger coal ships were probably berthed in the marshes towards the mouth of the haven. All carts coming over the Stone-bridge, no doubt from the marsh, with coal were to pay a toll of 4*d*. in 1514. Coal was too valuable to be left lying in the open, and merchants always stored it in warehouses in the town. For the inhabitants at large, the mayor fixed the price of coal and turves landed at the haven either at the common staithes or, if the water was deep enough, at Simwhite-bridge. The bellman went round the town to proclaim the price which had been fixed, and selling was allowed to begin one hour after he had done so. This, at any rate, was what the borough custom required. Coal was sold not only by merchants and ship-owners, but also by the mariners, who received 'portage' coal as part of their wages. Sometimes owners were forbidden to buy back the portage coal from the crew, but usually they were allowed to buy any unsold portage coal, and the mariners were not otherwise allowed to sell to those who did not live in the liberties of Grimsby. Probably most of the coal was shipped by Newcastle owners, but Grimsby men were also active in the trade. In 1527, for example, Michael Mason, Richard Empringham and John Barnardeston, the two latter being members of landowning families, hired Robert Page and his crew to sail to Blyth.[3]

A few men had begun to show an interest in the herring fishery. Thomas Chalender, buried in 1541 in St. George's aisle in St. James's, had a third share in a ship called the *God's Grace* which he left to his son, Edward, with the herring nets. This may have been the *God's Grace* of Clee, whose mariners in 1520 were fined for dropping ballast in the haven. The fact, as we shall see, that some Grimsby ships were well armed with guns by this time may have made them willing to risk hostilities with the French and Dutch herring fleets; but this is the only indication of an active interest in herring fishing.[4]

Much of the corn shipped from the haven still went north rather than to London. Robert Butler of Immingham contracted in March 1500 to deliver 120 quarters of barley to Mr. John Scott of Newcastle, at seven groats a quarter, and received five marks as God's penny to confirm the contract. Sir Christopher Ayscough in 1522 was concerned with Philip Hamby, gentleman, in dealings involving a sack of hops and the shipment of wheat and beans in a ship called the *Marie George*. A toll was levied in 1532 on twenty voyages by ships and keels taking a total of 3,078 quarters of corn from the haven. Of this amount forty quarters was shipped by Michael Mason in the *Leonard of Newcastle*. The *Great George*, the *Little George* and eight other ships were engaged in these voyages.[5]

The corn trade was regulated by the borough. At the house of Robert West, after an ordinance had been made in the mayor's court for measuring corn, Percival Banks, burgess and mercer, spoke abusively and said

> that it should be broken within a day or two and called the chamberlain fool for doing of his office. He would have his ship laden with corn this week, and then he should see who would ask him any, for he would pay none for any man. He has said aforetime that he is mayor now was never his mayor nor never should be.

The mayor was Peter Mason, whose son, Michael, was a corn merchant who in 1534 was licensed to export 200 quarters of wheat.[6]

Corn for the king's use was shipped from the haven, though often in a manner which made it seem a mixed blessing. At the direction of Richard Powell, the king's purveyor, in 1522, William Hatcliffe, the mayor, directed that the *Magdalene* should be loaded with eighty quarters of wheat belonging to John Allan and Richard Lucas. They were to be paid 7s. a quarter, but Lucas said he had been offered 8s. and refused to have his corn taken, saying that the mayor had no authority in the county. The mayor answered that he had the king's commission to value the corn. The mayor's sergeant, with the help of others, then arrested Lucas. Two years later Thomas Hatcliffe was commissioned to purchase corn for the king's forces in the north and in France. 1,158 quarters were milled at Grimsby and Skitter Mills, and carried to Berwick, Calais and Sandwich in the *Mary Grimsby*, the *Erasmus* and three other Grimsby ships, and in ships of Skitter Mills, Barton and Barrow.[7]

It was not to be expected that there would be no smuggling, and it is perhaps a little surprising that an accusation of doing a little in that line could be regarded as slanderous. It was held that John Best had misdemeaned himself before the mayor by calling William Beatniffe a false wretch, and saying that he had stowed sheep skins under his cabin. This was in 1526. By 1600 control was perhaps stricter. Benjamin

The Town in the Sixteenth Century

Richardson declared that David Maisterton had taken twenty quarters of beans and six of malt to Scotland from Stallingborough without paying any custom. Stallingborough was no doubt chosen as a place less likely to attract notice.[8]

Piracy and war at sea were still almost normal for seafarers, though there are signs that the armament of ships was beginning to make a significant difference. In 1523 so many Scottish ships lay at the mouth of the Humber that no shipmaster dared to venture out without assistance. Thomas Demilton, who did, was taken to Leith with his ship, the *Barbara*, and duly paid his ransom. Several Demiltons lived in Grimsby at that time. Robert was master of the *Mary Grimsby* in 1524, and in 1531 John Demilton was in the Isle of Man with a pirate named Kellwanton. He was obviously a pirate himself. When he fled to Grimsby and was arrested by Mr. John Heneage, his ship was found to be armed with a firkin of gunpowder, ten pieces of ordnance with their chambers, 1,200 pieces of pitch and resin, which would be used for setting fire to an enemy, three crossbows, eight bows and ten sheaves of arrows.[9]

In 1543 French and Scottish ships of war threatened the transport of corn from Hull and Grimsby to the king's forces on the Scottish Border. At the end of October 1544 a Grimsby ship bound for Newcastle, chased by a French or Scottish marauder, ran aground at Hartlepool as the only means of escape. The crew made a hole to sink her and came ashore in a boat, but the enemy were well provided with guns, and were able to take her off in spite of the arrows which were shot at them. The following day, 1 November, a Scottish ship attacked a crayer off Whitby, drove another aground at Robin Hood's Bay, and then attacked two Grimsby ships and one of York, all bound for Newcastle. One of the Grimsby ships was sufficiently armed to enable the other two to get away under the fire of her nine guns, but she and the York ship were driven on to the rocks, in the course of the fight, under high cliffs three miles from Whitby. Sir Richard Cholmeley sent men down with ropes to hoist the guns 600 feet to the top of the cliffs, but he had no powder, that in the Grimsby ship being either exhausted or ruined by the waves, and so was unable to turn them on the enemy.[10]

As always, anarchy at sea was a two-sided business, in which Grimsby men were sometimes the victims and sometimes the aggressors. The *Rose* of Grimsby, in 1549, with the *Michael* of Hull and a ship of Scarborough, successfully attacked a ship of Amsterdam. The goods of one of the owners, Nanmynk Clarson, were taken to Grimsby, and the Amsterdam authorities empowered a Hull man to act for him, which in all probability meant that he was to ransom the goods on the best terms he could manage. When French pirates brought a great ship of Lübeck to Grimsby Haven in June 1555, the owners asked the mayor of Hull to intervene. His letter to the mayor of Grimsby apparently produced no result. The merchants appealed to the Privy Council, and Christopher Ayscough of Bradley, Vice-Admiral of Lincolnshire, was summoned to appear before the Council and declare what he knew about it. In 1579 Richard Scarborough committed piracy against the *Boyer* and brought her to Grimsby. The merchants of the Steelyard on this occasion also appealed to the Council, and an order was issued that they should be compensated for the pitch, stockfish and other goods which had been taken. The matter was perhaps still not quite disposed of in 1581-2, when the chamberlains paid John Clatham 21*s.* 8*d.* for Edward Jackson's journey to London about the pirates.[11]

Certainly the interest of the town was such as to arouse deep hostility to the jurisdiction of the Admiralty. The Lord Admirals' authority seriously limited that of the borough court. In 1507-8, for example, John Taylor of Saltfleet Haven claimed a debt of 26*s.* 8*d.* from Brian Hansherd of Clee, and Hansherd's ship was arrested. He claimed, however, that the case could not be determined in the mayor's court but only in that of the admiral, so it was necessary to send the Deputy Steward to speak with Mr. John Heneage. When Heneage was elected High Steward in 1521 the mayor and burgesses had been engaged in business concerning the haven, and it was probably felt useful to have the vice-admiral on the side of the borough.[12]

To limit Admiralty jurisdiction in purely commercial matters, the use of weights and measures at the haven was carefully regulated. Four common measures were kept at the haven for the sale of coal, salt, lime and other things. Any man with a balance in his ship was required to land it upon the green shore clear of salt water. As far as possible selling on board ships was avoided, but in those cases where goods were sold on board, the heavy penalty of 20*s.* was held over those who sold by land measure instead of by water measure. A deep concern with the limits of Admiralty jurisdiction probably explains why it was found necessary to enter in the court book a record of matters relative to Hedon. In April 1541 the bosun of the *Michael* of Newcastle tried to kill Thomas Rutte, one of the owners, but was prevented by one of the bailiffs who was buying coal in the ship. Thomas Robinson, the sergeant of Hedon, made no arrest for this affray; but when the ship was aground

The Town in the Sixteenth Century 103

in the haven at low tide, with a cable fast in the ship and the other end on the green shore, the sergeant levied his staff and arrested the cable in an action for debt owed for victuals bought in Hedon. The plaintiff was John Underhill, another of the owners. Thomas Rutte denied that he ever complained to any officer of the Lord Admiral. Plainly they understood it all a good deal better than we now can.[13,14]

The officers of the Admiralty could be inconvenient because they had knowledge of matters which the men of Grimsby would have preferred to conceal. A Scottish ship with salmon came to the haven in November 1550 without any safe conduct, and there was a danger that the goods would be confiscated. This, and occasional piracy, made it unpleasant to have people in the town who would act for the Admiralty. Thomas Maddison's wife provided hospitality for the vice-admiral, and the chamberlains paid her 13s. 4d. for doing so. But in 1566 her husband, an alderman, twice left the hall when commanded to stay and wrote a letter to Lord Clinton, the Lord High Admiral, to the prejudice of the borough. In 1579 the mayor and burgesses actually disfranchised Richard Holmes because he had been acting for the Admiralty and Lord Clinton, at Tattershall Castle, wrote to signify that the penalties of his displeasure might be very severe. Yet although in most other matters the borough was infinitely pliable in the hands of magnates, in this it was prepared to put up a strong resistance. A letter, signed by the mayor, and thirty-four burgesses, was sent to him, insisting that they had acted strictly in accordance with their charters.[15]

The borough sometimes adopted an equally cavalier approach to officers of the Customs. In 1600 the mayor tried to insist that Anthony Atkinson of Hull, the head searcher, and John Johns of Grimsby, vintner and deputy searcher, should appear before him to be examined on oath on certain matters allegedly affecting the interest of the Crown. They refused. Legally the town was in a weak position. But Atkinson was seen to represent the ascendancy of Hull, which by now was felt to be a major cause of the difficulties of Grimsby merchants, and it was worth trying what could be done to harass him through his subordinates. Officious persons who made themselves sufficiently unpopular could always be arrested in a civil action, a device which was adopted against servants of the Admiralty. Indeed, after the election of the new mayor in September 1601 an attempt was made to use this quasi-legal trickery to persuade the Admiralty to moderate its demands. It was suggested that the mayor should be allowed to permit the Admiralty

H

court to sit in the town, and to direct that no one coming to it should be arrested for debt, on condition that Grimsby mariners were not put on 'foreign' juries or forced to make presentments of wrecks and royalties within the liberties.[16]

This was no more than a last brave effort for a dying cause. Year by year the haven was less frequented by shipping. In 1544, 1,509 fothers of lead had been brought to Grimsby to be sent abroad for the king's necessities, one-eighth of the whole amount to be sent. By the financial year 1571-2, the only vessels which used the haven were two keels, possibly with turf, another with lime, a crayer with salt, three ships, four hoys with coal and a Scottish ship with fish. In 1592 the port was sufficiently obscure for certain London merchants to hope to use Grimsby as a means of breaking the Hull monopoly of northern coastal trade. John Sibley and Robert Polsen, both of Thames Street, London, in August were admitted as burgesses of Grimsby. Each paid a fine of 50s., which was about double the fine usually demanded. By December the Hull merchants had made their complaint to the Privy Council and an order issued which put an end to any hope of London merchants trading through Grimsby. They had landed iron and other goods at Grimsby and had then shipped them to towns in the northern counties. It was ordered that except for coal and millstones no merchant of London or elsewhere should send any goods to any port or haven between Boston and Hartlepool unless he had first been admitted to the incorporation of Hull.[17]

As the shipping interest declined, the market, carefully regulated, was increasingly realised to be the main prop of what remained of the prosperity of the town. There were two weekly markets, on Wednesday and Saturday, beginning as soon as the mayor made his proclamation at nine o'clock at the market-cross, which stood where the road out of the Bull Ring now joins Flottergate and Victoria Street.* It was only on market days that 'foreigners' could sell bread or baked meats in the town. Except at the St. Bartholomew fair they were not allowed to keep shops selling bread, ale or victuals, and no inhabitant was allowed to let a shop to them for this purpose. Indeed the inhabitants themselves were forbidden to sell bread or baked meats from their windows, and were permitted to do so only in the market. The distinction between selling from a window and selling in the market must sometimes have been a subtle one. Market stalls were not physically very different from shops,

---

* The cross was partly of timber. In 1559-60 the chamberlains procured spars, boards and nails for the cross.

The Town in the Sixteenth Century   105

and except in the Bull Ring, medieval encroachments had narrowed the market place to the width of a street.

Fishermen were under a particular temptation to sell their catch at the haven and as soon as their boat came in, but they too were forbidden to sell except in the market. This regulation was strangely in conflict with the ordinances regarding the quartermen, who were required to supervise the sale of fish at the haven; but it was most often repeated in the latter part of the sixteenth century when the arrival of fishing boats in the haven must have been a great rarity. A regulation, aimed at the malpractices of country butchers, was proclaimed twice every year, to the effect that no sheep carcases must be sold in the market without their kidneys or suet.[18,19]

The mayor, with his servants, was the grand exception to all these rules. He alone was allowed to buy food before it came into the market, either personally or through his servants. When corn was scarce, however, no exception was made in his favour. At the Michaelmas court in 1556 an ordinance was made that no one, except strange mariners who came by water, was to buy corn or food in the market before eleven o'clock, under pain of losing whatever he bought. Yet in 1523, apparently a year of scarcity, corn brought to the market was reserved for victuallers until noon, after which time the rest of the inhabitants could buy what they needed. In 1534 people coming to the market from the country were not to buy any corn unless they had brought an equal quantity with them to sell. About 1550 the buying of corn in the Wednesday market was restricted. To allow time for all the country farmers to come in, corn was not to be sold before eleven in summer or noon in winter. Buyers could take only as much as they needed for a week for their household and guests; but when the clock struck two, anyone could buy as much as he wished, except on those occasions when a prohibition might be laid on those having much corn growing in the field or in store.[20]

Butchers were the object of a good deal of borough legislation. They were not to buy meat from country butchers for sale in the town, or to buy the skins of sheep and cattle. They were not to sell meat except in the market, and country butchers and others from the country were not to hawk from house to house. No butcher was allowed to sell corrupt flesh from any place where beasts or swine had died of the murrain. To ensure that they did not steal cattle and hide the evidence against them, they were forbidden to remove them from the commons except between 4 a.m. and 8 p.m. If a butcher wished to kill a bull, he was not to do so until it had been baited by dogs, as a public entertainment, in the presence of the mayor.[21]

The borough court issued orders relating to common rights with very great frequency, but only rarely paid any attention to the cornfield. Everyone had common rights, but less than a tenth of the householders held land in the fields. From the fifteenth century, the commons were stinted. At the beginning of the sixteenth the stint was one beast or cow for each householder with a whole toft. A burgess could keep a beast and either a horse or 2 cows, with 40 sheep if he had served as bailiff and 20 if he had not. Those who had been mayor could keep 2 beasts and a horse, with 60 sheep. Towards the end of the sixteenth century the stint was reduced. An ordinary inhabitant could now keep 5 sheep and a beast, a burgess 20 sheep and 2 beasts, a twelve-man 30 sheep and 3 beasts, an alderman 40 sheep and 4 beasts, and the mayor during his term of office 60 sheep and 4 beasts and a horse in the Little Field when it lay open, which was by no means every year. When it did, no sheep could be put there before Martinmas, and no oxen or steers above a year old.

The reduction in the stint had been made necessary by the enclosure of the West Marsh in or about 1514. After the enclosure of the West Marsh the commons were driven twice monthly, but the old fines, 1d. for each sheep, were not increased in spite of the fall in the value of money. Any renewal of a lease in the West Marsh had to be made with the consent of thirty burgesses three years before the expiration of the old lease. Formerly no person could let his common-rights to any other. This was known as 'gisting' or taking to half part, an arrangement under which the commoner and the owner of the animals shared the profits. Now, a small concession was made. Any burgess who was a poor and decayed person, but not other inhabitants, could let his beast-gates in the Little Field between Mayday and Lammas.[22]

The use of the commons involved the risk of animals straying into the town. No one was to allow cattle in the streets without someone to tend them, and if they rubbed down any walls—clearly walls of mud are intended—he was to repair them immediately. Since the marshes lay north of the town and all animals were kept in the town or in farmhouses to the south of it, there was a procession of pigs, sheep and cattle through the streets every morning and evening, and this regulation was particularly necessary. Pigs and cattle must be in the streets only at a lawful time, which meant when they were going to the commons, or returning, or, in the case of pigs, on Saturdays when the pigsties were being cleaned. The swineherd blew his horn at 7 a.m. and kept the pigs in the fields until 5 p.m. There was a neatherd also, and it was the duty of the common sergeant to distrain on the property of anyone who refused to pay the herdmen. The bailiffs took a fine of 1*d*. for each pig not properly ringed.[23]

There was no road from the East Marsh to the West Marsh except through the town, and there was therefore a common fold in each marsh for straying animals and those impounded by the chamberlains. Impounded animals were frequently unlawfully removed from the common folds by force. Whenever the gates or walls were broken, the chamberlains had to repair them within twenty-four hours. Nathaniel Lloyd deposed that Mrs. Jane Constable had been heard to say that she did not break the fold, but opened the lock, and that he also heard her say 'What, is Mr. Mayor's colours now up? Turd in his teeth!', a vulgar expression of ill-will frequently used. The borough also took fines for similar infringements at Clee. In course of time, with the West Marsh no longer common, the principal common fold was in the East Marsh at a point now recalled by Pinfold Lane, and a second pinfold for animals straying in the corn field was made near the Nuns' Farm, and in 1702 Christopher Chappell was presented for breaking it. Further, to put animals found straying in any place but the pinfold was an offence, in that if people were allowed to do so the distinction between stealing and impounding would often be a fine one.[24]

The commons were not only stinted. Only certain animals could be put on particular parts of them. In 1531 John Dale and John Blacklock kept sheep in the pasture called Haycroft, contrary to custom. An order of 1538 reserved the Little Field for geldings and oxen, but when in 1541 Stephen Bartholomew was found to have nine cows and twenty-three sheep there, and pigs which damaged the grass, he claimed that he was entitled to have thirty sheep and three beasts there. Geese, at one time allowed on the commons if their wings were clipped, from 1534 were to be kept on the land of those who owned them. The chamberlains, about 1550 were ordered to buy a common bull to be kept in the Little Field, but because Nicholas Reed had kept a bull through the winter, he was still allowed to keep it there. Anyone could gather rushes on the commons, but not elsewhere, except with the owner's permission, and although peat could be dug, it was an offence to dig for it, since the pits damaged the commons.[25]

As early as 1465, in opposition to the claims of the relatively few landowners, the borough had ordered that not only the marshes but also, at the proper season, the corn field was part of the commons of the town, to be occupied only under the jurisdiction of the chamberlains. In the Little Field, landowners were rather more privileged. Richard Thimolby was allowed to enclose his land there, and so withdraw it completely from the commons when it lay fallow. Crops there did not follow the ordinary rotation.[26]

Next, the West Marsh began to receive special treatment. In 1514, Philip Miffin, Peter Mason and three others were appointed by the mayor to supervise the enclosure of the West Marsh, and it was afterwards remembered that this had happened in Mr. Miffin's time, which suggests that he was the moving spirit. Even the west fitties, the sandy grassland, outside the sea-dyke near the Humber, subject to occasional flooding by the tide, were ceasing to be common. Michael Mason was given a year's lease, with an option to renew, of the west fitties, from the north-east corner of his own close. By 1560 the west fitties were farmed for 10s., and the West Marsh, by nine tenants, for £2 16s. 8d. Three of the tenants, Silvester Bellowe, Edward Sapcotts and Joan Barnardeston, were members of landed families. By 1565 the less valuable East Marsh began to be threatened. It was ordered that it should be 'sparred up' and that no one should have any sheep or other animals there from 11 November to 1 May, an order likely to have the effect that those who could not afford to hire grazing would have to sell most of their stock.[27]

It was not the landowners but the burgesses, except the really poor ones, who were the beneficiaries of these changes. Comparatively few orders were issued affecting the open fields. There were a few which were no more than reasonable steps to protect farmers.

Occasionally the gathering of peascods without the owner's consent was forbidden. Where land was sown with wheat, no one was to turn his plough or the cattle drawing it except on his own land. No one was to make 'scythe-paths' or ways to the windmill across the corn field, but to keep to the ancient ways and paths, lest farmers should suffer by having rights of way established across their land. No one was to tether mares of foals near strips from which the sheaves had not been removed, and people from Bradley must follow the highway with their carts and not a short cut across the field. But any landowner who encroached on common rights was strictly dealt with. John Sutcliffe, in 1587, had enclosed part of his land on the west side of the way going from the Nuns' Gates southwards, that is, in Scartho Road. He was ordered to remove his fences immediately and not to interfere further with commoners, under the exceptionally heavy penalty of £3 6s. 8d. As late as 1723 the chamberlains were ordered to impound the cattle put into the corn field before the harvest was completed by Mrs. Mary Allen and her sons of Abbey Farm, and Thomas Whelpdale of Bargates Farm.[28]

Considerable quantities of fish and game were taken in the commons, and there were one or two persons for whom this was the main occupation. People occasionally appear in the court rolls described as fowler. Arthur Cletter, who got his living by spearing eels, was forbidden to 'stang' for them in Lent except once weekly. He was not the only eel-catcher, yet he was a man of sufficient substance to have one daughter married to a Grimsby mariner and, more significantly, another married to a London grocer. The taking of wild fowl involved the digging of trenches and those who went wild fowling were required to fill their trenches in as soon as their sport was over. Nets of suitable mesh and lightness were required, and in his will made in 1578 Alderman Robert Wright mentions his stint-net and his plover net and a flight-net with poles and head-rope.[29]

All those who caught sakers, swans, cranes, goss-hawks and similar royal birds were required to present them to the mayor, under a penalty of 40s. In 1534 it was actually ordered that no one, whether he was a burgess or not, should take any fowl whatsoever, John and James Hatcliffe were commanded to present the two swans which they had taken to the mayor, and the chamberlains were directed to view all trenches which had been dug for fowling and to levy fines. This stern attitude was soon relaxed, though swans in the Haycroft always remained under special protection. As the use of firearms spread it was ordered that only those who were qualified by the statute should shoot with hand-guns or cross-bows except at butts or banks, and that no one should shoot at birds sitting on the church of St. James. St. Mary's was never protected in this way, probably because it was so dilapidated that a few stray shots would do no harm to its windows. In 1582 Christopher Harrington, Adam Sutcliffe and three others shot with hail-shot from a bombard, contrary to the statute, and William Cracroft, gentleman, with Richard Bacon, shot with a stone-bow at St. James's.[30]

It was believed that in 250 years 300 acres of marshland out of a total of 427 acres had been regained from the sea. Up to about 1580, high tides occasionally covered the East Marsh, and in 1612 a man of sixty could remember that at extraordinary spring tides the water had come over the West Marsh to Haycroft, Pitholme and the Salt Ings, which lay outside a bank west of the town which protected the Little Field from the sea. On the east side of the town Wellow Milne Bank extended south to the corn field, but a man of seventy-eight had seen a flood come into North St. Marygate. There were little hills in the East Marsh, perhaps the remains of salt workings, where people believed there had once been houses, but the only house which anyone could remember there was one belonging to Mr. Skailes, about the year 1570. Nevertheless, by the end of the century, the East Marsh was flooded much less frequently, and in 1599 it was enclosed and leased, the mayor and burgesses reserving forty acres of the fitties for themselves. The rest of the inhabitants were left to share no more than forty acres of the fitties worth only 6d. an acre, and remembering how they had once enjoyed common rights in all the marshes, murmured that 'they might perhaps live to see it so again'.[31]

The party responsible for the enclosure of so much common land included John Hatcliffe, mayor in 1596 when the enclosure began and the owner of Pitholme, Solomon Sutcliffe, William Kelk, gentleman and William Gower, each of whom was several times mayor. Their motive, it was said, was not only to enclose the East Marsh but also to lease portions of it to themselves at low rents. Several Exchequer actions were commenced against them. The first was in 1606, and there was another in 1609. In 1625 the opponents of the mayor and burgesses represented to the Exchequer that the inhabitants were too poor to defend their rights by litigation. Those who brought the action were of a very different kind. One of them was Thomas Philips, gentleman, owner of 160 acres, including the Nuns' Farm, and land in the Haycroft and Salt Ings. Another, Simon Patrick, owner of two messuages in Grimsby, was probably the son of Simon Patrick of Caistor, the Elizabethan translator and their leader, William Hatcliffe esq., of West Ravendale, was a decayed squire with a courtly background. He had been a fellow-commoner of Jesus College, Cambridge, in 1581, was admitted to Gray's Inn in 1586, was chief of their Christmas revels in 1588 as Prince of Purpoole, and is believed by Professor Leslie Hotson to have been the W.H. of Shakespeare's sonnets. The real grievance of these people was not that poor commoners were being robbed but that they themselves, as non-burgess landowners, were being treated in the same way.[32]

In 1615 the mayor and burgesses got an Exchequer verdict confirming their right to the marshes, and the 1625 action does not seem to have upset this. Nevertheless these lawsuits in the end brought valuable results to the commoners. The corporation never had the resources to fight a protracted and expensive lawsuit, and caution became necessary. What made caution possible was that the leases of closes in the East Marsh were short ones, and as they expired, much of the land became common again without any overt reversal of policy. The farmers and landowners were not able to push their claims very far until the enclosure act was obtained in the nineteenth century. But the commoners, whose stint had almost been extinguished by 1600, two centuries later still had extensive privileges which were an offence to all right thinking landowners: and as the numbers of the burgesses increased, they ceased to be a class sharply demarcated from the poorer townsmen.[33]

The borough strictly regulated certain aspects of the economic activity of the inhabitants. Glovers were not allowed to buy eggs in the market to use in their craft before noon. An ale-wife was bound to sell to anyone wishing to buy if she had four gallons in store. In 1503 three glovers were presented for practising their craft in the street all the summer, 'in the work of shaving called working upon the tree'. Richard Empringham, Christopher Holsworth and other tanners were not to buy the skins of dogs or sheep after Mayday. Richard Keith and others in 1565 were told that they must not hawk fish or other food in the country except at fairs or markets. And in particular the borough kept the right of expelling anyone from the town, and specifying the terms on which particular classes of people would be permitted to work.[34]

The threat of expulsion was occasionally used as the ultimate sanction behind the authority of the mayor and burgesses as when in 1500 Robert Page, who later occupied the common ferry, was ordered to leave the town with his family in eight days for not keeping his recognisance to be a good neighbour. Sometimes it was a desire to be rid of the poor, or of the potentially disorderly, which prompted the expulsion. About 1550, John Lowran's wife, and all other wives not with their husbands, were to go and join them before the end of November on pain of imprisonment. In 1587 Richard Hallay was to evict the sister whom he had taken into his house, widow Pasmore to evict the woman with child, John Ragge to evict a lame woman, Edward Clark, porter, to evict the persons whom he had lately harboured. Even John Skipwith, gentleman, under a penalty of 40s., had to evict a northern woman with her husband and children. Sometimes the borough desired to get rid of criminals. All stealers of eggs and other petty thieves were to be expelled within a week, as were receivers of stolen goods. Robert Beyk, carpenter, had to go before Whit-Sunday because of the misdemeanour of his wife and children, and anyone who harboured him was to be fined 20s. At Easter 1557 Agnes Walker was given five weeks to leave, because she had received goods stolen by the servants of Robert Hanslay, and Thomas Day was to reform his wife, a stealer of coal, wood, small ale and the like, or to quit the town. Occasionally an order was issued that anyone who had not laid in his supply of fuel for the winter was to be expelled. A man without fuel was a potential thief, and the more substantial burgesses had stocks of coal for sale which might easily be pilfered.[35]

The borough not only exercised the power to remove people from the town. It also tried to prevent the poor, the disorderly and the unattached from coming to live in it. From 1534 no house was to be let to more than one tenant, and no tenant was to sub-let. In 1557 landlords were to evict all idle beggars before Whit-Sunday, and to let houses only to men who could 'live of their own' or support themselves by work. During the annual fairs, people came to the town who would not have been welcomed at other times. In 1553, for example, the chamberlains distributed bread and flesh to sick folk at the fair on three occasions, but spent no more than 5s. on this work of charity. The problem was to prevent such people from becoming permanent inhabitants when the fair was over. In 1583, under a penalty of 40s., no one was to let a house or a shop to anyone not already an inhabitant without the consent of the mayor and his brethren. No one was to come to the town to dwell as a labourer unless the mayor admitted him and he paid a fine of 2s. Shoemakers, tailors, cobblers, glovers, smiths, weavers and similar craftsmen were admitted for 5s. if they were single and 3s. 4d. if they were married. Pedlars paid 5s., mercers and drapers 10s. and merchant adventurers and 'those that shall have any dealing in such like trades' 20s. When a labourer succeeded in becoming an inhabitant, he might soon have cause to regret it. Twice, about the middle of the century, ordinances were made that unless, for some urgent cause, the mayor gave his leave, no labourer was to work in the country when work was available in the town. By comparison, the restrictions on millers were mild. The miller at the haven mill was not to allow any doves or pigeons there, and every miller was 'to serve the inhabitants of this corporation each in his turn before any man from the country'.[36]

The borough required every able-bodied man over the age of sixteen to have a bow and four shafts to practise shooting on holidays, according to the statute.* Up to the end of the sixteenth century archers were shooting at butts, which it was the constables' duty to make, in the Little Field. Few other recreations were regarded as so innocent. Keepers of taverns and alehouses were to see that no unlawful games were played by craftsmen or servants, to allow no dicers or 'carders', or suspect persons to play after the bell had rung eight or 'misdemeaned' persons to stay there after nine out of their beds. And, naturally enough, they were not to give lodging to persons who might be suspected without notifying the mayor. If they could tread this narrow path, Sundays were much the same as weekdays. Business had to cease only in service time, when only strangers riding on urgent business could eat and drink in a victualler's house; and during time of divine service no one could keep open the doors of his coalhouse, warehouse or shop to sell anything.[37]

Even the respectable might offend. In 1520, William Toll, constable and burgess, played unlawful games at midnight in Stephen Rawden's house with the servants, and spoke malicious words to the watchman. In 1565 an alderman and a woman were among fifteen persons caught unlawfully playing cards, and the Rev. Robert Hundleby was one of seventeen who unlawfully played at bowls, occasionally a violent game. James Scopes, at the havenside in July 1523, caused an affray by striking William Bond violently with his bowl. Football too was frowned upon, and in 1589 the Rev. Robert Hundleby, still unregenerate, was one of the eighteen people who played football in the streets, contrary to the commandment of the mayor's lieutenant.[38]

At the same sessions, three men were presented as 'night-walkers'. To be found in the streets at night was always regarded as an offence, since in the absence of any effective police crimes against property were most likely to be committed in darkness. Arthur Hatcliffe, as well as being a footballer, walked abroad at night and 'behaved himself disorderly'. Margaret Smith, a widow, was caught at four in the morning, two days after Christmas 1580, when she went into Mr. Rose's ground 'and there found a chamber door standing on the sneck wherein was certain corn and opened the said door and did fill a bushel of corn into a sack that she did carry with her and that was the first time that ever she did so'. In 1587 Robert Harratt was suspected of going out at night to steal corn and bacon, but said he never went out after returning

* In 1516 John Atkinson, 'scoler' accidentally shot a girl with an arrow while shooting at butts in the garden. The surgeons of the town were sent for, and it was afterwards agreed that the fathers of the boy and girl should each pay them 10s. for healing her.

from work at 7 p.m., and that the corn he had, a mixture of barley, peas, wheat and possibly rye, consisted of a peck which he had bought from a poor man at Cabourne and a peck bought from another poor man. His wife had begged the bacon and three pecks of corn from good folks in the country. William Hallyday, in 1592, had a key which he had stolen from Henry Kirk's shop, and a key from a little hang-lock of his own, and used them to get into Mr. John Hatcliffe's shop two hours after midnight, and stole white and straw-coloured Milan fustian. He used the keys again one night in the same winter and stole Scottish linen, a buskin, two pieces of mockado, three hats, some ribbons, pins and a piece of yellow canvas.[39]

One night about Easter 1582 the servants of John Burnley went at night into the fields with spades and other engines and dug up a great glass and a pot of earth, and were suspected of keeping the treasure which they found. To make the disposal of stolen property more difficult tallow, which sheep stealers might be expected to have, and other goods, were not to be delivered at night. Constables and other persons in authority could lawfully go in the streets at night and listen at windows, but no one else was allowed to do so. In 1485 John Ranby, a weaver, complained that Joan Rawson came at night and stood against the wall of his house, clearly not a very substantial one, to overhear the counsel of his wife and himself.[40]

Occasionally a watchman was employed. In 1522 William Marn was hired at 4*d*. a day as a day watchman. At night,* the policing of the town was left to the constables and such townsmen as might be conscripted for the watch.

More reliance, perhaps, was placed on deterrence than on detection. Convicted thieves were whipped in the market. There was also a pillory in the market, and a pair of stocks. From time to time the chamberlains were ordered to keep them in proper repair, and also to erect the ducking-stool, called 'Cuckstoule', which stood against a pit, probably fed with water from the haven at a point where it was lawful to use the water for washing tripe.[41]

If all the by-laws relating to the streets had been enforced, the town would not have presented the 'very foul' appearance on which a Hull mariner commented in 1536. Two years earlier those selling fish in the

---

* James Scopes took only one turn to watch at night since the whole rota had served seven times. When the mayor met him in the street, and would have committed him to the town hall for contempt, he went into the churchyard and abused the mayor until he was forcibly led away.

market were forbidden to cast fish-guts in the street. Dung was not to be laid above Cowston Pit, where the ducking stool was. In the second half of the century we find orders for the common sergeant to sweep the market place and the Bull Ring weekly, for each householder to sweep the street against his house every Saturday, for blacksmiths shoeing horses to clean the street outside their shops twice a week, and for those delivering coal from carts to clear away the dirt. Butchers were commanded not to throw horns and guts into the street, and anyone scattering ashes, except in the 'dock' by Simwhite-bridge, on the south side of Chantry Lane, or in the low places in the Little Field between the butts, was to be fined 4d. for each scuttle-full. There was to be no dressing of corn in the streets, carts were not to stand there, stables were not to drain into the streets and the channels, from sinks in houses were to be scoured twice weekly. But these were probably counsels of perfection. Dunghills were left in the streets for week after week. Mr. John Kingston was fined 12d. 'because one swine of his lieth dead unburied, corrupting the town'. John Short cast dung and earth into Moody Lane from Mr. Sapcott's ground in 1565, and in 1582 the lane was again choked with ashes and rubbish.[42]

Because of the risk of fire no one was permitted to have a tenant living in a shop without a chimney. The use of fire-pots was common, as for most purposes this was the easiest way of lighting a fire, but flying sparks could be dangerous, and it was unlawful to carry embers from one house to another in a pot lacking a proper cover. Some houses were of brick, and so comparatively fireproof. When James Byrkes, a bricklayer, was admitted as burgess in 1515 he paid part of his admission fine by working at 'tiler-craft' at various places assigned by the mayor and chamberlains, and some of the houses belonging to the Rayner chantry had brick walls. But the basic structural material was still timber. In 1501 the servants of Alexander del See made two great pits in the common way against his close in Deansgate for repairing a wall, to the harm of all people coming to the town. This kind of digging was often necessary to shore up the posts of timber-framed houses, but those who did it were required by borough custom to fill in the hole and re-pave the street. Timber-framed houses with a thatch could be wholly destroyed by fire. Hence the frequent repetition of the order against fire-pots without lids.[43]

All the time the authorities were struggling against the appearance of waste plots and ruined houses in the town. The penalty of £10 could be inflicted on anyone who actually pulled down a house or building near the highway.* It was more difficult to prevent decay from natural causes. Nevertheless all those who failed to repair their decayed pentices in the market were threatened with a fine of 5s.: and in 1555 seven persons were given two years to rebuild on their waste plots. It is not likely, however, that the heirs of Lord Scrope, Lady Katherine Heneage or Mr. Christopher Hilliard who were among those named, could be coerced by the fear that the £10 fine might actually be levied on them.[44]

The houses of the wealthier inhabitants usually had a hall, still often the main apartment, one or more parlours, chambers above the hall and parlours, a buttery, a kitchen, a larder and a brewhouse.† A few people still kept weapons and armour in their houses. In 1578 a corselet and headpieces hung in Alderman Michael Empringham's hall, with a painting of the parable of the prodigal son. Richard Brather had a caliver, a bow and a javelin in his hall, but Brian Boulton kept his sword and dagger in the kitchen. Many households were distinctly rural.‡ David Ragge, a butcher and alderman, had fifty-five sheep, seven cows, a mare and a foal, which he kept in closes which he rented in the marshes. There were nine loads of hay at his house, and another in a chamber over his shop in the market place. Alderman Richard Thimolby who died in 1552 kept two cows, two pigs and a horse, in his yard as well as coal, and even one of his poorer descendants, a tailor, had six sheep and a pig in his yard. A rich man,§ such as Hugh Brown with 189 quarters of barley, beans and peas, might have to store most of his corn in the yard, but even he conformed to custom by keeping sacks of wheat in a chamber over the hall, and indeed most houses had some corn in an upper chamber where it was easier to keep it dry and free from rats and mice.[45]

This small, secluded, semi-rural society in a borough sinking into obscurity and corruption had one link with the great world of the

---

* In May 1516 the Prior of Ormsby undertook to rebuild his house near the market cross before Christmas, and to raise the front before the fair in August 'if any spars come to the haven in the mean season'.

† Some houses still had windows without glass. In 1522 arbitrators awarded to Mr. Fotherby the glass of a house which he had bought. It was clearly possible to claim that a man who purchased a house did not automatically acquire the window glass.

‡ George Clatam, a shoemaker, who rented six shops, provided for his young daughter by leaving money to buy a cow to be kept by her guardian.

§ Lyon Kirke, gentleman, was an exceptional householder. He had £80 in gold in his chests and trunks, the care of which in 1625 he entrusted to his niece, when he was sick and in danger of death. Mr. Waters, his physician, told her that her husband, Lyon Kirke's executor, was like to be cozened.

Renaissance. Players from London came almost every year. At the beginning of the sixteenth century the town had its own play of 'Holy John of Bower', and the Grimsby players had been rewarded with 6s. 8d. when they acted at Louth. Similarly, country players from Marsh Chapel, Kirton Lindsey, Stallingborough and Grimoldby had been rewarded when they visited the town, as were the minstrels of Hull and of Lord Darcy when they came in 1514, and the minstrels of the Duke of Buckingham and the Earl of Northumberland when they were at the Bartholomew fair in 1499.[46]

But there were also players of a different and superior kind. About 1550 the king's players visited the town, and in 1562-3 the Earl of Warwick's players came, followed by four different unidentified companies in the next year. Lord Mountjoy's players performed, or at any rate were rewarded, on Sunday 23 February 1572, the queen's players on the 11 June, and the Earl of Leicester's players on 6 August, when Burbage's father was already a member. The Earl of Worcester's company came in 1576-7, a year in which they were also at Stratford on Avon, and the Earl of Stafford's men were in the town in the same year.[47]

The chamberlains' accounts of the later part of the century do not distinguish between country players and true professionals. Perhaps the distinction was hard to make with such players as Mr. St. Paul's, who were rewarded in 1578-9, and Sir William Holles men, who often performed, concluding, as Alderman Fotherby used to relate, with a prayer for the queen and their patron.[48]

But every year, as far as we can tell, plays were put on by London companies, and people came in from the country to see them. A Nettleton farmer christened his son Tamburlaine, perhaps after seeing the play of 'Tamburlaine the Great'; and people came from as far as Caistor to see plays at Grimsby. In 1602 John Henchlawe of Grimsby and Nicholas Blunston sat together at the play, and quarrelled as they left. Two days later they met in Caistor market place. Blunston struck Henchlawe, who, incited by his father-in-law, drew his rapier and killed Blunston. He escaped to Scotland, persuaded James VI to intercede for him, and was finally pardoned in 1604.[49]

NOTES

1. LAO, Glebe Terriers, Walesby, 1577; GCB I, 172v; Chamberlains 8 Eliz.; CB (Misc.), 12 Hen. VIII, 4 June; GCB I, f. 238v.

2. GCB I, f. 161; Courts Leet, 1534, 3 and 4 Philip and Mary; CB (Misc.), 14 Hen. VIII, 29 July.
3. CB (Misc.), 8–9 Hen. VIII, June; CB (1562–75), f. 64v; CB (Misc.), 29 Hen. VIII, 11 Sept.; Courts Leet (undated), c. 1550 and 24 Eliz.; CB (Misc.), 27 Hen. VIII, 27 Feb. and 18 Hen. VIII, 9 April.
4. LAO/LCC, 1541, Thomas Chalender; CB (Misc.), 12 Hen. VIII, 18 Nov.; GCB I, 265v.
5. GCB I, f. 348; CB (Misc.), 23–4 Hen. VIII, Aug.; GCB I, f. 259.
6. CB (Misc.), 9 Hen. VIII; LPHVIII (1534), 1498–9.
7. GCB I, f. 225; LPHVIII (1524), 281.
8. CB (Misc.), 7 Dec. 1526; CB, Eliz. (fragment), 522v.
9. LPHVIII III, 3159; 3345; V, 379.
10. Ibid. XVIII, Part I, 141, 146; XIX, Part II, 514, 530.
11. HMC, 275, 255; APC V, 251; XI, 65; Chamberlains 5 Eliz.
12. CB (Misc.), 23 Hen. VII, 3 June 1521.
13. Courts Leet, Eliz., *passim*; Michaelmas, 3 and 4 Philip and Mary; GCB I, 275v.
14. GCB I, f. 235; CB (Misc.), 16 Hen. VIII, 15 Sept.
15. APC, NS, XI, 65; Chamberlains 1559–60; CB (1562–1575), f. 75; HMC, 256.
16. CB, Eliz. (fragment), f. 523, 540v.
17. LPHVIII XIX, Part I, 297; Draft Chamberlains' Account, 1571; GCB, f. 317; APC, NS, XXIII, 385.
18. Ordinances, 1498 and *temp*. Eliz.: Court Leet, Easter, 3 and 4 Philip and Mary; Courts Leet, Eliz., *passim*.
19. Court Leet, c 1580.
20. Ibid.; Court Leet, Michaelmas, 3 and 4 Philip and Mary; CB (Misc.), 15 Hen. VIII, 8 Dec.; Court Leet, 25 Hen. VIII.
21. Court Leet, c 1580; c 1550; Michaelmas 3 and 4 Philip and Mary; Court Leet c 1550 (H).
22. Ordinances 1498 and *temp*. Eliz.: Court Leet, c 1550.
23. Courts Leet, c 1580; c 1580–1600 (K); 25 Hen. VIII; GCB I, f. 156; CB (Misc.), 5 Hen. VIII, 22 Dec.
24. CB (Misc.), 4 Jan. I, 25 Nov.; SP, *temp*. Eliz.; CB (1693–1719), f. 282/473; Court Leet, c 1580; CB (1539–48), 9 May; 33 Hen. VIII.
25. CB (Misc.), 23–6 Hen. VIII, 11 Aug.; 26 Hen. VIII; GCB I, f. 261; CB (1539–48), 32 Hen. VIII, 15 March; Court Leet, 25 Hen. VIII: CB (Misc.), 20 Hen. VIII; Court Leet, c 1550 (D).
26. GCB I, f. 37v; Chamberlains 6 Hen. VIII.
27. GCB I, f. 158, 144; CB (Misc.), 5 Hen. VIII Jan.–March; GCB I, f. 229, 157v; Chamberlains 1560–1.
28. Courts Leet, c 1550 (D); Michaelmas 3 and 4 Philip and Mary; Easter 1587; CB (1720–38), f. 145.
29. Court Leet, c 1550; GCB I, 332v; LAO/LCC, 1578, 146v.
30. Courts Leet, 25 Hen. VIII: Easter, 24 Eliz.; c 1550.
31. HMC, 261; J. Thirsk, *English Peasant Farming*, 65–6; Grimsby Archives, Marshes Depositions.
32. PRO, E/112/92/465; CB (17th cent. Misc.), 31 March, 5 Jan. I, 7 March, 6 Jan. I; DNB xliv, 45; Fines, 201; L. Hotson, *Mr. W.H.*
33. HMC, 262.
34. Court Leet, c 1580; CRG, 19 Hen. VII, 12 Oct.; Courts Leet, c 1550 (D); 9 Oct. 1565.
35. CRG, 15 Hen. VII; GCB, 168v; CB (Misc.), 23 Hen. VII; Courts Leet, c 1550 (IF); Easter 1587; 25 Hen. VIII; c 1550; Easter, 3 and 4 Philip and Mary; c 1550 (B); c 1550 (D).

The Town in the Sixteenth Century

36. Courts Leet, 25 Hen. VIII; Easter 3 and 4 Philip and Mary; Chamberlains 1553; GCB, f. 333v; Courts Leet, c 1550 (H); c 1550 (IF); c 1550 (D).
37. Courts Leet, c 1550 (H); c 1580-1600 (K); c 1550; Oct., 1 Edw. VI; Michaelmas; 2 and 3 Philip and Mary.
38. CB (1562-75), f. 48v; CB (Misc.), 15 Hen. VIII, 4 Aug.; SP, 1.
39. SP, 5, 9, 3.
40. Court Leet, c 1550; c 1560; CB, 1 Hen. VII, 9 Nov.
41. GCB, 230v; CRG, 16 Hen. VII, April; Courts Leet, c 1560; c 1580-1600 (K); CB (Misc.), 14 Hen. VIII, 9 Sept.
42. Courts Leet, 25 Hen. VIII: c 1580-1600 (K); c 1550; Oct., 1 Edw. VI: c 1560; 9 Oct. 1565; Easter, 24 Eliz.
43. GCB I, f. 95; Courts Leet, *temp.* Eliz., *passim*; CRG, 16 Hen. VII, April.
44. Courts Leet, 16 Hen. VIII: Michaelmas, 2 and 3 Philip and Mary; 1580-1600 (K); GCB I, 164v.
45. LAO, Inventories, 20/126, 62/226, 62/11, 54/273, 132/279, 135/59; LAO (Calendars) Quarter Sessions, LSB, 1625/113; LAO/LCC, 1575, i. 70.
46. CB (Misc.), 19 Hen. VIII, 18 June; Chamberlains 7 Hen. VIII; Chamberlains 1571; Chamberlains 18 Eliz.; 6 Hen. VIII.
47. Chamberlains temp. Edw. VI, 22 Eliz. and 5 Eliz.; F. E. Halliday. *A Shakespeare Companion*, 535.
48. Camden Society, NS, LV, *Memorials of the Holles Family*, 42; Chamberlains 18 Eliz.
49. LAO, Register Transcripts, Nettleton, 1622, 1627; HMC, *Salisbury* XII, 563-4, Calendar of State Papers relating to Scotland II, 815; CSPD (1603-10), 142.

VIII

Holles, the Haven and the Civil War

In the decade before the Civil War Gervase Holles noted that the town had but one poor coal-ship and scarce mariners to man her. This was almost, but not quite, the whole truth. Though facilities for shipping were poor, water transport was so much cheaper than transport by land that any creek or haven, however bad, was likely to be used. Louth corporation had millstones from Newcastle landed on the shore at Somercotes, and Endymion Porter's agent tried to get barges from Hull to come to Somercotes to ship corn to Berwick. It was worth at any rate trying to keep the haven open and in 1606 a royal letter was obtained to the sheriffs and justices of Lincoln, Lincolnshire, Nottinghamshire, Derbyshire and the West Riding recommending assistance for the improvement of Grimsby Haven.

The mayor and burgesses could give a brief history of the haven's decline. Grimsby, they said,

is a very ancient borough and haven town and very useful to all those parts of the country aforesaid, and in or about the time of King Henry the Seventh of famous memory declined from that frequent course of trading which had formerly been used therein by reason of the decay and silting of the haven there, whereby the mayor and burgesses that then were of the said town were much impaired in their estates in labouring and in endeavouring almost to the utter impoverishing themselves in maintaining the said haven, and yet were not able to effect and accomplish their said desire.

Those proprietors who opposed the enclosure of the marshes gave a similar account, but blamed the enclosure:

Now, the same by means of the said enclosure it is so shelved and wrecked up that the whole trade of shipping and merchandise heretofore used is in effect utterly lost and decayed and most of the inhabitants of that town have in time past been merchants and tradesmen and now become tipplers and alehouse keepers.

In fact the natural accretion of land along the Lindsey coast, and the retreat of high-water mark both encouraged the attempts to enclose the marshes and led to the silting of the haven.[1] But in spite of silting, trade still continued at the haven. In 1611 Thomas Coulton of Grimsby was fined £30 for non-payment of customs on 1,000 deal boards. The fine was still unpaid in 1626 when Michael Cook, the king's footman, petitioned to have it granted to him. John Prime and Robert Latham in 1618 were fined by the corporation for buying barrels of herrings in a manner contrary to custom, and William Popple for buying fourteen barrels of salt. John Prime was also an inn-keeper who in 1633 was brought by messenger before the Lords of the Admiralty for acting as a marshal of the Admiralty without any warrant from the Earl of Lindsey, Vice-Admiral in Lincolnshire.

The customs of the borough were beginning to be seen as restricting the freedom of trade at the haven. It was becoming possible to ignore them. William Walesby, a merchant, in 1637, paid 5s. and was allowed to disregard the local custom and make the best bargain he could with fuller's earth, and for the same sum Christopher Bowman was given liberty to deal with a hoy-load of malt. In 1655 the corporation noted that the custom prohibiting the buying of a whole cargo by any inhabitant had been remissly laid aside for sometime; and it therefore resolved to take no action against Christopher Clayton who had bought a whole cargo of timber on behalf of his mother, Ann Alford, from Laurence Lamkey of Odwell in Norway. Clayton was not so much a timber merchant as a yeoman farmer with an interest in trade and shipping. He had land in Grimsby including closes at High Brigg, and Piper Creek Marsh, two houses, sheep, cattle and horses. He also owned Burnt House Farm at Holton-le-Clay. He had a one-eighth share in a pink, a one-sixteenth share in a new Grimsby keel, and a quarter share in the *Mary and Katherine* of Grimsby; and he traded in timber as well as in wool and salt.[2]

The trade in Scandinavian timber led to a conflict with the Hull Trinity House, the warden and brethren of which claimed that certain duties called primage, buoyage and beaconage were payable to them on goods brought to Grimsby by sea. The collector of customs at Hull had a deputy at Grimsby, and Hull Trinity House had its own deputy for the collection of these dues. In October 1632 this deputy, Edward Talbutt, notified Trinity House that Arthur Brooke, mayor of Grimsby had prevented the payment of primage of 40s. on 120 tons of fir deals and spars from the north of Norway in a ship of Grimsby formerly called the *Saint Peter* of Tunborow in Norway. Mr. Phillipps, part owner of the ship, paid his primage, but two of the Trinity House assistants were sent to Grimsby to take a distress. They tried to seize the ship's anchor, but a riot incited by Arthur Brooke* prevented them.³

There was no further dispute until May 1637, probably because no timber had come to the port in the intervening years. One ship's master named Rumflett was willing to pay primage. In May Moses Cook, the mayor, forbade Francis Plough, master of the *Gabriel* of Tunsborrough to pay 4s. primage on twelve tons of timber, and later in the year primage seems to have been refused on the cargo of the *Whitehorse* of Christian, of which a certain Evert Manson was master. Then in May 1638 a Danish ship came to Grimsby with timber. Trinity House sent its officer, Richard Clarke, to demand primage, and if it were refused, to arrest the ship by taking her cable or sails. Grimsby, having appointed its own collectors of primage, Robert Helme and Alderman Edward Popple, now resolved to defend the lawsuit which Trinity House was threatening to commence, and it was no doubt in connection with this that Gervase Holles, as mayor, went to London on the town's business in Michaelmas term. The action was finally tried in the Exchequer in May 1642, when Trinity House sent a brother to London to follow the suit. Not having much law on its side, Grimsby stated its case with eloquence:

> The town of Great Grimsby is and by all the time whereof the memory of man runneth not to the contrary hath been taken to be a port town of itself without dependence upon or relation to the port of Kingston-upon-Hull, for that the said town and port of Great Grimsby hath been of greater antiquity than Kingston-upon-Hull. It is most unjust and contrary to the franchises, charters and immunities of Grimsby aforesaid that any the mayor, burgesses or inhabitants hereof have received and accompted for the duty of primage in the bill mentioned to the said guild of Trinity House in Kingston-upon-Hull. The said town of Grimsby time out of mind hath or of right ought to have two collectors of the said duty of primage yearly chosen and sworn, who receive their power and authority from the mayor and burgesses of Grimsby.⁵

The verdict was in favour of Trinity House, which not only continued to appoint its collectors of primage, buoyage and beaconage but also, to make its triumph more bitter to Grimsby, was able to find Grimsby men willing to accept the office. In 1643 Thomas Beatniffe,

---

* Arthur Brooke was never mayor again. He was disfranchised in February 1637 for breach of his burgess oath, and died the same year. He was a man of fairly meagre estate, with personal property of less than £30. But he was described as a gentleman, and his house contained some of the trappings of gentility, such as a picture and four escutcheons, a chronicle in French, a rapier and a dagger. He was also a small farmer and a dealer in timber and iron.⁴

vintner, a person so obscure that in Hull his name was thought to be Beatrisse, was succeeded by William Brighouse, gentleman, who was followed by Gregory Greane, mariner, whom Alderman Nicholas Permiter succeeded in 1655. Each collector took 3s. 4d. for each pound of primage which he collected, and half the buoyage and beaconage; but Nicholas Permiter wanted to pay a lump sum and make what profit he could. Trinity House declined to accept this arrangement—a clear indication that the dues and the shipping which paid them were not yet negligible. And there were even some circumstances which could persuade a Trinity House man to change his allegiance and adhere to Grimsby. In 1644 William Crewe, an elder brother, was deprived of office because he had lived with his family at Grimsby for two years and had become an alderman. He was mayor in 1648.[6]

It seems unlikely that ships from Norway actually entered the haven. The timber was probably brought ashore in barges from ships lying at anchor in the Humber. In 1639 Holles said 'there was one that whilst he was mayor did suffer the haven to decay', and Ald. Heaton, mayor in 1629 and for a second time in 1643, said that if the mayor meant him, it was untrue. In 1641 the corporation petitioned the crown for assistance, setting forth that the decay and silting of the haven was the principal cause of the impoverishment of the town. Even small ships could reach the town bridge only with great difficulty, where formerly there was enough water to float a ship of three or four hundred tons. The inhabitants, already put to heavy expense in repairing the church which had recently been damaged by storms could not without assistance find the £2,500 or more which would be necessary to clear the haven. Letters patent were granted to the corporation authorising them to solicit alms and benevolences. The times were not propitious, and no further effort was made until the Restoration, but hope was not yet abandoned, and in December 1641, when ground near the Stone-bridge was leased for a water-mill, it was stipulated that if a new haven was made William Barnard should take down as much of his mill as was thought to stop the course of the water, receiving a proportionate reduction of his rent.[7]

The condition of the haven did not affect the roadstead out in the Humber where ships could lie at anchor off Grimsby. When the trained bands were raised in 1639 for the war with Scotland, Sir Anthony Irby marched the Holland forces to Grimsby with a heavy escort, fearing disorder and mutiny on the march. Various contingents were quartered near the town, ready to embark at twenty-four hours' notice, and the delay was long enough for the corporation to honour the commander-in-chief, and for some of his men to buy themselves out. At Great Coates Captain Hamond took money from some of the Grantham men to buy substitutes, including one from Scunthorpe. Clearly there was not much eagerness to meet the Scots; but for the corporation this was a remote prospect. They honoured Captain Jonathan Atkins by making him a free burgess. They put Francis Mussenden out of his office as Recorder for disregard and neglect, and elected the earl of Lindsey to his place. Then, a week later, Sir George Heneage having resigned, they elected the earl High Steward. The next day, 17 April, his forces began to embark in the roadstead and were gone by the 23rd; but arms for dispatch to the north were still at Grimsby more than a year later.[8]

In the early part of the seventeenth century it is difficult to separate the history of the town from that of the Holles family. Gervase Holles was very active when he served as mayor, but the family was really no more important than several others. But Holles wrote about his family, and about the town. The others were mute and inglorious. Freshville Holles, father of the antiquary, after serving for seven years in the Netherlands under Sir Francis Vere, came to live in Grimsby with his father, Sir Gervase Holles some time between 1593 and 1600. In 1600 he married Elizabeth, daughter and heiress of John Kingston of Grimsby, so that the ruins of the Kingston estate ultimately were added to that of the Holles family.

In 1608 Kingston and his son-in-law were involved in an affray with Thomas Clatham and Thomas Yarborough. Kingston had been a noted duellist as a youth, but no harm was done. In or about 1618 Freshville Holles, and Charles Garth, Rector of Bradley and formerly a soldier, were in a quarrel with Francis Guevara at Grimsby races, which seemed likely to lead to bloodshed but ended quietly. Holles the antiquary, Freshville's son, dismisses Guevara as a proud and insolent Spaniard. In fact, the Guevara's, protégés of the Earl of Lindsey and his family, owned property in Grimsby, and Sir John Guevara, father of Francis, had been second-in-command at the fortress of Berwick under Lord Willoughby. Freshville Holles lived in the White Friars at Grimsby with his father-in-law, who died in 1617. In 1627 he was elected alderman and became mayor, much to the anger of his father, Sir Gervase, who thought the office degrading to a gentleman of his rank.[9,10]

The young Gervase Holles succeeded to an estate in Burgh-le-Marsh, and on the death of his grandmother, to the Kingston property in

Grimsby and Humberstone. He had been educated in Grimsby at the grammar school, first under William Dalby, who also taught him music, and then under Herbert Hindmarsh, Vicar of St. James's. After this he spent three pleasant years with his uncle, John Holles, Earl of Clare, and in 1628 was admitted to the Middle Temple. After his father's death, he made extensive alterations to his house in Grimsby. Some rooms were wainscotted, and all were given deal boards in place of the old floors of plaster. A staircase was put in place of the old stone newel to the gallery and the upper dining room, and the garden was walled with stone. From the turret which he built, he could see the sea and the racecourse, and as far as Louth and Beverley. Yet after all this expense, to further his career and be close to the leading members of his family, in 1634 he removed to Mansfield in Nottinghamshire.[11]

His *Memorials* say nothing of why he changed his mind yet again and returned to Grimsby. By 1636 he was mayor for the first time, and rather more conscious than others had been of the dignity of his office. An order was made re-affirming the traditional duty of members of the corporation to attend the mayor to church.* Each alderman was to wear his gown, of a sad colour, and come to church in an orderly manner, on Sundays, Wednesdays and festival days, or pay a shilling fine. At the same court Francis Wickham said that the mayor did him wrong, and before he could receive Holles' pardon several gentlemen had to intercede for him, and he was forced to express sorrow for his fault and make public submission. A few weeks later Christopher Harling was ordered to be taken into custody by the bailiffs for opprobrious speeches which he made in court. Instead of putting him in the gaol against the town hall, the bailiffs went to a tavern with him, and for this contempt of the mayor were fined £20 each, and though the fines were reduced to £1, this was still, for Grimsby, an exceptionally heavy penalty.[12]

In 1637 John Guevara, the bearer of a name Holles was not likely to love, made an affray with bloodshed on Robert Brather. For some reason, however, Brather was no admirer of Holles. When John Howard, a butcher, was drinking with others at Brather's house, during Holles second mayoralty, Brather said that Mr. Mayor was a knave. Wishing to develop this topic, Matthew Maddison, a joiner,

---

* The vicar at this time was Lemuel Rampayne, formerly Rector of Broxholme. He picked up a ghost story from his patrons, the Monsons, about apparitions seen in the churchyard of Burton-by-Lincoln, and Holles recorded it in his antiquarian notes. He became a burgess in 1637.

proposed the health of the mayor, and to this Brather, now properly incensed, said: 'He would not pledge it. He was as good a man as Mr. Mayor, and a turd in his teeth, he cared not a fart for him.' A jury found him guilty and Holles not only deprived him of his status as a burgess, but also prohibited him from keeping his common alehouse for allowing disorder there. He was left to depend on his trade as a shoemaker, and when his kinsman, Alderman Brather, spoke unfitting words and did not hold his peace when the mayor commanded him, he was fined £20, a sum afterwards reduced to £1.[13]

Perhaps Holles was trying to enhance the status of the whole corporation. During his first mayoralty three gentlemen were made members of the corporation as twelve-men. One of them, Edward Boraston, was afterwards Holles' deputy, another Robert Barne,* was probably a cousin, and the third, George Needham, was also a relative. All three were admitted without any obligation to attend the mayor at the church in their gowns, except at their own pleasure. Needham and Barne were both resident in the town. In 1637 Holles also caused Sir Henry Radley of Yarburgh and Marmaduke Darrell of Horkstow to be admitted as aldermen. Both were to be active royalists during the Civil War. Darrell was brother-in-law of James Harrington, author of *Oceana*.[14]

In 1635 Grimsby was assessed to pay £15 ship money, as against £70 for Boston and £195 for Lincoln. The assessments were the same in 1636. Assessors were appointed in January 1639 to raise £6 'for His Majesty's ship of war', and in March there was a further assessment of £15 for maintaining soldiers and providing a navy. Accoutrements for land warfare were less expensive than the navy. The corporation in 1617 owned a caliver and a musket. Edward Popple, Holles' deputy in 1637, raised 26s. 8d. for parading and dressing the towns arms, which were 3 corselets, 3 pikes, 4 headpieces, 1 sword with a scabbard and 3 without, 3 belts, a musket and its rest, a mould for making bullets, a bandolier with 5 charges, 4 knapsacks and a bag for shot.[15]

In the Long Parliament† the borough was represented by Holles, and by Sir Christopher Wray, who proved a zealous supporter of Parliament against the king. Sir John Jacob, later a royalist, had thirty-four votes and Wray only twenty-three, but Jacob was returned for

---

* He was a grandson of a Lord Mayor of London, and of Edwin Sandys, Archbishop of York.

† The election described here was actually for the Short Parliament, but there was apparently no further election held at Grimsby in 1640.

Rye and Wray took his place. Wray had done legal business for the corporation.[16]

There was one other candidate, who received thirteen votes—Sir Gervase Scrope of South Cockerington, who had strongly opposed ship money but supported Charles I in the war, serving with Sir John Hotham, and against the Scots at Newark. Indeed, except for Wray, all the persons now prominently connected with Grimsby were to show themselves royalists. The Earl of Lindsey, killed at Edgehill, was High Steward until Sir Charles Bolle of Thorpe Hall, Louth, took his place. Bolle was an active royalist, and so was the Recorder,[17] Francis Halton, who had been baptised in St. James's in 1598 and became a free burgess in 1637.* Holles' friend, William Booth, who as late as 1651† was regarded as a person likely to help in a royalist plot to seize Boston, was probably the same person as the William Booth of Killingholme arrested on the order of Parliament in 1642 for obstructing the parliamentary deputy-lieutenants in viewing the militia at Caistor and saying 'that things should never go well as long as King Pym governed'. Booth was an alderman, elected in 1639 when it was decided that there should be an additional six non-resident aldermen. He paid £21 to Holles for a lease of the West Fitties 'to be disbursed for and about the town's occasions' and in June 1640 he and Holles were in trouble with Paul Willett, Vicar of St. James's, for laughing in church. Booth was so closely allied to Holles that it was an offence to say so during Booth's mayoralty: 'Richard Portas hath the fine of £20 imposed on him for divers contentious words spoken against Mr. Mayor, namely that there are two mayors, Mr. Holles and Mr. Booth.'[18]

There were three occasions during the war when there were skirmishes in the vicinity of Grimsby. In February 1643 a force from Hull attacked Thorganby Hall and carried William Caldwall‡ off to Lincoln. The royalists from Newark raided as far as Louth in September 1644, and again from Newark, on 18 June 1645, a force of cavalry under Captain Wright routed 200 Parliament troops at Riby Gap, leaving their leader, Lt. Col. Harrington, among the dead.[19]

It is difficult to know where the sympathies of the corporation lay. Perhaps it was safer not to have any, or to keep a mild royalist sentiment

* He was probably the son of Sir Roger Halton of Great Carlton. He was a gentleman pensioner of Sidney Sussex college, was admitted to the Inner Temple in 1624 and called to the Bar in 1633.

† In 1649 he was known at Grimsby as Col. William Booth.

‡ In 1641 he arbitrated between Thomas Phillips, late of Nuns' Farm, and Edward Popple.

under the firmest control. After the Newark raiders had reached Louth the corporation resolved to suspend the payment of the fee-farm rent still held by the bailiffs for the last three years 'seeing the times are so dangerous, it being demanded by both armies'. Francis Halton, though notoriously a royalist, kept his place as Recorder until 1646. Perhaps there was substance in Alderman Sea's contention 'that Mr. Mayor is a cavalier and all his followers, therefore take him away', words for which he was disfranchised. It was not until 1648, when assessments were being made for the quartering of soldiers, that the corporation recognised who had won the war and authorised William Beardshaw, the town clerk, to pay the fee-farm rent, accumulated over a period of five years, into the Exchequer.[20]

The attitude of the town was necessarily equivocal, but the loyalty of several of its inhabitants to the king was well attested. James Hardy,* captured when Cromwell and Manchester took Lincoln in May 1643, and then a prisoner at Boston for two months, redeemed his estate for £120. Phillips Weslyd, of the Nuns', married Elizabeth Skinner of Thornton Curtis, a member of a Puritan family, but was a captain of horse for the king from September 1644 to October 1645. When his fine was assessed at £368, he protested that £1,300 had already been plundered from him. Part of his estate, inherited from Thomas Phillips of Grimsby, lay under the control of the Newark garrison. Much of his land was at Winthorpe, and at Burgh-le-Marsh, where he had bought a farm from Richard Todd of Grimsby. His son, William Weslyd, also fought for the king, and surrendered at Winceby. The fine hardly impaired the wealth of the family and they continued to live at the Nuns'. In 1657 William Halton assaulted Phillips Weslyd, and Weslyd tried to ride over Thomas Newark. Charles Weslyd, obviously of the same family, was mayor in 1654 and in 1659 was the victim of an affray by a notorious termagant named Ann Dutch.[21]

Gervase Holles became a captain of foot in Sir Lewis Dives' regiment in August 1642. He was at Edgehill and was commissioned to command his own regiment. He fought at Newark, Belvoir, Adwalton Moor and Newbury. When he tried to compound for his estates in 1645 he claimed that he had protected the Parliament's friends and had voluntarily surrendered to the Earl of Manchester two years previously. He took up arms once more in the second Civil War and was a prisoner at Colchester. After his release, he remained on the continent until the

* In 1647 the Grimsby Sessions fined him for buying corn and sending it away in keels. He became a burgess 6 June 1647.

Restoration, though still active in royalist politics. He had already sold his Grimsby house to Richard Broxholme before the war. Because he was so active in the king's cause, the Committee for Compounding assessed his fine at one-third of the value of his estate and fixed it at £860. He refused to pay, but his wife was allowed to enjoy a fifth of the income.[22]

Holles had attended the King's Parliament at Oxford, and the House of Commons deprived him of his seat. Col. Edward King of Ashby-de-la-Launde hoped to be chosen for the vacancy. He was a son-in-law of Sir Edward Ayscough of Stallingborough and was one of those indicted for high treason by the Lincolnshire royalists in 1643. Cromwell had sent John Lilburne to report on his trustworthiness as governor of Boston, and Lilburne reported secretly that he believed King responsible for the loss of Crowland and Grantham, and for the failure to take Newark. Col. King's own private scapegoat was Lord Willoughby of Parham, whose conduct of the war in Lincolnshire he criticised in such terms that the House of Lords committed him to the Fleet prison and ordered him to make a public acknowledgment in vindication of Lord Willoughby's honour in Boston on a market day. This led to a quarrel between Lords and Commons, and he was released by order of the lower house.[23]

It may be supposed that King had made enough enemies to stand in the way of his election. To make it still more difficult, he was opposed by the other member, Sir Christopher Wray (1601-46) of Ashby-cum-Fenby and Barlings, grandson of the Elizabethan Chief Justice. Three generations of Wrays had sat for Grimsby, and Sir Christopher was determined to have his son, William, as his fellow member. Wray was in an excellent position to achieve this ambition. He had been an opponent of ship money before the war, had held various commands under the Long Parliament, and was now high in the confidence of its leaders. Since April 1645 he had been a Commissioner of the Admiralty, and in December was to be appointed one of the Commissioners with the Scots before Newark. In October Col. King gave £10 to be made a free burgess, but William Wray, though not yet a burgess, was returned as the new member to replace Holles.[24]

According to King's account William Wray, a captain in the parliamentary forces, was 'yet an infant and beyond seas'. Indeed he was in Italy, with the diarist, John Evelyn,* and with the poet, Edmund Waller. His election was procured by sharp practice. Sir Christopher

* Evelyn describes him as 'a good drinking gentleman'.

caused King to be summoned before the Northern Committee at Westminster to answer certain charges. When he presented himself, there was no one to bring proof of the charges, and he was allowed to return to Lincolnshire. When he reached Grimsby he found that Sir Christopher, by threats, had forced the mayor to hold the election six days previously, and by improper practices had obtained votes for his son. It was more than a year before William Wray came to Grimsby and was made a free burgess, presenting £10 to the town and £10 for the repair of the school house.[25]

On the death of Sir Christopher Wray in 1646 Col. King was again disappointed. The member chosen was Col. Edward Rossiter of Somerby near Caistor, perhaps the most successful of the Lincolnshire soldiers who served Parliament.* Five month's later King's courtship of Grimsby was rewarded when he became Recorder in place of the royalist Francis Halton. The corporation was careful to note not only that Parliament had declared Halton to be incapable of holding office but also that he had in fact neglected his office for several years past in breach of his oath. This would look better if the royalists were to win in the end, and perhaps Edward King had not yet begun to acquire the reputation, which he certainly enjoyed posthumously, of being almost a royalist himself.[26]

For Grimsby the period of the Interregnum was uneventful. Wray sat as the borough member in 1654 and 1656. In 1653 Col. Robert Overton at Hull hinted that he was holding the press gang as a threat over the head of the Mayor of Grimsby. Ann Dutch bit off a piece of Paul Underwood's ear, and told Robert Kitchin that he was a housebreaker and might go break another. The sessions jury which presented the lack of a ducking stool also presented in 1646 that John Taylor had two farms and lived in one, and that William Lusby who had three farms kept house in none of them. Mr. Alford held 40s. bequeathed to buy a cup for a horse race every Thursday in Easter week.†[27]

Church rates were levied just as regularly as in the years before the war. The corporation in 1645 declared it lawful for the churchwardens to take proceedings against anyone refusing to pay dues or assessments, and in 1647 it was decided to distrain upon the goods of those in arrears with their payments. An assessment of £10 for the repair of the church

---

* In 1660 he met Sir Philip Monckton and Lord Clare in Sherwood Forest 'though it was his marriage night' and arranged to remove his troops from Stamford to Lincoln and join the king's friends in order to promote a Restoration and frustrate Lambert.

† This money was eventually used to buy a salver for the race.

was made in 1648, and another of £15 in 1651. More surprisingly, in 1647 Edward Popple was indicted at the borough sessions for obstinately staying away from church for a month. Puritan toleration of Protestant non-conformity was yet to come, but the more obvious kind of Puritanism had already arrived. Elizabeth Mossum, after a fortnight in the House of Correction for fornication with Matthew Madison, was to stand in repentance in the open market. Robert Cook not only had to pay 2s. weekly for the maintenance of his bastard child, which can hardly have been an unexpected penalty, but also had to make a public confession on the next market day, wearing a white sheet. The next year two disorderly persons were sent to the House of Correction and William Crawfurth was forbidden to brew because he had allowed shuffleboard to be played in his house. Thomas Sea, a Puritan who in 1639 had taught in a school without being licensed, lodged information against three men who, one Sunday in 1655, carried hides and put them in the fresh-water haven, and much reviled him when he rebuked them.[28]

The town was a little more active in church affairs than in normal times. The borough court selected a new parish clerk, Walter Lloyd, in 1653, and his successor Philip Cave in 1658. William Smith was hired for 40s. a year to maintain the church clock and bells. Henry Dean contracted for half as much to keep all the church leads in repair, and then, having repaired the windows for £5 17s., arranged to keep them in repair for another 20s. a year. On the eve of the Restoration the corporation authorised Mr. Clayton and Mr. Heaton to collect tithes and see that the cure* was served.[29]

NOTES

1. HMC, 249; PRO, E/112/93/627.
2. CSPD (1625-6), 527; CB, 3 March 1618; CSPD (1633-4), 77, 108, 150; CB, 6 June 1637; HMC, 284; LAO, Lincoln Wills 1679, 279.
3. Primage Case Papers A and B; F. W. Brooks, *The First Order Book of the Hull Trinity House*, I, 14.
4. HMC, 282; LAO Lincoln Consistory Court Administrations, 1637/178.
5. Primage Case Papers A and B; F. W. Brooks, op. cit., 29 and 55; CB, 22 May 1638, 14 Feb. 1639.
6. F. W. Brooks, op. cit., 44, 61, 67, 108, 128.
7. CB, 7 Sept. 1639; Lincs. Notes and Queries I, 136-40; CB, 13 Dec. 1641.
8. CSPD (1639), 19, 20, 49 and 69; CSPD (1639-40), 451; CSPD (1640), 247; LAO Monson, 19/7/2/1; CB, 9 and 16 April 1639.

---

* Paul Willett had ceased to be vicar by 15 December 1660, and the benefice may have been vacant on 20 March when this order was made.

9. CB, 28 June 1608-9; Holles, Memorials of the Holles Family (Camden Society, Vol. 55, 1937), 193, 194, 196-7; LAO, 2 Ancaster; G. Archives, Concords 233, 239, 248.
10. Holles, op. cit., 204, 221-2, 228; CB, 21 July 1629.
11. Ibid., 229-30.
12. CB, 22 Nov. 1636, 20 Dec. 1636; Alumni Cantabrigienses, Part I, iii, 416.
13. CB, 20 June 1637, 6 Oct. 1638, 30 Oct. 1638.
14. CB, 28 March and 11 July 1637; Holles, op. cit., 236; MLP, 102.
15. CSPD (1635), 364; CSPD (1637), 2; CB, 15 Jan. and 12 March 1639; CB, 14 Oct. 1617, 16 May and 3 June 1637.
16. CB, 24 March 1640; HMC, 257.
17. CB, 28 Sept. 1641, 23 April 1639; Alumni Cantabrigienses.
18. HMC Portland I, 586; 'A Declaration of the House of Commons in Vindication of Divers Members . . .', July 1642; CB, 16 April and 7 May 1639, 16 June and 17 March 1640, 10 July 1649.
19. Lincs. N. and Q. I, 72-4; CB, 6 Jan. 1641; CSPD (1644), 545.
20. CB, 1 Oct. 1644, 12 and 18 August 1645; 1 Jan. and 14 Nov. 1648.
21. Calendar of Committee for Compounding, 1449, 1085, 1513; LAO/LCC Wills, 1661, 996; HMC, 284; CB, 29 March 1659.
22. Lincs. N. and Q. II, 35; Holles *Memorials* viii, ix; Calendar of Committee for Compounding, 1056; CB, 15 April 1645.
23. CB, 14 and 21 Oct. 1645; P. Thompson: *History and Antiquities of Boston*, 773-4; W. Haller, *Tracts on Liberty in the Puritan Revolution*, I 171-2; Lords' Journals VI, 575-6; Commons' Journals IV, 738.
24. DNB xiii, 77; CB, 14 and 21 Oct. 1645.
25. C. Dalton, *A History of the Wrays of Glentworth* II, 66; CB, 17 Nov. 1645; CB, 4 Sept. 1649; Diary of John Evelyn (Everyman Edition), 217, 226, 231.
26. CB, 3 March and 4 Aug. 1646; CSPD (1676-7), 178.
27. CB, July 1654 and 29 July 1656; CSPD (1652-3), 356; CB, 15 Oct. 1646; CB, 1 Sept. 1646, 2 Oct. 1677.
28. CB, 1 April 1645, 10 Oct. 1647, 23 Oct. 1648, 19 April 1651, 23 Jan. and 30 Sept. 1647, 5 Jan and 11 April 1648, 7 May 1639 and 9 Oct. 1655.
29. CB, 21 June 1653, 16 June 1657, 21 Feb. 1659, 12 Oct. and 20 March 1660.

IX

Restoration and Electioneering

Col. Edward King sat for Grimsby, with Sir William Wray, in the Parliament of 1660 which recalled Charles II to the throne. In 1647 he had obstructed the collection in Lincolnshire of assessments for the army, but never carried his opposition so far as to put himself in danger. For the time being, however, he ceased to play any part in politics, until in March 1660 he became a Commissioner for the Militia. Then, as member for Grimsby he spoke words in the House of Commons which many years later caused Edmund Calamy to record that 'he was the first in the House of Commons as was commonly reported and believed that moved for King Charles' Restoration'. The most he ever claimed for himself was that he had been active in promoting the Restoration. A royalist version of his role was given by Mr. J. Worsley, a 'learned and ingenious clergyman', to Abraham de la Pryme in 1697. 'He started up when he heard the motion made of bringing him (i.e. Charles II) in, and declared that though he was not against it, yet he would desire them that, considering they had all been in rebellion against him, they should take care to bring him in upon such and such articles that he might not hurt them.' According to Worsley, Monk's view prevailed, and King's speech was afterwards the reason for his being sent to the Tower.[1]

The Grimsby members in the Cavalier Parliament were Gervase Holles and Sir Adrian Scrope, both royalists of the deepest dye. Col. King's very moderate royalism was insufficient to recommend him to the borough, but he still had his adherents. Another royalist, John Bolle, produced letters-patent appointing him High Steward in March 1661. He never seems to have fulfilled any duties in connection with his office, whereas King did occasionally sit at Quarter Sessions as Recorder, and in 1661 presented £10 for the repair of the vicarage-house. In official quarters he was in the deepest disfavour, more particularly as he now dedicated himself and his knowledge of the law to obstructing the persecution of nonconformists by Sir Edward Lake, the Vicar-General of the diocese. In the autumn of 1666 on instructions from the king or the Duke of York he was imprisoned at Lincoln by

Sir Anthony Oldfield and Sir Robert Carr, for refusing to give a bond for his good behaviour. These embarrassments, however, did not prevent him from presenting himself once again as a candidate at a Grimsby election. The seat formerly held by Sir Adrian Scrope was now vacant, and King found himself opposed by Sir Henry Bellasis of Worlaby, another person of distinguished royalist connections who may perhaps be regarded as the official candidate. Bellasis was elected, with twenty-nine votes, but the fact that King had twenty-two votes may indicate the beginnings of a genuinely political opposition in the town.[2]

In February and March 1666 King had been in the Tower, and though a prisoner, he was allowed to consult the records kept in there and to carry on his researches into Temple Bruer and Ashby-de-la-Launde. Two of his daughters were married to London merchants and in 1670 it was said that he himself was daily on the Exchange, promoting sedition. There was an order for his arrest, for encouraging unlawful conventicles, yet the corporation still thought it appropriate to employ him on legal business in 1671, and to allow him to take to London certain Exchequer acquittances for the fee-farm rent dating from the time of Elizabeth. He kept his office as Recorder until his death at Ashby in 1681.[3]

Col. King never again, after 1666, contested an election in Grimsby, though there were several opportunities. In 1667 Sir Freshville Holles, only son of Gervase, the other member, stood against Sir Philip Tyrwhitt of Stainfield for the seat formerly held by Scrope. He had annoyed Samuel Pepys by playing the Lincolnshire bagpipes, and the diarist was not inclined to judge him favourably. In Pepy's coach he told him that his ancestors had been parliament men for Grimsby for 140 years, which Pepys correctly described as one of his romantic lies, and that his own election would cost him as much as it had cost his predecessor, namely £350 for ale and £52 for buttered ale. This went down in the diary as 'one of his devilish lies'. It is all too likely that it was true. At the election Tyrwhitt* had twenty-six votes and Holles twenty-three.

Tyrwhitt was returned as the new member, but in November 1667 a committee of the House found that he had not been duly elected and that Holles had. Sir Freshville Holles' naval commission makes it reasonable to regard him as the official candidate, and when a Dutch cannonball ended his short life at the Battle of Solebay, official pressure

---

* Sir Philip Tyrwhitt was a member of a Roman Catholic family. His confessor in Lincolnshire, Father Jenison, was a victim of Titus Oates in 1679.

was brought to secure that the new member also should be agreeable to the Crown. Lord Fanshawe's brother, Charles Pelham of Brocklesby, and Major Broxholme pursued their campaign of feasting and caressing the voters, but only the two last named actually stood as candidates. Gervase Holles could not at first bring himself to take an interest in the election, but in the end sent his man, William Griffith, to help in the choice of a loyal member.[4]

Broxholme won the election with twenty-nine votes as against twenty-one for Pelham and represented Grimsby until his death. He was a member of a local family, and had recently lost his estate at Barrow in consequence of deficiencies in his accounts as receiver-general of taxes in Lincolnshire. At the time of his election, therefore, he was probably without any source of income other than his pay as a major of foot in Sir Thomas Slingsby's regiment. If he was ever likely to waver in his loyalty, he must have remembered that proceedings were still pending against him for the debt which he still owed. They were suspended in 1674, but could have been re-opened if he had been an unreliable member.[5]

On the death of Gervase Holles in 1675 Sir Christopher Wray* of Ashby-cum-Fenby, the fifth member of his family to represent Grimsby, stood against Mr. Bertie. He had forty-one votes and Mr. Bertie fourteen, but the sheriff of Lincolnshire returned Bertie as duly elected, possibly because a Bertie was more likely to support the Crown than a Wray. A committee of the House of Commons voted that Wray should take his seat, but its recommendation that the sheriff should be taken into custody was negatived.[6]

In 1679 there was no contest and Broxholme was returned with George Pelham of Gray's Inn. It was Charles Pelham of Brocklesby, however, who signed Pelham's election bond. In the same year George Pelham became High Steward of the borough. Broxholme, now promoted to lieutenant-colonel, was elected Recorder in succession to Edward King and was mayor in 1681-2. He died in 1684, and his monumental inscription in the church at Barrow described him as 'a true son of the Church of England, in which faith he died, and a loyal subject to the King, which he manifested in several parliaments'.[7]

Sunderland in 1685 asked the Earl of Lindsey, Lord Lieutenant and Lord Great Chamberlain, to back the election of St. Leger Scrope at

---

* Circa 1670 his mother published a pamphlet alleging that William Balantine, a Scot, and others, had tricked him when he was only eighteen into marrying a French girl of bad reputation.

K

Grimsby. There seems to have been no contest, however, and those returned were Sir Thomas Barnardistone of Ketton in Suffolk, connected with the Barnardistone's of Great Coates, and Sir Edward Ayscough of South Kelsey. Ayscough certainly and his colleague presumably were favourably regarded by the Crown. Broxholme's office as Recorder was taken by George Pelham, and at the same time Charles Pelham of Brocklesby became High Steward.[8]

The handful of Grimsby non-conformists played no part in any of these elections. There were in all eight families which had one or more nonconformist members. Only one alderman, Francis Morley, had any connection with nonconformity, his wife being an absentee from church. At the first visitation after the Restoration, Edward Lake, the Vicar-General, suspended Edmund Popple for non-attendance at divine service and Elizabeth Weslehead* for refusing to pay church rates. In 1675 he found three absentees from church, one man reputed to have bought goods from an excommunicated person, and the church pavement in need of repair. Under the 1672 Declaration of Indulgence Martin Finch, once Vicar of Tetney, was licensed as an Independent minister at his house in Grimsby; but this congregation does not seem to have survived the renewal of persecution, and Finch spent much of the rest of his pastoral career at Norwich, where the chapel now called the Old Meeting was built for him. It was believed in 1676 that there were eight nonconformists in Grimsby as against 160 Anglicans. There were no Catholics. It is to be presumed that only adults were counted. In 1678 there were only three and in 1679 only six absentees from church.[9]

The hope once entertained of raising charitable subscriptions for the improvement of the haven had proved fallacious. For a while the corporation simply treated it as a drain and tried to make each frontager responsible for that portion which adjoined his property, as when in 1645 four men were fined 40s. each for failing to scour it and make it sixteen feet wide. But in 1660 the changing times inspired the inhabitants to try again and, at a general meeting in the town hall, to pass the following resolution:†

We the mayor, aldermen, twelve men and twenty four men‡ and we the inhabitants of Great Grimsby having and claiming to have common of pasture

---

* This is no doubt the same name as Weslyd, but the other Weslyd's were great loyalists and preferred to spell their name in such a manner as to conceal their ancestor's fancied resemblance to a weasle. † Slightly condensed.

‡ A term used to denote the other burgesses. The number was by this time probably a purely notional one.

in the East Marsh, having seriously considered the great damage and hurt which this our ancient and once flourishing corporation of Great Grimsby hath sustained by reason that the creek or haven is so silted and landed up that no ship or vessel can come into the harbour to load or unload upon any occasion whatsoever to the great decay of trade which hath happened thereby, and being resolved by the blessing of God to recover the said haven, do hereby agree to inclose and lay in severalty all the aforesaid Marsh and to let and dispose of the same either for ninety-nine years or three lives for the raising of money for cleansing and opening of the said creek and for no other purpose whatsoever.

Seventy-seven persons subscribed their names to this resolution, thirty-seven by signing and forty by making their mark.[10]

This was as unavailing as all previous efforts had been, but it was still possible for a ship to enter the haven in certain states of the tide even if it could not get as far as the town. Captain Thomas Skinner in September 1666 informed the Navy Commissioners that when his ship lay in Grimsby Roads he was attacked by a Dutch sloop which chased him into the creek where, with the help of the townsmen, he was safe. After three days he got out again and sailed up the Humber to Hull, but because there were enemy sloops and men of war at the mouth of the river he dared not sail for Chatham with his cargo of timber. His reason for taking his ship, the *Black Dog*, to Hull, may have been that even in the lower part of the haven he did not feel safe from the Dutch; but at any rate the tide had allowed him to get in. In July the men of Grimsby and their mayor, Thomas Heaton, were unable because of the tide to get out of the haven to defend a ship of Bridlington, and the *Thomas and John* of Boston, both of which were captured by a boarding party of twenty-four men from a Dutch hoy.[11]

In August 1667 an English warship, the *Swallow*, was anchored off Grimsby. Captain Bernard Ludman had with him a Dutch ship of thirty guns, the *Sea Ruter* of Camphire, which, in company with four other British vessels, he had captured after she came out of Bergen with two other Dutch warships, part of the squadron which had crossed the Atlantic after burning English ships in Virginia. But although there were occasional victories such as this, along the coast there was considerable fear of the Dutch. The militia was called out for coast defence. Sir John Monson reported from Grimsby that their courage was high; but the only actual success he could point to was the capture of an old Roundhead, Major Edmund Rolphe, who was reputed at one time to have offered to assassinate Charles I. Since the Restoration he had been a prisoner in Carisbrooke Castle, but he escaped, and when recaptured was acting as surveyor for the estate of Lord Colepeper of Thoresway. He was now held prisoner at Grimsby and was in very low spirits.[12]

Men were pressed for the navy in 1672 at Grimsby, Saltfleet Haven and Boston. In June a Dutch vessel came into the river almost as far as Grimsby. No one dared put to sea, and people living near the sea banks along the Lindsey coast arranged to keep watch at night against parties of Dutch marauders. Some of the enemy ships drew so little water and could come so close to the shore that at high tide people were afraid to be seen on the sea banks. But in Grimsby, admiralty jurisdiction and the state of the haven were the matters of the deepest concern. In 1669 the mayor was faced with the possibility of a prosecution by the Vice-Admiral of Lincolnshire about a wreck cast ashore within the liberties of the borough. The corporation decided that the necessary funds for defence should be drawn from the town chamber; but the cost of any further attempt to clear the haven could not be met out of the ordinary financial resources of the town. In 1675, having noted that the haven was 'very bad' the corporation decided to lay a special levy of £3 on each alderman, £2 on each twelve man, and £1 on each ordinary freeman; but even with sums as modest as this it was necessary to give the mayor and justices power to exempt those thought too poor to pay.[13]

It was not only that the town really was poor. It was also the case that some of the wealthier people, such as the Weslyds, were not burgesses and so could not be forced to pay by the ultimate threat of being disfranchised. This, rather than the real poverty of the town, would seem to explain why by 1679 no more than £135 had been spent on the project in spite of the fact that £35 was taken out of the common fund and Sir Christopher Wray had paid what was then the exceptionally heavy admission fine of £40 when he offered himself for election as a Member of Parliament.

The corporation seems to have had much the same attitude to the haven as a rural parish to its roads. Something must be done about it occasionally, but not very much. It was a natural phenomenon rather than a work of human contrivance. The politics of admitting freemen and making mayors were much more important, and perhaps even by this time more profitable to those directly concerned with the management of the borough. Many of the inhabitants were much more concerned with farms and common rights than with the sea, and even those men who owned shares in ships were usually farmers also. So long as the haven remained usable at all there was no occasion for deep concern.

And it was usable. Three men were fined for buying corn and sending it away from the town in keels, and a Waltham merchant, Thomas Markham, shipped twelve lasts of beans from Grimsby to Newcastle in the *Charity* of Bridlington. Traffic such as this was relatively insignificant, but it was as much as was needed by the largely rural community which now lived in the borough. If corn could be got away and occasional shipments of coal or timber brought in, few people would complain. There were a few other pickings also. From 1698 there was a customs' sloop based in Grimsby to prevent the landing of French goods between Wells and Flamborough Head. Alderman Brasse was given the opportunity of victualling the sloop in 1703 at 5*d*. or 6*d*. a day for each man. The offer was politically inspired; and as a correct politician he replied that these terms were too low, there was no one to be responsible for distributing the victuals equally, and he was not in a position to oblige the commissioners. He would, however, undertake to supply biscuit, oatmeal, cheese, beef, beer and pork at contract prices so long as his bills were settled promptly each month and such incidental costs as boat-hire allowed.[14]

This, however, was after yet another attempt to improve the navigation of the haven. Since in the seventeenth century ships could no longer reach the town, they were moored some distance to the north, at a jetty in the marsh, perhaps near Piper Creek on the west side of the haven.[15]

The diarist antiquary, Abraham de la Pryme, visited Grimsby for a day in 1697 and commented on the wretched condition of the haven. He was told, incorrectly, that it had once been a fine river up which large coal-ships could sail as far as Aylesby. This could never have been possible, though the cut made in the fourteenth century may have enabled small boats to get into the Freshney from the haven. As a high churchman he was inclined to see the misfortunes of Grimsby as a punishment for sacrilege committed at the Reformation, but as a fellow of the still young Royal Society he pointed to coastal erosion as the immediate and material cause of the obstruction of the haven. He was told that about the time of Elizabeth the sea began to destroy the cliff at Cleethorpes, carrying away pieces as big as churches at every high tide. The cliff had once made a comfortable bay and protected the haven. Now, there was only one good house in Grimsby, built recently in brick for a parliament man. The inhabitants were too poor to keep the church in repair, though some householders had paid up to £5 a year in church rates. The market was held in the streets, as there was no proper market place.*16

The one sign of improvement which the diarist could see was that for the last two or three years one of the borough members, public spirited and 'of a noble soul', had been exerting himself for the improvement of the town. He was trying to establish a woollen manufacture and had brought from Oxfordshire a maker of rugs and coverlets, giving him accommodation in his house rent free. He was interested in the possibility of expanding the fish trade, and five large fishing vessels were being built at Stockwith and elsewhere to sail out of Grimsby. Above all, he was trying to make the haven navigable as far as the town once more, with a new sluice and excavations to make the haven ten yards wide. De la Pryme told those who explained all this to him that it would never succeed unless they also made a staith at the foot of the Cleethorpes cliff to check further erosion.

The parliament man whose public so impressed him was Arthur Moore (c. 1660–1730), one of the Grimsby members since 1695. He was the son of a man who had some humble connection with the gaol at Monaghan, in Ireland. He himself had begun as a groom or a footman, but in some way had managed to make a fortune. De la Pryme's account suggests that he had interested himself in the economic improvement of the town as soon as he was elected; but the corporation was not involved until September 1696 when Henry Hildyard of Kelstern and Christopher his son, owners of land in Little Coates, agreed to allow the diversion of the Freshney into Grimsby to supply fresh water and to improve the town. The intention would seem to have been to re-excavate the cutting which had existed since the fourteenth century in order to bring more fresh water into the haven and so prevent silting.[17]

In 1697 Moore advanced £200 on mortgage, part of which was immediately delivered in a bag to Mr. Clayton and the rest spent on iron, brick and the wages of labourers. Moore's interest was sufficiently urgent for him to send a man named Terne to act for him, and for Terne to ride from Lincoln through such a snow storm that he resolved never so to tempt Providence again. The reason for his haste was what

---

* The present-day Old Market Place did not exist except as a topographical expression, and the reason for this was that in relatively prosperous medieval times market stalls had been converted into shops, and then into shops with houses above.

he described as the haven affair, but there were other matters demanding attention. Moore's fellow member, Sir Edward Ayscough, had bought a share in a ship in which some of the leading burgesses were interested. Moore had been less prompt with his assistance, and some were blaming him for the loss of an opportunity for a Rotterdam voyage. Moore's well-wishers were interested in his transactions with the blanket-men and advised that most of his great house should be turned over to them and a single apartment made habitable for himself.[18]

Moore's strongest interest was in the haven project. He advanced £320, and the West Marsh was mortgaged to him. By May 1700 Ald. George Clayton, described as 'expenditor for and disposer of the undertaking of making a sluice and scouring the haven', was ordering labourers to block the old course of the Freshney in order to divert it into the new sluice. The additional flow should have begun to clear the haven of mud, but in 1701 and 1702 it became clear that it was impossible to prevent the stream from seeping through into its old bed. The scheme was failing and the corporation noted that in spite of the new works the haven was becoming 'stranded, silted and choked up'. With no visible effect on the haven, it was decided that for two years money should be raised for further works by tolls on salt, coal, timber, fuller's earth, iron, lime, tiles and groceries coming to the town by water.[19,20,21]

There was still the painful contrast between the occasional keel or hoy which came to Grimsby and the vast quantity of shipping to be seen in the Humber. Storms in the North Sea on the assemblage of a convoy caused whole fleets to anchor in Grimsby Roads. In August 1702 two hundred colliers were anchored off Grimsby waiting to be convoyed to the Thames by two Dutch warships. Even so, a French privateer was able to sail in and take the *Robert Ducke*, a ship of eight guns which fought for four hours until its powder was exhausted. Off the mouth of the Humber Captain Roger Dawson of Gainsborough was captured and ransomed.[22]

Some Grimsby owners had an interest in the convoys. George Clayton, whose son Christopher had a pass to go to Holland in 1703, thanked Arthur Moore for the trouble which he had taken with 'our convoy'. But in 1706 William Brasse complained that John Haines'. ship had been left out of the convoy and was anchored in the roads. 'If Captain Peppies had desired justice', he wrote, 'he ought to have convoyed Haines, but it is not Captain Peppies' design to do us any service. He would have us to be his slaves.' By far the greater part of the shipping in the convoys, however, belonged to Hull. Dislike of Hull may explain why John Shee, who had come from Holland, was arrested at Grimsby and later released by an order from the Secretary of State. Defoe observed that it was mainly Hull shipping which went to Holland from the Humber, and that during the war two Dutch warships were always sent as escort. He thought Grimsby a good town; but the roadstead was indifferent. In the great storm of 1703 nearly all the ships dragged their anchors and many were lost.*[23]

With the haven no more than a creek, however, most of the traffic, such as it was, was coastwise. It was still worth while to order the chamberlains in 1712 to distrain keelmen who refused to pay ringage and pallage or other dues, and three years later to put a toll of sixpence on every keel and a shilling on every larger vessel entering the haven. John Bristow, gentleman, claimed also to be a merchant trading in timber, coal, salt and iron. The *Newark* of Grimsby brought seven tons of fuller's earth for John Newark in 1702, and the *Prosperous* brought ten chalders of the same material for Thomas Newark in 1704. Thomas Driver shipped forty-six packs of wool in April 1722 and thirty-one packs in October, and Thomas Hodgson sent twenty-nine packs in the *Supply*. It was on such traffic as this that what had once been a flourishing maritime community now subsisted.[24]

NOTES

1. CJ IV, 738; *Acts and Ordinances of the Interregnum* II, 1435; A. G. Matthews, *Calamy Revised*, 321; CSPD (1665–6), 36, 296.
2. CB, 26 March 1661, 17 Dec. 1661; CSPD Addenda (1660–70), 226, 235; CB, 6 Nov. 1666; DNB xxxi, 409.
3. CB, 2 May 1671; LAO, Wills, Lincoln, 1680, 336.
4. S. Pepys, *Diary*, 28 Sept. 1667; CB, 10 Sept. 1667, 24 Oct. 1667; *Records of the English Province of the Society of Jesus* XII, 615; CJ IX, 224; CSPD (1672), 555, 619.
5. CB, 4 Feb. 1673, 17 Feb. and 26 Aug. 1679; LAO Calendars, Cragg, 5/1/7; Calendar of Treasury Books, IV 564, V i 211, VI 233.
6. CSPD (1670), 641; CB, 27 April 1675; CJ IX, 330.
7. CB, 17 April and 30 Sept. 1679, 8 Feb. 1681.
8. CSPD (Feb.–Dec. 1685), 407; CSPD (1683–4), 82; CB, 1 March 1685, 15 April 1684.
9. LAO, Archidiaconal Visitations, Vij, 1675–6, 41, 44; Ibid. (1662), 14; CSPD (1672), 574; Matthews, op. cit., 196.
10. CB, 12 Aug. 1645; CB (Misc.), 12–13 Chas. II, f. 42.
11. CSPD Addenda (1660–85), 163; CSPD (1665–6), 544.

---

* But this was perhaps the most violent storm ever recorded in Britain. The navy lost fifteen ships and 1,500 men.

12. CSPD Addenda (1660-85), 211; CSPD (1667), 229.
13. CSPD (1671-2), 29, 170, 498; CB, 17 March 1669, 17 Nov. 1674, 26 Jan. and 9 March 1675, 4 Nov. 1679.
14. CB, 5 Jan. 1647; LAO Calendars, Cragg 3/91; Calendar of Treasury Books XIV, 129; Brasse to Moore, July 1703.
15. CB, 21 Jan. 1662, 23 Dec. and 30 Nov. 1684.
16. Surtees Society *Diary of Abraham de la Pryme*, 153-6.
17. DNB xxxviii, 340; HMC, 259.
18. CB, 13 July 1679; Terne to Moore, 26 Jan. 1698.
19. CB, 27 Sept. 1698, 13 Oct. 1699.
20. CB, 12 Aug. 1701, 23 June 1702.
21. CB, 7 Dec. 1703.
22. CSPD (1702-3), 222.
23. Ibid., 321; Clayton to Moore 23 March 1702/3; CSPD (1698), 82; Daniel Defoe, *Tour Through England and Wales*, Letter IX, VI: G. M. Trevelyan, *England in the Reign of Queen Ann: Blenheim*, 317-18.
24. CB, 26 Feb. 1712, 28 Feb. 1715, 29 Nov. 1709; PRO, E/190/338/10, E/190/335/6, E/190/356/3.

X

The Parliamentary Borough 1688–1782

In May 1688 Grimsby was facing the crisis which most boroughs had faced in the last three years. *Quo Warranto* proceedings had been launched as a first step towards cancelling the charters. It was decided to take counsel's opinion, the mayor signing this resolution with his mark; but on 15 September 1688 a new charter was issued superseding the old. The Revolution came so soon afterwards that this made no practical difference. In the 1689 Parliament the borough was represented by Sir Edward Ayscough of South Kelsey and Sir Thomas Barnardiston of Ketton, Suffolk. Ayscough was probably a sound Revolution man, and Barnardiston, as grandson of the Puritan Sir William Armine and nephew of the ultra-Whig Sir Samuel Barnardiston,* is likely to have been a Whig himself.[1]

Yet in all probability the complexion of Grimsby was distinctly Tory. Shortly before the election of 1690 Lord Lexington, Mr. Matthew Lister of Burwell and Mr. Hildyard were in Grimsby drinking to King James and swearing at the name of King William. At the election Ayscough kept his seat, but John Chaplin† (1658–1714) of Tathwell took the place of Barnardiston, who never again sat for Grimsby, though he remained Recorder of the borough.[2]

In 1695 Arthur Moore was returned unopposed with Ayscough. With the appearance of Moore, Grimsby politics acquired a new dimension. Aspirants to a seat in Parliament were prepared to bid high for the favours of the electors. With the stagnation of trade the perquisites of borough politics were growing ever more attractive to those of the inhabitants, probably about one man in four, who were so fortunate as to be freemen. And Moore was a politician of a more brilliant kind than any who had yet represented the borough. He was a man of strong intellectual interests, a friend of the economists Gregory King and Charles Davenant, was in the confidence of the Tory leaders, became a Commissioner of Trade and Plantations in 1710, was a

---

* A director of the East India Company.

† Son of Sir Francis Chaplin, Lord Mayor of London and brother of Sir Robert Chaplin who represented Grimsby in Parliament from 1715 to 1721.

The Parliamentary Borough 1688-1782   145

director of the South Sea Company and was the negotiator mainly responsible for the commercial clauses of the Treaty of Utrecht. Grimsby had never until now enjoyed the patronage of such a politically exalted person; and he, on his side, had to continue to deserve the confidence of the freemen in order to survive as a politician.*3

A determined effort was made in 1698 to prevent an election being held, perhaps in order to provide time for a rival candidate to make his appearance, since in the event only the two candidates, Moore and Ayscough, presented themselves, and were returned unopposed. Bedell Hastings, the mayor, went off to London, deliberately leaving no deputy to serve for him, so that there could be no one legally qualified to receive the writ for the election. William Joad saw him in London, and the mayor told him that he would never return. A letter asking him to come back for the election produced the same reply. He had even removed the mace and the seals, which were eventually returned by his wife. The analogy with the flight of James II in 1688 was all too obvious, and it was declared that the mayor had 'absconded and deserted the borough and abdicated the government thereof'. Moore and Ayscough signed the resolution, and the same day were declared to have been duly elected.[4]

Ayscough died at Grasby on 2 October 1699. Sir Thomas Barnardiston, the Recorder, had died in 1698. Lord William Pawlett was elected to succeed him and made Richard Robinson his deputy. Robinson now came forward as a candidate to succeed Ayscough. He was opposed by Thomas Vyner, and by the young Sir Thomas Barnardiston, son of the late Recorder, and Moore decided to put his interest behind Barnardiston. Charles Bransby, Moore's agent in Grimsby and the tenant of his house, was delighted with his patron's decision:

Your appointments [he wrote], and my own inclinations jump together. I have all along been ready to serve the Barnardistons by inclination, not dint of interest, and now I am glad to have an opportunity so fairly offered me. It has vexed me to see such juggling in former vacancies. Some here are endeavouring to frighten him with their industrious inquiry after his father's arrears and also his own at the last election. 'Tis the most matchless piece of ingratitude that I ever yet observed that some who have lived upon his bread should now desert him and besides espousing a contrary interest should do him

---

* Moore's intellectual ability was perhaps inherited by his third son, known as James Moore Smythe, who had enough success as a dramatist to incur the enmity of Pope. Cf. *Epistle to Arbuthnot*, 'Arthur, whose giddy son neglects the laws. Imputes to me and my damned works the cause.'

those ill offices as the mustering of such claims as these.... All agree that nobody is to be chosen here but who Lord Pawlett should nominate for they all have it from his lordship's own mouth.[5]

The election was hotly contested, and in the end it was Thomas Vyner who won in spite of the opposition of Moore and Lord Pawlett. There was considerable intimidation. William Newark was said to have advised Robert Godhelp, about four days before the election, 'to come away to them from the dove-cote and set it on fire'. Thomas Stephenson, an alderman, with his wife and his son were arrested with Thomas Dutch for pulling down the gable end of Mrs. Troth Wolby's dwelling house. All the rioters were supporters of Vyner; and immediately after the election eight civil actions were commenced in the borough court, all of them against men who had voted for Vyner. Three of the actions were brought by Charles Bransby, who shortly afterwards had the gratification of seeing Sir Thomas Barnardiston elected High Steward in place of the deceased Sir Edward Ayscough.[6]

In the 1699 election Moore seems to have acted on the advice of Charles Bransby, who proposed to spend £10 on a tankard and spoon and pretend they were a gift from Moore's wife to the mayor's. At the same time Bransby gave some sound advice about the next general election:

> I differ with your opinion about leaving the freemen to make up their bills after a dissolution. You will find 'em exorbitant and not to be borne withal. Pour money upon 'em by way of loan and they will take your money before anybody's. A handsome treat proportioned to every house too is necessary; but pay and go, or else deferring they will be filled with their old conceits of never being paid and talk as largely as they and their old captains have formerly done.

It was all the more necessary that his interest should be carefully tended as he was now in conflict with George Clayton, probably the most influential of the townsmen and hitherto his supporter. The corporation asked Moore to waive his privilege as a Member of Parliament so that Clayton could recover the £50 awarded to him in an action against another alderman, James Jefferson, who was nominally Moore's servant; and in 1699 they allowed Clayton to begin an action at common law against Moore and Alderman William Brasse. For the time being Moore had little to worry about. Through Brasse he was giving employment to eight shoemakers, though not to another who had only just been made a freeman and could be put off for a year. They drank his health, Brasse told him, and worked with a great deal of cheerfulness. This was in the summer of 1700 when Evan Lloyd,

The Parliamentary Borough 1688–1782

himself a shoemaker and a Moore supporter, was mayor. When the election came in December Clayton was mayor and Moore lost his seat to William Coatsworth, Thomas Vyner retaining the seat which he had won at the by-election.[7]

Moore was without a seat for rather less than a year. At the election of December 1701 William Brasse, so much indebted to him, was mayor and the shoemakers were still grateful. Moore was again elected, Coatsworth kept his seat, and Vyner came at the bottom of the poll with twenty-two votes. Thereafter Moore kept his seat until 1715. Clayton was against him in the election of 1701 and again in 1702, but for many years Moore's interest was supreme. In the election of 1705 he was returned with Coatsworth, defeating John Chaplin and Thomas Vyner, the latter having only a single voter. There was no contest in 1708, Moore and Coatsworth retaining their seats, but in 1710 Robert Vyner took Coatsworth's seat. Coatsworth was still determined to be in Parliament and was a candidate in a by-election at Boston, where he pleased the electors by describing their borough as a lady and Grimsby as a whore. Moore was satisfied with the result and immediately after the poll wrote to Harley to assure him that he was confident that Vyner would join him in all measures for the public service.[8]

As the time approached for the election of 1713 it became clear that it would be held under a mayor, Matthew Wardale, who was not only hostile to Moore but had also spent heavily in canvassing for the mayoralty for the express purpose of injuring him. Moore had once been his landlord and he was persuaded that to speak of being revenged upon Moore would endear him to the freemen. In working for the mayoralty, he scattered money in alehouses and allowed gleaning for peas on his strips in the open fields, a most unusual liberty, and also promised a great pea-feast at the end of the harvest. Moore had been defeated in 1701 when the mayor was against him, but before the election of 1713, at which Moore was returned with Coatsworth, the mayor was in some way won over and gave one of his votes to Moore and the other to Sir James Clarke.[9]

Though the support of the mayor did not save Moore, at the next election in 1715, the mayor's influence at elections was already so strong that it was worth making considerable efforts to gain his support.

Our sordid mayor [wrote Bransby] is the very tool of Clayton, but it will be necessary to send him the quarter of malt I proposed to him. It will be expected the freemen be kept cheerful to prevent a mutiny amongst them or the encouragement of any pretender.

For the greater part of twenty years Moore's interest was so deeply intrenched that he had little trouble from mayors or pretenders. He owned much property in the town: between 1696 and 1711 he bought the Nuns' Farm with land in Wellow, Weelsby, Little Coates and Laceby, from Cyriack Weslyd, a house which had once belonged to Gervase Holles, various closes from the corporation, a house in the market, and a malt mill in Brighowgate. For nine years he allowed the corporation to withhold the interest on his mortgage, until in 1706 it was decided to let him take the land and cancel the debt. Clayton spoke of him as threatening the people, and no doubt some harsh language was used before the mortgage was foreclosed, but he softened the blow in 1707 with the gift of a silver decanter.[10]

Moore for some was a landlord deserving a vote at each election, until a better landlord should appear. For others he was a kind of cornucopia. He continued his patronage of the shoemakers, paying £370 in 1706 for 2,000 pairs shipped to London. The masters of several cornships obtained favours through his interest with Prince George. Mr. Harland desired his place in the excise to be at Barton instead of at Grimsby. Elizabeth Spurr begged for assistance in apprenticing her son to Samuel Harneis, a barber in Mark Lane. A supporter was given a suit and a hat for Easter to prevent him from discrediting the cause by looking ridiculous in his rags.* Modd's situation was so miserable that nothing would do him any good but the mortification of a gaol, but money was needed for Newarke, in spite of his ingratitude, to preserve him a little longer from destruction. A debtor, in prison and with a fever, needed £6 to get him out, and a merchant coming to London with malt, peas and tallow needed £30 to save him from arrest for a debt owed to the keeper of the *Black Boy*, Thames Street, New Billingsgate.[11]

This flow of patronage was channelled through Moore's man of business, Charles Bransby, town clerk and deputy-comptroller of customs. When George Clayton, still opposed to Moore, was mayor in 1704 Bransby was disfranchised for bringing actions at common law against two freemen† which should have been brought in the borough court, but in 1705 a writ of *mandamus* restored him to his privileges as a burgess. He became an alderman in 1708 and was elected mayor in

* This voter had once lived in a dove-cote.

† Few actions of any importance were now tried in the borough court and burgesses were increasingly resorting to the common law to adjust their differences. In 1714 it was decided to bury in oblivion the trespass of those burgesses who had sued others outside the borough court.

3. Old town hall and market place from roof of the Corn Exchange, c. 1860. This town hall, an eighteenth-century brick structure, including a gaol, stood on the site of the fourteenth-century timber-framed hall

The Parliamentary Borough 1688-1782　　　149

1709, 1710 and 1714. Moore at one time suspected him of fomenting litigation to further his private interests as an attorney, but Bransby claimed that he did no more than was necessary to secure control of the town for his patron. His desire to have Moore made an alderman was opposed by Brasse who said he remembered Sir Freshville Holles being an alderman when he was also one of the borough members and knew the folly of it. However, it should be possible to get rid of Lord Pawlett and let Moore replace him as Recorder. Nothing came of this, but on the death of John Chaplin Moore did become High Steward in 1714.[12]

Bransby looked for his share of favours. In 1710 he hoped to be under-sheriff to Marmaduke Darrell, and there was some prospect of his being made receiver-general of taxes in Lincolnshire if his father-in-law could put up the security for him. His hopes were disappointed, and in 1712 he was asking Moore to use his influence with Lord Ancaster to have him made Clerk of the Peace for Lindsey in succession to George Davenport.

I am now more unfortunate than any of my profession. Brackenbury of Spilsby, his lordship's steward of courts was drowned in salt water at Scarborough about three weeks ago. Davenport drowned in ale. Wickham went to heaven in a string and Jolland is said to have endeavoured and desired to go that way out of the world as most eligible, is not yet gone but is expiring and can't subsist a week. These four leave abundance of business behind 'em of one kind or another, and in case this cannot be compassed nothing can happen to me otherwise but from the favour whereon as I have had a long dependence so I do continue in the same. Though I have grown old in your service yet I promise myself you will sometime find something suitable to the capacity of, honoured sir, your obliged servant.

A year later he was still complaining that he was 'cloistered up', blind to everything but Moore's interest, and especially the management of the Nuns' Farm.*[13]

But Moore's long reign at Grimsby was now ending, and not even the most careful management could save his seat. In 1714 he was alleged to have been involved in a trading venture to the prejudice of the South Sea Company. Accusations of corruption by Moore appeared so nearly to involve Bolingbroke, his great patron, that the last session of Parliament in Ann's reign was hastily brought to a close. Moore was expelled from the South Sea Company, and called the directors a

---

* More than £200 would be needed for oxen, a clear indication that they were still used for ploughing in the Grimsby fields.

parcel of rascals. At the election of 1715 Moore and Coatsworth lost their seats. One of the new members, Robert Chaplin, was a director of the South Sea Company, and the other, Joseph Banks, held South Sea Stock, a situation which strongly suggests that Moore's former associates were anxious to punish him for his misdeeds, and for his free-trade ideas, by turning him out of his seat.[14]

But Moore's interest was still far from dead, and his enmity was still to be feared. Coatsworth had contented himself with petitioning against the return of Banks and Chaplin, on account of bribery and corruption, but thereafter abandoned Grimsby. Moore had a grimmer way of making himself remembered, by making an awful example of William Kitching, an ex-mayor who had supported him in previous elections and deserted to Banks and Chaplin in 1715. By the autumn Kitching was a prisoner at the suit of Moore and Bransby. Each year, until October 1720, he was handed over from one set of chamberlains to the next and kept in custody; but Bransby died, another election was approaching, and it was thought fitting to release him.*[15]

There had been complaints about Moore's neglect of his office as High Steward, neglect which was probably no more than a drying up of the source of patronage. When he failed to appear to hold a court in 1720 George Clayton was chosen to keep it, and the town agreed to indemnify him. And now, with the collapse of the South Sea Company, Moore savoured revenge on his old enemies and for a year regained his seat at Grimsby. For his share in the scandals of the South Sea Bubble Sir Robert Chaplin had been expelled from the House of Commons. Moore appeared at Grimsby to contest the seat, took the oath as High Steward which until now he had neglected to do, and had his son, William, admitted a burgess for £20 so that he also should be able to stand in the general election which, under the Septennial Act, must be held in 1722. In the by-election he himself was elected with fifty-six votes as against fourteen for his former colleague Robert Vyner.[16]

In the 1722 election Moore lost his seat and withdrew from politics. It was not so much the mismanagement of his interest which cost him the election as the fact that he and his son, William, had to fight five other candidates. Charles Pelham and Benjamin Collier were elected. Moore had seventeen votes, and William Moore one vote only, his father's. Joseph Banks too had only a single vote, perhaps because he

* It was perhaps possible for him to carry on his business as a butcher during his imprisonment. As a burgess he was entitled to be in the hall rather than in the gaol, and he had two shops under the town hall.

The Parliamentary Borough 1688-1782   151

was known to have been a stockholder in the South Sea Company. John Page had fifteen votes and Matthew Boucherett* nine. Moore remained High Steward, but began to sell some of his Grimsby property and took no further interest in the borough.[17]

In the courses of the eighteenth century parliamentary elections became the most important common concern of those who lived in Grimsby. Not every one was able to vote, but any male non-voter could look forward to the possibility of qualifying for a vote by marrying the widow or daughter of a freeman. For most the perquisites of elections offered the most immediate prospect of a temporary escape from poverty. The Methodist Conference of 1763, having passed a resolution against bribery, went on to say, 'Let this be particularly observed at Grimsby and St. Ives.' Wesley himself must have known how strong the temptation was in a town so sunk in decrepitude. 'It is no bigger', he wrote, 'than a middling village, containing a small number of half-starved inhabitants.' It reminded him, rather oddly, of Purrysburg in Georgia.[18]

In a situation like this it was not difficult for a family a little richer than the rest to become predominant by sheer ruthlessness, thus ensuring that they would become the channel through which funds dispensed by parliamentary candidates would have to flow. This was the happy position which the Claytons made for themselves. Litigation and the threat of imprisonment for debt was the method they employed. A Clayton prisoner was in a different category from any other. In 1702 a William Simpson, arrested at the suit of George Clayton, escaped from prison. The chamberlains were ordered to make diligent search for him, put him in the great low prison and leave him chained to the great stone until he revealed the names of those who had helped him escape. The system worked and the Claytons continued to gain in political stature.[19]

By harassment of refractory voters, and by their position as the

---

* Matthew Boucherett was a keen Whig, thought by some to have been responsible for the victory of Robert Vyner in the 1724 county election when he defeated Sir Neville Hickman with the help of a rumour that the latter had drunk the Pretender's health at Gainsborough. The rumour was spread by the circulation of an affidavit about the incident sworn before Boucherett, and because of his involvement Boucherett found it necessary to print a personal statement defying all who threatened him: 'I am the son of a divine of the church of England and educated in its most excellent doctrine and discipline. I shall always be ready to sacrifice my life and fortune in defence of it, King George and the Protestant interest, against all opposers. And I disdain to fear the threats of being chained in the middle, or be forced to leave these kingdoms, or my estate, or be hanged . . .' He was an unsuccessful candidate at Grimsby in 1741 and petitioned against the return.

wealthiest family in the borough, the Clayton's dominated the corporation, and from 1727 to 1772, one of the borough members, at least, was a Clayton nominee. They were connected by marriage with the Hildyard's of Kelstern, and in the middle of the century the second Christopher was a client of the Duke of Newcastle and had a profitable place in the Customs. In most other places they might not have counted for much, but Grimsby was now a very poor market town and its business community, apart from the Claytons, who were the only merchants, consisted of four millers, two bakers, seven victuallers, who were probably no more than innkeepers, and eight shopkeepers. Christopher I farmed the Chantry Farm, once held by Arthur Moore's agent Bransby, and he had shares in ships bringing timber from Frederikshall in Norway. Christopher II, his nephew, brought timber from Langsound in the Norwegian ship *Fortuna*, and imported redwood from Christiansand. Israel Bartram, of the Nuns' Farm, claimed the beaconage-toll which the priory had enjoyed before the Reformation, and tried to assert his rights by taking timber from one of Clayton's keels. But the corporation supported Clayton, and no more was heard of this claim. Christopher II also had London business interests, and had tea shipped from Bengal by his brother David, a Grimsby freeman and a lieutenant in the service of the East India Company, who died in the Black Hole of Calcutta.

Ultimately the Clayton interest descended to the Tennysons, who had married into the family, but they were now about to come under the shadow of a much greater person. Christopher II was really no more than a manipulator of elections and a London merchant who happened to have property and relatives in Grimsby.[20-24] He was not in any real sense a landlord. But Charles Anderson Pelham (1749-1823) was, and was able to take the parliamentary borough away from him completely. He succeeded to the Brocklesby estate in 1763 and became a Member of Parliament for Beverley in 1768. In 1772, Lord Luxborough having died, he was unanimously chosen Recorder of Grimsby. At the general election his brother, Evelyn Anderson, was returned for Grimsby with Joseph Mellish. The election was virtually uncontested since there was only one vote for anyone else—a vote ironically cast by Christopher Clayton for Charles Anderson Pelham.[25]

For the rest of the eighteenth century, and indeed even up to the reform of Parliament, Pelham candidates triumphed at almost every election. After 1782 the Pelham interest was virtually managed by the town clerk. William Hildyard, though related to the Claytons, was a

The Parliamentary Borough 1688-1782   153

member of an older and more distinguished family. The new town clerk, George Babb, had been employed in Hildyard's office and was a complete *parvenu* not likely to question the orders of his political masters. He was elected on the death of Hildyard with 183 votes. Main, George Tennyson's partner, received forty-two votes, and Tennyson one. To make Babb a member of the corporation Samuel Parker took Hildyard's place as alderman. Now that he was a twelveman, Babb was eligible to be an alderman himself. Another alderman, T. Hesleden,* who had gone to live either in Norfolk or in East Yorkshire, resigned his place, stating not only that he lived too far away to perform his duties, but also, rather oddly, that his present situation rendered him legally incapable of holding any office. Babb glided peaceably into his vacant seat.[26]

NOTES

1. CB, 18 May 1688, 1 Jan. 1689; Maddison, *Lincolnshire Pedigrees*, 98-100.
2. HMC, Duke of Leeds, 35; CB, 3 March 1690; Maddison, op. cit., 236-7.
3. CB, 29 Oct. and 1 Nov. 1695, 20 July 1698.
4. CB, 20 July and 2 Aug. 1698.
5. Maddison, op. cit., 67; CB, 22 Aug. 1699; Bransby to Moore, 30 Oct. 1699.
6. Sessions Papers, 1699; CB, 8 Nov. 1699, 4 June 1700.
7. CB, 2 Nov. 1698 and 13 June 1699; Brasse to Moore, 5 and 13 July 1700.
8. CB, 1 Dec. 1701, 20 July 1702, 9 May 1705, 6 May 1708, 6 Oct. 1710; Bransby to Moore, 11 March 1711; HMC, Portland, IV, 608.
9. Bransby to Moore, 12 Aug. 1712; CB, 1 Sept. 1713.
10. Bransby to Moore, 11 March 1712; LAO Calendars, Yarborough, 197; CB, 10 Dec. 1706; Bransby to Moore, 26 July 1706; CB, 7 Oct. 1707.
11. Brasse, 10 July 1703; P. Thompson, 23 Feb. 1702/3; Bransby, 28 May 1703; E. Sparr, 19 March 1702/3; Bransby, 17 April 1706, 1 Dec. 1710; Brasse, 23 Feb. 1708/9.
12. CB, 20 June 1704, 6 Feb. 1705, 8 June 1714; Bransby, 26 July 1706, 1 Dec. 1710.
13. Bransby, 11 March 1711.
14. HMC, Portland, V, 531; J. W. Hill, *Letters and Papers of the Banks Family*, xxii-xxiii; CB, 29 Jan. 1714/15.
15. Bransby, 30 May 1707; Calendar of Treasury Books XXIX, Part II, 199, 321, XXII, 294; CJ XVIII, 28; CB, 9 Oct. 1715, 7 Oct. 1720.
16. CB, 11 Oct. 1720, 10 and 11 Feb. 1720/21.
17. CB, 20 Feb. 1721/22; Stamford Mercury, 12 March, 1724; CJ XXIV, 27, 41.
18. Hocken, *Brief History of Wesleyan Methodism in the Grimsby Circuit*, London, 1839, 33; J. Wesley, *Journal*, ed. Nehemiah Curnock, London, 1909, V, 164-5.
19. CB, 24 Oct. 1702.
20. CB, 7 Oct. 1726; LAO Calendars, Yarborough, 224-7.
21. CB, 23 April 1734; LAO Reports II, 7; CB, 4 May, 1741, 5 June 1747.
22. CB, 19 Sept. 1752, 16 April 1754, 24 March 1761, 3 Dec. 1762; Namier and Brook, *The House of Commons 1754-90*, I, 326-7.

---

* Probably a son of the Rev. W. Hesleden who was vicar from 1750 to 1774.

23. HMC, 284; CB, 28 Oct. 1741; LAO Reports VIII, 9; LAO, Tennyson–Deyncourt 3/16, 121/30 and 120/5/3; CB, 22 Aug. 1758.
24. CB, 10 Dec. 1734, 2 Oct. 1753; LAO, Tennyson–Deyncourt 121/30; CB, 20 April 1752.
25. Complete Peerage, Yarborough; CB, 21 April 1772.
26. Vouchers, 1780–1; CB, 1 and 8 Jan. 1782.

XI

Returning Prosperity

In the first part of the eighteenth century the corporation was orthodox in religion, gave the church no trouble, and was quite willing to fall in with the bishop's scheme—a purely temporary one, as it proved—to annex the Grammar School to the vicarage of Little Coates. Some repairs were carried out on St. James's, but in 1791 the Hon. John Byng found it damp, dirty and blocked by galleries—and the whole borough wretched and living only by corruption. There was no licensed meeting house in the town in the first part of the century, and the corporation made life hard for nonconformists, notwithstanding the Toleration Act, by prosecuting selected individuals for being absent from church. One of them, Elizabeth Stephenson, spent five months in the town gaol in spite of the fact that her husband was an alderman.[1, 2, 3]

Until the appearance of the first Methodists there was no serious challenge to the established church. People went from Grimsby to Epworth, an extraordinary undertaking, to hear John Wesley preach in June 1742, and again in January 1743, when one of them was William Blow. This man, the earliest identifiable Methodist in Grimsby, was a cordwainer and a freeman, who took his first apprentice in 1741, and others in 1746, 1749, 1757 and 1759. He was a chamberlain in 1751, a bailiff in 1752, and in 1756 was defeated by only two votes for a vacancy in the corporation. In 1764 he took as his apprentice Amos Appleyard, one of the founders of Methodism in Cleethorpes.[4]

Blow gave hospitality to John Nelson whom Wesley sent to Grimsby in February 1743. Plainly there was already a congregation there—'some people that had once run well but were turned out of the way by one that had come down from London'. The intruder was apparently some kind of Antinomian. A man and a boy had been sent to bring Nelson, and the journey from Epworth, on foot, took two days. He was allowed to preach in a school which held several hundred people. The schoolmaster warned him that he might be mobbed, but everyone behaved quietly.* His hearers became so numerous that for

---

* Hocken says: 'The schoolmaster's name was Francis Walker, an Arian in principle; and the school room formed part of extensive premises called Torret Hall, which was

several days he stood on a table at Blow's back door to preach. The vicar and three men came as near as possible to play quoits, but failed to disturb him.⁵

John Wesley made his first visit in October of the same year, after a dangerous crossing of the Trent at Owston Ferry which he risked in order not to disappoint the congregation. He preached in the evening, moving into the street as the house would not hold a quarter of those who wished to hear him. This was on a Saturday. He again preached on Tuesday and Wednesday and then set off to Newcastle with William Blow. A woman, a converted sinner, rode pillion behind Blow to return to her husband in Newcastle.⁶

John Nelson's next visit was probably in March or April 1744.*

When I came to Grimsby [he wrote in his autobiography] the minister got a man to beat the drum through the town and went before the drum and gathered all the rabble he could, giving them liquor to go with him to fight for the church. No one offered to touch Blow's house till I had done preaching. Then they broke the windows, till they had not left one whole square about the house; and as the people went out, they abused them, till some of the mob began to fight their fellows for abusing the women, so that most of the people got away while they were fighting one with another. Not long after, the minister gathered them together again and gave them more drink; then they came and broke the stanchions of the windows, pulled up the paving in the streets which they threw in at the windows, and broke the household goods in pieces, the parson crying out: If they will not turn out the villain that we may put him in the black ditch, pull down the house!

An appeal was sent to an alderman to stop the riot, which lasted from seven until midnight. The alderman, however, was of much the same mind as the parson.

He would do nothing [Nelson continued] but lend them his mash-tub to pump the preacher in . . . The parson said to the drummer: I will reward you for your pains, but be sure to come at five in the morning, for the villain will be preaching again then. So the drummer did, and began to beat just as I was going to give out the hymn. When he had beat for near three quarters of an hour, and saw it did not disturb us, he laid down his drum and stood to hear for himself,

---

converted into a house of industry and afterwards into the present (1839) Granby inn, and the town's court house. The large dining room occupies the place of Walker's school, and the rooms in the house of industry were entered on the outside by a flight of steps from Bethlehem St.' Francis Walker was a freeman and voted for Boucherett in 1741.

* But Hocken says June 1743.

Returning Prosperity 157

and the tears presently rolled down his cheeks. When I had ended he expressed great sorrow for what he had done to disturb us.*[7]

When John Wesley made his next visit to Grimsby, after an interval of four years, many of his hearers were drunk, and a drunken alehouse keeper encouraged their rowdiness; and when Charles Wesley preached in 1747 rotten eggs were thrown at him as he left Blow's house. Later in that year a deputation went to consult Wesley at Grantham, but missed him; and Thomas Meyrick wrote to him from Epworth that Methodism was in danger of disappearing from Grimsby, the leaders having left the town because of unemployment.[8]

But it seems that the tide was now beginning to turn for the town as well as for the Methodists. In 1748 Wesley preached in the town hall which dated from the fourteenth century and was then almost at the end of its life. He noted that he was in an upper room, with many people on the stairs. The vicar, he said, still bitterly cursed the Methodists, but had been unable to prevent them from spreading. Most of those who came to hear him in 1751 were serious, though a good many were drunk. The next year the room where he preached was overcrowded, and he also preached in the open air, at the end of the town, to almost all the inhabitants. By 1753 he had an assistant in Grimsby, Thomas Capiter, to whom he sent advice about preaching. Capiter was said to have been a sailor before he became a farmer, or perhaps a bailiff at the Nuns' Farm. According to a later tradition he was tarred and feathered at Cleethorpes and pressed on board the warship *Princess Caroline* off Spurn Point, but was able to secure his release because he already had a certificate of discharge from the navy. He died in 1772.[9]

Through the exertions of Thomas Capiter, and possibly with the patronage of Lord Luxborough a new room was built for £78 in Blow's yard, and Wesley preached there in 1755. On his 1759 visit he regarded the room as a chapel (it had been registered with the diocesan authorities) and in the empty ground of the old St. Mary's churchyard, standing on scaffolding against a brick wall, he addressed a crowd which he was told was almost the largest ever seen in the town.[10]

---

* Nelson was more fortunate than another Methodist, Thomas Mitchell. He also preached at five on a Sunday morning in August 1751 at Wrangle and was arrested by the constables who led the mob against him. After being kept in the alehouse until four in the afternoon he was ducked in a pond, covered with white paint, and ducked again so that he almost drowned. A friendly villager gave him shelter but the mob drove him out of the village, crying 'God save the King, and the Devil take the preacher.' Mitchell afterwards wrote: 'In Lincolnshire I found a serious people and an open door, but there were many adversaries. This was the most trying year which I had ever known.'

By 1760 Elizabeth Blow and two other women were walking out to North Thoresby on Sunday afternoons to hold prayer meetings. Eventually Wesley told John Peacock, his assistant in Grimsby, to stop women preaching in his circuit. In 1762 Thomas Carlill, a pipe-maker in Bethlehem Street, began to preach in the district. At Waltham a hive of bees was flung into his meeting. When Wesley, in 1766, found that Grimsby so oddly reminded him of a town in Georgia, he was satisfied with the spiritual state of the Methodists, though the town was so poor. People who came to live in it, as in many parts of Lincolnshire, were likely to be attacked by the ague. Charles Atmore, who followed Peacock, suffered frequent attacks, and was advised by Wesley how to treat himself. There was trouble, too, with Calvinist preachers of Lady Huntingdon's connection, Beaufoy and Wrenn, who were also active at Keelby and Tetney. Wesley expressed his affection for Grimsby on the occasion of his 1780 visit, but was still worried about the Calvinists; and in 1786 the Calvinist minister disturbed his preaching in the market place. Methodism, however, was now firmly rooted, and its adherents were eventually to take over the government of the town. The corporation allowed them a space in front of their meeting house for a nominal rent, and in 1788 the vicar invited the now aged Wesley to preach in St. James's.[11]

At some time in the middle of the eighteenth century there was a change in the fortunes of the community. In the time of George I the vicar* estimated that there were only ninety-eight families in the town, and the parish registers seem to show a population of no more than six or seven hundred. In 1676 Grimsby may have been smaller than Clee, about half the size of Caistor or Stallingborough and one-sixteenth that of Boston. By the time of the 1724 county election there were five inhabitants who held freeholds in other parishes,† but in this respect the town was no different from such a village as Barrow or Goxhill. The place was so sunk in poverty that even a member of the corporation could find it hard to make a living. John Kemish, a twelveman, declared to Thomas Skelton that he could live better out of the town than in it, and was deprived of his place.[12]

Even so the corporation was increasingly concerned with the qualifications which made a man a freeman, enabling to earn some of his bread by voting, and with the disqualifications which could cast him

---

* This was Thomas Fairweather, Rector of Scartho, where he lived. He was the son of a Barton yeoman.
† East Halton (two), Waltham, East Butterwick and Frieston.

into voteless darkness. In 1728 Richard Urrey, a baker, under threat of 10s. a month fine for trading when not a freeman, was made to buy his freedom for £15; but this was the last occasion on which the freedom was sold to anyone other than a parliamentary candidate. Henceforth a man could become a freeman only by being born the son of another freeman, marrying his daughter or widow, or being apprenticed to him. Becoming a felon, or later, becoming a pauper, made him a non-freeman for ever. John Turner, a mariner, and Sarah his wife, convicted in 1730 for stealing a sheep, were burned in the hand and the husband disfranchised, as John Appleyard, a fisherman, had been in the previous year for stealing wheat. Six years later Sarah Turner was again convicted of felony and became the only person ever sentenced by the borough quarter sessions to seven years' transportation to one of His Majesty's American plantations.*[13]

A freeman could become a foreign freeman by non-residence and so temporarily lose his privileges. It was decided in 1738 that all those were foreign who lived in Wellowgate beyond the former boundary which had marked the liberty of Wellow Abbey. No foreign freeman could vote in any election, but he could be returned to the call-list of freeman after coming back with his family and residing for three months. John Coulson, however, who lived at Usselby, tried to return to the borough to qualify himself, and the corporation wished to remove him to prevent from gaining a poor law settlement in the parish of Grimsby.[14]

The regularity of general elections under the Septennial Act led to difficulties, never fully resolved, about the necessary period of residence. In 1769 the period was increased to three years and thirty-four freemen were peremptorily declared to be foreign;

> the corporation having found great inconvenience and very great hardships accrued to the resident freemen from a vast number of foreign freemen crowding into the borough one year before an election who have been absent the other six years without paying scot and lot, or doing the usual rights and services of every resident freeman viz. attending the mayor at full courts and other services and undergoing corporation offices according to their burgess oath.[15]

There were cases, however, in which a special indulgence could be shown to returning absentees. William Bates was reinstated as a freeman as soon as he began to reside again, in 1788, because he was able

---

* Apprenticeships to freemen were recorded more often about this time; e.g. in 1743, of Dymocke Williamson to Charles Newarke, surgeon and apothecary.

to show that when he was struck off the list he was an N.C.O. at the headquarters of the North Lincolnshire Militia, unable to leave his post without a furlough. The case of Matthew Empson was even harder. He was struck off during the Seven Years' War when he was taken by a press-gang from H.M.S. *Frederick*, and was twelve years in the navy. It was decided that his absence from the borough had been involuntary and that his name could go on the call-list immediately, only three days before an election. The town presumably still had a number of more-or-less seafaring persons who could attract the attention of the navy. In 1738-9, for example, the mayor entertained the captain of the *Salamander* when his press gang came ashore with a lieutenant, and the captain of the *Greenwich* who came with a warrant for deserters.[16]

This was about the time when the population, and perhaps the prosperity of the town was beginning to increase again. Nevertheless the prospect of becoming a freeman was perhaps still the strongest reason for seeking to live in Grimsby and the attractions were to become even greater. In 1754 it was found necessary to restrict the opportunity of gaining the freedom by marriage:

> Whereas by the courtesy of this borough any person marrying a freeman's daughter (she being born in the said borough) hath been admitted to his freedom thereof; and whereas it is found by experience that this indulgence hath been a means to induce the freemen's daughters to marry very young to their great prejudice; therefore at a full court it is unanimously agreed upon that no person who shall for the future marry a freeman's daughter shall be admitted to his freedom thereof until such time his wife shall have attained the age of twenty-one years and hath been resident according to the usual customs.

This resolution was signed by Ralph Tennyson the mayor, Christopher Clayton his stepson and forty-one others. Whatever difference it made to the daughters of freemen, it did not affect the marriage rate. In the previous decade there had been forty-one marriages at St. James's: in the succeeding decade there were seventy-one.[17]

But, as has been said, by the middle of the century the tide was turning. The register of baptisms indicates that the population was now again approaching one thousand. In 1761 it was decided to hold the weekly market on Friday instead of on Wednesday and to advertise the alteration in the *Gazette* and the *Stamford Mercury*; and at the beginning of 1765 Hildyard, the town clerk informed the corporation that a number of gentlemen had met at Caistor to consider the making of a turnpike from Grimsby Haven towards Louth and Caistor. The borough members were informed, the corporation gave concrete proof of its support by allowing the trustees to take 144 square yards of the Chantry Close for the road, and in the course of the year a turnpike act was obtained.

The turnpike ran from a place, north-east of the town and near the haven, called Upper Sands End, entered the town over the bridge then called Seamour White bridge,* turned down George Street, reached the Bull Ring through Osborne Street, Bethlehem Street and South Saint Marygate and proceeded along Bargate, eventually coming out at Wold Newton. There was nothing peculiar about the route through Grimsby, but a road to such a remote spot as Wold Newton can only be explained on the assumption that the aim was to take a metalled surface to a point on the wolds where there were unmade roads on a reasonable chalk surface reaching towards Louth and Lincoln and open in most seasons. It was also intended, at first, to have a branch of the turnpike turning off westwards through Laceby towards Irby in order to improve the road from Grimsby to Caistor, but nothing was yet done about this.[18]

By the end of 1767 subscribers had raised £5,460. The largest sum, £880, came from William Hildyard. Charles Anderson of Manby, the future Lord of Yarborough, and Joseph Mellish, one of the borough members, each contributed £600, presumably for political reasons. There were only two other subscribers not resident in Lincolnshire, and only one of the Lincolnshire people who subscribed, William Neve of Louth, lived more than five miles from the road. Edmund Turner of Kirmond was the only subscriber of the same standing as Anderson and Mellish.

When Hildyard died, George Babb, who succeeded him as town clerk, became also clerk to the trustees. Frequently meetings of trustees were called and then postponed because too few of them appeared. No doubt from the point of view of the unfortunate subscribers, their enterprise was a failure. Until 1791 their dividend was rarely as much as three and a half per cent and was sometimes less than two per cent. After the original £5,460 had been spent, and even of that sum very little can have been left for the road after the expenses of obtaining the act had been met, only insignificant sums were available for road work. A surveyor was employed, but his duties were part time only and he was largely concerned with enforcing the obligations of various parishes

* This was the bridge formerly called Simwhite-bridge, where the Riverhead now is.

to repair the road. When the trustees received a windfall of £20 in 1793 they decided to share it among the parish surveyors of highways, but only after they had put the road into repair.[19]

Grimsby was still in a remote corner of the kingdom, as Holles had long ago observed. Even in 1772 when Mr. Gregory of Harlaxton wanted to send a pointer bitch to Christopher Clayton he had to send her via Gainsborough and then by slow stage-waggon, the whole journey taking nine days. By 1780, there were no more than five people in Grimsby with man-servants (no more than in Brigg) as against twenty-seven at Gainsborough. Yet, however little immediate improvement the turnpike brought, it came at a time when population was slowly increasing. George Tennyson was having warehouses built by William Lumby of Lincoln, and in the course of 1780 the old fourteenth-century town hall was demolished and a new hall and gaol erected.* The old structure, timber framed and tiled, and with some in-filling of brick between the frames, had become dangerous. Occupiers of shops under the hall were given notice to quit, £200 was raised on mortgage for the new work, and the prospect of a new gaol prompted the constables of Wellow-with-Weelsby to pay gaol fees owing since 1769 and those of Clee to pay arrears dating back to 1773. By 1788 the prospects of building at a profit were such as to induce seventeen freemen to take leases of waste ground, for fines totalling £231, against the turnpike and the haven side. The men who embarked upon these ventures were no doubt aware of the negotiations which had been going on since 1787 for the employment of an engineer to turn the haven into a dock. The stagnation of trade was nearly at an end.[20]

Clearly the Grimsby Haven was a factor which had brought about the construction of the turnpike, but it was not until 1783 that it was thought worth while to erect the East Bar to ensure that the inhabitants paid toll, at the rate of twopence for a cart and a half penny for an ass or a horse, when unloading vessels in the haven or carrying sand from the shore. For seventy years or more the haven had been largely neglected, though small sums were spent on its maintenance every year. It was only in 1753 that the corporation spent £53 on the clough-doors and £57 on the West Marsh banks; and the borough members, Gore and Lock gave £100 for the improvement of the harbour. They stipulated, however, that it was 'to be wrought for by the resident

---

* An L-shaped building 63 feet by 63 feet in the present-day Old Market Place about 160 feet due east of the south transept door of St. James's.

Returning Prosperity 163

freemen' under the supervision of Samual Spendlove, chamberlain and church-warden, and they were probably more concerned with their own electoral prospects than with the haven. The resident freemen might work well, but their important qualification was that they alone could vote. Some, however, were seafaring men. There were sixteen mariners among the freemen in 1790 and two fishermen. All the freemen, however, stood to benefit from any real improvement of the haven, and in 1787 the first tentative steps were taken.[21]

In 1787 Samuel Parker consulted Jonathan Pickernell of Whitby about plans for a dock. Parker was a glazier who had become an alderman in the reshuffling of seats which had been necessary when George Babb was made a member of the corporation. Pickernell had been resident engineer under Smeaton in the building of the Tyne bridge at Hexham, and in the period when he was corresponding with Parker was designing the town hall at Whitby. He produced two alternative plans for a dock: one for the use of merchant shipping would cost about £50,000, and a larger one, suitable for naval use, would cost twice as much. Samuel Parker must have known that there was little prospect of raising such a sum in Grimsby, but he had a strong following in the borough and probably hoped to be able to capitalise his political influence. At any rate, towards the end of 1788 a meeting of ninety freemen at the Queen's Head instructed him to approach Robert Wood and William Wellesley-Pole, who were to be the Tory candidates in 1790, and thanked him 'for his steady perseverance in the measures he has taken for the freemen's relief under the injuries of which they have long complained'.[22]

If it really was Parker's strategy to use the political ambitions of wealthy men to promote his own schemes for a dock, the election of 1790 sufficiently explains why plans remained in abeyance until 1794. Pole and Wood were much more interested in winning an election than in promoting the construction of a dock, and the same was no doubt true of North and Harrison their successful opponents. It was not until 1794 that the scheme began to move again, i.e. a year after the attempt to unseat North and Harrison had failed and in the very year when Mr. Anderson Pelham, at last ennobled as Lord Yarborough and no longer needing to return two members for Grimsby, was prepared for a compromise with the managers of the rival interest in the borough.

Just before Christmas another engineer, John Hudson, was asked to estimate the cost of improving the haven, and reported that it could be made three feet deeper, with a pier and mooring posts, for £4,500. Pickernell, who had been sounding the opinion of possible supporters at Hull, Scarborough and Whitby was sure that this estimate was too low. George Tennyson, a much more substantial person than Samuel Parker, was now sponsoring the plans for a dock, but even so, until they had learned from experience, nearly everyone who was involved in the scheme regarded Pickernell's informed estimate as inflated, an opinion which in the end was to lead to his dismissal.[23]

In November 1795 a public meeting was held at the Granby inn to consider applying to Parliament for an act to improve the haven. The corporation was favourable, but at a full court the disorder among the freemen was such as to prevent proper consideration of anything. The matter was referred to a committee consisting of the aldermen, the common councilmen and twenty four freemen, an arrangement which suited the interest of George Tennyson. As a landlord he was not the equal of Lord Yarborough. 'A thing which I think very dangerous', John Lusby advised him, 'is the attempt to vest the power in the gownsmen for Lord Yarborough has such a command there by means of farms low rented etc. etc. that he might now do anything he pleased, and should your interests ever be separated I am well persuaded yours as well as the corporation's would feel the injury.'[24]

As yet, however, there was no fear that conflict between Tennyson and Lord Yarborough would arise. Babb, the town clerk and virtually a Yarborough nominee was afraid that Lieut. Colonel Loft, who had designs on the borough might persuade the corporation to petition against the bill which was about to be introduced to incorporate the Grimsby Haven Company. Babb saw North and Harrison in London before the second reading when North warned him of the danger of opposition from Hull; and he warned Tennyson that political rivals in Grimsby might gain support from Hull:

Thorold I find was twice at Hull before he went up to town, and as he is somewhat intimate with Harrison the Collector there, I am afraid he went purposely to stimulate him to opposition, and who from his official situation, which by this undertaking may be rendered less lucrative, and from his being a holder of several dock shares, will scarcely want any additional incentive. It has escaped Thorold's own roof that his errand there was solely for that purpose and since his return from town he scruples not to say that it is now in their power to hinder the bill from being passed. Two or three days ago there was a cabinet council held at Waltham, which consisted of Loft, Thorold, Anningson and Haddelsey, since which Anningson has been heard to say that the bill will not be passed . . . It should seem that it is to be strangled this session to make room for one of their own.

But there was no strangling and the bill was finally passed in May 1796.*²⁵

In earlier attempts to keep the haven navigable those who provided money seem to have done so largely for political reasons. Now, however, though the new Haven Company was bedevilled by politics, subscribers were inspired by the hope of profit and by the expectation of improving their property in the Grimsby area. The act of 1796, amended in 1799, authorised the company to raise a capital of £50,000. Most of this was subscribed by people with local connections. Sir Henry Nelthorpe subscribed £500, George Tennyson £2,000, and William Lumby (who had designed Tennyson's Grimsby warehouses) £200. Not much of the capital came from people in the borough. The corporation had £2,000 in shares, Richard Nell, a corn and timber merchant £200, and Babb himself £100; and there were one or two others. The Reverend Marmaduke Alington of Swinhope held £1,000 and was chairman of the company. Lord Yarborough and Mr. G. B. Heneage subscribed £1,000 each. Both could expect a considerable improvement in their property even if the company were only moderately successful. £3,000 came from J. J. Angerstein, the founder of Lloyds, who had estates in north Lincolnshire and was brother-in-law of Ayscough Boucherett of North Willingham, who had political ambitions and invested £2,000. John Henry Loft put in £1,000 because he hoped to represent the borough in the House of Commons, and William Mellish £2,000, because he already did so. Possibly Mellish could have afforded more. He had been a director of the Bank of England since 1792 and was to be Governor.²⁶

But it was only with great difficulty that this capital was raised. Those who first invested imagined that a total of less than £10,000 would see the work done, and Babb was speaking of a four per cent dividend as a certainty and eight per cent as probable. Gradually it appeared that civil engineering cost a great deal more and was much less simple than the company had been inclined to believe; and in the end it became obvious that the original subscribers had no hope of saving their investment except by doubling or even quadrupling it. 'I must confess to you', wrote Angerstein in 1800, 'that I have now no

---

* 36 Geo. III cap. XCVIII: 'An act for widening, deepening, enlarging, altering and improving the haven of the town and port of Great Grimsby in the county of Lincoln.'

opinion at all of the Grimsby business. It seems badly managed and I never hardly remember an instance where a scheme is set on foot and so many repeated calls made.'[27]

In the end the dock cost about as much as Pickernell had originally predicted, but although he remained their consultant for a while, the company at first aimed at something much more modest than his plans. Babb insisted that something less than £8,000 would be needed. As an attorney, he clearly felt himself superior to any engineer and competent to criticise his schemes. At first he was quite confident that no lock would be necessary. With the haven properly deepened Grimsby would be in the same situation as Hull before its dock was opened in 1779. Someone perhaps explained to him that geography made it impossible to make the old haven anything like the River Hull, because he was soon converted into a firm believer in a lock, but relying on John Hudson's opinion he still maintained that the capital required would be less than £8,000. Pickernell was quite firm about what was needed:[28]

I can see no more in Mr. Hudson's plan than to clear and open the old channel which of course will be of some trifling expense and advantage to the present trade which is now established in Grimsby, but as for further trade and commerce there will be very little chance, neither can it be expected without some accommodations for such ships as are employed in the coal trade, Baltic trade and coasting trade in general. The above mentioned trade requires water sufficient at all sorts of tide so as to admit ships of seventeen or eighteen feet draught to moor within the pier-head in safety. Vessels will not attempt to go into a small cut like that Mr. Hudson speaks of without a pier, for in case they should miss the entrance and stick fast on the side of the haven it would be ten to one she would overset.[29]

After the Haven Company Act had been passed, Babb found the earliest opportunity to rid himself of Pickernell. 'From the first', he told him, 'your view has been to make a job of the business.' A quarrel was provoked about Pickernell's expenses, and he was dismissed, but the plans which he had prepared for the company were retained and another engineer named Pilley was entrusted with their execution. Pickernell protested at the injustice of these proceedings. Within a month the company was regretting its choice. Heavy rain was causing the banks of the new excavations to slip and by August 1797 the slips were so serious that John Lusby, who was superintending the work advised Tennyson that the subscribers were desperate and were clamouring for John Rennie to be called in as consultant. 'They think', he complained, 'that another site for the lock ought to be chosen. They all think of themselves as engineers and it begins to be an unpleasant business, but Mr. Rennie may bring some improvement.'[30]

Some time during 1798 Rennie came to Grimsby and prepared plans, including a new diversion of the Freshney into the haven. By the end of 1799 the company began to feel that the dock was nearly complete and could be opened to shipping. Rennie insisted on the proper completion of the entrance lock and its return walls, which the directors of the company were inclined to think could be curtailed. 'I beg to entreat', he wrote to Tennyson, 'if the subscribers have any regard to the stability and success of the work they will let their engineering knowledge be displayed upon other parts of the work.' By the end of 1800 the dock was ready. Forty ships could be accommodated in water eighteen feet deep, and in a depth of fourteen feet there was space for sixty more. George Tennyson was having a quay built on his frontage, and the corporation had decided to have a quay opposite the site chosen for the new market.[31]

One last hurdle had to be cleared before the dock could be used. There was a deputy-customer, a deputy comptroller and a coast waiter at Grimsby, but since 1792 the collector of customs at Hull had insisted that all vessels for Grimsby should go to Hull to obtain customs clearance. There was a strong feeling that many people in Hull would like to prevent the development of the new port, and in fact the directors of the Haven Company had hoped to induce merchants to leave Hull and settle in Grimsby. Only one, however, J. C. Brandstrom, had done so, and these hopes were largely disappointed. Hull had nothing to fear and no opposition was raised to the establishment of proper customs facilities at Grimsby. The entry of the first ships in November 1801 was celebrated with a musical accompaniment and liquor for the workmen.[32]

NOTES

1. *Torrington Diaries*, 1954 edition, 367; CB, 14 April 1668, 4 May 1703, 20 Dec. 1720, 19 Nov. 1723, 18 Jan. 1726.
2. CB, 1 June 1714, 8 Aug. 1707, 17 July 1713, 24 Oct. 1703, 10 May and 11 Oct. 1706.
3. CB, 3 June 1701, 13 July and 8 Oct. 1708, 1 Feb. 1709/10, 17 April, 19 June and 2 Oct. 1711, 6 Oct. 1713; LRS IV, 33, 136, 22.
4. Hocken, op. cit., 9; CB, 11 May 1741, 9 Aug. 1748, 18 Aug. 1749, 25 Oct. 1757, 12 June 1759, 29 Dec. 1764.
5. T. Jackson, *Lives of the Early Methodist Preachers chiefly written by Themselves*, I; Hocken, op. cit., 12.

6. Wesley, *Journal*, III, 104–6.
7. T. Jackson, op. cit., 277–80.
8. Wesley, *Journal*, III, 171–2, 279; Hocken 25.
9. Wesley, *Journal*, III, 360, 524, IV, 20; Wesley, *Letters of John Wesley*, Epworth Press, 1931, 97; Hocken, 21; Wesley, *Journal*, V, 479.
10. G. Lester, *Grimsby Methodism*; Wesley, *Journal*, IV, 228, 307.
11. Hocken, 31; Wesley, *Letters*, VII, 8; Hocken, 27–8; Wesley, *Letters*, VII, 124; *Journal*, VI, 242; Hocken, 37–8; *Journal*, VI, 285, VII, 172, VI, 326; CB, 19 Sept. 1786.
12. *Alumni Cantagrigenses*, I, ii, 118; *Lincolnshire Notes and Queries*, XXVI, 33–50; CB, 27 Nov. 1711.
13. CB, 6 and 13 Aug. 1728, 28 Jan. 1729, 3 and 17 Feb. 1730, 11 Oct. 1743.
14. CB, 16 Jan. 1738.
15. CB, 27 June 1769.
16. CB, 29 July 1788, 15 March 1768, 12 Aug. 1740.
17. CB, 23 April 1754.
18. CB, 28 July 1761, 1 Jan. 1765.
19. Turnpike, 1 March 1791, 13 June 1794, 10 June and 25 Sept. 1791.
20. LAO Reports, XIV, 28; *Lincolnshire Notes and Queries*, IV, 201–7; LAO Reports, VIII, 9; CB, 4 and 11 April, 11 July 1780, 29 July 1788.
21. Turnpike, 10 July 1789; CB, 11 July 1780, 20 March 1749, 5 Oct. and 21 Dec. 1753, 19 June 1790.
22. Samuel Smiles, *Lives of the Engineers* (1864 edition), II, 151; TC, Pickernell to Parker, 6 Nov. 1787; TC, 13 Dec. 1788.
23. TC, Hudson, 20 Dec. 1794, Pickernell 5 and 6 Jan. 1795.
24. CB, 3 Nov. 1795; TC, Lusby, 6 March 1796.
25. TC, Babb, 26 Feb. 1796.
26. TC, Squires, 10 Aug. 1805.
27. TC, Angerstein, 10 Feb. 1800.
28. TC, Babb, 4 and 13 Oct. 1795.
29. TC, Pickernell, 6 Jan. 1795.
30. TC, Babb, 18 Aug. and 1 Sept. 1796, Pickernell, 25 Oct. 1796, Lusby 20 Nov. 1796 and 26 Aug. 1797.
31. TC, Rennie, 26 Nov., 16 and 17 Dec. 1798, 23 Dec. 1799, 30 Jan. 1800; CB (Memorial to Treasury), Dec. 1800; TC, Plaskitt, 24 Jan. 1801.
32. CB, Dec. 1800.

XII

The French War and the Growth of the Town

The new dock proved to have many imperfections, and in the winter months the absence of a pier at the entrance deterred all but the most intrepid shipmasters from entering it. Yet, in the circumstances, it was marvellous that anything had been achieved at all. The dock was made not only during a major war, but also at a time when the corporation and at least half the inhabitants were more obsessed with elections than at any previous time. It was only in 1790, 1793 and 1796 that there were actual parliamentary elections, but in a town constituted as Grimsby was there was nothing which could be done which did not have some bearing on election prospects. Those candidates who had the mayor on their side were likely to win, and the mayor was elected annually by the freemen. Further, the mayor must be one of the aldermen selected by their brethren, the freemen simply having the choice of which man it was to be. The party, therefore, with a majority among the aldermen had a flying start at any election.

For twenty years or more this party had been that of Mr. Anderson Pelham, the future Lord Yarborough. He was the principal owner of property in and around the borough, owning the bulk of that which had once belonged to Arthur Moore and then to Sir Thomas Sutton, to which, in 1793, he added Grimsby Farm and Bargates Farm. He was probably opposed to electoral bribery, as later his son certainly was, since his property was sufficient to give him control of the aldermen and common councilmen; and it may be that those freemen, probably a majority, who cherished corruption saw this plant withering under the rising sun of the house of Brocklesby. They were not, however, without hope. Alderman Samuel Parker, who had first put himself in touch with Pickernell the engineer was the leader of a popular party which aimed to throw the election of the mayor into the hands of the freemen, irrespective of nomination by the aldermen. In 1786, as champion for the freemen, he opposed the decision to take counsel's opinion as to the power of the aldermen to grant leases of the West

Marsh to themselves. Three years later he had a clear majority at the mayoral election, but was not, of course, elected.¹

The corporation on its side was closing its ranks. The aged and possibly unreliable William Lusby was given a pension of 5s. a week for life to persuade him to resign and allow the Reverend William Thorold, a more solid man, to take his place as alderman. But prospects were much brighter for Parker's party. Christopher Clayton still hoped to keep his interest in the borough alive, and could only do so through them. Better still, there were hopes of Treasury backing for attempts to upset Mr. Anderson Pelham's control. He, after all, was a Whig, and two sound government men were needed. In the early part of 1789 Samuel Parker returned from London and immediately went to see his friend, Hildyard Marshall, alderman and apothecary. 'Very great news, doctor,' he said. 'I have been with Mr. Pitt and he has taken the borough into his own management, and we shall have little or nothing to do with it.' As it turned out, however, they had a great deal to do with it, and the management by Pitt was not very apparent.²

The great object of the reds, the party of Parker, Clayton and Tennyson was to capture one or both seats from the blues. John Harrison had been one of the borough members since 1780. Although he had a fine country residence at Bishop Norton, built by Carr of York, his family was not an ancient one and was rumoured to have been founded by a coachman who grew rich by hiring out horses for stage coaches. His colleagues, Dudley Long North (1748-1829) had represented Grimsby since 1784 and for the rest of his life remained an ardent Whig, sitting for various other boroughs after he had finally abandoned Grimsby. Their opponents were the Hon. William Wellesley-Pole (1763-1845), Wellington's elder brother, a naval officer and a member of the Irish Parliament, and Robert Wood, who owned the house in Putney where Edward Gibbon was born. None of these titans had the slightest interest in Grimsby except as a place that happened to have parliamentary representation.³

Since this election was afterwards investigated by a committee of the House of Commons in considerable detail, its events are more fully known than those of any previous election. The natural delicacy of the members of the committee made them reluctant to inquire too closely into corrupt practices, and there is a certain lack of clarity about the evidence here; but it seems that the great hope of the reds lay in bribery, while the blues, controlling the corporation, could admit as many new and doubtful voters as their cause required. For some time before the election Michael Plaskitt, a carpenter, with the backing of Samuel Parker's 'Red Club' arranged for free distribution among the freemen's families of corn and meat, and of coal, which the freemen had to carry from the boats which brought it to the haven.

At the election itself Pole and Wood were deeply implicated in bribery. Pole took Edward Richmond into the cellar at the *Compasses* and gave him a £50 note to vote red but to keep wearing the blue colours. As Richmond could not read the landlord had to be called in to assure him that the note was genuine; and Richmond, taking the red money, treacherously voted blue. At the *Queen's Head* Margaret Burton heard Pole say: 'Good God, we shall lose the election! We'll give to the amount of fifty or one hundred pounds to as many as will do.' She told him she could get him a voter for less than that, but found she could not do so as two men were guarding his door to ensure his neutrality.[4]

The reds had been active also in seeking out non-resident freemen. Wood went to see John Gresham, a journeyman carpenter, at Fulham. 'He said he belonged to the court party,' Gresham declared, 'which had such places as Customs' and Excise's. If I would vote for him it was in his power to get me a place of that sort.' Wood also invited William Rodenhurst to his house at Putney to explain to him the advantages of voting red rather than blue, as he intended. Rodenhurst, however, was merely a potential voter. When he had lived in Grimsby as servant to Christopher Clayton for four years he courted Ann Cook, the daughter of a common-councilman. Clayton used to tell him that if he married the girl and became a freeman he would have £20 at every election. He had no poor-law settlement in Grimsby, however, and even when the girl became pregnant her mother would not consent to the marriage. Disappointed, and considering himself ill-used by Clayton, he left the town. Before the election Mr. Pelham's party brought him up from London to pay his addresses once more to Ann Cook. He was received coldly. She threw a pitcher of milk over him and her brothers threatened to kill him. Nevertheless she agreed to marry him and he went to Brigg for a special licence. Knowing that Rodenhurst would vote for the blues, George Tennyson, Clayton's nephew, offered him £50 to delay the wedding until after the election. Clayton tried the effect of swearing at him, while Pole offered him a place in the East India House. Rodenhurst was unmoved, but would have been wiser to yield. Tennyson won over the family of the bride, stopped the preparations as she was dressing for the wedding, kept her locked in

Samuel Parker's parlour until the crisis was over, and dismissed the groom with a guinea to help him back to Greenwich.[5]

Red agents even risked physical injury in their attempts at bribery. Michael Plaskitt went to the home of a known blue, Edward Wardale, and offered £50 if his son would vote red. The offer was not accepted, and Plaskitt was in some danger from the mob outside. 'He did not', said Wardale, 'want to get himself into a hobble. We did not wish to hurt the man. We let him out at the back door and he jumped over the garden wall.'[6]

But all this was in vain. Samuel Parker, Robert Lusby and two other aldermen supported Pole and Wood, but the rest were staunchly blue. With a blue mayor, the issue could hardly be in doubt. New freemen, most of them blues, were admitted up to the eve of the election, and residence qualifications were manipulated in the blue interest. The future Lord Yarborough had no property in Wellowgate, and since 1788 no freeman living there south of the stone marking the abbey boundary had been entitled to vote. Simon Spenceley's house was divided by the boundary, but he was careful to keep his bed on the north side.* But a serving man from Brocklesby, a stocking weaver from Westminster, a tile-maker from Deptford and forty-five other manifestly non-resident voters were admitted to vote for the blues. This power to poll non-resident freemen was exercised with discretion. Pole and Wood were allowed the votes of a London bricklayer and a Nottingham framework knitter and eighteen others equally disqualified. But at the end of the day North and Harrison had 140 votes and Pole and Wood 135. Clearly everything had turned on the essential blueness of the corporation.[7]

This victory, however, was too narrowly won for the comfort of the blues. Pole and Wood petitioned against the return, and until the decision of the House was known it was necessary to be ready for a fresh election; and at any time the simple mortality of aldermen might change the balance. In an aldermanic election the blues might fail to round up their non-resident voters, and three defeats would be enough to take the corporation away from them. The reds could dare to hope,

---

* This disqualification of freemen living south of the boundary had been introduced in 1713 but had lapsed in 1783. John Brown, who was eighty in 1790 could remember how in 1727 a man who owed him money had escaped arrest by retiring beyond the stone. He was naturally sensitive about the boundary and informed the Common's committee that a person apprenticed to a freemen did any work outside the town during his apprenticeship he did not qualify for the freedom. There was no other support for this rigorous interpretation of the custom relating to apprenticeship.

The French War and the Growth of the Town 173

and Pole invited George Tennyson to collect evidence for the petition to unseat North and Harrison.

> I am very strongly of the opinion [wrote Pole] that it would have a powerful effect with a committee if we could prove that Pelham's house was open during the whole contest and that freemen were entertained without reserve. I believe Nicholas Atkinson, who was, as you may remember, kidnapped by them, could say much upon that head. There are some charges of Parker's which I should hardly think it safe to pay at present, and the account is so confused that I don't understand it. Unless you undertake the discharge of these accounts it will be impossible for Mr. Wood and I to get clear of them as we ought. I have given you credit on my bankers. We cannot venture to keep up any expense in the town except the Club.*8

William Atkinson of Brocklesby was believed to have had an offer from the blues of any sum he cared to name if he would undertake not to reveal his knowledge about the election. He feared that Mr. Pelham would turn him out of his farm if he did not comply, but he was bold enough to ask the reds for £15. They, however, feared that he might be a Pelham spy; but before they could make up their minds there was a fresh panic when Alderman Leigh unexpectedly died of the gout.9

The balance of parties was too delicate for either to risk an immediate contest. To win the vacancy, the reds would need the support of Samuel Parker's club. He was not wholly trusted and was in any case more concerned with fostering his club than with getting Pole and Wood elected. In 1791 he had a poor rate quashed on the grounds that two of his voters were not rated and were thus disqualified and that seventy-three men without property had been rated simply so that they could vote. Whatever the risk, however, he had to be trusted. At the mayoral election he again demonstrated his power to regiment voters when 107 freemen voted for his candidate, who was not, of course, elected, while the candidates properly nominated by the aldermen shared no more than sixty-seven votes between them. Pole saw that it was necessary to let Parker select his own candidate to be alderman, but as Parker explained to Tennyson, money was what was really needed.

'If we were in possession of a little powder and shot', he pleaded, 'we should be able to beat them on any ground.' Tennyson, however, could offer only £100, whereas the blues, after waiting a whole year, paid £20 to each young freeman and Samuel Gooseman led numerous deserters away from the ranks of the reds. Mr. Pelham's men were

* Slightly condensed.

elected.* Tennyson and the reds contemplated an action for bribery against the town clerk to restore the morale of their party and upset the blues; but early in the new year Samuel Parker died, and the reds saw themselves fighting a losing battle. When Joshua Plaskitt, a red, claimed to be admitted a freeman by marriage, the spirits of the blues were so high that they rejected him on the specious ground that he had neglected the ancient custom, never hitherto mentioned in any record now surviving, of visiting each of the aldermen and common councilmen to solicit his consent and support. Perhaps it was known already that Pole and Wood intended to give up the fight. Even when the House of Commons declared the election of 1790 invalid there was no red triumph. North and Harrison were returned without a contest.[10]

There was a pause in the conflict to control the borough. Christopher Clayton was dead and Tennyson, his nephew and heir, stood in his place as the only challenger to Mr. Pelham who had now become Lord Yarborough. Both were ready to compromise. In 1794 the election of Ayscough Boucherett as High Steward, and of two aldermen and two common councilmen took place without a contest. The calm was broken in 1795 by the appearance of Lieut.-Col. John Henry Loft and his threat to the interest both of Lord Yarborough and of Tennyson. In September he went to Portsmouth with his regiment but left his band-master to canvass on his behalf and spread the rumour that Tennyson was now working for the election of Ayscough Boucherett. Nothing, he assured Boucherett, would be nearer his heart than to see him in Parliament if his pecuniary situation permitted it. He intended to support the nominees of Lord Yarborough who, however, treated him with coldness and caution; but his situation was such that he felt it urgently necessary to gain the alliance of Lord Yarborough, whatever the injury to his own feelings might be.† He now made a formal offer:

I got to London last night and called at your lordship's door this morning. I have great reason to think myself neglected and contemptuously treated by Administration. I don't think it right that my little interest in the borough

---

* An aldermanic election necessarily created a vacancy among the common councilmen which also had to be filled.

† Lord Yarborough's relatives exaggerated Tennyson's humble origins. 'I have heard my grandmother, Lady Netthorpe,' wrote Sir Charles Anderson, 'say that she recollected old Tennyson sweeping out the office of the attorney at Barton. I think Marris was the name. He afterwards went to Grimsby and got on in the office. It is pretty clear that the Deyncourt assumption and the baronial hall etcetera are as great an imposition as was ever practiced upon the public.'

The French War and the Growth of the Town 175

should be taken by force from me, and I have now to propose to your lordship, if you have not already settled with Administration, to join with you in bringing in two members. Whatever your lordship agrees I shall be perfectly satisfied with but I would much rather show Administration that we have power and spirit enough to resent their ill-treatment.[11]

The ill-treatment was of a peculiar nature. Since October 1795 Loft had been enlisting freemen in his regiment so that they could earn the bounty as volunteers and be discharged as soon as they had voted for him in the impending parliamentary election. Even so experienced a politician as the town clerk was astonished. 'The freemen', he wrote, 'continue enlisting and by being sworn in preclude all chance of return, as they take it for granted a non-compliance with his expectations at the election will prevent their having a discharge which of course they expect to be given immediately afterwards, so that the only hope will be the strong probability of overturning this new and gross mode of electioneering.'[12]

To check Loft, it was suggested that ejectments should be served on those Tennyson tenants who had joined the regiment, and the bell-man was sent round the town to cry that some legal means was about to be found of getting them out of the army. Tennyson even hoped that the pressure he could bring to bear was strong enough to cause some soldier-freemen to vote against Loft, who remained in Louth but kept up the spirits of the party by sending the bell-man round to announce a treat. The corporation was against him, and two of his freemen were disqualified because although their names appeared in the rate-book they were rated for single rooms only 'used but occasionally for the purpose of acquiring a right to vote as freemen at the ensuing general election'. This left a margin just sufficient for the election of Ayscough Boucherett and William Mellish, the candidates sponsored by Tennyson and Lord Yarborough. They demanded a poll and received the same 131 votes each. Loft had 130 votes, and his colleague, Robert Home Gordon, 128, and their only consolation was that they would have been elected if the mayor had not rejected the votes of paupers from Waltham, Tetney, Grasby and Market Rasen. But even for the victorious candidates there were drawbacks. Boucherett was soon complaining of the expense of the constituency. Both members sent £20 for Babb to distribute among the voters. Babb told Boucherett that this was but a drop in the ocean, and the member complained of the injustice of having to distribute money equally to all voters and not merely to those who had voted for him.

In the end the need for domestic economy was to force him to give up his seat.[13]

By the spring of 1802 Loft had found an ally in Mr. Robert Sewell of Ongar, and both were canvassing Grimsby freemen who were living at Hull. At the mayor's court held on the eve of the election all four candidates were represented by counsel, Sergeant Vaughan acting for Boucherett and Mellish, and Mr. Clark for Loft and Sewell. A large number of new freemen were admitted (no fewer than thirty-two by virtue of marriage to freemen's daughters) but the mayor, John Simpson, refused to accept several of the names put forward by Sergeant Vaughan. Vaughan therefore claimed that *none* of the newly admitted freemen should be permitted to vote, but the mayor allowed all their votes. Three freemen from Cleethorpes, four from Hull, and others from Laceby, Hilbaldstow, Goxhill and Gainsborough, as well as some from London, were all allowed to vote. A pauper from Healing, however, who had promised to repay the overseer 'if he was lucky at the election', found that his luck did not hold. A Wesleyan minister, the mayor and nine others were forced to swear, before voting, that they had not been bribed. Loft topped the poll with 146 votes, Ayscough Boucherett, with 144, kept his seat. Sewell and Mellish had 143 votes each.[14]

Colonel Loft celebrated his victory by issuing an address to the voters. 'Your steady and upright conduct', he declared, 'has convinced our opponents and the country at large, that honest men, however poor, are not to be frightened by tyranny, enslaved by oppression, or bought by bribes; and that independence and integrity are more frequently found in the huts of the peasant than in the mansions of opulence.'

But his victory was short-lived. Mellish and Sewell petitioned against his return. The Commons found that Loft was guilty of bribery and corruption and that John Simpson, as mayor, had corruptly rejected votes and had admitted freemen improperly. Mellish was declared to be elected in place of Loft and the mayor was summoned to the bar of the House and committed to Newgate, where he remained until May 1803. Boucherett resigned his seat in July 1803 and Charles Anderson Pelham, eldest son of Lord Yarborough, was returned unopposed. Loft petitioned against the return, alleging that the mayor caused the election to be held in such haste that he himself was unable to reach the borough in time, but he allowed his petition to lapse.[15]

The French War and the Growth of the Town 177

This, then, was the political scene in the years during which Grimsby was again being made into a port. By February 1802 it seemed to the corporation that development had gone far enough. The two hundred yards of quays which the Haven Company had constructed were likely to be all that would ever be needed, and the company could very well renounce the right to take further land for quays. Private individuals, on the other hand, let their optimism run away with them. 'The port of Grimsby', an advertisement announced, 'being the nearest port to the Dogger Bank in the North Sea, and very convenient for the fishing trade, it is intended this season which commences with Lent to supply this part of the country and neighbouring counties with cod, haddock, ling, butts, skate *etcetera*, two cobbles being already engaged for that purpose. The advantage arising from the selection of Grimsby is that when the north-west or north-north-west winds prevail, which frequently happens during the fishing months, boats find no difficulty in making this harbour when it is impossible to make any other up the river.' The corporation paid a bounty of 10*s*. to the first cobble in any week to land fish,* but the great days of fishing were not to come for another fifty years.[16]

Ships of a kind never previously seen in the haven were now entering the new dock. In September 1803 there was the *Peggy* from Quebec, the *Sovereign* from Halifax and the *Agenoria* from Rostock 'with His Majesty's cream coloured horses'. The dock was closed for a while for the excavation of another three acres for wharves and warehouses. When traffic started again in July 1804 one ship entered from Gallipoli, one from Memel, and five others from the Baltic. In the course of 1805 sixty-eight ships came to the dock bringing timber, tar, linseed, wheat and whale-oil, and one, the *Amelia*, brought two hundred tons of kelp from Galway. Their total tonnage was 17,786. But 1805 was an exceptionally good year, and the number of ships using the dock could fluctuate remarkably. In 1807 there were only eleven, in 1811 thirty-five. These figures relate only to ships landing goods at Grimsby. The number of vessels taking cargoes from Grimsby was always smaller—three only in 1807 as against sixteen in the previous year and six in 1811. Grimsby, in other words, could not attract the flood of manufactured goods from Yorkshire and the Midlands shipped from Hull; and the total receipts from dock dues, which began at £280, had risen to no more than £933 in 1805.[17]

But although Grimsby still ranked very low as a port, it could now

* In 1814 those receiving the bounty were William Dickson and John Cammish.

begin to grow again. The population of 1,524 in 1801 rose to 2,747 in 1811. No real fortunes were made, but at least the townsmen were given new ways of earning their living. The corporation offered land near the dock to be used by J. C. Brandstrom as a ropery, and in 1803 Mrs. Peasgood paid a fine of £100 for a ninety-nine year lease of land for her ropery. The reading room of the *Queen's Head* was used each morning as an exchange for merchants, ship-owners and masters and the *Yarborough* packet now sailed daily to Hull with a postal bag. Mary Babb, widow of the town clerk, acted as agent for Garfitt's Bank—until she secretly and without security advanced nearly £2,000 to Richard Marris, a tradesman who became a prisoner for debt in Lincoln castle.

'The borough', Loft wrote to Tennyson, 'is certainly one of the first situations in England for a mercantile situation (*sic*), and I am sorry to see it so thrown away for want of a little common exertion. Was this used, your property alone in it would be worth at least £8,000 per annum.' Tennyson was well aware of it, and began to take an interest in whaling. The *Bernie*, originally a prize taken from the Spaniards, of 265 tons, was bought in 1803 from Mr. Atkinson of Hull by Mr. Marshall and his partners and was fitted out at Grimsby for a voyage to Davis Strait, returning in August. Under the same master, Hornby, she sailed again in 1804 and returned, a 'full ship', with eight whales. In 1805 she completed her voyage as early as 22 June and had nine whales. In the next season she caught five whales, and at the end of August 1807 arrived from Greenland, again a 'full ship' with whales and 262 seal-skins.[18]

In 1807 a second whale-ship, the *Earl Fauconberg* began to sail from Grimsby. She was a vessel of 331 tons, built at Whitby in 1765 and formerly sailed from Hull. After her first voyage from Grimsby to Davis Strait she docked with eight whales, three walrus, one bear and three hundred butts of blubber. Each season both ships continued to sail from Grimsby until the *Bernie* was lost in the ice late in May 1813, the *Earl Fauconberg* bringing back her master and crew. In 1816 the *Earl Fauconberg* too was so badly damaged by ice that her crew almost decided to abandon her off the Humber; but in 1818 she not only made her usual voyage to Davis Strait but also in the autumn brought a cargo of timber from Memel. Her master valued his one-and-a-half shares at £450, but could not foresee that her end was near. In 1820 he visited an Eskimo settlement, apparently abandoned on the approach of the ship, in latitude 73° 20', on the east coast of Baffin Island. This was her last successful voyage. With six other whalers she sank in Davis Strait in 1821. The crew reached safety, and Charles Cooper, the master, carried on business in Grimsby until 1851. With the loss of the *Earl Fauconberg* the brief history of the Grimsby whale fishery ended.[19]

The war with France had a greater effect on shipping than on any other aspect of the life of the town. To celebrate Lord Howe's victory in June 1794 the corporation had given a hogshead of ale to be drunk by the public, illuminated the town hall, and gave twenty guineas to the fund for national defence. In 1798, after deciding to give £100 to assist the government in the national emergency,* the members of the corporation changed their minds and gave the money to provide uniforms for 'an armed association of volunteer corps of infantry for the defence of the town and neighbourhood, a preference being given to men of the most sober, peaceable and industrious character'. A further £150 was given in 1804 to the Grimsby Volunteer Infantry, for clothing and incidental expenses, and two years later a sum was given for celebrations on the feast day when the colours were presented to the volunteers. Because, however, of a dispute with Mr. Stockdale, the Vicar of St. James's, they proposed to march to Waltham and have their colours blessed there.[20]

There was one privateer which sailed from Grimsby during the war, the *Minerva* of Liverpool, under Captain Oxley. There was a French privateer off the mouth of the Humber in April 1805, and the armed ship *Duke of Kent* put out to investigate. Later that year the *Humphries*, bound from Grimsby to Quebec was taken in the Atlantic by a Spanish privateer which plundered her and allowed her to proceed. The following year the collector of customs, the mayor, the town clerk and three others were appointed prize-commissioners for the port.[21]

The news of the surrender of the Danish fleet at Copenhagen, published in the *London Gazette* two days later, was brought by the gunbrig *Cruizer* which arrived at Grimsby with dispatches on 14 September 1807. The crews of the two whale-ships volunteered to go to Copenhagen to assist in bringing the Danish ships across the North Sea. In November a French privateer, *L'Actif* captured two ships off the mouth of the Humber and took them to Dunkirk. Little more than a week later Lieutenant Milne in the *Carrier* captured her off the Dogger Bank and brought her into Grimsby. A detachment of the

* In September 1799 sick and wounded troops from Holland were expected to be landed at Grimsby and barracks were cleared to provide space for them.

Voluntary Infantry marched the twenty-nine prisoners as far as Brigg on their way to the great prisoner-of-war camp at Yaxley. At Sleaford they made an unsuccessful attempt to escape.* The same winter the Grimsby Volunteers escorted another thirty-three prisoners landed by the sloop *Ringdown*.²²

Throughout the war convoys were assembled off Grimsby, but after Trafalgar no considerable escort was required. In September 1812, for example, the cutter *Princess of Wales* assembled the convoy, and in December 1810, the sloop *Woodlark*, which almost occasioned the death of a Grimsby man and woman when their boat overturned as they were attempting to sell goods to her. Running a bumboat was not the only way of turning the war to good account. Prizes were frequently brought in and could be profitably bought. In August 1809 the gun-brig *Wrangler* brought in two Russian prizes which had been employed in provisioning the Russian forces in Finland. William Richardson in 1808 bought corn from the Danish prize *Hercules*, intending to send it to Hull for export to Sweden; and in 1811 R. Drewery bought the prize *Toujours Fidèle* and re-registered her as the *Expedition* of Grimsby.²³

By reason of its proximity to Germany and the Baltic, Grimsby occasionally had the earliest news of developments in the fight against Napoleon. On a Sunday evening in August 1809 the Duke of Brunswick landed at Grimsby from the frigate *Musquito* after fighting his way to Cuxhaven where the *Musquito*, operating from Heligoland, had overcome the garrison and spiked the guns. The *Cruizer* again arrived with dispatches in November 1812, and a courier immediately left in a post-chaise and four for London. In March 1813 the Danish ship *Alsen*, of eighteen guns, arrived under a flag of truce and the captain, accompanied by Lieutenant Southcott, at once set off for London with dispatches which were believed to contain proposals for the withdrawal of Denmark from the war. So much of Europe still remained under Napoleon, however, that the shortest route from central Europe and the Balkans still lay through Grimsby, and on 9 June a messenger arrived with dispatches from Vienna and Constantinople. A few days later two transports, the *Campbell* and the *Charles*, were at Grimsby with detachments of the German Legion destined for war on the continent. But there was now a state of war with the United States also, and the *Beaver* arrived from the coast of Norway with the news that Commodore Rogers in U.S.S. *President*

* A sentry was sleeping against the exit of their escape tunnel.

The French War and the Growth of the Town 181

was cruising to intercept the whalers homeward bound from Greenland.*[24]

The end of the year saw a vessel lying off Grimsby with Spanish deserters from the army of Napoleon; and in April 1814 the mayor was informed that a treaty of peace with France had been concluded. The corporation met at the *Granby* inn and decided to illuminate the town on Saturday. The vicar, however, protested, so the illumination was fixed for Friday, and the corporation walked in procession with a band. But because the war with America continued warships were still needed to escort merchantmen. In August 1814 a Baltic convoy was assembled and Lieutenant Price of the *Cruizer* requested the mayor to inform the mayor of Hull that he intended to sail as soon as the wind was favourable.[25]

With the final collapse of Napoleon, the corporation decided to give £30 'for the benefit of the families of the slain and wounded of the British army at the glorious battle of Waterloo': and Captain Mott was proud to tell his neighbours not only that he himself had arrested Parker, the leader of the Nore mutiny in 1797 but also that his son was now first Lieutenant in the *Bellerophon*, the ship on which Napoleon embarked after his capitulation.† Few of the freemen had seen active service. Thomas Potts and Richard Jenny had been struck off the call-list in 1803 because they had voluntarily enlisted on board a man of war. In 1815 three freemen, one of whom had been in the navy, returned to reside, and in the following year two returned from the army and one from the navy. John Leonard returned in 1817 after five years as a barrack sergeant at Plymouth.[26]

The town was growing throughout the war years. It was noted in 1794 that some freemen were enclosing and building upon plots by the roadside on the pretext that these had been properly allotted to them by the manor jury, and that recently this practice had greatly increased. One freeman was ordered in 1796 to pull down the house which he had illegally built in the East Marsh, and the next year four others had similar orders served on them. As the dock neared completion the corporation decided to lay out building lots for freemen in the East Marsh. This automatically reduced the area of common, but as the common-rights of non-freemen in the March had already ex-

---

* Danish privateers were still active. One of these captured the Swedish ship *Neptunis* when it reached Grimsby after being rescued by the gun-brig *Vixen*.

† His monumental inscription in the church at Old Clee says that he was an honest man and a post-captain in the Royal Navy. In fact commander was his highest rank.

tinguished, there could be no effective opposition. The lots lay along the turnpike road from the gate at the entrance to the East Marsh to the point where the road turned east to Cleethorpes.* Each lot was of twelve by thirty yards on a ninety-nine year lease. The mayor chose his own lot, and the rest of the freemen balloted. Non-freemen were allowed to bid for any lots not taken by Christmas. Lessees were to build houses within ten years and the houses were to be of two storeys or more. The corporation filled in any pits in the area. No slaughter houses were to be built fronting the streets.[27]

It was felt that this unprecedented leasing of land might result in those freemen with poor-law settlements in other parishes acquiring a legal settlement in Grimsby. Counsel's opinion was taken and the corporation was assured that a building lot would not confer a settlement. In 1802 the lessees were offered easy terms for converting their leases into freeholds, and in 1803 further lots behind the original lots were laid out and offered to freemen, though others could bid for them if the freemen did not take them.[28]

George Babb and his partners in the brick company, who had proposed to make a fortune out of clay excavated for the dock, were given a lease of land against the turnpike for their tile-kiln and drying sheds. From 1797 George Tennyson consolidated his estate near the dock. In 1811 he bought land at Freeport Wharf, and he had building leases from the corporation, letting the houses to carpenters, joiners and masons. A new market place was laid out in the newly developed area and Thomas Cook, a stonemason, was given a lease as a reward for his services in building an obelisk and a cistern in the new market. But, in spite of the covenant in the leases, not much building took place, and in 1802 the term during which buildings must be erected was extended from ten to twenty years. Most of the land was used by the lessees to grow potatoes, cabbages, turnips and carrots, and the corporation had to agree to pay the vicar £16 a year on condition that he claimed no tithe in this area. By 1819, however, it was necessary for the chamberlains to make a well and a pump in Lower Burgess Street; and in 1825, by a vote of seventy-five to sixty-nine, the freemen agreed that more of the East Marsh should be set out in building lots of 360 square yards for those freemen who had never had one.[29]

The corporation began to take an interest in paving and lighting. In

* The building lots laid out between 1799 and 1825 lay in the area now bounded by Victoria Street, Pasture Street and the railway, where the street pattern has been much modified by re-planning.

1800 the pavement in front of the town hall was flagged and kerbed, and 325 yards of the streets were laid with gravel. Those freemen who were smiths were invited to tender for placing twenty-four lamp-irons at various places in the town and James Bunch of Lincoln provided globes with burners to light the streets during the winter, with twelve spare globes in case of accidents. A lamplighter was employed at 7s. a week, but the next winter the chamberlains were told to agree on the lowest terms with anyone who would agree to light the lamps and provide the oil. And from 1800 a fire-engine was maintained by the corporation.[30]

The corporation realised also that the growth of its revenue now permitted it to pay the two sergeants rather more. The common sergeant up to this time was paid by fees of 8d. from each freeman and 1s. from each alderman, which he had difficulty in collecting, and was expected to dine at the mayor's table on Sundays. Now he was given a salary of £10 a year instead, and the salary of the mayor's sergeant was increased from £2 to £10. The reason given for this generosity was the heavier burden placed on him by 'the increased number of the freemen, the more dispersed situation of their habitations, and the greater frequency of full courts', factors which reflected the heightening of political tension rather than the real growth of the community. The salary of the town clerk went up to £20, though his fees made his office worth a great deal more, and the gaoler, who had little to do, was given an extra £10 to sweep and cleanse the pavements in the centre of the town. And thirteen new prayer books, to be left in the care of the parish clerk, were bought for the use of the corporation.[31]

It was at this time too that some improvements were made in the grammar school. The master, Thomas Wilkinson, received a salary increase of £7 a year, and in addition to his proper duties was to teach reading and writing to ten children of the poorest freemen. He also did a certain amount of work for the corporation as a land surveyor, but for this he received additional fees. In 1803, the year of his death, a brick school-room was built for him, eighteen by fifty feet and ten feet high. Two candidates for the vacancy were referred to the Rev. Mr. Gray of Waltham. He found both suitable, and Samuel Bucknall of Carlton-le-Moorland was appointed at £40 a year. The appointment was made by election, eighty-two freemen voting for Bucknall and seventy-one for his rival.[32]

The master was given a house free of tax and window duty and was allowed thirty-five days holiday each year in addition to Saturday afternoons and Sundays. All but twenty of the children were to pay him fees of 5s. a quarter, and he was to teach reading, writing and arithmetic, with Latin if required. For a while some of the children were taught by the widow of his predecessor, and the corporation paid her £10 a year. Bucknall's appointment ended in 1808 when he was dismissed for cruelty and gross ill-treatment of the children.[33]

The way was now open for the most colourful personality who had ever conducted the school, George Oliver. He was born at Papplewick in Nottinghamshire, and educated in Nottingham. His father was rector of Lambley and later of Whaplode. He himself applied unsuccessfully for the Grinsby post in 1803. At that time he was clerk to an attorney at Holbeach, but by the time of his marriage he had become usher in the Caistor grammar school. At Grimsby his talents came into full bloom. In 1808, although he was not ordained until 1813, he was provincial grand chaplain to the Lincolnshire freemasons and preached at their service in the cathedral. He produced a treatise on education with a dedication to the mayor and burgesses of Grimsby, who decided to frame it and thank him for his services to the school. Smedley's company of players in 1812 performed *Wonder! A Woman Keeps a Secret* 'by desire of Mr. Oliver and the young gentlemen of the corporation school' and also a comic interlude, written by Oliver himself, called *The Thespian Barber or Rhyme without Reason*. And in 1817 he published his inaccurate and wildly imaginative *Monumental Antiquities of Great Grimsby*.[34]

The Rev. Joseph Stockdale, Vicar of St. James's, who was also Vicar of Clee and Rector of Waith and of Muckton made him curate of St. James's in 1814, and on his death in 1815, Oliver became Vicar of Clee also. These promotions meant that he could largely ignore attempts to control his conduct of the grammar school. His position was more comfortable than that of any of his predecessors. To make up his salary to £137 10s. a year the freemen were no longer to have £25 shared among them at the mayoral election, and the mayor gave up his own salary of £50 which he had enjoyed since 1804. The numbers in the school were restricted to seventy children of freemen, and it was expressly stipulated that the master must not take fee-paying pupils. He failed to get an increase of salary in 1812, and three years later was found to be taking fees for teaching fifteen children, whom he was required to remove in six weeks. But in 1816 he was again formally thanked for his conduct of the school, and three years later the freemen elected as school visitors cleared him of a charge of 'immoderate correction'.[35]

When Smedley's company performed for Oliver in 1812 they had already been visiting the town for four years. At the theatre, behind the *Golden Fleece*, facing Burgess Street, they performed during the races. An ordinary was held at the *Granby* each day, and there were donkey races, sack races, jingling matches, a greasy pole and hog-tail catching, with cock-fighting at the *Crown and Anchor*. The race-course was used in 1804 for a five-mile running race between a butcher and a cordwainer, for £20. The butcher won in just under half an hour after the cordwainer retired exhausted in the last half mile. Hawkes, a gunsmith, in 1809 undertook for a bet to walk seventy-two miles daily for a fortnight on an uneven piece of ground in the East Marsh. A magistrate stopped him from performing on a Sunday and he gave up the following Tuesday. The chamberlains in 1811 and 1812 were authorised to spend £20 on improving the race-course in the East Marsh up to the old haven, and in 1821 to contribute £50 for a plate to be run for annually. The course still needed improvement in 1827 when in a field of three horses for the Members' Plate two fell into a sandpit and did not finish.[36]

The East Marsh, though still a common and being built on, was the place for recreation. Fireworks were prohibited there after a complaint that squibs had been let off near haystacks. In 1823 all who played cricket either in the East Marsh or in the Little Field were threatened with prosecution, but people were daily playing cricket in the East Marsh in 1836. A deputation from the cricket club presented a petition, but were refused leave to play. The freemen's stock were being injured, and all games were again forbidden in the Haycroft, the Little Field and the East Marsh. It was not until 1844 that the cricket club was at last given permission to play in the Marsh; but every year the bell-man was sent round to cry a prohibition against bonfires in the Marsh streets on Guy Fawkes' day.[37]

For many years yet the markets were still held in the streets in the oldest parts of the town. The fish and pig markets were in the Bull Ring, the latter outside the *Fox* public house, until in 1816 it was decided by a vote of eighteen to nineteen to move it into the yard of Bransby Harrison.* A few of the ancient street and market ordinances were still enforced. In 1814 a butcher named Easter was threatened

---

* A member of the corporation, said to be the grandson of the inventor of the marine chronometer.

with prosecution for causing a nuisance with the offal from his slaughter-house, and in 1820 the chamberlains were ordered to display a notice in the market 'that no shopkeeper, huckster, or other person shall purchase any butter, eggs, fowls, fruit or vegetables intended to be resold by them previous to the hour of twelve o'clock'.[38]

As the town grew, the problem of poverty became more intractable. In 1783-5 the cost of relieving the poor of Grimsby had been no more than £63 a year. In 1802-3 it was £258. As a means of alleviating poverty without any charge to the rates the corporation in 1800 tried the effect of buying £100 worth of flour to be sold to the inhabitants at cost price. It was decided a year later to form a union with adjacent parishes for the maintenance of the poor and Lord Yarborough was invited to give a piece of land, in exchange for other land, for the site of a house of industry. The land was in the end acquired from George Tennyson in exchange for the Coal Hill and other pieces of the bank of the old haven. Builders were invited to submit tenders for erecting the house, and Tennyson was appointed visitor and John Squire guardian under the Poor Act of 22 George III. Within a year there were thirty-one paupers in the house, ten of whom belonged to Grimsby. By 1823 there were about a hundred and there was a treadmill to keep them busy. It could be used for grinding corn, crushing bones for manure, which was becoming a thriving business in the town, working a circular saw or turning a grindstone. 'Its adoption', wrote a local enthusiast, 'in all houses of industry will no doubt speedily ensue.' The hopes of such visionaries were disappointed. A few years later Sarah Hardy, mistress of the house of industry, woke Sarah Wardale, one of the paupers, stripped her, tied her to the treadmill and flogged her. The case was removed from the Grimsby quarter sessions to the King's Bench, and Mrs. Hardy was sent to the Louth house of correction for four months. Nothing of the original house of industry now remains, but some of the houses built as an extension to it prior to 1837 can be seen as the row now called Alfred Terrace in Brighowgate.[39]

The population changes which obliged the town to modify its traditional attitude to the poor also necessitated an alteration in common rights. Because these rights were regulated by a full court in which only freemen could vote, their rights were carefully fostered while those of non-freemen were treated in a cavalier manner. The most privileged freemen were, of course, the members of the corporation. The greater part of the West Marsh had been reserved for them and they held it on leases of twenty-two years. On the death of an alderman or councilman the lease passed to his heir, and it sometimes happened that there was no lease available for a newly elected member. For the rest of the freemen there were only eight plots available to them in order of seniority, and a poor freeman would sometimes sell his turn several years before it came due. In 1783 the system was reformed. The freemen's plots were vested in trustees for the benefit of all of them, and leases to members of the corporation were to be terminated by their death. Samuel Parker would have preferred to put them on the same footing as other freemen and in 1786 opposed a decision to take counsel's opinion as to the power to grant leases.[40]

Non-freemen were finally deprived of their common rights in the East Marsh in 1788, though they could still enjoy common rights elsewhere if they occupied ancient toftsteads. Even so, it became necessary to reduce the stint in the East Marsh and the Little Field. An alderman could keep twenty-four sheep instead of forty-five, a councilman eighteen instead of thirty, and an ordinary freeman twelve instead of fifteen. The freemen would not consent to any more drastic reduction of their stint.[41]

Occasionally there were conflicts with the farmers, who, if they were not freemen, enjoyed only the most restricted rights of common. In April 1814 the sheep of a farmer named Bowling were found in the fallow field and were impounded by the chamberlains. He was the tenant of Tennyson who had bought the Chantry Farm in 1800 in the mysterious absence of any other bidders. It had been sold to him without common rights. Acting for Tennyson, Joshua Plaskitt applied for the release of the impounded sheep on the grounds that his employer did have common rights in respect of other land called Foxtail and Rye Hill Leas. This, however, amounted to no more than three acres and in the corporation's view gave him only three sheepgates. Tennyson refused to give up the fight. He persuaded his friend, Ayscough Boucherett, the High Steward to appoint Plaskitt as his deputy to hold the next court leet.* Plaskitt duly held the court as deputy high steward and refused to swear the jury selected by the chamberlains and proceeded to select a jury and appoint his own set of manorial officers. If he had been allowed to do this unchallenged, the Tennyson faction would have been able to regulate the commons in their own interest. The corporation steeled itself to resist. The town clerk was instructed to search the records going back to the sixteenth century for precedents and found that courts leet had frequently been held by the mayor

* It was usually held by Nicholson, the deputy recorder.

without the High Steward or his deputy. Indeed he would have had some difficulty in finding anything else. He waited upon Lord Yarborough, who was recorder, to confer with him on counsel's opinion as to Boucherett's conduct, and a lawsuit was commenced against Boucherett in the King's Bench. From the point of view of the corporation the affair ended satisfactorily with the accidental death of the High Steward when the pole of his curricle broke on Willingham Hill. George Anderson Pelham, Lord Yarborough's younger son, and certainly no Tennyson man was appointed in his place.[42]

All this had arisen out of a single dispute about a farmer's rights of common. The corporation was equally determined to prevent any farmer from curtailing the rights of the freemen. During the quarrel with Tennyson it was resolved to defend the right of the freemen to stock the fallow field, that is to enjoy common rights in an area where the great majority of them had no land, and to take legal action if any animals were impounded by the farmers. During the spring two farmers impounded cattle and horses in the fallow field which they claimed had been damaging their corn. After a noisy meeting with the mayor and the town clerk they agreed to release all but a single horse which would be made the subject of a test case. For its part the corporation agreed that it would not indemnify any freeman whose stock was found straying from the fallow into the corn and that no one was to leave any animals in the fallow field at night until the corn was cleared.[43]

With a full knowledge of what had happened to commoners in those Lincolnshire villages already enclosed, the majority of the freemen were deeply suspicious of any moves towards enclosure and full individual ownership of land. There was even hostility to the enclosure of Clee where the freemen had no common rights but where the corporation was still lord of the manor. In 1812 a Mr. Hepworth was appointed to act for the corporation in the proposed enclosure of Clee, but in 1814 the bailiffs deliberately absented themselves so that no proper court could be held to carry the matter further. The following year a majority decided to oppose a bill for the enclosure of Clee, Cleethorpes and Thrunscoe, fearing that it might endanger their common rights in the East Marsh. It was not until 1838, long after the Grimsby enclosure act that the new corporation was approached by Mr. Thorold of Weelsby and agreed to the enclosure of Clee with compensation for their manorial rights, and in 1841 they accepted the proposals of the other Clee landowners for an enclosure act.[44]

The growth of Cleethorpes had made the freemen all the more sensitive about their common rights. As that hamlet became a fashionable sea-bathing resort and its population grew, the men of Cleethorpes also were interested in common rights. The bell-man was sent round the town in 1822 to summon a special court to consider what to do about the action of the Cleethorpes shepherd, William Osborne, who had driven the stock of the freemen from the common beyond the blue stone. It was decided to employ two men to tend the stock and keep them in the disputed area. Two years later George Babb, the second town clerk of that name, was ordered to defend an action at the assizes arising from the impounding of horses at Cleethorpes. Damages of £40 were awarded against the corporation, each side paying its own costs. In 1829 several men resorted to self help and forcibly removed animals from the pinfold at Cleethorpes. Nine of them were imprisoned in the house of correction at Kirton Lindsey for the old common law misdemeanour of pound-breach. They were regarded as monuments of civic virtue and the corporation allowed them up to 10s. a week each during their confinement. This was followed by a civil action at the Lincoln Lent assizes in 1830 to decide whether the disputed land, which had been gradually left by the sea, belonged to the corporation as lords of the manor of Clee or to Richard Thorold as Lord of the manor of Cleethorpes. The verdict again went against the corporation, and it was found that £400 would be needed to meet the costs of the lawsuit.[45]

None of this made it easy to consider enclosure dispassionately. Some of those who desired enclosure undoubtedly intended to extort rather more than their legal rights and in the end certainly succeeded in doing so; but the majority of the freemen could not extract any value from their rights unless they too acted illegally. The 1831 census showed that only fifty out of a total of 772 families were employed in farming. Few of the freemen can have had stock of their own, and it was well known that they were tempted to take payment for depasturing the animals of other men as their own.[46]

An anonymous address from 'A Burgess' was circulated in the town declaring that the case coming on at the assizes about the impounding of horses at Cleethorpes was of less importance than the fraudulent stocking of the commons. There were three hundred burgesses and only fifty used their common rights; but a proper enclosure could give every burgess an annual rent in lieu of these rights, and it would also be of great advantage to have the land exonerated from tithes and especially from those on cabbages and potatoes.[47]

In 1826 the mayor received a requisition signed by seventy-two burgesses asking him to call a full court to consider enclosure. The signatories included a wine merchant, the collector of customs, the chief mate of the revenue cruiser, a confectioner, and of other persons unlikely to have any strong interest in agriculture. But three substantial farmers signed, and fifteen members of the two associations for the prosecution of felons. The mayor summoned a court, only to find that there was still a majority against enclosure; but, as the town clerk was to tell the municipal corporation commissioners in 1834, bribery was used to win a majority and in February 1827 a full court decided by 166 votes to 30 to petition Parliament for an act to enclose and to exonerate from tithes. The petition was presented a fortnight later, and with the passage of the act John Burcham of Coningsby, an employee of Lord Yarborough, held his first sitting at the *Granby* as enclosure commissioner on 14 July. In August all occupiers were ordered to follow the usual course of husbandry and in October he decided to ignore all claims of non-freemen to common rights. This was hardly an injustice since, lacking any corporate protection against the farmers, it is doubtful whether any non-freeman would venture to use his rights.[48]

Within a year Burcham had decided on the main features of his award, though it was not issued until 1840. Long before then the freemen had repented of their conversion to enclosure. In 1830 one of the farmers, who was also a freeman, was punished for his zeal in the cause of enclosure and was disfranchised for fraudulently putting sheep on the commons in the name of another. The vote, 117 to 9, showed the strength of feeling, which was not diminished when he was restored to his privileges by a *mandamus* from the King's Bench. More feeling was aroused in 1832 by the circulation of a handbill which stated, erroneously, that the time had expired in which Burcham must make his award, and that his powers had therefore lapsed. The author, said the *Stamford Mercury*, 'is an inhabitant who has for many years proved himself the staunch friend of the freemen in the independent interest of that borough'. This meant, of course, that he was an opponent of Lord Yarborough, in whose interest, according to the municipal corporation commissioners, the enclosure had very largely been manipulated.[49]

The freemen of the next generation, finding their franchise much less valuable than that of their ancestors, instead of blaming the Reform Act of 1832, blamed Lord Yarborough, who had, of course, been in

The French War and the Growth of the Town 191

favour of it. 'There is not a municipality in England', declared Newby, a radical, 'where the people have been so robbed as in Grimsby.' His colleague, Hopkin, was more specific and even less accurate. 'Does Lord Yarborough', he asked, 'consider that we in Grimsby are ignorant of the manner in which he has obtained a considerable amount of the property which he holds in and around the town? General Loft once told me that the field over which the foot road to Scartho passes was obtained for £30 and a few barrels of ale given to the freemen, who, it appears, borrowed that sum of money when they were in need and the beer was given them to befool them into signing the land away.' This became part of the mythology of the freemen, as remote from history as the Havelock stone.

NOTES

1. LAO, Calendars, Yarborough, 197, 224–7, 229–33; CB, 24 Oct. 1786.
2. CB, *ante* 8 Jan. 1787; Election Minutes.
3. Maddison, op. cit., 464; DNB xli, 153; lx, 223; Namier and Brooke, op. cit., III, 657.
4. Election Minutes.
5. Ibid.
6. Ibid.
7. CB, 29 July 1788, 13 Jan. 1712/13, 19 June 1790.
8. TC, Pole, 23 Aug. 1790.
9. TC, 21 Nov. 1790; TC, Parker, 17 Dec. 1790.
10. CB, 12 July and 20 Sept. 1791; TC, Pole, 21 Dec. 1791; TC, Hall, 10 Dec. 1791; TC, Vine, 2 Jan. 1792; CB, 18 Sept. 1792, 17 April 1793.
11. CB, 26 Sept. 1794; TC, Babb, 27 Sept. 1795; TC, Boucherett, 8 and 9 Oct. 1795; LAO, Anderson Commonplace Book; TC, Tennyson, 19 March 1796.
12. TC, Babb, 13 Oct. 1795.
13. TC, Babb, 27 March 1796; CB, 16 Jan. and 30 May 1796; TC, Boucherett, Feb. 1800.
14. LRSM, 23 April 1802; CB, 8 and 9 July 1802.
15. CJ LVIII, 13, 56, 269, 384, 422; LRSM, 25 March 1803; CJ LVIII, 661.
16. CB, 9 Feb. 1802; E. Leary, *Date Book for Lincoln and Neighbourhood*, Lincoln 1867, 244; Vouchers, 1813–14.
17. LRSM, 30 Sept. 1803, 27 July 1804, 7 Feb. 1806.
18. CB, Oct. 1801 and 11 Jan. 1803; LRSM, 21 Feb. 1805, 27 July 1804, 22 March 1811, 4 Feb. 1803, 26 Aug. 1803, 28 June 1805, 4 and 11 Aug. 1806, 3 Aug. and 4 Sept. 1807.
19. LRSM, 26 July 1802, 28 Aug. 1807, 11 Aug. 1813, 6 Sept. 1816, 20 Nov. 1818, 29 Dec. 1820, 12 Oct. 1821, 14 March 1851; TC, Veal, 23 Jan. 1819.
20. CB, 16 June 1794, 15 May 1798, 9 Oct. 1804, 17 June 1806; LAO, Tennyson-Deyncourt 2/6/32 and H/1/4.
21. LRSM, 1 Feb., 9 April and 20 Sept. 1805, 13 June 1806.
22. LRSM, 18 and 25 Sept., 20 Nov. 1807, 17 June 1808.
23. LRSM, 16 Sept. 1812, 7 Dec. 1810. 23 Aug. 1809; PRO, Customs, 94/19/523, 94/21/94 (ex inf. Dr. G. Jackson).

24. LRSM, 14 and 21 July, 18 Aug. 1809, 27 Nov. 1812, 12 March, 11 June, 14 July, 3 Nov. 1813.
25. LRSM, 20 Nov. 1813; Vouchers, 1813–14.
26. CB, 8 Aug. 1815; LRSM, 20 July 1815; CB, 5 July 1803, 3 Oct. 1815, 14 May 1816, 21 Feb. 1817; James Dugan, *The Great Mutiny*, 317–18.
27. CB, 30 April 1794, 12 Dec. 1796, 16 June 1797, 12 Nov. 1799.
28. CB, 5 Oct. 1802, 11 Jan. 1803.
29. CB, 29 Aug. and 16 Sept. 1800; LAO Reports II, 7; CB, 27 April 1819.
30. CB, 13 Oct. 1800, Oct. 1801, 6 Oct. 1800.
31. CB, 16 and 30 Sept. 1800.
32. CB, 2 Feb. 1802, 11 Jan. and 20 Sept. 1803.
33. CB, 17 May and 27 Sept. 1808.
34. CB, 13 May, 1809; DNB xlii, 143: Vouchers, 1802–3: LRSM, 18 April 1805; E. Leary, op. cit., 266, 296, 299; 26 Feb. 1811; Playbills, 1812.
35. CB, 27 Jan. 1812, 3 Dec. 1816, 16 Nov. 1819.
36. LRSM, 15 April 1808, 27 June 1817, 6 April 1804, 30 June 1809, 4 June 1811, 19 May 1812, 25 Sept. 1821; LRSM, 15 June 1827.
37. Vouchers, 1822–3; CB, 21 May 1823, 5 July and 9 Aug. 1836, 3 Aug. 1844.
38. CB, 18 April 1815, 28 May 1816; Vouchers, 1813–14; CB, 24 Oct. 1820.
39 *Abstract of Returns relative to the Expense and Maintenance of the Poor*, 1803; CB, 1 Sept. 1801; LRSM, 1 Jan. 1802, 28 Feb. 1823, 30 Nov. 1827.
40. CB, 10 June 1783, 24 Oct. 1786.
41. CB, 29 July 1788, 12 Nov. 1799.
42. Vouchers, 1813–14, 1799–1800; CB, 5 Oct. 1814; Vouchers, 1814–15; LRSM, 22 Sept. 1815; CB, 3 Oct. 1815.
43. CB, 1 Nov. 1814; Vouchers, 1814–15; CB, 18 April 1815.
44. Vouchers, 1822–3; CB, 27 Jan. 1812, 25 Oct. 1814, 18 April 1815, 7 June 1838, 9 Nov. 1841.
45. Vouchers, 1821–2; CB, 6 June 1822, 20 July and 23 Nov. 1824, 8 Sept. 1829; LRSM, 12 March 1830.
46. CB, 26 Aug. 1823.
47. Skelton, *Proof Book* (Grimsby Borough Library), 3 July 1824.
48. CB, 1 Oct. 1826; Skelton, 1826 and 1830; CB, 8 Feb. 1827; LRSM, 2 March 1827; Enclosure Minutes.
49. CB, 12 Oct. 1830, 26 April 1831; LRSM, 20 Jan. 1832.

XIII

The Last Days of Corruption

To the freemen of Victorian times, the beginning of the nineteenth century seemed a silver age. The old corporation had never been more deeply sunk in political corruption than in its final decades. Lord Yarborough, it was well known, had alternative means of winning voters but there was bribery at every election. In 1805 he made one of his rare appearances in the town, dining at the *Ship* with nearly a hundred gentlemen after John Lusby had been sworn as mayor. At the election of November 1806 both his sons were returned without a contest. Col. Loft had come forward as a candidate, but recognising the struggle as hopeless, he wrote to Tennyson from Healing to tell him that he did not intend to go to a poll, so that Tennyson would not be put to the expense of enrolling more freemen.[1]

Lord Yarborough was less fortunate in the 1807 election. His elder son, with 138 votes, was returned with William Ellice, who had 142; but his younger son had only 122 votes. Loft was again in the fight, and with 137 votes had no reason to despair. Thirteen actions for bribery were in the cause list for the Lincoln summer assizes, though none of them came to trial. Loft petitioned against the return of Pelham, alleging bribery and that he himself had the same number of votes when the mayor improperly admitted a person to vote for Pelham. The House unseated Pelham and declared Loft elected. The church bells were rung at Louth when the news was known, and he made a triumphal entry into that town. Shortly afterwards he was promoted to the rank of major-general, and in 1809 the corporation of Grimsby resolved 'that the main street leading from the east bar to the lock be henceforth forever called Loft Street in honour of Major General John Henry Loft M.P.'[2,3] He owed his position to his defiance of the Yarborough interest; but Lord Yarborough still controlled the corporation, and Loft knew that his own reign would end at the next dissolution of Parliament.

Already, before Pelham was unseated, John Peter Grant began to canvas the electors, presumably in the hope of capturing Ellice's seat. He gave £100 for a new market house, and a relative, Captain Cook, added another £50. His interest in the borough was managed by the new town clerk, William Frazer. It was said to be Frazer's habit to hold meetings of Grant's supporters the day before a full court to decide on how they should vote. Free drink was available for them at the *Granby*, and at the *Bricklayers' Arms*. On one occasion they drank all night and were still drunk when the court met in the morning.[4]

Frazer's opponents tried shock tactics to remove him. Frazer, a barrister, of Grey's Inn, had opposed William Marshall (1759-1826) the collector of customs, in an action at the assizes. Marshall's son-in-law, George Hewson, challenged Frazer to a duel, and Frazer's acceptance of the challenge required some courage, since Hewson was a naval captain.* Grant appeared as Frazer's second and after a harmless exchange of shots Hewson said 'Well, there's the first broadside' and demanded that the shooting should continue until one of them fell. Grant refused to allow this and Hewson assaulted him. An action at the assizes ensured that Grant got 40s. damages. There was really very little that Sergeant Vaughan could do for Captain Hewson, so he did his best to impugn the patriotism of his opponents.

He described him [wrote the *Stamford Mercury*] as having been a lieutenant on board Admiral Collingwood's ship, the *Royal Sovereign*, in the glorious battle of Trafalgar, and he made a powerful appeal to the feelings of the jury in behalf of the sensitive honour of a British naval officer. Although Captain Hewson was, on his proper element, more than a match for the foes of his country, he had unfortunately fallen in with a nest of hornets at Grimsby, men who went to fight with a pistol in one pocket and a writ in the other.[5]

As it had proved impossible to frighten Frazer out of the town, Major General Loft himself appeared at a full court in August 1809 where, seconded by Lusby who was now the postmaster, he persuaded a majority to vote for Frazer's dismissal. Frazer and Grant therefore started legal proceedings against the corporation and tried to prevent it from using corporate funds in the action. In February 1810 a writ of *mandamus* from the King's Bench restored Frazer to his office. To revenge himself he procured indictments for perjury against some of Loft's adherents, though he did not actually prosecute them, and started an action for conspiracy against Loft.[6]

The case came on at the assizes in March 1811. Frazer's claim failed for technical reasons, but the publicity afforded by the trial had its intended effect. This time he enjoyed the advantage of being represented

* He eventually became vice-admiral.

The Last Days of Corruption

by Sergeant Vaughan, who spoke eloquently of the rancour and ill-nature which, he said, were so often found in a borough.

Mr. Frazer [he said] is a man of character, a man of conciliatory manners, a man of talents. For my own part I am surprised to think how he got to Grimsby . . . I wonder that a residence in Grimsby does not bring ill-health upon everyone. Gentlemen, you have only to look at Maj. Gen. Loft as a confirmation of what I have to say. Look, gentlemen, how sallow he is, how much he looks like a man who has lived in the air of Grimsby. He is just returned from visiting his constituents. Twenty campaigns would not have such an effect on him. There is no oxygen, gentlemen, in that air. A man cannot be florid and healthy long.[7]

In 1812 Grant, with Sir Robert Heron of Stubton, headed the poll with 210 and 192 votes respectively. Loft's following fell to 97, and a certain E. J. Collett, who must have been a politician of great ineptitude or of outstanding purity, received only twelve votes. Loft petitioned against the return alleging not only bribery but also that the mayor had stationed armed men at the door of the town hall to prevent his supporters from entering to vote. His witnesses were summoned to Westminster on a Speaker's warrant, but Loft's shortage of funds forced him to abandon his petition. He met his witnesses at London Bridge and told them that he could not pay for their homeward journey. They in their turn petitioned the House for relief and a committee, of which Grant and Heron were members, was appointed to consider their claim. Loft sent a letter to vindicate his own conduct but failed to appear, and his address could not be found. The House voted £120 to the witnesses, the committee observing: 'If no public relief can be extended to these unfortunate persons there is no alternative but that of removing them to their parish, by order of magistrates, if they are not arrested at the suit of their creditors.'[8]

After this Loft could expect no support in Grimsby. One of the supporters of his petition, Charles Lowcock, was punished when he was elected bailiff in 1814 by being forced to prove that he had a settlement in Grimsby. Frazer, Grant's lieutenant, was less fortunate. In an action at the assizes in which he was instructed by a woman who had been brutally beaten by a farmer when she was gleaning at Clee, the farmer was represented by N. G. Clarke, K.C., who had frequently acted for Loft. The case was a hopeless one, so on the instigation of Loft's brother-in-law and of an assistant whom Frazer had dismissed for dishonesty, he tried to excite prejudice by abusing Frazer's professional conduct. Unable to obtain an apology from Clarke, Frazer wrote a letter to him, which he also published in the *Stamford Mercury*, calling him (in capital letters) 'a base, a pusillanimous, and a vile calumniator'. He must, he said, defend his character 'to return to that town in which so much asperity and party dissension prevail, to meet all that goading sarcasm not uncommon in country towns'. In his trial for criminal libel he was defended by Brougham whose address in mitigation resulted in a fine of £20 and a month's imprisonment in the Marshalsea. He retained his office in Grimsby, acting through a deputy, until 1824.[9]

It was clear to everyone that both Grant and Heron were Lord Yarborough's men. 'We have been lucky, this time', the Hon. C. A. Pelham wrote to John Heaton, 'my father having carried two members at Grimsby and one at Beverley, and no opposition for this country.' Heron, many years later, gave a different account of what had happened:

> Lord Yarborough, who after immense sums of money thrown away, had lost the borough by bad management, though he possessed an over-ruling property in it, and even a considerable popularity in it, at length abandoned it ... I told everyone who asked me the whole truth as to my principles, political or religious. All who were concerned for me assured me that such conduct would ruin me. It has, however, hitherto appeared that my simplicity of manners and conversation has been perfectly approved at Grimsby.[10]

In 1817 a meeting, at which the mayor took the chair, presented a petition to the House of Commons against placemen, pensioners and the Septennial Act, 'such long parliaments being the cause of corruption'. The petitioners also deplored the recent attack on the Prince Regent. A rival meeting in the town, on the same day, presided over by Captain Mott, deplored the attack in more enthusiastically loyal language which could not, however, bear comparison with the fulsome address of the Louth warden and assistants who hailed the Regent as the deliverer of Europe through his 'consummate wisdom and unshaken fortitude'. This was no more than an interlude in the serious business of borough-mongering. As soon as Grant and Heron had been elected, Charles Tennyson, younger son of George Tennyson, had declared his intention of standing for Grimsby at the next election.[11]

In 1818 Sir Robert Heron withdrew from Grimsby to contest the county. Charles Tennyson sent a Christmas gift of coal to the voters and his generosity was thought to have eclipsed that of Grant. He was advised to spend £160 on four pecks of corn for each voter—'better

The Last Days of Corruption 197

than a drunken feast and far less expensive, besides the great benefit to wives and children in keeping husbands and fathers at home or work, instead of carousing a whole night'. Fazakerley and Grant, however, raised the bidding with a distribution of tickets for two stones of flour and a stone of beef. Lusby therefore urged Tennyson to stop thinking about corn and give to each freeman a stone and a half of flour and the same quantity of beef. He ought to come to Grimsby immediately, with a silk banner at least six yards by four.[12]

Charles Tennyson's campaign was managed by Joshua Plaskitt, collector of the dock dues. The fight was expected to be a hard one, because even with government backing Tennyson had been unable to find another candidate to support him. Plaskitt's temper was greatly tried by some tactless words of Tennyson about electoral purity, and he was already impatient because the candidate was unwilling to start his canvass in holy week and thought it unwise to arrive on the 1st of April. Tennyson succeeded in mollifying him, and since Babb, in Lord Yarborough's name, was trying to get him dismissed from the dock company, there was no safety for him except with the Tennysons. Babb, as Fazakerley's agent was 'very busy in catching the young voters as they come in', and Fazakerley was again distributing beef and flour. In June Tennyson asked Sergeant Vaughan to come up as soon as possible as the writs were issued and there would soon be a court to admit freemen. Ninety-five were admitted in spite of Grant's objections to three of them.[13]

The election was held two days later. One of the blue voters, a watchmaker, was disqualified as he was held to have been convicted of perjury. Fazakerley and Tennyson were at the head of the poll. A friend who congratulated Tennyson on his victory had been in great suspense. 'When I left you on Tuesday night', he wrote, 'I felt much for your anxiety of mind, having witnessed some attempts of venality in my way to my lodgings.' Tennyson issued his address in celebration of his victory a few days later. 'I found you', he declaimed, 'depressed by frequent failure of attempts on your behalf such as mine, and by the retrograde condition of your commerce and your prosperity. I may boldly pronounce that for you a new era has commenced.' For his own part he inaugurated it by standing as sponsor in ninety-two christenings in St. James's and giving a bottle of wine to be kept for each child.[14]

There was still the chance that Tennyson might be unseated by a petition, and Grant's agents began to harass some of the Tennyson camp with actions for bribery. Plaskitt was so alarmed that he tried to flee to America with some of the cash belonging to the dock company, but Tennyson met him in Liverpool and persuaded him that his fears were groundless and that he could safely return to his friends. Unity was essential because if there were a petition, it would be difficult to organise a counter attack.[15]

Lord Yarborough had, in effect, lost one seat, but had certainly not lost the borough. Within a few weeks of his victory Tennyson was informed that Babb* had been elected mayor 'by the genial and beneficial influence of Brocklesby House'. In December there was a hotly contested election of an alderman. When the poll was almost complete and each candidate had 142 votes Babb, as mayor, was said to have assaulted one of the aldermen. He wished to adjourn the court until the next morning, but the tumult among the freemen, who closed the town hall door and began to break the windows, was so great that he was unable to do so and the poll continued until Goulton had been elected alderman and Veal common councilman in Goulton's place. Both were Tennyson men. The reds, however, suffered a defeat when Squire, another Tennyson man, was dismissed from his place as registrar of the court of requests, 'almost', as George Oliver wrote 'without a charge against him. A more vile and scandalous transaction has not taken place in Grimsby for many years'. But the defeat was not really serious. Tennyson was advised that Squire had brought his downfall upon himself by drunkenness and villainy, but in spite of this, and in spite of Lord Yarborough's efforts to assemble forty magistrates and gentlemen to vote against him, he was reinstated.[16]

Tennyson could not feel secure until the election petitions had been settled. Oliver, his father's curate at St. James's, was sure that Fazakerley had come out at the head of the poll by bribery, though it was not certain that evidence could be found. He thought that the best way for Tennyson to secure his interest would be to build houses on his Grimsby estate and divide the rest into small farms which could be let to sons of Lord Yarborough's tenants. He reminded the new member of his promise to give £20 to the National school, Fazakerley having already redeemed his promise. But everyone knew whose side Oliver was on. If there was no news of a petition against the election, wrote Captain Miller, commander of one of the revenue cutters, 'my friend Oliver and self intend doing ourselves the pleasure of astonishing the natives on Monday morning by firing a royal salute from Mr. Oliver's

* The son of George Babb mentioned above.

garden, having fixed two of my swivels there in stocks made on purpose, the salute to be answered by twenty-one guns from the Lock Hill'.[17]

There was a petition, got up by Dr. Bell on behalf of Grant, but it was not presented in time to stop the cannonade. There was also a counter-petition against Fazakerley, but both were allowed to lapse and for a while the members could enjoy their position free of distractions. Fazakerley, even before the petition, had thought it safe to break his promise to give a pound-note to each of his voters. Tennyson was perhaps less secure, and as a supporter of the government was more happily situated for distributing favours. Prize-money was obtained for one freeman. Another, a plumper* for Tennyson, was not only got off from a sentence of transportation, but was also appointed a harbour pilot, in which capacity he could be more useful than in Australia. Marris, another zealous friend, wanted to be made an excise tidesman at Hull. Tennyson was assured that in his day Loft had got one of these places for his servant, and that Marris understood the duties perfectly. He was also expected to show an interest in a proposal to reopen the *Queen's Head* as a respectable inn.[18]

Marris, disappointed in his hopes of leading an outdoor life as a tide-waiter, hoped to be made a permit-writer in the excise. 'The late officer', Tennyson was informed, 'was a man of very dissipated habits and his death was expected for some time.' Joseph Benton also wanted a place on the excise. He had a large family connection. Another voter who had been employed during the election might go over to Grant if his account was passed, in spite of the fact that he was a tenant of the Tennysons. Mr. Smelle, a minister of the Countess of Huntingdon's Connection, was made happy with a promise of a contribution for his school. Edward Brown, the tide-surveyor claimed that no officer in the kingdom was paid less and asked that an increase of salary promised in 1810 should be obtained for him. It had been useless for him to petition when both members had been in opposition.[19]

The only weakness immediately visible in Tennyson's position was that the best inns were controlled by the blues. The *White Hart* had just been bought for Lord Yarborough, whose position was dominant in the old town, and this was all the more harmful because a depression of maritime trade was causing tradesmen to move back from the new town near the dock, 'almost like wildfire or as removing from a contagious disease'. Tennyson's advisers urged him to strengthen his

* A plumper was a voter who voted for one candidate only.

position by buying property unostentatiously. A few thousand pounds discreetly spent would be the soundest of investments if it helped to prevent future contests, and he could always have the *Queen's Head* until an inn closer to the town hall could be found.[20]

The reds scored a brilliant success in September 1819 with the election of their candidate, Goulton, as mayor. It had long been the custom for the aldermen to deprive the freemen of any real choice by nominating one candidate who was so obnoxious that the other was bound to win a majority. This was the tactic which failed in 1819. Goulton was unpopular, but the Tennyson managers were able to exert enough pressure to get him in, and the blue leaders could do little more than threaten that Goulton's brother, a Yarborough tenant, would lose his farm. Immediately after the election Tennyson's attorney, Daubney wrote:

> After Goulton's brother left Grimsby on Monday night a special messenger was sent to him at Croxby with a notice to quit his farm. Our Mr. Goulton was called up in the middle of the night at three o'clock in the morning. His brother produced this notice-to-quit and by all means endeavoured to terrify him. On his way to the town hall, near the *Black Swan*, he was again beset by his brother and Howson, and he again resisted, though he entered the hall with evident tokens of agitation. All the blues who are not tied hand and foot are ready to run. You must have the goodness to send Mr. Goulton a haunch of venison. They have always been in the habit of having one from Brocklesby for what they call their mayor-feast. Howson has threatened to discharge every tenant that sells Goulton his corn or buys coals of him. I must find out some expedient to counteract this if possible. I really do not feel a doubt that we shall by perseverance and industry make the borough yours, or at least wrest it from Lord Yarborough.[21]

With a red mayor, Tennyson had no difficulty in heading the poll in the 1820 election with 227 votes along with his colleague William Duncombe, who had 204.[22]

Yet, in spite of the usual triumph of corruption, there was some political feeling in the town, and the sentiments of Charles Tennyson were not wholly to the taste of his supporters. In 1819 there were rumours that he favoured Catholic emancipation, and he was warned that this was a cause obnoxious to his most respectable constituents. There was no difficulty when the members were asked, on the discovery of the Cato Street conspiracy, to present a loyal address to the Regent, 'expressing their loyalty to the king, attachment to the constitution and laws of the country, and abhorrence of the means that have of late been taken to raise up sedition, treason and rebellion'. But Tennyson was known to support the measures which the government proposed to take against Queen Caroline, while Lord Yarborough's support of the queen earned him great popularity. What hurt Tennyson still more was that on the death of an alderman his own candidate was beaten by 187 to 113. To save himself from further odium he thought it necessary to write a pamphlet for his constituents explaining that although he had voted with the government he was opposed to any further action against Caroline.[23]

In Grimsby George Oliver also was in trouble about Queen Caroline. On her death the corporation ordered their pew to be hung with black cloth. Oliver told the sexton to remove it, and when reprimanded by the corporation he replied that he was answerable only to the bishop and was determined to prevent

> a mockery of divine ordinances. When the late Queen Charlotte died, who was *undoubtedly* a most virtuous and irreproachable female, Mr. Oliver had the greatest difficulty to prevail upon the officers of the corporation to put their pews in mourning, though they were already furnished with black cloth for that purpose; and on the day the Queen was interred he believes, if his memory does not fail him, that the corporation was engaged in political controversy at the very moment when divine service was performing in the church as a mark of respect due to so solemn an occasion as the committing an incomparable and universally lamented Queen to the bowels of the earth.

Though Oliver came close to losing his appointment in the ensuing controversy, all this had been forgotten when the 1826 election was fought.[24]

But it was fought without Tennyson, who preferred to be returned for Bletchingley, where his family also had property. In Grimsby he would have found the red attitude repugnant to his principles. They pursued a virulently anti-Catholic campaign inspired in part, at least, by the fact that G. F. Heneage, one of the blue candidates, was a recent convert from Roman Catholicism. A person describing himself as an independent burgess asked the electors whether they really wanted Catholics to sit in Parliament:

> Will the avowed friends of popery or decided supporters of Protestantism be the proper persons to aid the continuance of the glorious system of religious toleration and preserve our children and grandchildren from fire and faggot? Gentlemen, the innocent blood of our ancestors shed by popish secular authority calls upon you.

Another, who called himself a freeman, was equally impassioned:

> By giving power to Roman Catholics you are taking murderers into confidence, and the murderers of your forefathers will become the executioners and enslavers of your children.

And a song, exhorting the freemen to break their servile chains (to be sung to the tune of *Rule, Britannia*) spoke of 'how Latimer there lit the torch which burns on Grimsby's lowly plains'.

This may have won some votes. It certainly did not win the election, since Charles Wood and G. F. Heneage, both Yarborough men, won by a majority of over a hundred. There was only one red candidate, Sir Thomas Philips, whose campaign was managed so inexpertly that nine of his bandsmen were brought from Louth.[25]

In 1830 one red, Captain George Harris, was returned with the blue Charles Wood, secretary to Lord Grey, and Heneage lost his seat.* It was believed that the reds owed their success to the intervention of the officers commanding the two revenue cutters. Charles Wood's carriage was stopped by a party of seamen with Harris and one of the officers looking on. The intention was to throw him into the river, but he was not in the carriage at the time. Four brass blunderbusses and a musquetoon were landed from the *Greyhound*, and were fired some time during the day, and Lieutenant Howe posted seamen at the toll-bar to prevent red voters from being kidnapped in blue coaches. For their part the blues believed that some of their men had been made dead drunk and held on board the *Greyhound* until the voting was over. Daubney, no longer a red, wrote a letter to the *Globe* which caused Lieutenant Howe to sue him for libel. Howe maintained that all his actions constituted lawful assistance to the government candidates, and was awarded £10 damages.[26]

In 1831 Wood voted for the reform bill and Harris against, and after this there could be no doubt that the freemen, threatened with the demotion of the borough to a single-member constituency, would desert the blues. The corporation, through Harris, presented a petition against the awful and impending change. Grimsby, they said, was a town of great antiquity, offered considerable advantages as a port, and as a result of a house to house inspection by the minister and churchwardens was found to contain 4,006 inhabitants, which should be

---

* His defeat was attributed to the fact that Daubney not only would not pay the voters enough but also insulted them by saying, 'Damn them, they may be bought like sheep at Smithfield when they are wanted.'

enough to qualify it as a two-member constituency. Moreover, the town was rapidly progressing and as a result of the enterprise of the Haven Company: and they continued:

> The inhabitants of Grimsby have been distinguished for their loyalty and attachment to the constitution of this country. At this moment the borough of Grimsby contains 383 resident voters who return their representatives to parliament by the unbiassed exercise of their elective franchise. Your petitioners view with sentiments of regret and deep apprehension the proposed curtailment of their birthright and chartered privileges and humbly pray that your honourable house will discountenance that part of the measure calculated to disfranchise the children and posterity of your petitioners.[27]

In the election of May 1831 the blues Gronow and Hobhouse were doomed from the beginning. According to Gronow, Lord Yarborough personally asked him to stand and made him promise that he would not in any circumstances give bribes. He attributed his defeat to this promise, and remarked that Shelley, formerly member for Gatton, was notably polite to him throughout the election because he had been wrongly informed that Gronow might shoot him. The members of the corporation were overwhelmingly for Lord Yarborough's men, but Harris and Shelley were returned. Nevertheless there were reformers in Grimsby. A dinner held in Marshall's granary to celebrate the passage of the great reform bill was attended by the mayor and the town clerk with Charles Tennyson, now himself an ardent reformer, and the two county members, the Hon. C. A. Pelham, son of Lord Yarborough, and Sir W. A. Ingilby. Captain Maxfield was one of those who attended and in the new, enlarged constituency,* with the aid of the newly enfranchised £10 householders, he defeated the Tory Lord Loughborough by 298 votes to 132.[28]

In its last years there were few occasions when the old corporation needed to concern itself with matters not immediately affecting the political management of the borough. They were briefly alarmed in 1814 by a bank failure. £32 had been deposited in Streath's Bank for the payment of the fee-farm rent, and when the bank stopped payment the unhappy bailiffs asked the corporation for help. Even so small a sum as this could be a serious embarrassment in the unreformed borough. The corporation agreed to stand £10 of the loss, tried to force the bailiffs to pay the balance in Bank of England notes, and only

---

* In the new constituency, which included some of the adjacent villages, there were 656 voters of whom 353 were freemen and the rest £10 householders. Only 79 of the household voters lived in Grimsby itself.

agreed to meet its obligations when the lessees of fee-farm rent threatened a lawsuit. Three years later it was still trying to recover the whole sum from one of the bailiffs.[29]

The members of the old corporation might have been a little more flexible if the dock had lived up to their original expectations; but it had not done so, and the economy of the town was again sinking into stagnation. In part this was because of the imperfections of the dock itself. The absence of a pier at the entrance made it difficult for shipping to enter in bad weather. In the winter months of 1830, for example, only six ships entered, and three of them apparently did so only because of storm damage. General Loft in 1811 proposed a scheme to improve the dock at a cost of £35,000 and at a meeting in the town exhibited a model of a pier; and there was a proposal in 1813 for grounding a hulk at the entrance to serve as a pier, a dangerous plan which might have blocked the entrance entirely. Lord Yarborough was against it.* Ayscough Boucherett and the Tennysons favoured it and hoped, though vainly, that the ingratitude of the town would be remedied by the action of Parliament.[30]

The dock would no doubt have been busier but for the war and Napoleon's Continental System. The price of timber rose ten-fold during the war, and because the traditional trade with the Baltic was interrupted the *Amity* in 1812 brought timber, deals and lathwood from the Canadian port of St. Andrews. In that year the only ships from Europe were the *Elizabeth* and the *Fairfield*, both from Malta with wine, currants, sulphur and quicksilver.[31]

Peace brought some revival of trade. By the beginning of November 1816 the price of corn had risen so far that it became worthwhile to bring two cargoes from Holland. The price at Grimsby was 63s. to 84s. a quarter (and up to 106s. at Louth and 140s. at Gainsborough), when a year earlier it had been 48s. to 52s. There was a beginning also of the importation of bones from the continent for manure. In April 1819 alone the *Hoffnung* brought bones from Bremen, and the *Anna*, the *Friends* and the *Jane* from Hamburg. There were wild rumours that some of the bones were human and that pieces of shrouds had been found in ships' holds. At one time the Belgians were alleged to be the offenders. 'Our brave countrymen', said the *Stamford Mercury*, 'who fell at Waterloo and who were there consigned in undistinguished

---

* Even in the war years his eldest son spent much time at sea in his yacht, which was really a frigate, and it seems likely that the family was well informed about what the effect on the haven might be of a hulk at its entrance.

thousands to huge graves, have, after laying down their lives in defence of the liberties of their country had their ashes used for enriching the soil!' By 1834 there was an even more fantastic report that 200 tons of bones being discharged were those of the men who, with 30,000 horses, died from cold in a single night on the retreat from Moscow; and anyone inclined to disbelieve this could see that there were three steam mills newly established in the town for crushing bones, and for grinding corn and seeds.[32]

The *Riby Grove* traded regularly with Riga and Archangel, and there was a revival also of Mediterranean trade. In 1816 the *Amity* arrived from Licata and the *Albion* from Girgente, in 1817 the *Darlington* came from Smyrna, in 1819 the *Ruby* from Messina and the *Cyprus* from Smyrna, in 1820 the *Rambler* from Constantinople and the *Two Brothers* from Seville. The *Rambler* brought iron and cocoa, but much of this traffic was in fruit, and in the 1820s labourers at the fruit wharf of the firm of Todd and Wells were earning 3s. a day and three pints of ale.[33]

There was an occasional trans-Atlantic trade. The *Susan* in 1819 brought cocoa and brown plantation sugar from Trinidad. In 1818 the *General Ripley* discharged rice and staves from Charleston, South Carolina, and two years later the *Jubilee* came from Charleston, also with rice. There was even a small emigrant trade. The *Eliza* in the summer of 1819 embarked twenty-eight passengers for New York, and the *Farmer*, after waiting for six weeks, sailed with thirty-three. The steam packet in 1827 took 125 people to Hull on their way to America. Even a few Grimsby people emigrated and this gave Cobbett the occasion to include a favourable mention of Grimsby when he visited the town in 1830. The passage is worth quoting as a comment on Grimsby and perhaps also as an example of Cobbett's occasional gullibility. He met Joshua Plaskitt, who was a pillar of corruption in the cause of the reds, and judged him 'a man of as kind and benevolent appearance and manners as I ever beheld in my life'. He continues ' "What the devil", the reader will say, "should you want to recollect that place for? Why should you not want to forget that sink of corruption? What could you find there to be snatched from everlasting oblivion, except for the purpose of being execrated?" ' And he goes on to say that Plaskitt gave him a singular example of a republican virtue when he showed him the watch which had been found with his son who had been drowned in America and which honest freemen scorned to steal. The younger Joshua Plaskitt seems to have settled in America and was mate of the *Savannah*, lost off Long Island with all hands. The elder Plaskitt presumably intended to join his son when he fled in 1818, and his admiration of Cobbett probably explains why he then regarded himself as a persecuted radical.*[34]

Some ships had been built at Grimsby even before the dock was made as, for example, one of five tons in 1790 and another of nine tons in 1798. The dock brought slightly more activity, but even so, in 1813, an exceptionally good year, only three were launched and their total tonnage was only 212. Most of the Grimsby-registered ships were built elsewhere. There were fifty-six of them in 1813, totalling 2,523 tons, and seventy-one in 1824 totalling 2,782 tons. By 1818 the customs collected at Grimsby had risen to £130,000 and eighty-four vessels had discharged at the dock; and whereas in the early years there had been little outward traffic, in 1824 129 foreign-owned ships were cleared from the port and in 1826, sixty-seven, British and foreign.[35]

By 1819 the haven company dues at last exceeded £1,000. This was a very poor return on the original investment. Nevertheless it was proposed to raise another £10,000 to build a pier and for scouring and clearing the dock. The corporation decided to subscribe up to £800 from fines on the West Marsh leases and urged the company to carry out the improvements as quickly as possible. No pier was built, but by August 1825 the dock was temporarily closed and ships were discharging in the outfall. In December the work was complete and the harbour-master refilled the dock with fourteen to eighteen feet of water from the back drains.[36]

This very moderate prosperity was reflected in an increase of road traffic. The turnpike tolls, which had brought in £373 in 1804-5, in 1831-2 were leased for £565 a year, and dividends of up to five per cent were being paid; and since 1803 there had been a turnpike to Louth also. In 1824 when the powers of the Louth turnpike trustees were to be renewed the corporation formally opposed the measure in the hope of getting the Waltham toll-bar abolished. This did not happen. Louth was still nearly twice as big as Grimsby, with a flourishing London and Yorkshire trade based on its canal. But for Grimsby Hull was more important, and often more detested.[37]

In 1820 the corporation sent a memorial to the Treasury about a

---

* A more exotic transient than Cobbett was Count Capodistria, the Russian foreign minister, who arrived with Count Lieven, the Russian ambassador, on 5 September 1819. Capodistria left for Russia on board the new Russian frigate *Hector*, of sixty guns, in company with a sloop of war, and Lieven returned to London.

recent directive requiring coast documents to be provided for all goods sent up the Humber from Grimsby. This was seen as a victory for malicious persons in Hull. 'It appears to your memorialists', they complained, 'that your lordships have been wilfully and maliciously misinformed by some designing person or persons for the sole purpose of benefiting his or their private interests, of the situation of the said port and the practices falsely alleged to be carried on.' The practices referred to were, of course, smuggling. And in 1827 the mayor received a requisition referring to 'recent illegal and arbitrary attempts on the part of the port of Hull to infringe upon the rights and privileges of the town and port of Grimsby'. The privileged position of the Hull Trinity House was a permanent grievance. So many Hull shipmasters, as brethren of the guild, were able to bring their ships to Hull exempt from its dues. But at Grimsby in a single year twenty-one vessels coming into the dock paid £148 10s. 0d. to the Haven Company and £157 16s. 5d. to the Hull Trinity House.[38]

But as Hull grew more rapidly than Grimsby, the ferry to Hull became more important. The proprietors of the packet boat in 1812 were still required to acknowledge that the corporation held the monopoly of the ferry. Their vessel depended entirely on wind and tide, but the steam packet *British Queen* began to ply between the two ports after the war and in 1825 the corporation agreed to subscribe £100 to Croft and Morvinson's steam packet. This was the *Pelham*, built at Gainsborough, which made a ceremonial entry in May 1828 with a hundred gentlemen and the band of the 83rd Regiment from Hull. Salutes were fired at the lock and the customs' house and a dinner was given by the Apollo lodge of freemasons. She was also used for trips to Goole, for which the fare was 3s. with tea and coffee and a picnic lunch, and in the summer she offered excursions to Scarborough. In November 1826 the *Graham* packet which had just left Grimsby for Hull blew up in the river, killing four passengers. The crew were about to embark passengers from the *United Kingdom*, the Leith and London packet, and having turned off the cold water feed, put a weight on the safety-valve to keep up the boiler pressure.[39]

The plundering of wrecks was a profitable side-line for some of the inhabitants. Ships which were lucky enough managed to get into the dock. The *Thornton*, bound for Goole with timber, and the *Kamasda* from Gothenburg, both damaged off Spurn managed to do so in 1830, but in 1823 some ships were less fortunate. Thirty ships were ashore between Grimsby and Tetney Haven. The *Dispatch* of Woodbridge docked and the owner reported that he had only lost forty-five yards of chain cable to thieves.

I heard [he added] from a Lynn captain that within an hour after he and the crew were obliged to leave the ship she was boarded by sharks and the blocks cut from her rigging. Even the brass front was taken from the cabin stove. So much for Lincolnshire hospitality! Captain Smith of the *Jane* of Ipswich was wrecked on Cleethorpes and her hull and materials will be sold tomorrow. A schoolmaster robbed him of his spy-glass and other articles, for which he is now in gaol. A pretty rascal for the care of children in their education![40]

In spite of the presence of cutters of the preventive service, a good deal of smuggling went on. There was a rumour in 1822 that two cargoes of smuggled gin had been landed at Grimsby and safely conveyed inland. Thomas Lumley, who was at various times a grocer, a tallow-chandler and a nail-manufacturer in Grimsby and died at Caistor in 1848, was fined £1,500 for smuggling in 1826. His method was said to be to remove smuggled goods from a barn at Stallingborough to the tower of Aylesby church, and New Holland was said to have got its name from his trade in smuggled gin. The cutters *Lapwing* and *Greyhound* frequently brought their prizes into the dock. In 1822 after a chase off Whitby the cutter *Stag* brought in the *Agnes* of Flushing with a crew of twenty-five and 1,500 tubs of gin; and in 1826 the *Greyhound* captured the *Tartar of Nieuport* with tobacco and 700 tubs of gin. Shrewsbury, a veteran smuggler, was caught in Grimsby with three tons of tobacco and imprisoned in Lincoln castle in 1832.[41]

Under the old corporation the town was neither rich enough nor large enough for other crime to present much of a problem. Imprisonment in the town gaol was not really regarded as a punishment, and debtors were the usual inmates, with 4*d*. a day allowed to them by their creditors. There were rarely more than five prisoners. No work was provided and there were no bibles or prayer books and no chaplain. The police functions of the bailiffs had long ceased, but there were three annually elected constables under a chief constable appointed by the borough quarter sessions. When a woman, subsequently pardoned, was sentenced to transportation at the sessions in 1828 for stealing linen drapery the occasion was notable only because this was the first such sentence for almost a century. A match-seller in green spectacles who appeared in 1821 turned out to be a Bow Street runner who had followed his man from Lincoln.[42]

There were two associations for the prosecution of felons, as unofficial agencies for the prevention of crime, and it was their custom to advertise rewards for information. The rewards were not large, but in the early months of 1828 they amounted to £172, a sum perhaps large enough to tempt accomplices to proffer information. There had been an outbreak of agrarian crime, with mutilation of sheep and corn stealing. The Grimsby Old Association issued advice to the upholders of law and order:

> The General Committee understand that many of the inhabitants of the parish praiseworthily employ themselves in keeping nightly watch. They therefore beg to recommend to those who so praiseworthily employ themselves, not to go abroad in companies, or publicly, but to put themselves in some such secret situations as to see and not be seen; and that if they perceive any suspicious persons abroad, or any person about to commit an offence, not to cause interruption, but to allow the offence to be committed, taking care to be able to identify the offender; and he may be apprehended at leisure.[43]

During the rick-burnings of 1830 special constables were enrolled in the town, and the officers of the revenue cruisers had orders to give assistance to the magistrates to quell any outbreak of mob violence; but neither then, nor in the ensuing years, was there any arson in Grimsby. Potatoes were stolen, and sheep were killed at Weelsby, but there was no crime clearly attributable to the desperate poverty of farm labourers. A meeting was called at the town hall of those concerned to suppress disorders, but the disorders felt to be so important were merely those of drunken men in the streets.*[44]

The attempt to provide street lighting had been abandoned and some of the more timid felt that the streets were unsafe at night. One of the church-wardens, and the select vestry, in 1829 petitioned the bishop to have the evening service in St. James's changed to two-thirty in the afternoon. The curate, they said, was the only person opposed to the change. But the curate was George Oliver and he had no difficulty in producing a counter-petition with eloquent reasons for keeping things as they were. He claimed that Betts, the dissident churchwarden, had acted without the knowledge of most of the inhabitants, and that only six or seven members of the vestry ever came to church.

---

* The situation of the poor and the severity of the authorities appeared in the neighbouring village of Wold Newton. A labourer's wife, who had recently given birth to a child, resisted attempts to evict her from their cottage. Her landlord's men then proceeded to evict her by pulling it down over her head. Driven to despair, she set fire to the pile of ruins, and for this she was convicted of arson and sentenced to transportation for life.

Though not lighted [he went on] the streets are in good condition, and level, so that the old and infirm (with lanthorn) feel but little more difficulty at six than at two-thirty. Many, so long as they have an opportunity, will attend, either drawn by inclination or impelled by duty, but if servants are deprived of that opportunity of receiving religious instruction, their leisure hours may be spent in idleness, and they in the mean time exposed to evil temptation. The trifling expense of lighting the church is of no consequence compared with the general good that candle-light prayers are calculated to diffuse.[45]

But the darkness of the streets had its inconveniences and grave robbers could desecrate the churchyard.*

Some evil disposed person or persons [announced a poster of 1831] did on the night of Thursday March the 31st disinter the body of Mary Hollingshead, which was buried on the 25th day of February 1831, and with circumstances of great brutality, broke in the coffin lid and exposed the corpse to public view on a tombstone adjacent to the turnpike road, where it was seen on the morning of Good Friday.[46]

NOTES

1. LRSM, 11 Oct. 1805, 7 Nov. 1806; TC, Loft, 31 Oct. 1806.
2. CB, 8 May 1807; LRSM, 17 July 1807; CJ LXII, 579, LXIII, 117; LRSM, 4 March and 15 May 1808; CB, 5 Dec. 1809.
3. CB, 15 Dec. 1807, 4 Feb. 1808, 4 June 1811.
4. LRSM, 28 Aug. 1807; W. Kitching, *To the Free Burgesses of the Borough of Great Grimsby*, Hull 1810.
5. LRSM, 18 Aug. 1808; *Yorks. Archaeological Journal*, VII, The Marshalls of Pickering.
6. LRSM, 15 March 1811.
7. *Trial between W. Frazer, gent. and John Henry Loft M.P. and others for a conspiracy*, taken in shorthand by J. Worsley of Lincoln, London 1811.
8. LRSM, 9 Oct. 1812, 5 March 1813; CJ LVIII, 24, 205, 221, 242, 267.
9. CB, 20 Sept. 1814; LRSM, 18 March, 1 and 20 April and 29 July 1814.
10. Sir J. Heron: *Notes*.
11. LRSM, 28 Feb. 1817.
12. LRSM, 13 Feb. 1818; TC, Squire, 1 Feb. 1818; TC, Lusby, 11 Feb. 1818.
13. TC, Plaskitt, 10, 18 and 22 March, 29 and 30 April, 1 May, 1818.
14. CB, 15 and 17 June, 21 Sept. 1818; TC, Plaskitt, 1 Aug. 1818.
15. TC, Daubney, 1, 8 and 23 Aug. 1818; TC, Plaskitt, 1 Aug. 1818.
16. TC, Veal, 12 Sept. 1818; CB, 8 Dec. 1818; LRSM, 25 Dec. 1818; TC, Bell, 9 Dec. 1818; TC, Daubney, 1 Dec. 1818; TC, Lusby, 1 Jan. 1819.
17. TC, Oliver, 24 Nov. 1818 and Jan. 1819; TC, Miller, 28 Jan. 1819.
18. CJ LXXIV, 74, 84; TC, Daubney, 12 Sept. 1818.

---

* The regularity and speed of coach services to London led to some increase of grave-robbing. The guard of a Barton coach told the coroner that he frequently had corpses in the coach boot for sale to the London anatomy schools. For this reason he disinterred the body of his daughter and reburied her secretly in his garden.

The Last Days of Corruption 211

19. TC, Veal, 4 and 26 July 1819; TC, Daubney, 19 Aug. 1819; TC, Brown, 1 Sept. 1819.
20. TC, Squire, 23 Jan. 1819; TC, Daubney, 28 Jan. 1819.
21. *Reports of the Commissioners on Municipal Corporations in England and Wales*, 2250; TC, Cooper, 21 Sept. 1819; TC, Daubney, 22 Sept. 1819.
22. CB, 6–7 March 1820; LRSM, 17 March 1820.
23. TC, Veal, 4 July 1819; CB, 20 Nov. 1819; LRSM, 24 Nov. and 15 Dec. 1820, 5 Jan. 1821.
24. CB, 20 Aug. 1821.
25. Skelton, *Proof Book*, 4 March and 23 May 1826; LRSM, 4 March 1828.
26. Skelton, 12 Aug. 1830; LRSM, 13 Aug. 1830, 24 June 1831.
27. LRSM, 25 March 1831; CB March 1831, 84–8.
28. Mayors CB, May 1831, 100, 154; LRSM, 6 May and 19 Aug. 1831, 16 Nov. and 14 Dec. 1832.
29. CB, 13 Aug. 1814.
30. LRSM, 2 Dec. 1829, 30 Jan. and 20 Feb. 1830; Leary, op. cit., 278; LAO, Tennyson-Deyncourt, H/I/5, 8; CJ LXVIII, 367, 446.
31. LRSM, 9 Sept. and 7 Oct. 1812.
32. LRSM, 29 Nov. 1816, 23 April 1819, 3 Dec. 1824, 1 Aug. and 12 Dec. 1834.
33. LRSM, 26 July 1816, 19 Dec. 1817, 27 Jan. 1819, 5 April and 14 Dec. 1820; *The Sailor's Yarn, the Life of John Taylor*, Louth 1852.
34. LRSM, 6 Oct. 1819, 12 June 1818, 1 Nov. 1820, 11 June and 2 July 1819, 18 May 1827; Vouchers, 1803–5; Cobbett, *Rural Rides*; LRSM, 13 Dec. 1822, 10 Sept. 1819.
35. From information provided by Dr. G. Jackson; TC, Moody, 28 Aug. 1819.
36. From information provided by Dr. G. Jackson; CB, 30 Nov. 1824, 28 June 1825; LRSM, 26 Aug. and 16 Dec. 1825.
37. Skelton, *Proof Book*, 1831–2, 54, 250; CB, 16 March 1824.
38. CB, 22 Jan. 1820, 10 July 1827; TC, Brandstrom to Tennyson, 14 May 1825.
39. CB, 7 Sept. 1812, 28 June 1825; LRSM, 2 May, 1828; Skelton, *Proof Book*, 1828, 111, 123.
40. LRSM, 1 Jan. 1830, 7 Nov. 1823.
41. LRSM, 15 Nov. 1822; *Hull Advertiser*, 8 Dec. 1848; LRSM, 1 March 1822, 28 April 1826, 10 Aug. 1832.
42. *Reports of the Commissioners on Municipal Corporations*, 2249 seq.; LRSM, 9 May 1828.
43. Skelton, *Proof Book*, 1828, 8, 9, 13, 19, 30, 37.
44. LRSM, 10 Dec. 1830.
45. LAO, Daubney, II, 9–12.
46. Skelton, *Proof Book*, 1831.

XIV

The New Corporation and the Docks

With the Reform Act of 1832 the new constituency, including Grimsby, Great and Little Coates, Bradley, Laceby, Waltham, Scartho, Weelsby, Clee and Cleethorpes, returned only one member. After 1833 there was no contested election until 1852. The freemen now had to share the franchise with the £10 householders, and although bribery did not disappear, it ceased to have much significance in the life of the town. The new corporation, elected by the ratepayers, had no connection whatever with parliamentary elections, and very little with its predecessor. George Babb continued as town clerk, but only four of the twelve councillors of 1835 had belonged to the old corporation, and the four aldermen were all new. Only three of the new members were Tories, and only four were Anglicans. There were eleven Methodists and a Baptist. It was so far from radicalism that it refused to allow the teetotallers to use the school-room, and chased two Owenites from the town, and they departed 'without any further attempt to inculcate their blasphemous and obscene tenets'.[1]

The new corporation, with a revenue of less than £2,000, was not very active. It began gas-lighting in 1838, and appointed twelve part-time constables. By 1846 it decided to have a full-time force of one superintendant and three policemen, with the council-chamber as a temporary police station, and by 1849, with the growth of population, there were eight on the establishment.[2,3,4,5]

During the 1830's the population, which had risen from 3,064 in 1821 to 4,048 in 1831, declined and was no more than 3,700 when the 1841 census was taken. For a time it had seemed that the manufacture of ropes was going to bring prosperity. In 1830 a strip of ground in the East Marsh was leased to Capt. Harris, at that time one of the borough members, for a ropery.

For my more particular ideas [he wrote] I refer you to Mr. Thorp with whom I have opened my mind freely, well knowing that he is a friend of the poor and has the welfare of the port and borough at heart, and that no circumstance would delight it more than to see them progressively rise from obscurity to their ancient consequence and splendour.[6]

The New Corporation and the Docks 213

Though this was no doubt intended to strengthen his political interest, it was also a serious enterprise which was not allowed to lapse when he ceased to be an M.P. By 1835 a steam engine was in use at his ropery, and there was also an adjacent flax-spinning mill.

The town [a visitor reported] is likely to derive great benefit through the exertions of Capt. Harris R.N. who after having overcome great difficulties erected a range of buildings for the manufacture of New Zealand flax into sail-cloth, cordage *etcetera*. Every article the company fabricate they can render waterproof. The buildings have a very imposing appearance.

A London engineer named Smith also tried to establish a factory for making wire cordage for ships. The municipal corporations commission found the town prosperous, with labourers at the dock earning 12*s*. to 18*s*. a week, though there were usually twenty or thirty men without work, except during the harvest. The ropery works failed, however, and the decline in population was thought to be a consequence of this, and by 1841 125 houses, or about one in every eight were uninhabited.[7]

Hopes had been raised in 1831 by proposals for a railway to connect the town with Sheffield and a full court, seeing the probable advantages to the town, the landowners and the dock company, urged that the corporation should do all it could to encourage the project. It was, in fact, not only the absence of industries, but also the lack of good inland communications which limited the further use of the dock. The tonnage of Grimsby registered vessels remained practically stationary at about 1,400 tons, comprising thirty-seven or thirty-eight vessels. In coastwise traffic the goods taken from the port were roughly in balance with the goods brought in. But the town had practically nothing to offer for shipment overseas and the owners of foreign going ships could be fairly certain that nearly all their vessels discharging at Grimsby would have to leave in ballast. In 1844–5, for example, though it was a bad year, sixty-four foreign going ships discharged cargoes and all but one went away empty. In the previous year, a more typical one, the figures were thirty-seven and four. So the Grimsby trade remained an unprofitable one, and there was little to encourage shipowners to make more use of the dock.[8]

In 1844 a group came together, under the chairmanship of Lord Worsley, to form the enterprise which was to be incorporated as the Great Grimsby and Sheffield Junction Railway Company. The route between Grimsby and Gainsborough was surveyed in the autumn and a meeting of landowners assembled at the *Red Lion*, Caistor, with

Lord Yarborough, Lord Worsley's father, in the chair on 28 October. The proposals for a railway were approved and the route was considered at a second meeting held at the Grimsby town hall in November. In 1845 the corporation petitioned in favour of railways to connect the town with Lincoln, Gainsborough, Sheffield, Louth and Boston. At the same time the dock was about to be transformed. A new Grimsby Docks Company acquired the assets of the old Haven Company. Five of the directors, including G. F. Heneage and Lord Worsley, were also on the board of the railway company, and at their first general meeting, in the town hall, in October 1845, they agreed to amalgamate the dock company with the railway company, though there was one director, C. T. D'Eyncourt,* who opposed the move. They immediately decided to construct a new dock planned by James Rendel, with Adam Smith of Brigg as resident-engineer.[9]

The new dock was to be built far out in the Humber on land reclaimed from the foreshore. Work began in the spring of 1846 with the construction of a cofferdam 1,500 feet long, of three rows of piles of Memel fir. At high tide the outer face of this dam stood in twenty-five feet of water. Behind it, an embankment stretched to meet the shore on the east side, and on the west a wharf 2,431 feet long extended to the entrance of the old dock. By the end of 1848 the work of reclamation was complete and the dock was being constructed inside this area. Meanwhile an East Lincolnshire Railway Company had been formed and its line from Grimsby to Louth and Boston was opened on 1 March 1848 at the same time as the Grimsby–New Holland line of the Manchester, Sheffield and Lincolnshire Railway Company which had now taken over the Great Grimsby and Sheffield Junction Company. The line to Brigg, Barnetby and Market Rasen was opened on 1 November 1848. Trains started to run between Grimsby and Lincoln a week before Christmas, and to Sheffield through Gainsborough on 16 July 1849. In April the Prince Consort entered Grimsby in a special train from Brocklesby with Lord Yarborough,† the chairman of the company. They came to the dock entrance under triumphal arches and the royal train was drawn over the last part of its route by a hundred navvies. The Prince laid a ceremonial stone of eleven tons at the site of the lock gates, and a naval squadron from Sheerness, anchored in the river, fired a salute. By the beginning of 1850, however, some of the directors were thinking of curtailing the size of their new

---

* Formerly, as Charles Tennyson, M.P. for Grimsby.
† Formerly Lord Worsley. He succeeded his father in 1846.

dock; but 9,000 piles had already been driven, and on the advice of Robert Stephenson they decided that there should be no alteration of plans. Work continued, and in March 1852 the completion of the dock was celebrated at a banquet in a marquee erected in the larger of the lock-pits, attended by Lord Yarborough and three hundred guests. Water was let into the dock later in the month. The railway from the dock to the town station was opened on 1 August 1853, and on 14 October 1854 Queen Victoria and Prince Albert visited the town in the royal yacht, and the railway company's dock was rechristened the Royal Dock, the name by which it is still known.[10]

The consequence of all this was a rapid growth of population. By 1846 it was already noted that many houses were being built, and that proper paving and a new market place were necessary. 'What the sexton will do', observed the *Stamford Mercury*, 'with the dead bodies consequent upon an increased population, we cannot tell. It is the imperative duty of those who wish to preserve the health of the town, as well as to preserve the feelings of the survivors from outrage, to prepare for the emergency.' The number of houses almost doubled in a few years, and in 1848 there were 1,554, 600 of which it was thought had been built since 1844.[11]

For the first time the corporation had to concern itself actively and continuously with public health. In the days when the sanitary aspect of Grimsby was that of almost any village, the quality of medical practice had been low, and in 1809 two doctors, Bell and Lambden, summoned to the same confinement, had a fight instead of attending to the patient. But most people were content with the medical skill available, and continued to patronise dangerously incompetent inoculators long after the discovery of small-pox vaccination.

The delusion under which the lower orders of the community labour [wrote a doctor in 1816] cannot be more strikingly evinced than by the prevalence of that fatal disorder, the small-pox in the borough of Great Grimsby. Fourteen children had already fallen victims, seven of whom have suffered within the last sixteen days. The infatuated parents, with minds steeled against conviction, still continue to comfort themselves with this futile argument. *If it pleases God to afflict them and they die, all is well.* Natural affection seems to be absorbed in this deadly fanaticism, which depopulates the place and causes rational people to suspect that there is something more in this species of obduracy than a pretended resignation to the will of heaven.[12]

By 1830 there was again a severe outbreak of small-pox. Robert Richmond, M.R.C.S., offered free vaccination at his apothecary's shop

P

opposite the old St. Mary's churchyard. In the cholera outbreak of 1831–2 the town largely escaped because of its smallness and its isolation. Two cases were reported in July 1832, when there were thirty-eight deaths at Gainsborough, where river water was drunk, and 246 at Hull. With the appearance of cholera in London all vessels from the Thames were to lie in the wide hole in the outfall until they were checked by a doctor, and ships with suspected cases on board were to hoist the quarantine flag and lie in the river. Ships from Sunderland also were quarantined, and there was a voluntary board of health which could do little more than recommend cleanliness, temperance and ventilation.[13]

With the growth of population the death rate, 21 per 1,000 in 1841, was believed to have risen to above 40 per 1,000 in 1848–9. Official action was necessary. In October 1848 a number of ratepayers petitioned to the General Board of Health to send an inspector to inquire into sewerage, drainage, water supply and general sanitary conditions. An inspector, W. Ranger, was duly sent, and opened his inquiry in the town hall on 14 December, with the Earl of Yarborough among the spectators. His report noted at least 262 houses inhabited by over 2,000 people as dangerous to health. In Newbiggin there were new houses in a tanyard, with no back doors, and with scrapings from the skins and a tanpit against the front doors. At Cook's Buildings, where seventy people lived in twenty-four rooms, there was a cesspool under the entry, and none of the houses had a staircase, step ladders being used instead. Most of these slums were found crammed into plots of 360 square yards of the kind leased to freemen. Albert Buildings consisted of fourteen houses on 360 square yards, and there were many similar plots with from nine to sixteen houses. Harrison's Buildings, near the river, were seven houses built on sand with six inhabitants to each room.[14]

The sanitation of such houses was very much what could be expected. The report can be allowed to speak for itself.

The privy accommodation was described as most defective and inefficient. Moody's Entry, containing twelve houses and seventy-four inhabitants has a cesspool, privy and ash-pit in one. Paradise Place contains twenty two houses with seventy four inmates and has one privy only. Garden Street which has eight houses has no accommodation whatever. Brown's Yard has a privy to each house. Atkinson's Buildings are five in number; the number of inmates twenty-seven. There is a privy to each house under the floor of the living room. In one part of the town in one if not more of the houses the privy is in a garret up three pairs of stairs.

Water was drawn from wells, but there were also seven public pumps in the old town and two in the new, where the worst slums were situated. Washing facilities were consequently poor. For some reasons doctors 'greatly reprobated the prevailing practice amongst the poor of washing in their living rooms'. They wanted to see proper baths and wash-houses established. People who wanted a bath used the Humber. There were nine covered sewers in the old town and several in the new. None was wider than two feet and the narrowest, which hardly deserved the name, was only of six inches. Half an hour's rain was said to leave water standing two feet deep at the end of Silver Street, and an open sewer ran along one side of Loft Street. A sanitary committee formed in 1848 had persuaded the corporation to clear out some of the open ditches.[15]

Up to 1837 the parish officers had repaired only the roads in the old town, but in that year, after taking counsel's opinion, the corporation compelled them to maintain the new roads as well. A part-time surveyor and collector were employed, each at £15 a year. They spent £961 on the roads in 1848–9, and there was a highway rate of 1s. 6d. in the pound. But there were complaints that footpaths and roadways were almost impassable in December, January and February, and W. Colley Parker, a highly articulate freeman, said that in Fotherby Street his cart had sunk up to the axle-trees in mud, although it was empty at the time. But from September to May the streets were lit by eighty-four public lamps, each on an average seventy-three yards from the next.[16]

The inevitable consequence of Ranger's report was the application of the Public Health Act to Grimsby. This was opposed by Mr. Williams acting for Lord Yarborough and Mr. G. F. Heneage, proprietors respectively of 42 and 16 per cent of the land in the town, and in accordance with their wishes the council decided to oppose the application of the Public Health Act and to apply for an improvement act instead. Nevertheless in March 1851 the General Board of Health extended the act to Grimsby and constituted the council the local board of health. J. M. Rendel (1799–1856), who began life as a surveyor under Telford and was the civil engineer who planned the Royal Dock, was invited to prepare a plan for sewerage and water supply, and a surveyor named Micklethwaite was employed in 1851. In the following year the council decided to apply for a Grimsby Improvement Act to promote the health of the town and to enable them to provide a new burial ground and extend the market place. A meeting of the ratepayers voted to oppose this, and they signed a petition presented by Councillor Keetley, who was a shipbuilder, and three other councillors, reciting their objections to the act, which they had already made the subject of Chancery proceedings, on the grounds that it would cost £35,000; but the council refused to change its mind and the act was obtained in 1853.[17]

With a loan of £20,000 sanctioned by the General Board of Health, the local board decided to begin the main sewer and the waterworks under Rendel's direction, but in May 1854 the General Board had not yet given its approval to the plans and had to be reminded that now was the best season for work to begin. By the end of the year, however, conscious that this was the biggest corporate venture yet taken in the town, the local board asked its surveyor to prepare a more modest plan and only agreed to pay Rendel's fees when Micklethwaite assured them that his charges were such as were usually made by eminent engineers. Work on the sewerage scheme began at last in 1855, and land was bought near Littlefield Lane from Mr. Angerstein and Lord Yarborough for the waterworks. Contractors were appointed for the removal of domestic refuse, and the laying of pavements began in the old town and Loft Street with three inch Yorkshire tooled flags, curbs eighteen inches deep, and crossings of granite or Yorkshire ragstone laid in chalk or sand.[18]

Local doctors in 1854 complained that some deaths from fever had been caused by 'foul exhalations' from stagnant sewers, and before the works started by the local board were complete cholera had appeared at Cleethorpes. H. M. Leppington, the medical officer of the Grimsby district in the Caistor Union had warned the Board of Guardians about the sanitary state of Cleethorpes, and by early September there were forty-seven deaths from cholera. Grimsby once again escaped lightly. There were ten cholera deaths, but four were of people who had fled from Cleethorpes and four were on board a ship. And the good fortune of Grimsby continued through the 1850's, the death rate falling from 25 per 1,000 to 20 per 1,000. Much of this improvement was probably due to the age-composition of a population growing by immigration as well as by natural increase, but no doubt there was some gain from improved drainage also, and whereas malaria was prevalent before the filling in of open drains, it was now said to be less common. The council even felt that the results of the efforts which it had made as a local board of health entitled it to be exempted from the Public Health Act of 1848 and the Local Govern-

The New Corporation and the Docks 219

ment Act of 1858. It duly applied for exemption, Mr. Ranger again visited the town, and an inquiry was held at the newly built Corn Exchange; but for Grimsby, with its continuing growth of population there was no escape from rate bills and the nineteenth century. There was a drain in the East Marsh 'full of feculent matter which needs only a sight to convince any right-thinking person whether it needs covering or not'. The council was not exempted from any of its obligations, and continued to discharge them with something less than enthusiasm.[19]

Between the time when the railway and dock works had begun, and the 1851 census, the population had more than doubled. It was 8,860 in 1851, and then grew more gradually to 11,067 in 1861; and it was this growth rather than the reform of 1835 which forced the council to take its responsibilities seriously. The greater part of the increase of population had arisen from the migration of people to Grimsby, and many of the newcomers, 222 in 1851, were Irish. A very few, like Charles Blain who was born at Killibegs, were long established residents. Charles Blain was actually a freeman, having served an apprenticeship to his uncle. There was also John Campbell, the superintending constable, and Dr. Hennessy, a physician. But over two hundred of the Irish were poor, strangers and unpopular. In the exodus which had followed the great famine they were believed to bring disease with them. When an Irish woman died of fever in a common lodging house the Brigg guardians expressed their fear that the town might be 'infected by the influx of the poor, half-starved and fever-ridden Irish'. The Grimsby councillors were perhaps not unsympathetic, and dealt sharply with the town crier:

> At this meeting (on March the 15th 1847) Matthew Wardale the town crier attended to answer a complaint preferred against him for crying that a meeting would be held to drive the Irish out of the town, such cry having a tendency to cause a breach of the peace, when Matthew Wardale admitted that he had made such cry and expressed his regret, when it was resolved that the said crier be dismissed from the office of crier for his misconduct.*[20]

Among the newcomers many had found work in connection with the dock and the railway. One was an engineering surveyor, and Thomas Halloran was a contractor for the dock works. There were eighty-eight Irish labourers and twenty-six stonemasons. Many were single men under forty lodging with Irish families, in Lower Burgess

---

* Wardale was given his job back only a fortnight after his dismissal. He was not finally dismissed until 1857 for the offences of keeping a brothel and crying publicly that a Mr. Thomas West was lost, stolen or strayed.

Street, King Edward Street, Whitehall Yard and Irish Green. Henry Marchat and Thomas Thompson were tramps, aged twelve and thirteen.

In the population of 1851 there were also a few people born outside the United Kingdom. A glazier and a jeweller were Poles, there was a German teacher, a German musician and a grocer from Wisby in Sweden. A labourer, probably a soldier's son, was born in the East Indies; a housekeeper was born in Australia, and a man, born at Wainfleet, and with a Cornish wife, was a returned emigrant from the United States. Genuine natives—people born in Grimsby—were now a minority.[21]

The town had grown almost entirely because of the railway and the new dock. During the period of construction it was felt that Grimsby tradesmen were not sharing in the new prosperity in quite the way they had expected. Within a few weeks of the first piles being driven at the dock they complained that the navvies were paid fortnightly instead of weekly and were getting into debt. In 1850 there was strong local support for the stonemasons employed on the dock who were striking for 4s. 6d. a day and an end of payment by ticket. The tickets were not exchangeable for goods from Grimsby shops. A contractor was fined for threatening a picket with a pistol. There was a meeting at the Baltic warehouse in support of the strikers, with W. Colley Parker in the chair; and he won an action in the county court against one of the contractors' firms in which the judge strongly condemned the ticket system and awarded him the value of two tickets which he had exchanged for coal.[22]

The coming of the railway involved a change in the affairs of the freemen, whose common lands in the Little Field, Haycroft and East March had remained unaffected by enclosure. In 1846 the town clerk was instructed to engage Mr. Page of Beverley to decide what price the corporation ought to receive for land to be taken by the railway, and in 1847 the Manchester, Sheffield and Lincolnshire Railway Company was allowed, on giving an arbitration bond of £50,000, to occupy thirty-two acres 'in order to facilitate the completion of the Manchester, Sheffield and Lincolnshire Railway and the dock and works connected with that undertaking, and to enable the directors of the company to give employment to labourers and mechanics during the ensuing winter'. Legislation was necessary to decide on how the purchase price of the land should be shared. The Grimsby Pastures Act decided that the sum of £19,262 paid by the railway company should be used to pay the mortgage debt, legal costs and the cost of obtaining the act. The Vicar of Grimsby* received £3,408 and the lay impropriator £1,733. One-twentieth of the residue went to the corporation and the rest to the freemen, or more exactly, to the Pastures' Committee which they were to elect annually and which was to regulate the stocking of the commons and sell or lease common land for building, paying an annual dividend from the profits to freemen and their widows.[23]

The affairs of the borough had once revolved between the poles of the freeman and Lord Yarborough. The political power of the freemen had now disappeared, but Lord Yarborough, reincarnated as chairman of the MS and LR company, was just as resplendent as in the days when his father and grandfather had returned two members for Grimsby. In 1850 he viewed the works in company with the Earl of Zetland and the directors of the Great Northern Railway. On the surface, this was a friendly discussion as to how the MS and LR dock should be connected with the GNR line to London in order to make Grimsby into a fishing port. But until they reached an agreement on running rights, each company was trying to outmanoeuvre the other.

Your directors [said Lord Yarborough in his 1851 report] have felt it their duty to oppose a bill brought into parliament by the Great Northern company during the past session, by which they sought to gain running powers over your line between Grimsby and New Holland, with the right to use the works at the latter place, and to appropriate to their use a most important portion of the dock property at Grimsby, upon which they proposed to erect a rival scheme, and to make a new station at Sheffield.

Lord Yarborough was still the squire of Grimsby. He was expected to arrive in the Royal Dock towards the end of May 1857 in his yacht *Zoe* before cruising in the Baltic. He invited the corporation and the magistrates to a dinner at the Yarborough Hotel, and the yacht was to be open to the public. She was lost, however, by going aground in a calm off Happisburgh. There was no loss of life, but his lordship was too shaken to attend the dinner, at which Lord Worsley took his place. The corporation presented an address to congratulate him on his escape, and the public were able to see the two boats, in which he and the crew had left the yacht, on the lake at Newsham.[24]

Lord Yarborough lived long enough to see the fruition of his schemes and his satisfaction must have been largely altruistic, since

---

* The Rev. F. T. Atwood (1799-1856). He was born at Hammersmith where he was perpetual curate of St. Paul's from 1826 and spent most of his time. He had also been Vicar of Ludford and Sixhills until he became Vicar of Grimsby in 1831. He died at Grimsby.

very little of the new development was taking place on his land. On his death in 1862, the corporation fully realised the part which he had played in remaking the economy of the town.

It was resolved that the members of the council desire to record their high appreciation of the eminent late Earl of Yarborough to whose persevering and untiring energies must in very considerable degree be attributed the formation of the extensive docks and railways which have so largely contributed to the present extension and prosperity of the port of Grimsby.[25]

The change in the prosperity of the port had been noticeable for five or six years before the dock was open for shipping. In addition to material required for the railway, almost half a million cubic feet of timber had to be imported from the Baltic for the piling of the Royal Dock. In 1832 only forty-nine ships with foreign imports had entered the old dock, and even in 1845 there were only sixty-four. Now the numbers increased sharply to 204 in 1846 and 372 in 1847. There was a short period of depression with the completion of work on the Royal Dock. Except when the tide was favourable, only small craft could use the old dock which was becoming too shallow because of leaks in the dock gates. By the spring of 1853 the town was full of men without work, and it was said that in a single week thirty had left for America. But beneath the surface everything was changed, and the rest of the nineteenth century was to see such expansion that the old, medieval market town, which Grimsby had been for so long, was almost obliterated. By the 1860's over £1 million had been spent on the Royal Dock, representing an investment about ten times as great as that of the defunct Haven Company. In 1852 the North of Europe Steamship Company opened a weekly service to Hamburg with the *City of Norwich*, and a weekly packet-service to Rotterdam, the MS and LR having guaranteed a five per cent profit. The service to Hamburg was doubled in 1854, and by 1856 there were regular sailings to Königsberg, Memel and Tonning.[26]

Foreign trade increased markedly: 256 cargoes were imported in 1851, increasing to 503 in 1853; 32 cargoes were exported in 1851, compared with 166 in 1853. An analysis of trade for the first three weeks in August 1855 shows that exports consisted of coal, bale goods, cotton, salt, iron and machinery. Those which did not go to Baltic and Scandinavian ports went to Hamburg and Rotterdam. In the same period imports, mostly from the same places, were of iron, timber, wheat, linseed, hemp, flax and oil cake from Dunkirk. In the three weeks in question the largest ship in dock was the *Hamburg* of 534 tons, but most were of less than 200 tons, and one from Norway, with iron, was of 65 tons. A few ships sailed for more remote seas. The Grimsby brig *Anthracite* left for Australia in 1853, and she was again at Melbourne in 1856.[27]

The staple trades were timber* and coal. In the timber trade, even such ancient craft as the *Liberty and Property*, launched at Whitby in 1753, could be profitably employed. It was a seasonal trade, coming to an end each year shortly after the first ice appeared in the Baltic, though it was not unusual for the latest arrivals to have been sawn out of the ice. There was a good deal of unemployment each winter when the timber trade ceased, and the town was severely pinched by the effect of the Crimean War. Robert Keetley, the shipbuilder, bankrupted himself by litigation arising from his purchase of the Russian ship *Neptune*, claimed by the Admiralty as a prize. Imports of Baltic timber fell from 43,000 tons in 1854 to 17,000 tons in 1855. Though they did not arrive until the war was over, five ships came from Quebec with timber because of the shortage caused by the war, and linseed came from Egypt and Constantinople instead of from Russia. The MS and LR failed to persuade the Admiralty to use the Royal Dock for shipping stores to the fleet in the Baltic, though they sent coal from New Holland and Peto, Brassey and Company sent sleepers from Grimsby for the railway between Balaclava and Sebastopol. But the effect of the war was merely to retard commercial expansion. The tonnage of ships using the Royal Dock was 118,000 tons in the second half of 1855 and 162,000 tons in the second half of 1856. Over 4,000 bales of cotton were in the dock warehouses ready to go to Russia as soon as peace was proclaimed. The first four ships for St. Petersburg sailed on the first day of the peace, nine vessels left Archangel for Grimsby during the summer and a ship arrived from Taganrog with linseed in October.[28]

Towards the end of the war the Anglo-French Steamship Company had been formed with Lord Yarborough as chairman. In its first six months the company sent sixty-three ships from Grimsby, chiefly with coal to French ports from the south Yorkshire coalfield, then producing a million tons a year. Up to 3,000 tons a week could be exported from Grimsby. A Frenchman, M. Hippolyte Worms, was a major shareholder and by 1858 he was the leading exporter from Grimsby. In a sample period of six weeks from 3 March 1858 he sent twenty cargoes from the dock, including some to Greece and the Mediterranean, as

* By 1889 timber was being imported at the rate of over 300,000 tons a year.

against only four sent by other exporters. 46,000 tons of coal were shipped in 1856, 60,000 in 1857, 363,000 in 1875, and, in spite of increased facilities at Hull, 800,000 in 1890.²⁹

At almost every point the council was aware of the dependence of the town on the MS and LR. It opposed the Humber Conservancy Bill until it had had time to confer with the directors, and then, on the creation of the Humber Conservancy, paid £100 a year from 1868 to 1875 in order to be represented on the board. It acquiesced in 1868 in the company's intention to promote a bill to acquire corporation property in the West Marsh for dock and railway works, and when the company got its act, virtually allowed it to decide its own price for the compulsory purchase. In 1872 the council wanted the price to be settled by arbitration, but the company simply offered £300 an acre. At a public meeting the council was urged to accept, but John Wintringham, an alderman and J.P., and twenty-four others signed a memorial to the Treasury drawing attention to the fact that similar land had been sold twenty-eight years previously at £500 an acre and that James Reed, the mayor, who was port-master, and several other members of the council were servants of the MS and LR. The Treasury, however, gave its consent, and the MS and LR bought 105 acres for £31,500 in an area where land was soon to be worth £1,000 an acre.³⁰

In August 1873 work began on a cut one hundred feet wide with a lock of forty feet to connect the old dock with the Royal Dock, and this was completed in 1874. Even with the improvement of the old dock, however, further accommodation was needed. In 1856 £1,000,000 of British manufactures had been exported through Grimsby. By 1875, in spite of the disturbance of trade caused by war, the figure had risen to £10,000,000, and the tonnage of shipping using the port had increased six-fold in twenty years. Sir E. Watkin, chairman of the MS and LR began to see Grimsby as a great grain port, and a warehouse was started; and at the end of 1878 Logan and Hemingway were awarded a contract with over £50,000 to construct an eastern extension from the northern end of the old dock with a railway link to the main line near Great Coates. In 1879 the Prince and Princess of Wales* opened the canal linking the Old with the Royal Dock, and

---

* At the time of this visit a Grimsby skipper was entertained in the wardroom of a Danish gun-boat in the North Sea. He had hailed her in the mistaken belief that she was a 'coper', one of the vessels which plied a dubious traffic in drink. He was nevertheless supplied with meat, brandy and tobacco in exchange for fish; and one of the officers gave him a letter to Princess Alexandra. He delivered it at Brocklesby Park and was appropriately rewarded.

the Old Dock with its twenty-six-acre extension became the Alexandra Dock. The work was completed by 1880.[31]

The export of agricultural machinery from Grimsby had started as soon as the Royal Dock was opened. In 1853 steam threshing machines made at Lincoln by Clayton and Shuttleworth were sent to Hungary via Hamburg for Countess Esterhazy and Count Domini Zichi. By the seventies Thomas and Stephen Oates were sending locomotives to Poti on the Black Sea, and so much Lincoln threshing machinery had reached Russia that wheat coming to Lincolnshire from the Black Sea was found to be noticeably cleaner.[32]

The cotton trade had begun in 1858—that is to say, the importation of raw cotton as distinct from re-exports to the continent. The first shipment arrived in the *Sir George Rogers* from Mobile in February 1857, followed in March by the *Wolfe*, also from Mobile, with nearly 3,000 bales. She was the largest ship, just over a thousand tons, to enter the Royal Dock so far. The MS and LR built a warehouse to store 25,000 bales. In February 1858, 3,289 bales arrived from New Orleans, followed in April by 3,313 from Bombay. Even during the cotton famine of the American Civil War 7,038 bales arrived in 1863 and 35,215 in 1864.[33]

The emigrant traffic was a direct consequence of the railway and the Royal Dock. By crossing the North Sea to Grimsby and taking the train to Liverpool emigrants who could afford the extra cost were able to shorten the misery of their ocean voyage. The *Glen Albyn* brought possibly the first such band of 200 emigrants from Rotterdam in April 1854, and 160 more came from Hamburg a day later. Work began on converting the station on the dock into a temporary home for such travellers. In a single week in May the Hamburg and Rotterdam packets brought another thousand. Many of these travellers were Mormons. In April 1857 a vessel from Copenhagen brought 223 on their way to Salt Lake City via Liverpool, and 350 Mormons were reported as arriving in Grimsby two years later, many bringing aged parents with them to America. In 1871 the average of emigrants arriving was 200 a month, but 500 arrived in October and were thought to consist chiefly of peasants, including some well-to-do farmers, escaping from Prussian rule in Holstein and Alsace-Lorraine. The exodus of such refugees continued into 1872, with a surprising proportion of well-educated middle-class young men and women. There were refugees from Russia too, and in 1875 the *Halifax* brought 130 Mennonites on their way to Canada, 'leaving the soil of the Czar because their religion forbids them to carry arms'. By 1887 and 1888 emigration through the port had mounted to 10,000 a year. The superintendent of the Emigrants' Home and port interpreter for twenty years, Isaac Freeman, naturalised in 1871, was himself a refugee from Russian Poland named Beleveg.[34]

The railway and the Royal Dock had thus converted the town into a flourishing port, virtually without any industry or manufactures of its own other than those concerned with shipping. Since 1865 Grimsby had ranked as the fifth port, immediately after Glasgow, exporting in that year just over £4 million of British goods. The growth of population had reflected this commercial expansion. There were only 9,000 inhabitants when the Royal Dock was opened. There were over 40,000 when the Alexandra Dock received its first ships in 1880 and over 60,000 by the end of the century. But the commercial docks were only in part responsible for this great change. It was the fishing industry which gave the town its unique character.[35]

NOTES

1. Mayor's CB, 6 Jan. 1835; LAO, Daubney, IV/3/3; LRSM, 1 Jan. 1836; MB, 12 Aug. 1839; LRSM, 11 Sept. 1840.
2. MB, 1 Jan. and 9 Aug. 1836, 3 Jan. 1837, 1 Jan. 1839, 12 Feb. 1840, 3 Feb. 1851, 9 Nov. 1840.
3. MB, 14 Feb. 1837, 14 Aug. 1838, 5 Aug. 1839.
4. MB, 10 May 1836, 16 May and 23 Dec. 1837, 6 April, 7 June and 9 Nov. 1838, 16 March 1846.
5. MB, 1 Jan. 1836, 16 May 1837, 12 Nov. 1838, 1 Aug. 1839, 12 Feb. 1840, 3 Feb. 1842, 10 Feb. 1846; LRSM, 31 March 1843.
6. Mayor's CB, 1830, 68–73; LRSM, 24 July 1835.
7. J. Saunders, *Lincolnshire in 1836*, 144; 1851 Census, II; W. Ranger, *Report to the General Board of Health of a Preliminary Inquiry into . . . Grimsby* (H.M.S.O., 1850), 7.
8. CB, 20 Sept. 1831; Ranger, op. cit., 12.
9. George Dow, *Great Central*, I, 85; MB, 22 Jan. 1845; Dow, op. cit., I, 84; *Statutes of the Realm*, 9 and 10 Vict. c 268.
10. Dow, op. cit., I, 118–19, 123, 141, 151.
11. LRSM, 3 April 1846; Ranger, op. cit., 7.
12. LRSM, 17 March 1809, 1 Nov. 1816.
13. LRSM, 2 April 1830; Skelton, *Proof Book*, 1830; LRSM, 20 July 1832; Skelton, *Proof Book*, 1831, 22.
14. Ranger, op. cit., 13, 24.
15. Ibid., 27, 28–30; LRSM, 22 July and 28 Oct. 1853.
16. MB, 19 Aug. 1837; Ranger, 33, 31.
17. Ibid., 17; MB, 28 Nov. 1849; DNB xlviii, 10; MB, 17 Feb. 1853.
18. LBH, 7 March 1855; MB, 23 Jan. 1854.
19. LAO, Caistor Union Minutes, 27 May and 2 Dec. 1854; LRSM, 1, 8 and 22 Sept. 1854; Grimsby Independent, 22 April 1859.

The New Corporation and the Docks

20. CB, 1 Aug. 1820; LRSM, 28 May 1847; MB, 15 and 29 March 1847, 6 May 1839, 2 Feb. 1857.
21. Grimsby Borough Library, 1851 Census returns, micro-film.
22. LRSM, 17 July 1846, 8, 15, 22 Feb., 17 May 1850.
23. MB, 6 Oct. 1846, 20 Nov. 1847; *Statutes*, 12 Vict. c. 16; *Alumni Cantabrigenses* II, i, 98.
24. LRSM, 25 Oct. 1850, 29 Aug. 1851; G. Gaz., 22 May 1857.
25. MB, 3 Feb. 1862.
26. Dow, op. cit., I, 173-5; Ranger, op. cit., 12; LRSM, 18 March and 16 Sept. 1853.
27. G. Gaz., 19 Jan. 1854, 17 and 24 Aug. 1855; LRSM, 25 March 1853; G. Gaz., 12 Sept. 1856
28. LRSM, 24 June 1853; G. Gaz., 28 March 1856; LRSM, 17 Aug. 1855; G. Gaz., 1 Feb., 21 March, 11 and 26 April, 3 Oct. and 14 Nov. 1856; Dow, op. cit., I, 176; G. Gaz., 16 Jan. 1857, 18 May, 13 June, 1 and 22 Aug., 24 Oct. 1856.
29. G. Gaz., 5 Sept. 1856; G. Obs., 10 May 1876 and 31 Dec. 1890.
30. MB, 16 April and 10 June 1864, 24 Feb. 1868, 1 Feb. 1875, 14 Dec. 1868, 5 July 1872, 4 March, 13 Oct. and 8 Nov. 1873, 9 Feb. 1874; Dow, op. cit., II, 162.
31. G. Obs., 27 Aug. 1873, 10 May 1876; Dow, op. cit., II, 162 and 164-7; G. Obs., 22 July 1879.
32. LRSM, 25 March 1853, 18 Dec. 1870; G. Obs., 7 Feb. 1872.
33. G. Gaz., 20 and 27 Feb., 27 March and 3 April 1857; G. Obs., 10 May 1876.
34. G. Gaz., 14 April 1854; LRSM, 19 May, 1854; G. Gaz., 24 April and 5 June 1857; LRSM, 8 April 1859; G. Obs., 8 Nov. 1871, 21 Feb. 1872, 7 July 1875, 29 Nov. 1871.
35. LRSM, 6 Jan. 1865, 28 July 1880.

XV

The Arrival of the Smacks

There had been occasional landings of sprats in the Old Dock, but it was the construction of the Great Northern line to London which really made the town into a fishing port. Fishing with the beam trawl, known at Barking and Brixham since about 1800 had led the smacks from the Channel to the North Sea. As the yield of fish from the traditional grounds diminished, grounds further to the north were explored and by 1845 there were forty smacks fishing from Hull. It was at once realised that the position of Grimsby was more favourable if only the fish could be got to London. The town council made this point in petitioning of the East Lincolnshire Railway Company's bill:

> If this southern communication were obtained the immense trade in North Sea fish which now passes up the Humber for the metropolis must necessarily come into the port of Great Grimsby and be transmitted by this railway at a very reduced cost and in at most half the time that it now takes, and the commodious dock and other improvements now being made at Great Grimsby at a great outlay of capital will much facilitate such a traffic.[1]

Seymour Clark, manager of the Great Northern, persuaded his directors to give a bonus to the firm of James Howard and Company to bring their fleet of thirteen vessels from Manningtree to Grimsby. The first smack to make a landing was probably the *Princess of Wurtemberg* from Barking, whose skipper later emigrated to Australia and visited friends in Grimsby in 1880. It was in 1850 that she came from Barking. The new dock, and the railway to it, were not yet complete, and the first box of fish was taken on a cart to the town station, ceremonially escorted by a band,[2] or so he recalled in 1880.

Most of the earliest smacks to come to Grimsby were not equipped for trawling but for catching lobsters and line-fishing for cod. The vessels were fitted with wells from which the catch could be landed alive. When Harrison Mudd came from Brixham as a cabin-boy in one of these vessels the dock tower was only one-third built and they landed in the outfall of the Old Dock and sold the lobsters at Keetley's dry dock. In 1851 up to 7,000 lobsters from the coast of Norway arrived at a single landing and in the course of the year 50,000 were sent to London by rail. By 1853 the *Pearl*, a screw steamer, was bringing lobsters from Norway, discharging 7,000 and several boxes of salmon only eight days after sailing; and the Grimsby-built smack, *Thomas*, landed 20,000 lobsters after crossing the North Sea in fifty-three hours.³

Fishing vessels were built at Grimsby within a year of the commencement of the trade. The Great Grimsby Fishing Co., an enterprise jointly sponsored by the railways, ordered the *Thomas* from Robert Keetley and in May 1852 she was launched into the Old Dock. In the evening he gave a party for sixty of his men. Seven of the other eight vessels owned by the Great Grimsby Fishing Co. were built by Keetley, including the *John Ellis*, a schooner with an auxiliary screw, intended for lobster fishing and completed in 1853; and the *George*, a steam screw schooner with a crew of nine for collecting fish from smacks on the Dogger Bank. She appears to have been the first steamer used in fleeting, but when she sank two miles off the Humber after a boiler explosion in 1853, she was not replaced.⁴

At first, Grimsby was not so much a fishing port as a place from which smacks were trying their luck before moving elsewhere. At the end of each season many of the lobster fishers left Grimsby for the Scottish cod and herring fishery. But very soon the advantages of Grimsby began to attract smacks from other ports. From Hull it was necessary to tow smacks to sea when the wind was unfavourable. Grimsby was on the coast. The advantages were not overwhelming, and for much of the nineteenth century Hull kept pace with Grimsby as a fishing port; but the growth of the industry at Hull did not in any way retard it at Grimsby. There was nothing to tie vessels to one particular port. In 1856 there were hopes, wildly exaggerated, that a hundred or more smacks were about to transfer from Barking to Grimsby. In actual fact fourteen smacks sailed from Grimsby for Iceland and nine of them were from London. Many smacks were expected to leave Hull when the first Grimsby fish dock was opened. It was said that they could land their fish and be back on the fishing grounds in the time which it would have taken them to sail up the Humber to Hull. But in the first year of the fish dock only five transferred from Hull to Grimsby.⁵

The Alward family may be cited as an example of how Grimsby ultimately profited from the migration of smacks. Robert Alward and his brother William were among those Brixham fishermen who had begun to trawl in the North Sea and were looking for a new base. In

1850 they took their two smacks to Scarborough and remained there several years but found the local inshore-fishermen ill-disposed and the harbour too open. One son, James, moved to Hull. George Alward left Scarborough and came to Grimsby in 1856, and his object, to use his own words, was 'to better their condition, which was the object of all who migrate from place to place'. Soon afterwards James joined him, mainly because of disputes at Hull between masters and men as to the use of ice and steam cutters for fleeting, both of which had been tried at Grimsby. The feeling at Hull was so intense that in James's opinion smacks had secretly visited Grimsby to obtain supplies of ice.[6]

The smack *Surprise* was the first, it was believed, to use ice at sea in 1858. Previously it had been used for keeping the fish fresh as it was sent to London. It appears to have been in this matter of preserving fish that Grimsby for a long time enjoyed its greatest advantage. Cod were brought alive in the wells of smacks and could be kept alive in the fish dock until the market was ready for them, in floating cod-chests. There were complaints that because of the shallowness of the dock the water soon became too warm and the fish died; but this happened only in the hottest part of the year, and at Hull there was no water in which cod could be kept alive. Up to 400 cod-chests were at one time in use, and some of them survived into the twentieth century.[7]

At first smacks used both the Royal Dock and the Old Dock. In the first three months of 1854 105 departures of smacks were reported by the dock-masters, and in the last quarter there were 211 departures. The names of smacks were not usually reported, and it seems likely that there were really no more than about a dozen of them. By 1857 movements reported would indicate that up to fifty smacks were using the port. When George Alward migrated from Scarborough, he believed there were only twelve cod-smacks and ten trawl smacks. These, however, were vessels permanently based on Grimsby, and they alone cannot have caught the 1,500 tons of fish which were sent away by rail in 1856. There must have been almost as many belonging to other ports but landing at Grimsby, and some of these, in the following years, would leave their home port and become permanently based on Grimsby.[8]

The railway to London had brought the smacks, but it was the construction of a fish dock by the MS and LR which enabled the industry to grow. Work on construction of the dock, east of the new Royal Dock, began in the summer of 1855. In the course of the year a lock-pit and an entrance pier were made. There was a set-back when part

4. Norwegian ice-barques in dock at Grimsby at the time of the 1897 Jubilee

The Arrival of the Smacks

of the embankment fell in but the new dock was ready in March 1857. 'On Saturday last', the *Grimsby Gazette* reported, 'the fishing dock was opened to the entrance of fishing smacks, so that the nuisances on the Royal Dock, which have long been complained of, will now be avoided.' The town was to grow rich out of the nuisances.[9]

In the first year of the fish dock the tonnage of fish dispatched by rail more than doubled, to 3,400 tons. There is no means of knowing how much greater the total catch was. In the earliest years the tonnage sent by rail was probably nearly the whole of it; but in course of time a considerable proportion of the catch was never included in the railways' fish statistics. Apart from the small amount consumed locally, increasing quantities were smoked or salted, and in many years at least an equal amount caught by Grimsby crews was sent direct to Billingsgate by fast cutters to avoid railway freight charges. Certainly the 8,500 tons carried by rail in 1862 and the 19,400 tons five years later was not the whole of the fish caught by Grimsby smacks. Until 1864 the greater part of the fish-carrying trade was in the hands of the Great Northern. By then, however, fish was ceasing to be purely a luxury for the London market, demand was growing in the industrial north, and the MS and LR began to get a good share of the trade.[10]

The fish dock and the shore facilities were entirely the concern of the MS and LR. In 1858 the company built the first twenty-five houses for fishermen near the dock. There was a thatched ice-house beside the dock and the Deep Sea Fishing Co. advertised for carters, labourers and bargemen to collect pond-ice. In March 1857 the barques *Amphion* and *Lehman* arrived with the first of the regular cargoes of Norwegian ice— 460 tons from the port of Drobak. The ice-trade grew with the same rapidity as the fish trade, and a second ice company was formed in 1864. The fish dock, of six acres, with the pontoon or floating fish market, cost the MS and LR no more than £12,000. Within two years of its opening smack-owners and fish merchants were complaining of its inadequacy and asking that it should be enlarged to accommodate 500 smacks. It was not until 1866, however, that the MS and LR felt it necessary to begin to enlarge it. A new lock-pit was started in 1869, and, as a token of its involvement in the traffic, the Great Northern agreed to reduce its rates for carriage to London by 2s. 6d. a ton.[11]

Though the trade always complained of its treatment by the MS and LR, Hull smack-owners were even more discontented and many migrated to Grimsby. Although between 1860 and 1881 the total of Hull smacks increased by 243 per cent, 18 per cent of them moved to other ports, principally Grimsby. It was felt that facilities at Grimsby were better. 'The Hull Dock Company', said a witness for the Hull and Barnsley Railway bill, 'does not care a straw about fishermen.' For cod-fishing in particular Hull was at a disadvantage. By 1872 there were eighty Grimsby vessels line-fishing for cod and thirty more sailing from the port. Each cost £1,500 and had a crew of ten or a dozen. But the number of trawling smacks had increased to 371, and conditions of service in them were so much more attractive that it was becoming difficult to obtain crews for the cod-liners.[12]

In the fifties there was a social and a topographical gap between the fishermen and those who were running the town. The fish dock was on the remote outskirts, a mile or more distant from the homes of the middle-class. The weekly newspaper barely noticed its existence and was much more concerned with the patricians of church and chapel than with the wandering proletarians from the south who might easily disappear with their fishing craft as suddenly as they had come. But instead more and more of them came every year, and fortunes began to be made. The first fish-merchant to become a councillor was elected in 1858. Ten years later John Gidley became the first smack-owner to gain election. By 1873 four of the sixteen councillors were smack-owners. A number of freemen, who presumably were not newcomers, owned smacks, and much of the capital for new smacks came from local residents in the form of mortgages which were yielding ten per cent interest until 1878, but thereafter more usually seven per cent. In the seventies it had become impossible to find magistrates who clearly had no interest in fishing. The economy of the town would have collapsed without it. W. T. Lundie, headmaster of the old Grammar School, thought that two-thirds of the inhabitants gained their livelihood from the fish trade. Probably half the inhabitants would be a more reasonable estimate, 3,400 men and boys went to sea in smacks and another 100 in ice-barques and steam-carriers. There were 564 shipwrights, sail-makers and others working on the repair and construction of fishing vessels, 400 persons, including women, employed in forty-one smoke-houses, 400 labourers on the pontoon where fish was landed and marketed, and 161 people working for subsidiary companies.[13]

Though there were a few wealthy smack-owners, in the days of sail ownership was very widely spread, and it was very much easier in fishing than in most industries for a worker to become an employer. A good apprentice would probably become a skipper. It was easy for a skipper to obtain a mortgage to buy his own smack, and with luck he could pay it off in a few years. Unfortunately the life-history of the majority of smack-owners must always remain unknown, but what is known suggests that nearly all of them were self-made men in the Samuel Smiles tradition. Henry Smethurst, the biggest owner, claimed that he once took three boys from Louth workhouse. One was drowned and two became owners. J. W. Wilkin, a New Clee smack-owner, in applying for two apprentices from Caistor workhouse, described himself as one of the workhouse master's old scholars and assured the guardians that they could therefore be certain that the boys would be well-treated. J. Plastow was an apprentice from Hackney workhouse in 1854, serving under Robert Hewitt at Barking until 1861. He saved £20 in two years and came to Grimsby. As a skipper he saved another £65 in eight months, put down a deposit for a smack which he bought for £750, and paid off the mortgage and interest in three years. For another two years he still went to sea, until he had saved £700 and could have a second smack built, and he then stayed on shore as a fish salesman and ultimately the owner of several smacks. George Fellowes first went to sea in 1840 when he was apprenticed at Ramsgate. When he was out of his time he moved to Hull, becoming a skipper there in 1847. His service as a skipper was an exceptionally long one, and it was not until 1864 that he came to Grimsby and began to buy a smack on mortgage. As soon as he was clear of this debt he bought other smacks, no longer went to sea, and became president of the Smackowners' Mutual Insurance Co.[14]

For a skipper to become an owner, it was almost essential for him to be a teetotaller. Earnings were high, and the moral tone of the town was such that a fisherman with money had the strongest temptations put in his way to spend it on drink and prostitutes. It is not suggested here that the majority of skippers and owners were total abstainers, but the leaders were. The conditions under which apprentices served were such that a boy who took to drink was not likely to become a skipper, —one who drank could legally barter fish for drinks with liquor traders at sea. Significantly, Thomas Campbell, who was to become one of the most successful owners, as early as 1854 had a smack named the *Abstainer* and the vessel which brought the Alwards to Grimsby was named the *Sons of Rechab*. Harrison Mudd, one of the founders of the North Sea Steam Trawling Co., and chairman of the Coal, Salt and Tanning Co., was a fervent teetotaller, especially in his youth. When he was fishing in the Faroes in 1860, each Sunday he was in harbour, he hoisted what he described as the Bethel flag on his smack, and held

Primitive Methodist services on board her, in which denunciation of strong drink was an important part of the doctrine preached. Three other vessels, he wrote, had Bethel flags, but twenty-seven had no praying man on board. 'I am sorry to say', he added, 'that the monster strong drink has sometimes held sway over many here.' Henry Smethurst, who with his son-in-law Carl Magnus Mundahl owned fifty smacks, was just as fanatical; and the humbler fishermen ordinarily held their meetings at the Temperance Hall.[15]

But as the pioneers grew rich, there was less plain-living and there were those who were intensely critical of them. When the Smack-owners' Association was trying to convince the public that they were doing badly, some critics laid the blame at their door. 'The trade flourished for many years', a fisherman complained, 'and many have done well, but there is no class of people in this town who have lived so fast and wasted so much.' A shipwright carefully itemised the sins of the owners:

Me and my mates think we can tell them several reasons that the smacks won't pay. One is that when they are launched they at once load them with mortgage deeds down to Plimsoll's mark, so that they are unable to carry large houses and servants, horses and carriages, and foundation stones* etc., and allow them to drink champagne. Put their smacks in dock, scrape all the mortgage barnacles off them, and give them a clean bottom; keep less servants, less horses and carriages; drink less champagne and wine; lay less foundation stones, unless, indeed, it can be done honestly and fairly.

This, however, was criticism of the leading owners. Few of the smaller owners can have afforded much ostentation.[16]

Until the smacks were entirely replaced by steam trawlers at the end of the century there was a certain community of interest and outlook which fishermen shared with most owners. The great majority of fishermen were skippers and mates, and had every reason to expect that they could become owners themselves; and many owners could look back on the time which they had spent as fishermen. As late as 1889 there were 292 smack-owners each of whom had only one vessel. In the seventies several owners were members of the Trawl Fishermen's Union. J. Gidley, the president and J. Plastow, the vice-chairman, were both owners. Fishermen had their own grievances, such as the employment of Dutchmen and of too many apprentices, and the payment of mates in some vessels by wages instead of by the almost universal

* Presumably the writer meant chapel foundation stones and was referring to the fact that most owners were nonconformists.

share system; but they also had other grievances which put them firmly on the side of the small owners. Too much of the profit, they felt, was being skimmed off by the shareholders of the Grimsby Ice Company. Ice was being brought from Norway at the rate of over 50,000 tons a year. It was sold to smacks in 1876 for £1 1s. a ton, but to inland customers at 15s.; and it was believed that when ice was put on board smacks, sixteen cwt. counted as a ton, and that certain favoured owners were given a secret bonus of five per cent. In the previous year the price had actually been advanced from 25s. to 30s. a ton. 'Why', asked Gidley, 'should fishermen, who were the very backbone of the ice-trade be thus imposed on?' It was also believed that the larger shareholders were pressing for a higher price to reduce the fishermen's profits and give certain owners who happened to be shareholders a concealed profit in the form of higher dividends on their ice shares. The company admitted that it did not sell ice freely to all customers, but it denied the existence of fraudulent discounts, and defended its prices on the grounds that there were unpredictable fluctuations, depending on the severity of the winter, in the supply from Norwegian lakes. High profits, the company maintained, were justified by the risks of the trade. There were the risks to the ice-barques at sea, and the ice-houses were on dock land rented from the MS and LR on three-month leases.[17]

NOTES

1. CMD, vi; LRSM, 18 March 1838; MB, 2 March 1846.
2. G. Obs., 17 Jan. 1872, 22 Sept. 1880.
3. LRSM, 27 June 1851; Fishing Trades Gazette, 16 Dec. 1905; Mudd's MS in Hull Times, 31 March 1923; LRSM, 27 May and 3 June 1853.
4. LRSM, 29 May 1952; G. Alward, *The Sea Fisheries of Great Britain and Ireland* (Grimsby, 1932), 193; LRSM, 2 May 1856, 18 and 25 March 1853.
5. LRSM, 17 Aug. 1855, 1 Aug. 1856; G. Gaz., 5 June 1857.
6. Alward, op. cit., 337, 195; G. Obs., 19 Aug. 1891, 13 Dec. 1876.
7. Mudd's MS; Alward, op. cit., 201; G. Gaz., 12 June 1857.
8. G. Gaz., 1854-7, weekly shipping notes; CMD, App. 30.
9. G. Gaz., 22 June 1855, 7 March 1856, 13 March 1857.
10. CMD, App. 30.
11. G. Gaz., 6 Feb. and 3 April 1857; LRSM, 26 Feb. 1864; Alward, op. cit., 203-4; Grimsby Independent, 11 March 1859; Dow, op. cit., II, 162.
12. G. News, 19 May 1882; CMD, App. 30.
13. MB, 1 Nov. 1858, 2 Nov. 1868, 3 Nov. 1873; CMD, App. 37, 217-30; Alward, op. cit., 206-13.
14. CMD, 57/2258, 67/2538, 39/1630; G. News, 21 July 1882.
15. Grimsby Free Press, 20 July 1860.
16. G. Obs., 2 April and 24 Sept. 1879.
17. Alward, op. cit., 217; G. Obs., 2 Feb. and 23 Aug. 1876, 17 March 1875.

XVI

Police and Public Order

When the smacks first came to Grimsby the town was still almost rural in appearance. In 1833 a fox, pursued by the Brocklesby hunt from near Barton, had swum across the dock, taken refuge under a pile of timber, and escaped after being fed. The hunt continued to meet in the sixties and seventies in the Old Market Place. In 1876 they killed a fox from Bradley near the bridge in Flottergate; and such leading townsmen as Dr. Keetley regularly rode to hounds. When there were complaints that the Gas Company were slow in laying mains in new streets in the West Marsh, they explained that the labourers had demanded a ten per cent wage increase and had gone harvesting when it was refused. As soon as the harvest was over the men would come and work at 3s. 6d. a day and the pipes would be laid. Even as late as 1886 the council still thought of the town as small enough to justify the appointment of a new town crier after the 'capabilities' of the applicants had been tested. And when the first park was to be created, Dr. Keetley protested that the town was too rural to need one, and that the scheme was really intended to benefit the estate of the donor. 'There is', he said 'as much necessity for a park in Grimsby as in Switzerland. Its surroundings are park-like and the whole scheme is a building speculation, the Board of Health making the roads instead of the landowner.' No one else ranked Grimsby with Switzerland. In any case, Dr. Keetley was a leading Conservative and the donor of the land was a Liberal; but Dr. Keetley was too honest to allow political prejudice to cloud his judgment and would not have suggested corrupt motives unless he knew the moral quality of the town council, which he did all too well.[1]

A Hull journalist gave a depressing account of the appearance of the town in 1875:

There is no centre to the town. There is certainly a small market place, but it is quite at one end of the town, and there is another market place, styled new, which does not seem to be patronised at all except on Saturday nights, and then chiefly by cheap-jacks, try-your-weights, paltry shows and punching machines. The town is straggling, without order or method in construction. Freeman

Street is by far the most compact and uniform, and should properly be the main artery of the town; but Victoria Street, which takes precedence by inheritance, is a long, winding, rambling place, with dirty hovels, good houses, gaunt timber yards and modern cottages all jumbled together in a manner very offensive to the eye. The road to Cleethorpes is spoilt by ugly gaps, or short rows of dirty shops falling to pieces, and the causeway in front rotting into gaping holes.

As to the quality of local government, he added: 'Perhaps Grimsby may be a little worse than other towns in this respect of internecine quarrelling, though my own impression is that few places could equal it.'[2]

In providing the amenities and the administration necessary for a large town, the council was handicapped not only by the very limited sphere of competence which the nineteenth century assigned to local government, but also by the fact that for many years it was dominated by those who had grown up in the pre-railway age. Chief among these was the town clerk. This office was held when the period of expansion began by George Babb, a henchman of Lord Yarborough. When he died in 1861 his successor was William Grange (1821–1913), who held office until his death. He was a freeman who had been articled to Babb and had been his partner since 1857. In his days as Babb's managing clerk he had made many long journeys by stage-coach in connection with the affairs of the Haven Company; and though, according to his lights, he served the town well, as town clerk he was in a sense a survival from the days of the stage-coach. He and his partner, J. Wintringham, were the leading solicitors in private practice. They were joint secretaries to the Waterworks Company and solicitors to the Anglo-French Steamship Company; and Wintringham was chairman of the Gas Company. By 1887 it was felt by some that the town clerk could not properly hold office while his firm also represented numerous concerns which had official dealings with the corporation. A resolution was tabled that he should devote the whole of his time to his official duties; but the understanding between the town clerk and the members of the council was perfect, and support for the resolution evaporated in an atmosphere of mutual congratulation. If responsibility for what Grimsby became can be assigned to one man, it must be assigned to William Grange.[3]

In Babb's day, the council envisaged little more than the improvements needed for a market town. It was decided to allow farmers and corn merchants to use the town hall as a temporary exchange each Friday, until a proper corn exchange could be provided. A Tudor-classical design by Bellamy and Hardy of Lincoln was accepted and a builder named Good contracted to erect it in the market place for £3,519; but he seems to have bankrupted himself in the attempt as it was completed by his assignees, Wilkinson and Marshall, for £300 above the contract price. The corporation waived all penalties so long as it was completed by February 1857. The southern half served as a butter and poultry market, and the Rifle Corps used a room near the entrance to store their weapons. Having done so much for the farmers, the corporation waited until 1875 before providing a better site for a cattle market on Lord Yarborough's land in Brighowgate, a site which in the present century became the bus station. They decided in 1860 to provide a new town hall to replace the modest Georgian building in the market place, and selected a new site in the Six Acres, on the edge of the built-up portion of the old town. Mr. Heneage was asked to allow a road to be built over his garden ground in Victoria Street to give access. Bellamy, Hardy and Giles of Lincoln, joint architects with Fowler of Louth, provided a design for a large grey brick structure in the style which was then regarded as Italian, and John Brown completed it in 1863 at a cost of £6,494. The building still stands, with later additions at the back, and still serves its original purpose. The old town hall stood until 1868, when the materials were sold by auction. For the last three years of its life it provided a home for the Grammar School which then moved into two new school houses on either side of the new town hall.[4]

 The corporation property in the West Marsh was separated by the Old Dock from the new town in the East Marsh, and if houses were built there, their inhabitants would only be able to reach the Royal Dock and the fish dock by making a long detour through the old town. By 1868 the demand for building land was such that the corporation realised that it could dispose of its land to builders very profitably if only the dock were not in the way. It was therefore decided to have a swing bridge across the dock and to meet the cost by selling land. The contract was let to Head, Wrightson and Co., of Stockton-on-Tees for £5,200, and the bridge was opened in 1873. In the same year a new market for the most populous part of the town was opened on the freemen's land in Freeman Street, and the same firm built a long footbridge across the railway to New Market Street, giving direct access to the Freeman Street market both from the old town and from the West Marsh. In consequence of these developments, it was possible to begin to dispose of building lots in the West Marsh on ninety-nine year leases, the builders undertaking that each house should have not less than eighty square yards of land. Even in the oldest part of the town population was growing, and the last vacant spot in the former St. Mary's churchyard was built on in 1872.[5]

The act which the town had obtained to make it possible to have the bridges also envisaged a park in the West Marsh. With the sale of 100 acres there for railway and dock extension, the possibilities for a park were limited, and the council began to look round, not very energetically, for a park elsewhere. They wanted, but could not get, the southern slopes of Holme Hill, which were already planted with trees. For several years in the summer months, Alderman Wintringham opened his grounds each Thursday afternoon at the abbey. A flag was hoisted at opening time, and anyone was admitted who had obtained a ticket from a councillor. Land beside the Freshney in the West Marsh was leased in 1874 to the trustees of the new hospital at a nominal rent, and it was decided to make a 'public promenade' along the stream, and this was planted in 1877. Edward Heneage of Hainton gave land for a real public park, the present People's Park, in 1881. He was Liberal M.P. for Grimsby and as a ground landlord had benefited more than any other from the expansion of the town. Objectors, who were mainly Conservatives, maintained that the spending of £6,000 on the park would indirectly benefit the estates of Mr. Heneage and of Alderman Wintringham; but any public improvement was bound to enhance the value of someone's property, and Mr. Heneage's gift must be seen as an act of enlightened generosity. The park was opened by the Duke and Duchess of Connaught in 1883. After another thirteen years in the House of Commons and conversion to the cause of Liberal Unionism, Mr. Heneage eventually became a peer; and by that time the corporation had at last decided to create another small park, the Duke of York's Gardens, in the West Marsh.[6]

The Great Grimsby and Cleethorpes Tramway Co., undertook in 1876 to lay a public tramway from the southern end of the town at the Wheatsheaf in Bargate up to Humber Street, near what was then the eastern boundary. Though they made their proposals in 1876 it was not until 1880 that a thousand tons of granite sets were brought from Aberdeen in the steamers *James Hall* and *Duchess* and the work of construction began. At first the government inspector refused to pass the line as properly laid, as the sets were not laid down in the way specified in the plans submitted to Parliament. After some hasty and expensive improvisation, the line was finally accepted as properly laid and the first horse-trams began to run in June 1881. The Tramway Co., was seen as a blessing by the corporation not simply as a public utility but also because the company was responsible for part of the cost of road maintenance. The state of the roads was that which was then usually found in towns—a surface of water-bound macadam, full of holes and occasionally dangerous to fast traffic, with deep pools in the winter and clouds of dust in the summer. People complained that mud was ankle-deep at the Central Market, and in many parts of the town the granite crossings at intersections were the only place where the road could reasonably be crossed on foot. Blinding clouds of dust were felt to be the worst nuisance, and it was often suggested that the streets should be watered twice a day in dry weather to lay the dust instead of only once. A steam-roller to consolidate the road metal was considered, but the resolution was deferred for six months. By 1883 the corporation did have its own steam-roller and was prepared to lend it to the Criterion Tennis Club at a fee to be fixed by the borough surveyor.[7]

As the town grew, the risk from fires increased, and the old volunteer fire-brigade was no longer felt to give proper protection. The fire-engines had been made under the care of the man who attended the pumping engine at the cemetery. They had arrived quickly when the first Theatre Royal was burned down in 1855, but, said the *Stamford Mercury*, 'their utter inefficiency was never more apparent'. However, this was a pretty severe test of efficiency; the theatre was a wooden building coated with tar. An insurance company prudently hedged its risk by presenting a fire-engine with a steam pump, and for many years the volunteers continued to use this. It was not until 1877 that the council decided to have a fire-brigade with a superintendent and seventeen men.[8]

The electric telegraph had appeared in 1856, with offices in Victoria Street linked with Hull, and two years later the Electric Telegraph Co., was allowed to put poles in the Six Acres. The mayor used the telegraph in 1859 to send for a special train to take him to Hull to meet the Harbours of Refuge Commission, only to find that they were not concerned with any harbour south of Filey. The first postal pillar boxes were put up in 1860. A telephone was demonstrated at a lecture in the town hall in 1878, with the mayor in the chair. The phone was connected to another in a dentist's house in Victoria Street, and ladies and gentlemen almost stopped the proceedings as they pressed round to try it. The MS and LR began to use the telephone in 1881 at the docks, the goods warehouse, the engine sheds and the main office.

Telephones were installed generally in 1888 when the corporation allowed the wires to be carried under the foot-bridge over the railway. By 1893 it was possible to make calls to Hull.[9]

A Siemens electric arc light was demonstrated as an entertainment at the music hall in 1878. A portable steam engine was started outside the theatre to supply current, and suddenly the audience was astonished by a hissing noise and a blaze of light which dimmed the gas jets. There was a fire later in the week caused by a short circuit and an escape of gas. In 1882 the Cleethorpes Local Board had the main streets lit by arc lights, which were more spectacular than reliable. In Grimsby it was not until 1891 that electric lights were put in the town hall, and councillors soon complained about the dimness of the bulbs.[10]

The police force grew with the town, and the ordinary policemen had a hard time. A constable on night duty was attacked by a crowd of fishermen and his staff was taken from him in January 1858. He seems to have been the first victim of the violent habits of some of the fishermen. They, and still more the shore-bound parasites who lived off them, were to present the most intractable of police problems. They were violent, immoral and in some cases well able to tempt the police with bribes. To keep and recruit a fully efficient force was almost beyond the capacity of the chief constable and the watch committee. The temptations were too many, good men too few, and good men and bad could never be certain of the temper and prejudices of the watch committee. The independence of the force, however, was never threatened except in 1854 when Lord Annesley, the borough member, was asked to oppose any measure to consolidate it with the county force. The chief constable remained answerable only to the watch committee and the Home Office inspectors.[11]

When necessary he was able to bring police from outside. Fifty came from Hull during the 1862 election, but even so the rioters sacked the Yarborough Hotel. Another election riot damaged the Royal Hotel in 1877. The police were reproached for their conduct in 1862, and it was said that the introduction of men from Hull influenced the temper of the rioters. But the authorities were unlucky rather than inefficient—elections in Grimsby were still the signal for a return to the state of nature. In 1865 they were lucky and there were no mistakes. Voters were alleged to have been kidnapped by Tories and taken to sea in fishing boats, but this was the kind of thing which always happened before the Ballot Act. There was no riot: the police were backed by a detachment of the 17th Hussars.[12]

From the first establishment of a regular force in 1846 it was hard to maintain proper discipline. Opportunities for other work were sufficiently numerous to take much of the sting out of the ultimate penalty which could be inflicted for indiscipline—dismissal from the force. The sergeant and two constables were dismissed in 1853 on the complaint of the superintendent. Handbills were circulated stating that there were posts now available for a sergeant and three constables. Later in the same year two men were reprimanded for being drunk on duty and one of them was dismissed when he was found drunk again. This was bad enough, but still more serious was the unrebutted allegation that the superintendent himself had a criminal record. Such things were not unknown in the early days of some borough forces, watch committees no doubt acting on the principle that a reformed thief would know the habits of others not yet reformed. At any rate in Grimsby, one of the radicals, Thomas Newby, declared that the superintendent, Isaac Anson, had once been convicted for stealing lead. The minutes of the watch committee required him to 'clear his character from such an imputation' but contain no evidence that he ever did. His career lasted only another two years. Three constables were dismissed in 1858 for disobeying a sergeant and the superintendent was accused of stealing a ham. At first the committee decided 'that Mr. Anson had acted in the matter respecting the ham in accordance with his duty as police superintendent'. But there were more complaints from seven different constables, and as the easiest way out the committee decided to dismiss the whole force and get a new one. There was loud applause from the public benches in the council chamber.[13]

The new force was bedevilled by town politics. The new superintendent owed his position to the radical party of T. Newby and W. Colley Parker, who were both also savouring their recent triumph in electing their candidate as churchwarden. There was a rowdy dispute at a meeting of the watch committee in 1859 to appoint a sergeant. The mayor refused to put a motion, his opponents seized the minute book, and he loudly called on the superintendent to do his duty. There was a fight on the floor and the superintendent finally handed the book not to the mayor but to Parker, who sat on it. This superintendent survived a feud of twenty years with the committee and retired at sixty-five because of his declining health. There were few high-lights like this in his career, but the atmosphere was always much the same. His successor, Job Waldram, had been a sergeant under him.

Under Campbell and Waldram the inspectors of constabulary regularly reported the force as efficient, though their private communications with its head may have been to a rather different effect. Much of the surviving evidence points to extraordinary laxity. The police career of Benjamin Coo is almost classical. He was appointed in 1860 and reprimanded after only five days for drunkenness and playing dominoes in three different public houses while on duty, and was fined 10s. He was drunk again in 1863 and finally dismissed for drunkenness in 1864. He had precursors in the force. Sergeant Hardcastle had been invited to resign nine months after his appointment, but before he had gone the drunkenness of the constables drew attention to the scarcity of reliable men and he kept his position until 1860 when, after being suspended for insubordination and misconduct, he resigned. P.C. 22 Loft was requested to resign for being found drunk and asleep on the steps of the Corn Exchange. Constables were constantly being warned, fined, or dismissed for similar offences, or for being too drunk to come on duty; and the press reported cases of policemen fighting one another, coming out of brothels and trying to blackmail publicans. No doubt the press often reported the complaints of a single biassed councillor as objective truth, but all too often the minutes of the watch committee contain evidence that their complaints were believed to be true. And even in perfectly straight-forward matters, men were constantly found not to be doing their duty properly. In 1859 constables were reprimanded for allowing prisoners to go at large instead of putting them in the lock-up; and in 1875 P.C. Bates was 'cautioned not to allow prisoners to get drunk from their friends or otherwise whilst being carried to Lincoln gaol'.[14]

Drink was, of course, partly the root of the trouble. In a drinking community it was hard to find sober individuals who would make good policemen; and as the force was then organised, their duties obliged a few men to spend a good deal of time in public houses. The corporation, by a vote of five to four, adopted the Publc House Closing Act of 1864, and public houses were closed from 1 a.m. to 4 a.m. Under the Licensing Act of 1871 the borough magistrates closed them from 11 p.m. to 6 a.m. Some constables were said to be too arduous in watching public houses to see whether the law was being broken. It was an offence for them to drink on duty and for a publican to serve them. The watch committee ordered the men to wear armlets when on duty so that no publican could commit the offence unwittingly. But too many felt that free drinks were one of the attractions of being in a disciplined force, and most of them, including the sergeants refused to have anything to do with the armlets. The old system was equally attractive to some of the publicans. In 1879 the committee deplored the conduct of the landlord of the *Leeds Arms* in giving presents to policemen, and the men were warned that any of them who accepted would be dismissed.[15]

In spite of many lapses, the borough police, in its own fashion performed the duties for which it had been created, and numerous others which fresh legislation imposed on it. The police were made responsible for seeing that the Freeman Street market was closed at 11 p.m. on Saturdays. They inspected premises in the West Marsh where explosives were kept, had two ropes 'for the purpose of lassoing mad or dangerous dogs', and from 1874, when Mr. Boterill of Cleethorpes Road received the first one, they were responsible for petroleum licences. The first police station had been at the old town hall. When the new town hall was opened in 1863 the new station was there, but the cells were too far from the most troublesome part of the town; so a branch lock-up was opened in King Edward Street and from 1890 was connected with headquarters by telephone. Occasionally constables were required to go on duty in plain clothes, and sometimes, probably worried about possible damage to their clothing, they refused. The first two plain-clothes men were appointed in 1878, though very shortly the chief constable reported that one would be enough. The behaviour of criminals was a more eloquent testimonial than the routine reports of the inspectors of constabulary. By 1878 it was commonly said that much of the criminal population had moved outside the boundary and were living in New Clee, and the county magistrates for the Bradley Haverstoe sessions were reminded that the densely populated streets and terraces of their area were not properly policed.[16]

Brothels, not always distinguishable from other resorts of entertainment, gave less trouble to the police than public houses, but only because it was extremely difficult to prosecute a brothel-keeper successfully. Alderman Smethurst in 1882 tentatively suggested that licensed prostitution, under the Contagious Diseases Act, might have to be considered. He claimed that the immorality of the town was such that parents were afraid to allow their daughters to come and work in it. He believed the watch committee had not done its duty and said that he saw scores of girls as young as fifteen 'roaming the streets in a life of vice and degradation, running by scores from one public house to another and becoming reduced to such a state of degradation as is horrible to see'. They were very often a cause of men employed by him failing to go to sea (though with equal propriety he could have said that it was fishermen who caused the degradation of the girls). As a smack-owner he lost heavily, but as a leading nonconformist he was obviously afraid of religious opinion, and when his proposal was attacked he hastily dissociated himself from it.[17]

The powers of the police were insufficient to deal with the evil. In 1880 the chief constable had been ordered to 'get up at least two cases against brothel-keepers and prosecute them at the next quarter sessions'. This was difficult, as complaints from householders were necessary and they were not easy to procure in the worst districts of the town. The watch committee, however, was able to reprimand a sergeant for having a woman of loose character as his housekeeper; and when Smethurst made his complaint the chief constable claimed that he prosecuted more brothel-keepers than any other chief constable in the country. He may well have done. The Victoria Music Hall was a place much frequented by prostitutes. Policemen were forbidden to attend the music hall or the theatre on duty or in their own time. Frederick W. Hoffman, the manager of the music hall, had formerly worked at Cardiff and Liverpool. When he applied for a renewal of his licence in 1883 the magistrates refused because of his 'defiance of the authorities' and because the police objected to the way in which the hall was managed. Within a week the hall, fully insured, was burned down, and Hoffman's foresight had its reward. The manager of the Theatre Royal had asked to have a constable attend each performance, but this was refused until 1891 when he was allowed to have a constable so long as he contributed 15s. a week to his wages.[18]

Such was the moral quality of the town, and more particularly that part of it nearest to the docks into which, year by year, the fishing industry was bringing hundreds of lads, most of whom were homeless and all in need of some degree of care and supervision. Attention must now be given to these lads and to the way in which the community discharged its responsibility to them.

NOTES

1. LRSM, 13 Nov. 1833; G. Obs., 8 March 1876, 15 March 1875; MB, 14 May, 22 Sept. 1886, 30 Sept. 1881.
2. G. Obs., 26 May 1875.
3. G. News, 13 June 1913; LRSM, 6 March 1868, 7 April 1865; G. Obs., 4 May 1887.
4. MB, 17 Feb. 1854, 16 May and 6 Aug. 1855, 8 Nov. 1856, 5 Oct. 1858, 27 April 1860, 15 Oct. 1875, 5 Sept. 1860, 15 March and 5 Aug. 1861, 31 March 1865, 1 June 1868; VCH, 482.

5. MB, 13 Aug. and 14 Dec. 1868, 29 April and 5 May 1870; 19 May 1871, 3 Feb. 1873, 12 Aug. 1872, 16 May 1873; G. Obs., 6 March 1872.
6. MB, 20 Sept. 1875, 2 July 1877, Aug.–Sept. 1881.
7. MB, 15 May and 22 Sept. 1876; G. Obs., 14 July 1880, 27 April and 8 June 1881; MB, 1 July 1881; G. Obs., 9 June 1875; Highway MB, 2 April 1883.
8. LRSM, 26 Jan. 1855; MB, 5 Feb. 1877.
9. MB, 10 July 1858, 27 April 1860; G. Gaz., 9 May 1856; G. Obs., 27 Feb. 1878, 18 May 1881, 17 May 1893; MB, 18 May 1888.
10. F. Baker, *The Story of Cleethorpes*, 143; MB, 23 Feb. 1891; G. Obs., 30 Sept. 1891.
11. MB(WC), 4 Jan. 1858.
12. MB, 19 Nov. 1877; LRSM, 14 July 1865.
13. MB(WC), 25 April and 3 Nov. 1853, 11 June and 1 Sept. 1856, 19 and 29 Nov. 1858.
14. Ibid., 5 May 1860, 9 March 1863, 8 May 1864, 10 and 17 Nov. 1859, 21 March and 27 April 1860, 8 March 1859, 3 May and 5 Aug. 1875.
15. Ibid., 6 Feb. 1865; G. Obs., 21 July 1875; MB(WC), 6 Jan. 1879.
16. Ibid., 5 May 1873, 18 March 1874, 17 Oct. 1889, 3 Nov. 1890, 17 Dec. and 18 Nov. 1878.
17. G. News, 6 Jan. 1882.
18. MB(WC), 6 Dec. 1880, 3 Jan. 1881, 1 Dec. 1882, 17 Nov. 1891; LRSM, 2 and 9 March 1882.

XVII

Smacks, Apprentices and Owners

To the end of the century the demand of the fishing industry for lads was almost insatiable. There were times when, to outsiders, it appeared to be consuming lads as an engine used coal. It simply could not go on without them. But the lads were not precisely consumed. Many broke their indentures and ran away. As many or more survived their apprenticeship, became fishermen, and even rose to be skippers and smack-owners. Many died at sea; and many were marked by the diseases they contracted on shore and the harsh treatment they experienced in the smacks. A majority, perhaps, became the future citizens of the town, local government electors, members of clubs and co-operative societies, fathers of the generation which served in mine-sweepers and stormed Hohenzollern Redoubt; and some lived long enough to serve in the Great War themselves.

Until the nineties, hardly a smack could have put to sea without them. In a crew of five, three would be apprentices. There were instances where the skipper was the only person on board who was not an apprentice; and, though very rarely, a smack was known to sail manned entirely by apprentices. In 1872 the apprentices out-numbered the fishermen by 1,350 to 1,150. They were bound for five or six years, sometimes as early as the age of twelve. 229 were indentured in 1868, 424 in 1872 and 576 in 1877. Partly because of the expansion of fishing, they were being enrolled at a rate more than sufficient to maintain their numbers. By 1877 there should have been 2,259 apprentices, if all those enrolled had stayed at sea, and the total labour force should have exceeded 5,000. In fact, it was under 3,500—1,794 apprentices and 1,676 men. It is clear that many deserted or disappeared from the industry in other ways; but for those who remained, the chances of rising to be a skipper were good, though on the whole a boy was more likely to be drowned than to become the owner of his smack. The minority of boys who lived with their parents when not at sea received wages, rising from 9s. to 14s. a week. Other apprentices were paid as their masters thought fit, and it was the general opinion that they had more pocket money than was good for them.[1]

About half of them lived in their masters' houses when not at sea, but the proportion was declining as many smack-owners ceased to act as skippers. Sometimes other lodgings in the town were provided, but very often a boy was given money and told to provide for himself. Swanston and Stoneham, who reported on apprenticeship for the Board of Trade concluded 'that in too many cases he would appear to be regarded as merely part of the machinery for taking fish'. The chairman of the Smack-owners Association in 1878 looked back with regret to the days when they could apprentice lads from the families of their neighbours, and lamented that they had first been driven to recruit from workhouses, and then, when slanderous reports had almost stopped up that source, they had been compelled to go to reformatories and take 'lads, who had been convicted of practices of the worst kind'.[2]

The slanderous reports had some foundations, though it took poor-law guardians a long time to realise this. The Bethnell Green guardians sent a committee in 1873 to look into the condition of their boys in Grimsby. Though they complained that boys were not properly supervised on shore, for the most part they had nothing but praise for the system. They had sent fifty-six boys to Grimsby in five years, and only five had been imprisoned. They were always highly regarded by their masters. In the smacks their sleeping accommodation was the same as the skippers'. In their lodgings they had a feather bed with sheets and blankets of good quality. All had the same suit of clothes—a blue braided jacket with a velvet collar, a black silk vest, blue or black trousers, sometimes with a stripe down the middle. None of the boys questioned wanted to return to the workhouse. They had meat, pudding and potatoes every day at sea. Some of the smacks were so beautifully fitted out that they were like gentlemen's yachts, and some no doubt were, as it was the time of the annual cleaning and refitting, when a regetta was usually held in the Humber. The guardians were perhaps inclined to see the system through the eyes of the alderman who stressed the admirable qualities of owners and told them that few of the apprentices in prison had come from workhouses. But they were not altogether uncritical. They favoured a proposal, cherished by the Smack-owners Association, that skippers should be required to hold a certificate. They felt also that boys should not be apprenticed until they had been to sea in winter, and that there should be some provision for amusement and recreation, since the attractions of the beershops, and of the theatre with its spacious bar, were proving far too strong.[3]

Nevertheless many boards of guardians were beginning to look askance at fishing, particularly after a local government board inspector had told the St. Pancras guardians that they were acting illegally in sending boys to be apprenticed more than thirty miles away. Some unions continued to evade the law by having the apprentices bound on ordinary forms, in which the guardians were not named as parties in the indenture; but for many years the Caistor board, in whose area Grimsby was situated, refused to provide apprentices altogether. The chairman observed that boys were needed on the land and that there were rumours of cruelty to them at sea. When they did agree to let a boy go on trial to a smack-owner, Harrison Mudd, now one of the Grimsby guardians, urged that ordinary forms of indenture should be used; but other guardians felt they had a parental responsibility which they could not devolve upon the Grimsby guardians and magistrates. When a circular about the need for lads in the navy was received from the local government board, the chairman said that they would be more useful on the land. Mr. Wintringham, for Grimsby, retorted that boys trained as farm labourers were likely to end their days in the workhouse which first launched them into the world and every effort should be made to get them into the navy or merchant service. As it was, there were no pauper boys ready for employment, and too many of the guardians were like Satan rebuking sin. Four years later they were prepared to send two boys to Mr. Satchell, a New Clee smack-owner, who undertook to board them in his own house. Mr. Mudd assured them there was now less reason for supervision by the guardians as apprentices were now under a Board of Trade inspector. He did not tell them that this inspector had gained all his relevant experience as secretary of the Smack-owners Association; nor could they foresee that regulations by the Board of Trade was to make little real change in Grimsby. A few years later they were furiously angry with Satchell for abandoning a boy who had fallen ill at sea and refusing all responsibility for his treatment in the Caistor workhouse hospital.[4]

By 1876 press reports about Grimsby had proved so damaging that the supply of labour from workhouses had almost ceased. Only eight of the 534 apprentices indentured in that year came from workhouses, and in the following year only two out of 560. However, workhouse boys had generally been very small, and some owners were aggrieved when they had to deal with guardians who refused to put down any money to clothe the boy for his new life. There were other sources of supply, and they were glad to turn to them. Many lads were sent by the Essex magistrates from the Enfield reformatory, and the superintendent of mercantile marine thought them the best boys. In 1883 Bernard Monds, a missionary among the fishermen, shared this view. Many boys came from the Shoe Black Brigade and from the Discharged Prisoners' Aid Society, and he told a Commons select committee that when they turned out well, they were better than workhouse boys. The select committee was told that boys were again coming from workhouses and that some guardians made an annual visit of inspection.[5]

The select committee was in part an inquiry, not very assiduously pursued, into abuses of the apprenticeship system in the various fishing ports of England and Wales, and in part a forum in which the leaders of the industry were able to ventilate their grievances and do what they could, by plain speaking or otherwise, to repair their tattered reputation. It was a pretty delicate business. Sometimes it seemed best to stress the virtues of the system, the noble qualities of the lads, and the careful treatment they received. Thomas Freer, a skipper for twenty-six years and a teetotaller who wore the blue ribbon when he appeared before the committee, thought that apprentices were dealt with too gently. 'I should like apprentices', he said, 'to go through the same hard rule as we went through. They are too well treated, I think, now. They are more like gentlemen's sons than apprentices to the fishing trade.' On the whole, however, it was easier to dwell upon the shortcomings of the apprentices. 'The conduct ashore', an anonymous magistrate wrote, 'of this increasing class of boys is becoming a serious social problem'—a phrase which to Victorians carried an imputation of prostitution and disease.

It would be vain and Utopian to seek to do away with the amusements which have such attractions for boys fresh from the discomforts and hard life of the fishing grounds. We may keep a check upon the character of the amusements and insist that the places of amusement are closed in reasonable time. Beyond this we cannot go. Many of these poor lads are parish apprentices. It must therefore rest with the parish authorities to turn out better boys, and there is ample room for improvement in this direction.[6]

The select committee asked the chief constable whether the bad fishing boys, who were, he thought, about ten or twenty per cent of the whole group, were worse than in other classes and he answered emphatically:

I do think so. They are more difficult to deal with. They are nearly all from the dangerous classes. They are street Arabs from large towns, convicted over and over again. They are tramping thieves without a bit of shoe on their foot or clothes on their back very often. They get well fed and then there is no holding them. I believe smack-owners take a class of boys that no one else would look at. Their feet are in a filthy condition. They have to scrape it off them and put them into a bath before they go into the house.

He said that a large proportion of the boys had been in prison before they came to Grimsby, which was 'the very best place for a tramping boy to come to be reformed'. Older apprentices frequented brothels. Henry Smethurst complained that too many of his apprentices had venereal disease and that he found it expensive to provide medical attention for them. Some were of the opinion that lads went to prison at Lincoln to be cured by a doctor and that a training ship in the Humber—often urged as a panacea—would become a floating hospital for the casualties of love.[7]

The problem would have been more tractable if apprentices had been properly accommodated between voyages, but most of them were not. Many were in common lodging houses, the master paying the lodging-house keeper £1 a quarter and 6d. for each meal eaten by the apprentice. Others had quarters in beer-houses, and Stoneham and Swanston in 1878 found that too many lads were simply given money and left to fend for themselves. They were completely uncared for until wanted for the next voyage, and often spent the money on 'debauchery'. 'It is useless', noted the *Grimsby Observer*, 'to disguise that many mere boys are tempted away to their ruin, and that night after night they are absent from their lodgings, and are literally kept in hiding by prostitutes until discovered by the police.' Under an act of 1880 the corporation could have enforced the licensing and inspection of lodging houses, but failed to do so. It was easier to leave alone, and to fall in with the view of the majority of smack-owners who hypocritically opposed licensing on the grounds that no system would work unless apprentices were compelled by law to live in licensed lodgings. Henry Smethurst, J.P., an alderman and chairman of the school board, told the select committee that he had 80–100 apprentices and two or three lodging houses 'where the people take them in entirely for me, and others are distributed about, two and three and four in a house'. He was asked whether he supervised the lodgings personally, and answered that he had several men, four or five at each house, not skippers, but men working on the land. His vagueness about how many apprentices he had raises the suspicion that these men were not supervisors at all but simply other lodgers. Smethurst was not the only owner to give vague answers about how many apprentices he had. Bernard Monds, the missionary, thought the best system was that of indoor apprentices living with their masters, and that many who were called indoor apprentices were nothing of the kind, but were boarded out with widows and lodging-house keepers.[8]

The county prison was an essential adjunct to the Grimsby system of apprenticeship. Under the Merchant Shipping Act of 1854 (17 and 18 Vict. c. 104) owners could order the arrest without warrant of apprentices and others who deserted their ships. Offenders were tried summarily by magistrates and committed to their ship, or, if they refused, to prison. As early as 1864 it was noted that many apprentices were deserting from smacks and that some were persuaded to do so by other owners who were short of men. In the sixties the borough magistrates were quite commonly gaoling deserting apprentices, and soon the ritual of imprisonment had become so deeply embedded in the system that the younger Smethurst could publicly take pride in the fact that less than half of his apprentices, twenty-one out of sixty-five, had been to prison.[9]

It was the imprisonment of apprentices which, with allegations about cruelty at sea, for several years almost stopped the supply of apprentices from workhouses. In 1873 several national newspapers printed a paragraph about Grimsby fisher-lads from the *Lincolnshire Chronicle*:

Lincoln rings with indignation at the treatment these lads receive at the hands of the authorities. The lads are brought by train, which generally arrives about 9.30 p.m. and are heavily chained together, in numbers from three to five, and in this way are marched through the busiest part of the High Street of our city for more than a mile to their destination.

The clerk of the Holborn Union visited Grimsby and the superintendent of police showed him the chain, which he called a light one, of $\frac{7}{8}$-inch diameter, with four or five handcuffs attached. The use of such chains, it was explained, was fairly general. One policeman could take charge of several prisoners, so reducing the cost to the public. When the Home Office prohibited the chaining of apprentices, they were taken to prison from the station in the horse omnibus, until other passengers began to object too strongly.[10]

The number of apprentices sent to the Lincoln prison each year rose from 20 in 1872 to 132 in the following year and 244 in 1877. More than half the sentences of imprisonment passed by Grimsby magistrates were on fisher-lads. Stoneham and Swanston thought that the magistrates should be free from all personal interest in fishing, but regretted that this was impossible, as almost the entire community was interested. Indeed, of the seventeen men who were magistrates in 1881, eight were clearly financially interested in fishing, and the five who were described as of independent means may very well have held mortgages on smacks. One, at any rate, who looked thoroughly independent, Edward Bannister, was so far involved that in 1881 he became a director of a new steam-trawling company. He was probably the anonymous magistrate whose opinions on the morals of fisher-lads have been quoted above. Like others, this magistrate saw it as his duty to use his office to force lads to go to sea, and he pointed out that 200 of the 471 lads who had been brought before the bench in 1877 had returned to their smacks.[11]

In dealing with apprentices magistrates were not often oppressed by the solemnity of their task. They would cheerfully present offenders with the choice between the sea and the county gaol, and they would refer jokingly to the exercise which they would get on the treadmill. One example of magisterial behaviour will serve as an example of what was all too common. The presiding magistrate was the mayor, Captain James Reed (of the Volunteers) who, as portmaster, was not clearly free from all interest in the case. The offenders were two apprentices who complained that they were insufficiently clad. One said that when they were fishing off the Faroes there were only three shirts and two pairs of stockings full of holes to be worn by five apprentices, presumably on a cod-liner. He was given twenty-eight days hard labour. The other said that he was ashamed when a man in the street asked him whether he was wearing a rag or a shirt. 'What has that got to do with going to sea?' the mayor asked. 'Many people have got ragged shirts.' With this judicial aside on the state of society, he dismissed the lad with a caution.[12]

The one magistrate who did protest against the system was Dr. T. B. Keetley, a surgeon, a former mayor, an amateur pugilist and a leading Conservative. At a rate-payers' dinner in 1875 he responded to a toast to the magistrates, and took the imprisonment of apprentices as his theme:

He thought it was a great mistake for them continually to be bringing their apprentices before the magistrates. How was it possible to make a bad boy a good one by affording him only ten minutes in which to determine whether he would go to Lincoln or serve his employer? He thought there was too much sending to Lincoln with regard to these boys. He knew of boys who were badly treated and kept three or four days on deck with their boots full of water, and he found there was often a greater amount of intelligence in the lads than in the skippers themselves.

Smack-owners, mainly his political opponents, were present, but no one protested against his views. And James Alward, a pioneer smack-owner, was another whose conscience was stirred:

As at present conducted [he was reported as saying], the trawl fish trade of the port—he did not profess to know anything of the cod trade—was a disgrace to any civilised country. The number of convictions which took place year by year before the magistrates for keeping the trade in existence was becoming greater and greater. It appeared to him that the trade only survived by means of magistrates, policemen and prisoners. They could not find a similar state of things existing in any other fishing port in the kingdom.

In fact, as was pointed out by a magistrate, the situation in Hull was no better. Yet there were no such convictions of apprentices in Scots or Irish ports, and very few were imprisoned except at Hull and Grimsby. Soon the system was to survive only at Grimsby, and even Keetley and Alward would be found passing sentences of imprisonment on deserters.[13]

The county magistrates were critical of Grimsby. When the prison chaplain made his annual report to them in 1877 he observed that many lads who chose to come to prison rather than go to sea did so because of ill-treatment and lack of proper clothing. The chairman, Sir Charles Anderson, then noted that almost a thousand Grimsby apprentices had been in the new prison since it was first opened. It was doubtful, in his opinion, whether many of the pauper apprentices could be considered as free agents, and that the attention of the Home Secretary should be called to the situation. The threat of official intervention stung the Smack-owners Association into life. The chairman, Harrison Mudd, declared that the chaplain's report did them a great injustice. The source of much of the trouble, he said, was that vessels were springing up like mushrooms and they were glad to get men and boys from anywhere. They ought themselves to approach the Home Secretary, and they might get government assistance in establishing a training ship; but James Alward again spoke of imprisonment as a great evil and asked what good an official inquiry could possibly do. It could only, in his words, expose their own rottenness. He remembered the years when no lads were sent to prison, but now they had sunk into as bad a state as that of the merchant service before Plimsoll began his agitation.[14]

The Home Secretary agreed to meet a deputation, and they were introduced to him by Sir E. Watkin, M.P., chairman of the MS and LR, and by his son A. M. Watkin, member for Grimsby. The deputation (H. Smethurst, H. Mudd, W. Moody and J. O. Hawkes) assured the minister that the remarks of the Lincoln chaplain, which had received wide publication, were entirely unfounded, and the prejudice they had caused had largely stopped recruitment from workhouses. Consequently they were now taking apprentices from the lowest strata of society, and the immorality to which they were exposed on shore frequently led them to desert, so that the unhappy owners were compelled to take them before a magistrate. Yet short sentences and mild treatment in prison removed all deterrent effect from prison sentences. A few weeks later the Grimsby case was again put to a select committee by Edward Bannister, who represented the magistrates and maintained that apprentices were not ill-treated, and were not sent to prison without good reason. The reason, he explained, why boys were not imprisoned at such ports as Yarmouth and Sheringham was that they were not apprentices—an admission almost as damaging to his case as his insistence that boys often ran away from their Grimsby masters to take service in Scarborough and other ports. The governor of Lincoln gaol, examined on the same occasion, said that prison life did great harm to a boy without preventing him from deserting again. Even boys of twelve had been sent to him, but no boys ever showed marks of ill-treatment. He failed, however, to mention that when boys were released from his custody they were left to walk back to Grimsby. They often applied for a night's lodging to the relieving officer at Market Rasen, but it was his rule to refuse them.[15]

The Home Office was sufficiently concerned to send Stoneham and Swanston, whose report has already been referred to, to Grimsby. They drew attention to the case of one apprentice who had been imprisoned twenty-two times. Some boys, they found, saw no disgrace in going to 'Lincoln College', as they called the prison. To avoid going to sea some would destroy ship's property or even mutilate themselves. It was quite understandable, their report said that in bad weather a boy with venereal disease should prefer prison to life at sea in a smack. The people of Grimsby could have averted the demoralisation of the boys if they had exerted themselves in time. The owners who profited from the exploitation of apprentice labour owed it to them to provide proper and decent lodgings. They, and indeed the whole community, the report concluded, had failed to discharge their responsibility.

There must have been some feature peculiar to fishing which caused so many lads to prefer imprisonment. There was indeed. The peculiarity of the industry was not only to be found in the hardships of a seafaring life, but also in a very considerable risk of death, and, for some, very rough treatment and exposure to insane cruelty. The hardship was unavoidable. The crews of smacks spent longer uninterrupted periods at sea than most merchant seamen. Fishing stopped only in a storm, or when there was too little wind to draw the trawl. The hardships cannot be measured except in the numbers of apprentices running away from them. The dangers, however, can be measured in the casualty lists, though until 1880 loss of life at sea from fishing vessels was frequently not reported to any official agency.

Even from incomplete statistics, it seems that 1865 was probably the worst year. In a February storm forty men and boys were drowned, and it seems likely that the losses for the whole year would amount to fifty or more. In the eighties losses were to be much higher than this (e.g. 120 in 1883) but by then the total labour force had grown fourfold. Grimsby was more dangerous than other fishing ports. For the period 1884-91 the loss of life each year was 11 per 1,000 men employed in Grimsby smacks, as against 7·5 per 1,000 men employed in all other fishing ports; and average Grimsby losses were probably a good deal higher than 11 per 1,000, a rate based on the assumption that 6,000 persons were employed in the smacks. For the period 1880-95 the annual loss of life among Grimsby fishermen certainly exceeded 12 per 1,000. If a boy remained at sea as a fisherman it was probable that he would be drowned or killed before he was 60.[16]

The risk of death was particularly great for an apprentice. Ignorance and lack of supervision killed many lads. It was thought that at Grimsby washing decks was particularly dangerous. The bulwarks were only two feet six inches high, and a sea could easily take a boy overboard. 'I think with a little care it might be avoided,' said Bernard Monds. 'Lads do come fresh to sea and are told to clean the decks. They throw the bucket overboard. They have no idea of the resisting force of the sea. They put the rope round their hands, and if they do not pull the bucket up, the bucket will pull them down.' There was also danger in ferrying boxes of fish in small boats from the smack to the fleet carrier. At Hull, where the practices were very similar, Councillor Ansell esti-

Losses at Sea from Grimsby Fishing Vessels

1876	15	1886	46
1877	30	1887	67
1878	23	1888	62
1879	34	1889	70
1880	63	1890	127
1881	83	1891	43
1882	72	1892	55
1883	120	1893	78
1884	76	1894	81
1885	62	1895	80

mated that less than five per cent of his apprentices were lost; and of ninety-seven lads apprenticed from the Hull and Sculcoates workhouses, four or five were lost. After a boy had survived his apprenticeship, the risk was not quite so great. Stoneham and Swanston thought the life a healthy and hardy one. The boys they saw were well fed, and did not give the impression of being afraid or ill-treated. The skippers, from the same social class as many of the boys, were rough but not unkind, and Monds, who spent a month at sea each year, knew of no cases of cruelty.[17]

Others, however, were fairly sure that there was a good deal of cruelty. Isaac Miller, superintendent of the Fisherlands' Institute felt that although most boys were not exposed to cruelty, it was not exceptional. He had seen boys with their eyes so swollen that they could not see through them. Flint, one of the Bethnell Green guardians who made his own private investigation, thought the apprentices neglected at shore and ill treated at sea. The magistrates abetted the owners, and he mentioned an instance of boys who went to the police to complain of cruelty. Their protests were ignored and they were sentenced to fourteen days imprisonment for desertion. A skipper was, however, fined for blacking his apprentice's face with a frying pan and then putting a line round his neck to make him think he was going to be hanged. The Beverley guardians had very great difficulty in cancelling the indentures of a boy, said to be very unsatisfactory, whose face had been rubbed with herring heads by the third hand, and who had then been lashed by the skipper and made to take sixty casts with the forty-fathom lead, and carry the anchor stock for two hours. Two Norwich boys of fifteen who had been taken by a smack-owner for a trial trip were left with no means of getting home when they decided not to be bound apprentice; and Flint heard of an apprentice, driven to desert and imprisoned for twenty-one days only seven weeks before the end of his time. When the skipper and mate of the *Effort* were fined for assaulting an apprentice, the surgeon who treated him said that his thigh was so badly injured that at first it had appeared broken.[18]

It is difficult to know just how prevalent cruelty was. What is certain is that people generally thought it was far too common and that in some cases it may have caused the death of apprentices. The select committee of 1882 was not convinced, though it did refer to the conviction of two hands on the *Achievement* of Grimsby for 'cruel, base and disgusting treatment of two lads', and to the murder of two lads in a Hull smack. Two pauper apprentices committed suicide within a few days of one another in 1873. Frederick Donker, serving as cook in the *Jubilee* of Grimsby, was from St. George's-in-the-East workhouse. He was only sixteen when he jumped overboard off Flamborough Head after the skipper had beaten him with a broken hand-spike. Frederick Brewer, a pauper boy from Dover Union, jumped from the smack *Wilberforce* of Grimsby after being beaten for upsetting a tin of paraffin. The skipper of the *Jubilee* was charged with manslaughter and the St. George's guardians decided to send no more boys to Grimsby until after the trial. He was not convicted, as the judge advised the grand jury to find no true bill. In Lincoln gaol, where the chaplain frequently heard complaints of cruelty at sea, Edward Powell, aged fifteen, told the chaplain that the skipper treated him violently, and he died of an abscess at the base of the skull. This, if treated as a dying declaration, could have brought about an indictment for murder; but at the inquest his master, H. W. Earle, described him as a very untruthful boy, and no proceedings were instituted.[19]

In 1878 the Smack-owners' Association complained to the Home Secretary

> that owing to the rapid growth of the trade and in consequence of certain prejudices which exist in many parts of the country against the fishery we have been unable for several years to obtain a sufficient number of apprentices from Union workhouses or from other places where boys of a fair, respectable class can be found.

The Board of Trade was on the whole inclined to give the industry a clean bill, but even so the Board found it necessary to issue new regulations in 1880. Boys were no longer to be left to find their own lodgings, they were to come under the supervision of the superintendent of mercantile marine, and skippers and mates were to be required to hold certificates. George Swanston, the official whose inspection had helped to spur the board to take action, pointedly refused to give any opinion as to the conduct of the magistrates and told the Association that they had 'had the privilege of dictating their own terms'. So the owners were left to reform themselves, and proceeded to found the Fisherlads' Institute on a site in Orwell Street given by Col. Tomline.[20]

For some time there had been concern about the skippers' lack of education. Many were illiterate, could not keep a log, and had no knowledge of the principles of navigation. They found their way by dead reckoning and by feeling the sea-bottom with the lead. Indeed knowledge of the nature of the sea-bed under the smack was far more important than knowledge of latitude and longitude. Nevertheless it was feared that ignorance could be very dangerous as the smacks were driven further to the north in search of fish and that men of the quality of those who were now taking smacks to sea would be unable to pass on their knowledge to apprentices in the traditional way. As the industry expanded the demand for skippers was so great that there were instances of apprentices in command of smacks. The time had now come, it seemed, for the provision of a more formal nautical education which would somehow produce better skippers and raise the moral tone. This was emphasised by Mr. Daubney at the laying of the foundation stone of the Fisherlads' Institute:

> It might be asked why these lads needed special attention. The reason was this. They were all untutored and uneducated. Most of the men and a large proportion of the skippers had been drawn from the same sources, and they had not had the advantages which it was proposed to afford the boys in the institute. The boys could learn nothing from them either by precept or example that would tend to elevate their moral and social conduct. When these boys were properly educated they would in due course of time take the place of the men and skippers under whom they now served. The improvement that would be effected must of necessity be of very great advantage to fishermen and to society generally.

These great aims were to be achieved economically. The Fisherlads' Institute, opened by Lord Yarborough in 1880, cost about £3,500. This was less than the cost of three new smacks or of one of the new steam trawlers; and the expenditure on it each year was less than one per cent of the railway freight charges.[21]

It was not to be expected that the institute would be an instantaneous success. When the select committee came in 1882 a member visited the institute and found forty lads there. He then went on and saw 'another house of another sort not far away, with a fair mixture of members of the other sex'. There were 150 lads there. But Isaac Miller, superintendent of the institute, thought that three quarters of the lads frequented it, perhaps going on afterwards to the other place.[22]

For some years smack-owners had been anxious to see the certification of skippers and mates introduced. From 1875 the Smack-owners' Mutual Insurance Ltd. had issued its own certificates, and had suspended them when necessary; but the fishermen were opposed to the system as they felt the owners might withdraw certificates for reasons not connected with misconduct or incompetence, and the strongest of the mutual insurance clubs had refused to adopt it. Harrison Mudd in 1878 had told the Home Secretary that 'the greater part of the fishing smacks now belong to men who have no practical knowledge, and many of the fishermen never served any apprenticeships. They enter the trade from 18 to 20 years of age and soon offer themselves as captains.' To his brother owners he had expressed himself more robustly, saying that 'many of the skippers knew no more of courses or distances than the man in the moon. Government should come to their help and establish an official system of examination, so that before a man took charge of property to the value of £1,400 and several lives, he should give some evidence that he was qualified'. In 1880 the Board of Trade at last complied with the wishes of the owners. Those who were already skippers or mates were given certificates of servitude. Future applicants were required to submit themselves to an oral examination, and courses of instruction were offered at the Fisherlads' Institute.[23]

The trade thus gained one real victory in 1880, but suffered also an apparent defeat. The Merchant Shipping Act of that year was intended to stop imprisonment for desertion. Owners were empowered to use the police to put lads on board instead of charging them, courts were given a discretionary power to annul apprenticeships, and a lad could give forty-eight hours notice of his unwillingness to sail, and so protect himself against liability to be brought before the magistrates. It was quite clearly the intention of Parliament to put an end to the whole shameful system of using the courts to man the ships, but many owners felt that they could not operate without it. A circular from the Board of Trade showed how an attempt could be made to evade the law and allow Grimsby to keep its peculiar institution. Owners were advised that if an apprentice gave the forty-eight hours' notice required by section 10 of the Act this might be interpreted as a breach of his indentures to be dealt with under section 248 of the Merchant Shipping Act of 1854. The Hull stipendiary clearly thought this was bad law and would only convict lads of genuine offences. He imprisoned thirteen in 1881 and three in the next year. The Grimsby justices, and William Grange, their clerk, took a different view. They were well aware that no lad would ever be in a position to appeal against a conviction, and if he refused to go on board he was guilty of disobedience to a lawful order. Major Reed (he was to be a colonel eventually and his judicial talent has been noted above) was questioned on this point by the 1882 select committee.

Most of these lads were sent to you for disobedience to lawful orders?—That must be the charge, and personally I ask when a boy is brought before us whether he has been ordered to perform any duty and has refused.

So in 1881, 158 Grimsby lads were sent to the Hull prison, and 121 in 1882.[24]

Nevertheless the owners had avoided defeat only in so far as lads were still being sentenced, probably illegally, to terms of imprisonment. But now Grimsby stood alone in its dishonour. If a lad got away from the town, it was usually impossible to bring him back again. C. M. Mundahl, Smethurst's partner and son-in-law was as vague as everyone about how many apprentices he had. He thought between forty and fifty, but twenty had run away. George Fellowes said that formerly no hands had been employed, but only apprentices, but now they had virtually freed themselves. The numbers of those indentured each year declined from 508 in 1878 to 280 in 1881 and 380 in 1882, by which time only 800 were still serving in smacks. Imprisonment, said Fellowes, was the only cure, and plainly the ease with which apprentices were escaping was making it much less economic to employ them. It was necessary to employ weekly hands instead, and James Alward thought that there were now a thousand of them serving in the place of apprentices.[25]

The trade again hoped for state intervention. Edward Heneage, the member for Grimsby, and Edward Birkbeck asked questions in the House about the losses caused to owners and crews through delays in sailing caused by desertions. To the general public this was not the most anomalous aspect of the industry, nor did it seem so to Joseph Chamberlain when, as President of the Board of Trade, he received a deputation of owners from Hull, Grimsby, Yarmouth and other ports. They spoke with feeling of their losses, but Chamberlain gave them no comfort:

> Then you mean to tell me [he said] that one fourth of the whole of the people engaged in your fishing business break away from their engagements with their employers. Surely such a state of things does not exist in any trade or business. What can be the reason of it? Either the men do not like your bargains, or they must be the very worst class of men to be found. What you say is this, that unless you have the power of summarily taking a man up and putting him into prison you cannot get him to carry out his bargain—that you cannot get men to work except under threats of imprisonment. That would be reducing matters to a state of serfdom. As to the apprenticeship system, I am not sure it is not a system more honoured in the breach than in the observance. We hear of the most cruel treatment of apprentices being common amongst smack-owners in Hull and Grimsby, and I have been told by some of the largest owners engaged in the fishing trade that they are not sorry the system is broken up.[26]

Nothing would move him from this position and some Grimsby men, who had hoped for benevolent government intervention, showed their alarm. With Chamberlain at the Board of Trade, *laissez-faire* might after all be best. They addressed a letter of protest to the great man, and after thanking him for his patience and courtesy went on to say:

> We the undersigned smack-owners of Great Grimsby, representing 672 smacks, beg leave to state from the knowledge, which many years of experience has given us the opportunity of acquiring, that in our opinion if the apprenticeship system were to be allowed to die out or become unduly trammelled with Board of Trade or other control, the effect on the trade would be most disastrous. It is to the apprenticeship system that the trade must look for a regeneration.[27]

They had, however, brought the danger upon themselves by asking for state intervention and they had to face the select committee of 1882. There was very little to fear from this paper tiger. The members of the committee were C. Norwood, M.P., E. Birkbeck, M.P., E. Heneage, M.P., Alderman Leake, mayor of Hull and Thomas Gray, secretary of the marine department of the Board of Trade. Gray was the official who had given the friendly hint as to how the imprisonment of apprentices could be continued in spite of the legislation designed to end it, and there was a general disposition to discover interpretations of the facts which would be favourable to the owners.

Before their sittings began Norwood, as chairman, explained to Heneage that one of their tasks would be to find the best way of protecting owners against losses caused by desertions. Their inquiry began at Hull in September and they came next to Grimsby for two days before visiting other fishing ports. They sat in the police court at the town hall and examined a number of owners, skippers and apprentices. The atmosphere of the police court, and the presence of their masters, may have inhibited the apprentices, who at any rate said they had nothing to complain of. One of them when asked whether 'he had anything to say as representing his class' perhaps understood the question. He answered that he had not.[28]

The committee produced much of the evidence which has been cited above, but with very few reservations they commended the apprenticeship system. In retrospect, we might think them more humane if they had done otherwise. But they were practical men in a harsh world, and perhaps they could not damn an industry which had given jobs and sometimes a genuine career to youths who might have been thought destined for a life of crime alternating with imprisonment. The decline of the system continued, and fishing became increasingly dependent on weekly hands who were often regarded as morally inferior even to the apprentices. Fewer apprentices went to prison, but the proportion of those who did tended to rise. In the seventies the numbers imprisoned each year were 12 to 13 per cent of the whole. In 1887 the proportion was over 14 per cent. As prison was no deterrent, eager reformers recommended birching as better and cheaper. A skipper was hanged for murdering an apprentice—and the skipper's insurers proudly advertised that out of generosity they had met his widow's claim. There were still complaints about cruelty to lads, but the superintendent of mercantile marine, their official protector, thought that the patience of skippers was quite remarkable since there was more malicious damage to ships' stores in Grimsby than in any other port. He was glad to say that in the whole of 1887 there had been only one conviction for cruelty, and to reduce one to a lower figure, he pointed out that the perpetrator was an Irishman who really belonged to Hull.[29]

Although from time to time there were complaints about depression in the trade, it grew from year to year and by now was qualitatively quite different from what it had been when the first fish dock was opened. By 1881, 861 smacks were registered at Grimsby, 625 of them were still in service, and there were many registered in other ports but

S

sailing from Grimsby, and over 50,000 tons of fish were caught. Over a fifth of the smacks in England belonged to Grimsby, and they caught a third of the fish landed in England and Wales. The old fish dock had been inadequate for a long time, and in 1877 a second fish dock of eleven acres was opened. This cost the MS and LR £23,000, and the return on the investment was probably a good one since in 1879 railway freight charges amounted to £100,000. Soon the trade had outgrown this dock also. In 1882 owners and merchants complained that on one November day seventy-five smacks had been unable to dock because of overcrowding, and said similar conditions were frequent every winter, though the MS and LR claimed that such overcrowding happened only when a long spell of easterly winds kept vessels in dock.[30]

By the eighties there were signs that the exploitation of the North Sea by smacks was near its limits and might soon become unprofitable. For each registered ton of smacks 2·4 tons of fish were caught in 1869, 2·3 tons in 1871, 1·6 tons in 1875 and 1·4 tons in 1881. These figures take account of cod-liners as well as of trawlers. Taking account of trawlers only, G. L. Alward told another select committee in 1893 that in 1875 an average smack had caught eighty-one tons of fish, and only about fifty tons in 1892. In 1875 nearly 39 per cent of the catch had been prime fish and that in 1892 only 21 per cent was prime fish. It was only very gradually that anyone became convinced that over-fishing was taking place, though the oldest pioneer clearly remembered that over-fishing in the Channel and the southern part of the North Sea had first brought them to the Humber. There were no restrictions on the mesh used in the nets or on the minimum size of fish sold. Complaints came from inshore fishermen in the older fishing ports, and at first Grimsby men felt that they only had to rebut these. The Sea Fisheries Commission visited the town for the first time in 1878. The commissioners were the naturalist, Frank Buckland, and Spencer Walpole, a former Home Secretary. Harrison Mudd told them that the trade was increasing, more fish was being caught in proportion to the men and ships employed, and Grimsby was sending fish to all parts of England, and to Hamburg, Rotterdam and Antwerp. James Alward said, a little more cautiously, that the trade was as prosperous as ever but that he felt the financial basis was unsound. Fish had been driven away from the old grounds, and in some places there were now fewer soles. Joseph Murrell, an owner for seventeen years, favoured the restriction of inshore trawling. When Buckland and Walpole returned in 1879 much the same views were expressed. Mudd said optimistically that 'there was quite enough fish in the sea to go on with and that the supply would be kept up'. But by 1881 experience had convinced some that the catching of under-sized fish was reducing stocks and a meeting of owners and fishermen at the Fisherlads' Institute declared that the supply of plaice, soles and turbot was falling off and that official protection of breeding grounds was desirable.[31]

By 1879 conditions were becoming critical for some of the smaller owners. Mudd knew of men owning as many as a dozen boats who had become bankrupt. They were paying too much in mortgage interest, and the catching of fish was becoming more expensive. In almost any other enterprise the owners could have tried to raise their rate of profit by reducing wages; but in fishing the great majority of those who were not apprentices were paid not by wages but by shares in the proceeds of each voyage. Any attempt to tamper with the share system would have led to such violent opposition that it was thought advisable to try an alternative approach. In the autumn of 1879 the Smack-owners' Association persuaded the shipbuilders to try to force their men to accept longer hours and so keep down the cost of repairing smacks. The men refused, and a lock-out began. When they tried to negotiate with their employers they found that smack-owners were at the meeting. But some of the shipbuilders were as much concerned with merchant shipping as with fishing craft. One employer, Mr. Hallett, took his men back on the old terms, and after a stoppage of three weeks, work was resumed generally without any extension of hours. The smack-owners had gained nothing but a good deal of bad publicity. Several of the shipwrights' leaders were victimised, and the men began to talk of starting a 'labour league'.[32]

The Smack-owners' Association had already hinted that fishermen were overpaid.

> The main evil our trade is now suffering from [said the first annual report] is the extraordinary outlay required to build, equip and maintain a smack, the latter item of which is mainly brought about by the character and want of ability on the part of a large number of persons who man the vessels. Whereas the scale of wages and shares paid to them by the owners enables them to live in a comparatively easy state, the owners on all sides are becoming bankrupt and insolvent. It becomes therefore a matter of self-preservation to bring about a more equitable arrangement.

What was now contemplated was an attempt to keep the smacks at sea for longer periods, and without any frontal attack on the share system, to reduce the value of the fishermen's shares by increasing the charge for the carriage of fish in fleet carriers.[33]

Formerly the majority of smacks spent no more than ten or fourteen days at sea and returned to port with their own catch. This was the system called single-boating. The alternative system was fleeting, with smacks fishing in groups of thirty or forty. Each night's catch was put on board a fast sailing cutter which then returned to Grimsby, and the profits of the whole enterprise were pooled among the fleet. Fleeting was unusual except in spring and summer. With the introduction of steam cutters in 1878 it became desirable to carry on fleeting all through the year so that the cutters would not have to be laid up. In the first winter this proved impossible. The fleet broke up in September and it was only with difficulty that twenty smacks were assembled for another short season of fleeting. When fleeting was to be resumed in the spring the men were so bitterly hostile that the police were called in to protect the departure of the thirty-two vessels ready to operate with the steam cutters. Fleeting went on through the summer of 1879, and by now the Ice Co. had five steam cutters, all built in Middlesbrough at a cost of £6,000 each. Feeling against them was mounting and some men said they preferred unemployment to working with the steam fleet in winter.[34]

The clash between owners and fishermen, however, was delayed until September 1880, when the owners tried to enforce fleeting all the year round, with many of the expenses of the voyage deducted from the fishermen's shares. They insisted that fleets should remain at sea for at least six weeks in the four winter months and for eight weeks in the rest of the year. The men would accept fleeting only between the beginning of May and the end of August. They had long suspected that the owners wished to set up a steam-cutter monopoly and so provide themselves with a means of levying an extortionate toll on all fish carried from the smacks; and their suspicion now seemed to be confirmed by the gummed-slip which the owners now attached to the official Board of Trade form on which all crews now had to be engaged. On this slip they found that a high proportion of the cost of nets, fish boxes and other equipment was to be deducted from their share in the proceeds of each voyage.[35]

The strike began with 90 skippers and mates, but within a week 250 had joined in, as smacks came in, and there were parades through the streets with a band. On the first Sunday 200 fishermen dressed in blue guernseys and smart trousers paraded twice from the club-room in

Kent Street to services in St. Andrew's church. Soon over 700 men were out and over 400 smacks were tied up in dock. Some owners did not wish to use the detested 'gum-slip', but the men refused to sail their ships, though they were sympathetic in cases of real hardship and did allow some smacks to sail, such as one which was the sole support of a widow and others which belonged to fishermen who were 'working them out' on mortgage. The strikers were sober and well behaved, and in the town there were very few who did not sympathise with them. Against the Ice Company, there was very strong feeling. It was seen as the evil genius of the owners, and was detested by many fish merchants, some of whom held its shares, because the cutters had been taking much of the catch to London. In the middle of September the smacks of the steam-cutter fleet came in and their crews joined the strikers. Even the despised third hands, who as wage earners were not affected by the 'gum-slip', supported the strike. Many had served their time as apprentices, only to find that other apprentices took their place and there was no opening for them as share-fishermen, and that owners spoke contemptuously of how they had taken them from the workhouse, the plough-tail and the streets.[36]

After three weeks the strike was over and the men had won. There were too many small and medium owners anxious about their financial stability. J. Meadows was the first owner to give in. The Smackowners' Association spoke of treachery and resolved 'that each member may get his smacks to sea in the manner he thinks best'. There was peace for another five years. There was no winter fleeting and the Ice Co. sold its steam cutters, but in 1885 a Grimsby company with fifty smacks bought five steam cutters and tried to resume winter fleeting. A strike, affecting between fifty and sixty smacks, dragged on through the autumn and winter, with the virtual defeat of the company. By January 1886 only eleven of its smacks were at sea with three steamers.[37]

The Trawl Fishermen's Society supported the strike on the grounds that winter fleeting was dangerous and that the owners were using the carriers to cheat the men. Apart from the dangers of boating fish from the smacks to the steam cutters, they stressed that in a storm the losses of fleets were heavier because of collisions between smacks. They pointed out that in the great storm of 1883 the Hull men were fleeting and their losses were heavier than those of the Grimsby men, who were not. As in 1880, they felt that the Ice Co. was really responsible for the strike. Dr. Keetley and Col. Campbell-Walker, the Conservative candidate, arranged for a deputation of fishermen to meet Edward Stanhope, President of the Board of Trade.* As far as the dispute concerned winter fleeting, Stanhope refused to interfere, but he sent G. J. Swanston to Grimsby to inquire into the other grievances of the fishermen. His report attributed the discontent in the industry to the fact that it had changed so much in recent years and that owners and men had become strangers to one another. He heard the complaint of the men that the owners were often financially interested in the firms which supplied stores and provisions to smacks at high prices, and that they made much of their profit through such firms; but he did not support the men's views that they were entitled to share in these profits. He noted that skippers had no control over the quantity or quality of the goods supplied to their smacks, and he thought that there was a good case for the Board of Trade to regulate the form in which the fishermen's shares were calculated at the end of the voyage. They were often given not more than a short, unsatisfactory memorandum showing proceeds from the sale of fish, the expenses of the voyage, and their individual shares in the balance. They were told that full financial details could be seen at the owner's office but feared they might be victimised if they insisted on their legal right to see them. He recommended that all settlements to share fishermen should be shown in detail on an official form. These and other recommendations were embodied in a bill rejected by the House of Lords, but passed into law in the following session.[38]

In spite of overfishing and labour troubles, the boom in smacks continued well into the 1880s. Ownership of a smack seemed a short cut to wealth. So many people wanted them that there was no spare building capacity in Grimsby, and vessels were built for Grimsby owners at Whitby, Burton Stather, Gainsborough and even at Altona on the Elbe. Nearly £1 million had been invested in them. The new vessels were much bigger and more expensive than those of the 1860s, and now cost up to £1,700 each. A hundred or more were fitted with steam capstans. 'We have to invest nearly double the money', said James Alward, 'and the men who do not contribute one penny to the outlay get the same money.' Owners with sufficient capital were increasingly tending to take their profits out of the industry indirectly through such concerns as the Coal, Salt and Tanning Co. which paid

* M.P. for the Mid-Lincolnshire division and second cousin of James Banks Stanhope of Revesby, who had made over his estates to him in return for an annuity. His monument is in the market place at Horncastle.

3 per cent, the Co-operative Box and Fish Carrying Co. with an 18 per cent dividend, and the Ice Co. which paid only 5 per cent but turned back a bonus to its trading members of 3s. 6d. per ton on the ice they bought.[39]

The Ice Co. had a bad name in labour relations. In 1886 it cut the wages of the crews on its ice-barques by 10s. per month, and broke the strike which this produced by bringing in men from Hull. And its directors were extremely shrewd business men. They foresaw that with the advent of the first steam trawlers, wooden smacks were likely to become of small value. They advertised the company was ready to buy smacks, and very soon had purchased sixty-six, of which fifty-eight belonged to directors. Other share-holders were indignant and appointed a committee which strongly censured this and other improprieties. Henry Smethurst, chairman of the company, was prevented by a sudden indisposition from attending the meeting at which this report was accepted. He and his son lost their places on the board, and the company proceeded to recoup itself by resuming winter fleeting which changed conditions now made it impossible for fishermen to resist.[40]

The weekly hands especially were lacking in any organisation which would enable them to oppose the demands of the owners. There was a proposal to remunerate them by a system of poundage, instead of by wages, with the object of reducing their earnings. Skippers and mates realised that they too were threatened but were afraid to support the hands. Only the continued high demand for labour saved them. The poundage system was not enforced, but the Smack-owners' Association expressed its conviction that earning must be reduced and blamed the lethargy and indifference of some owners. The weakness of the fishermen had been amply demonstrated. Winter fleeting, which had caused the strikes of 1880 and 1885, was resumed with hardly a voice raised against it, and it was a handful of steam trawlers which had brought about this change.[41]

A few iron smacks had been built, and a few had been fitted with an auxiliary screw, but they could steam at no more than five knots, and the experiment was abandoned. Old paddle-tugs were used successfully as trawlers from the Tyne and the Wear, and in Grimsby the tug *United* was converted to trawling in 1878. Originally the tugs had worked by towing smacks in weather too calm for a sailing vessel to move a net without assistance. They were less successful when used purely as trawlers. In 1880 the Danish steam trawler *Proven*, a converted vessel, appeared in Grimsby and aroused great interest. Like most of the earliest vessels of this class she had compound engines of 150 h.p. and steamed at ten knots. Clearly the steam trawler did not begin at Grimsby. It was not until 1881 that the Great Grimsby Steam Trawling Co. Ltd. was formed with a capital of £50,000 and several of the earliest smack-owners (W. Moody, G. Fellows, H. Mudd) as its directors. Mudd spoke at the launching of their first ship:

> The origin of the company was in consequence, he might say, of the success of steam trawling in other places, especially in the north of England. Himself and others of the directors had visited several ports where steam trawling was carried on, and seeing the fish delivered from the steam trawlers was superior in condition to the great bulk of the fish delivered at Grimsby, they felt that the trade and reputation of the port would suffer if they did not adopt some method which would enable them to compete successfully.[42]

Their first vessel was the *Aries*,* built by J. Charlton, who had built the first iron ship at Grimsby in 1863 and had launched his own steam trawler *Cecily* earlier in 1881. Their second trawler, the *Zodiac*, was built by Earle's at Hull. She and the *Aries* were also employed as carriers for a fleet of smacks in the summer of 1882. *Taurus* was built at Hull in 1883, and *Leo* by Charlton. Until 1890, when there were forty-two Grimsby steam trawlers, his yard was the only one in the port which could build them. He had built eight, and the rest came from Hull, Hessle and Beverley. The yard of the Box and Fish Carrying Co. was then opened at Lock Hill and the *Assyrian* was built there in 1890 followed by the *Brazilian* in 1891. By the end of 1892 there were 113 steam trawlers registered at Grimsby.[43]

The building of sailing smacks was abandoned and their unhappy owners competed to get rid of them. Already steam vessels from the Tyne and Wear had exhausted the grounds off Scarborough, and it was feared that the same would happen all over the North Sea. An old skipper, John Rutter, remembered how, when he was an apprentice, smacks used no ice, had only one mast, and rarely went more than ninety miles out. Fish was plentiful everywhere when he moved from Hull to Grimsby as a skipper in 1868. Now, he thought, steam trawlers were killing the trade. A smack might fish all over the Dogger Bank

---

* At the launching of the *Aries* a director prophesied that even the glories of steam would soon be dimmed. 'The time', he said, 'was probably not yet far distant when their vessels would go out filled with electricity and return with the treasures of the deep.'

and bring up nothing but dirt and weeds. They were having to fish 100 miles from Norway and were thinking of going to Shetland. This opinion was generally shared. Skippers who had become owners were only too glad to sell and seek employment from others. Thirty of them went bankrupt in 1887 alone. James Alward, the most informative of the owners, thought that 'a great deal of scheming and trickery was resorted to as a means of swinging clear of the general disaster. About a dozen individuals, smack-owners and schemers, are responsible for nearly all the evils which have so grievously affected the trawling trade of Grimsby for about ten years past.'[44]

But steam and fleeting were again making fishing more productive. By 1886 each ton of trawling capacity was producing 2 tons of fish as against only 1·4 tons five years previously. The steam vessels could trawl in a flat calm when the smacks lay motionless, and in all weathers could reach port more quickly than their competitors. They usually carried only two men who had served an apprenticeship, and by the time half a million pounds had been invested in steam there were fishermen to be seen every day tramping the docks in search of work. Inevitably many, in spite of the danger and hardship, were prepared to go fleeting in winter with the Ice Co. smacks. The Board of Trade in 1888, after consultation with the company, issued regulations to prevent loss of life in fleeting; but they were often ignored, and as the smacks struggled to survive, risks were taken and lives were lost. 'It was sad to think', said Mr. Porteous the superintendent of mercantile marine, 'that many of these lives had been wantonly wasted and thrown away.' But he blamed the fishermen more than their employers. At a meeting with Samuel Plimsoll at the Royal Hotel in 1890 a skipper asserted that smacks were now often sent out when they were unseaworthy, while others blamed the decline in the skill of the hands some of whom, they said, were not fit for ballast.[45]

Ships were spending longer at sea and going further north. Already in 1882 the cod-liner *Mari* had gone up to the edge of the ice, and the *John Ellis* with other cod vessels was fast in the ice for seven weeks. In 1890 the steam trawler *Sands*, given up as lost, spent a whole winter in an Iceland fiord after storm damage in the Atlantic. And James Westcott, an ex-apprentice, a skipper, and now an owner, said that he had lost men through collisions at night with screw steamers which, unlike the paddle-wheelers, could not be heard approaching. The Trades Union Congress, when it met at Glasgow in 1892, blamed the owners' mutual insurance clubs for the loss of life among fishermen and said that unseaworthy vessels were being sent to sea. At Fishmongers' Hall James Alward repudiated this attack on Hull and Grimsby practices. Their vessels, he said, were engaged in the most dangerous branch of the trade and constructed to ensure the utmost safety. But at the end of the year, Porteous again deplored the loss of seventy-eight lives, and regretted that all too often there were no life-lines and the life-buoy was kept below.[46]

There were still occasional shortages of labour in the trades which served fishing. The sailmakers struck in 1890 and got a wage increase of 1s. 6d. per week; but there was a considerable surplus of fishermen trained in sail. Too many apprentices were being taken on, and steam trawlers were reducing the demand for their skill. By 1892 over a hundred smacks had ceased to operate, and more than a hundred of the costlier and more productive trawlers had taken their place. There was very little hope that the men would be able to defend all their traditional privileges. A Fishermen's Trade Union, under the auspices of the National Federation of Fishermen was formed in 1890, distinct from, but not in rivalry with the Grimsby Trawl Fishermen's Society, whose members were chiefly skippers and mates. The employers were so sure of themselves that they refused to meet a deputation from the new union to discuss the general expenses charged to crews. By the end of the year there were 2,200 members, and sixty skippers were prepared to refuse to sail with non-union men; but one skipper, Roiall, was dismissed from the fleet working with the steam cutters because he had tried to get Yarmouth men into the union.[47]

Hull and Grimsby unions were working together for the first time, but felt themselves too weak to take up an aggressive attitude. They did little more than try to counter unemployment by asking that only fishermen should be employed on work in smacks in dock; but because of their links with other unions they hinted that they might think of a complete stoppage of the fish trade, to be brought about with the help of the railwaymen. Porteous warned the fishermen against those whom he styled professional agitators who organised strikes to cause disunion between masters and men. He thought that talk of a general stoppage was atrocious, and hoped that there would be a more kindly feeling and that the two sides would meet to discuss their differences. There was no strike until the spring of 1892 when 200 cod-men struck for an increase in wages after trying, in vain, for nine months, to persuade the owners to negotiate. The strike was easily broken. Some of the liners sailed as trawlers, crews were brought in from other ports,

5. An early steam trawler, the *Median*, with the bridge and wheel-house aft

and when the men gave in after three weeks many found themselves unemployed.⁴⁸

It was becoming clear why the owners had so often applauded the apprenticeship system as essential to the regeneration of the industry. G. H. Goodinson, secretary of the Fishermen's Federation, spoke of 'the grasping, slave-driving trading propensities of the owners of the last twenty years or so. Boys have been rushed into the trade along the lines of slave-dealing, and fishermen manufactured more rapidly than berths can be found.' With powerless unions and a surplus of labour the industry was able to carry through the transition from sailing smacks to steam trawlers without a major stoppage. In the course of the transition the number of apprentices declined. In 1889 Grimsby had 1,038 apprentices and the rest of the country only 720. The Ice Company was using them as a means of extracting profit from the last sailing smacks. By 1892 it had a capital of £150,000. More than a hundred smacks sailed with its steam-cutter fleet, and the whole of the catch was carried direct to Billingsgate. It had 182 apprentices* when it opened its Fisherlads' Home in Victor Street in 1891, hoped to have 300, and claimed to have more than any shipping company in the world.⁴⁹

It was rumoured that to keep their numbers down some skippers tried to frighten apprentices into deserting and passengers on the New Holland ferry often saw strings of lads handcuffed together on their way to the Hull prison. The superintendent of mercantile marine explained that many of these lads were picked up from the gutter and taken on by the owners out of kindness, but many ran away to Hull to work as hands and he thought that but for imprisonment apprenticeship would be at an end. The Hull prison chaplain told the Prisoners' Aid Society that Grimsby owners imprisoned eighty times as many apprentices as those of Hull: 196 Grimsby fisher-lads were imprisoned in 1887, and 96 out of a total of 887 in 1893. The Grimsby owners were fully aware that they owed the survival of their peculiar institution to a favourable interpretation of the law. At a banquet at the Royal Hotel in 1890, proposing the health of the magistrates, Alderman Mudd congratulated them on their excellent administration of justice, and noted that with the assistance of their clerk, William Grange, they had been able to preserve the apprenticeship system which in every other port was almost extinct. Clearly other ports lacked such excellent justices and so prudent a clerk.⁵⁰

---

* All were from workhouses as the experience of the company was that workhouse boys were the most tractable.

NOTES

1. CMD, App. 30, 317–20; G. Obs., 17 Sept. 1879.
2. Ibid., 16 Jan. 1878.
3. Ibid., 17 Sept. 1873.
4. Ibid., 1 Dec. 1875, 22 March and 10 May 1876, 10 March 1880.
5. Ibid., 17 April 1878; CMD, 44/1794, 2193.
6. Ibid., 54; G. Obs., 8 Jan. 1878.
7. CMD, 61–2, 2377–86, 1482–5, 2299–2301; G. News, 29 Sept. 1882.
8. G. Obs., 17 Sept. 1879; CMD, App. 37 and 1405–7, 2240–6, 1502–20.
9. LRSM, 5 Feb. 1864; G. Obs., 16 Jan. 1878.
10. Ibid., 9 Aug. 1876.
11. Ibid., 24 Oct. 1877, 9 Jan. 1878.
12. Ibid., 9 July 1873.
13. Ibid., 8 Dec. 1875, 9 and 16 Jan. 1878.
14. Ibid., 24 Oct. 1877, 16 Jan. 1878.
15. Ibid., 17 Feb. and 17 April 1878, 3 Jan. 1877.
16. CMD, xi, 38, 56/2197; G. Obs., 2 Jan. 1889, 15 June 1892, 27 Dec. 1893, 1 Jan. 1896.
17. CMD, 1591, 1502, 1499; G. News, 16 June and 22 Sept. 1882; CMD, 1452.
18. Ibid., 1584–6; G. Obs., 25 June and 13 Aug. 1873, 8 March 1876.
19. Ibid., 3 and 10 March 1873, 18 March 1874, 28 Feb. 1877.
20. Ibid., 26 May and 2 June 1880.
21. Ibid., 4 June 1879, 28 July 1880.
22. CMD, 1621–2.
23. G. Obs., 13 Feb. and 6 Jan. 1878; CMD, 1630–7.
24. G. Obs., 8 and 15 Sept. 1880; CMD, 1401.
25. CMD, ix; 1702; App. 47, 235; 1681–7; 1746–7.
26. G. News, 7 July 1882.
27. Ibid., 8 Sept. 1882.
28. Ibid., 15 Sept. 1882.
29. G. Obs., 11 Jan. 1888, 28 Dec. 1887.
30. Dow, op. cit., II, 164; CMD, 1384–8; App. 30, 204; G. Obs., 25 April 1880, 17 Dec. 1879; G. News, 8 Dec. 1882.
31. DNB, vii, 204 and lix, 209; G. Obs., 13 Nov. 1878.
32. CMD, 66; G. Obs., 1, 15 and 22 Oct. 1879.
33. Ibid., 12 March 1879.
34. Alward, op. cit., 221; G. Obs., 17 April, 11 and 18 Sept. 1878, 19 March, 2 April and 10 Sept 1879.
35. Ibid., 25 Aug. and 1 Sept. 1880, 2 Sept. 1879.
36. Ibid., 8, 15 and 22 Sept. 1880.
37. Ibid., 29 Sept. 1880, 6 Jan. 1886.
38. Ibid., 9 June, 24 Feb., 2 and 30 June 1886.
39. G. News, 6 Feb. and 15 June 1885; G. Obs., 24 Feb., 16 June, 6 Oct., 8 and 22 Dec. 1886, 11 Jan. 1888; Alward, op. cit., 217; CMD, vii , 14; 1743, 1820–1.
40. G. Obs., 5 May 1886, 7 Sept. 1887.
41. Ibid., 1 Dec. 1886, 28 Dec. 1887.
42. Ibid., 16 Jan. 1878; CMD, viii; HCP, 215.
43. G. Obs., 14 July 1880, 24 March 1881, 26 Feb. 1890; HCP, 9.
44. G. Obs., 13 Oct. 1886, 11 Jan. 1888, 22 July, 19 and 26 Aug. 1891.
45. Ibid., 18 May 1887, 7 Oct. 1891, 2 Jan. 1889, 26 March 1890.
46. G. News, 7 July and 15 Sept. 1882; G. Obs., 26 March 1890; G. News, 29 March 1893; G. Obs., 27 Dec. 1893.

47. Ibid., 10 and 24 Sept., 23 April, 19 Nov. and 3 Dec. 1890.
48. Ibid., 1 Jan. and 31 Dec. 1890, 13 and 27 April, 4 May 1892.
49. Ibid., 5 Aug. 1891, 20 Aug. 1890, 6 July 1892, 8 July 1891.
50. Ibid., 16 and 23 March 1892, 27 Dec. 1893, 26 Feb. 1890.

XVIII

The County Borough

In the second half of the nineteenth century, when Grimsby was expanding more rapidly than it had ever done, it enjoyed less formal independence than in the days of its decadence. The Municipal Corporations Act had taken away its separate quarter sessions and cases were heard at Lincoln until in the seventies the Lindsey sessions were held by adjournment at Grimsby; and for over sixty years, Grimsby paupers went to the Caistor workhouse and rating valuation was fixed by the Caistor Union Guardians.

When the Union was set up in 1837 Philip Skipworth esq., one of the Laceby guardians and chairman of the board, proposed that it should sit at Grimsby and use the House of Industry in Brighowgate as the workhouse. The borough council backed this scheme, and Mr. Betts of the Abbey Farm, a Grimsby guardian received a threatening letter:

We hereby give you this public notice from our meeting held last night, that if the poor of this parish be sent to Caistor Union we, thirty of our company, have determined to burn every straw of your property; and should it be that you catch the individual committing the incendiary, and you punish him, you may expect to be shot, and that the first chance after.

But the paupers went to Caistor, Mr. Betts was left undisturbed and a scheme of poor law administration, brought into existence when Grimsby was a mere market town, survived until long after it had become the largest place in the county.[1]

Edward Gulson, one of the assistant poor law commissioners, had already explained the principles of the new Union to a meeting at the *Red Lion* in Caistor—'that the condition of him who lives on the exertions of others should be somewhat less desirable than that of the independent labourer'. The poor were looked after with notable economy. In the first half of 1854, a hard year, the town was required to pay only £339 out of a total of £1,794. But for charity the poor rate would have been higher. The price of coal rose so steeply that the policy of dealers in holding back supplies was stigmatised as 'akin to locking up grain at a time of famine', and a voluntary committee was formed to bring a cargo from Newcastle and sell it at a price 20 per cent lower to save poor people from applying to the Union.²

For all purposes, and not merely for the poor-rate, the valuation of property in the town was the task of a sub-committee of the board of which no Grimsby guardian had ever been a member. The fact that in 1855 the deputy-overseer made off with £835 was by comparison a minor matter, as also was the virtual de-rating of the poorer inhabitants such as those of Whitehall Yard, 'a lawless class of persons with nothing worth the expense of summoning'. Matters were still further complicated by the different types of rates which could be levied for municipal purposes. Highway rates had been levied on all property, but as soon as there were public works of sewage, paving and water supply within the meaning of the Local Government Act of 1858, only a general district rate could be levied, and farm, railway and dock land was exempted from this as to three quarters of its valuation. The local opponents of rating in 1858 actually succeeded in getting a rate quashed by the Lindsey quarter sessions, and for a time there was no means of paying the Gas Co. But the major and recurring grievance was that the town had no say in rating valuation. A revaluation in 1874 had increased the rateable value of Grimsby property by an average of 15 per cent, but that of the railway by 1,000 per cent. To the corporation this naturally seemed an enormous wind-fall; but the MS and LR challenged this valuation in the courts and the Caistor Union refused to allow the Grimsby overseers to be parties in the action. It seemed likely that a compromise would be reached without any chance for the town to protect its interest. Regretfully the corporation had to base its rating demand to the MS and LR on a modest provisional valuation of £10,000 instead of the old one of £4,000.³

Increasingly the town was ill at ease in a Union dominated by squires and farmers. All meetings were held at Caistor, and there were times when some of the Grimsby representatives had to walk both ways, until in 1874 the corporation, to protect its own interests, offered them free transport in a 'covered-conveyance' once a month. Seventeen of the eighty guardians were tenants of Lord Yarborough. Not surprisingly, when a new poor-rate collector was appointed for the town the three Grimsby guardians had twenty-seven votes against them and the successful candidate had been a clerk for nine years in Lord Yarborough's estate office. The borough was paying just under a fifth of the total poor-rate in the Union and felt itself entitled to be represented by twelve guardians on a board of eighty. The board was prepared to agree that the number should be increased to eight, and the council was moved to instruct the town clerk to prepare statistics which would enable it to consider the desirability of applying for a separate Union.[4]

The logic of events seemed increasingly to be making this the desirable solution. With the growth of the town vagrants became more numerous. The workhouse was too distant and they had to be put in common lodging houses. When the Union proposed to set up a vagrant ward in Grimsby the Local Government Board inspector told them that he knew of no precedent. But there had to be a ward so that vagrants seeking relief could be given lodging, a bath, test work, and be searched for hidden money and valuables, and Grimsby was the only place to put it. Yet each year more and more of the inhabitants of the town had to be sent to the workhouse on Caistor moor, or to its infirmary. There were fifty-five there in 1872, and in addition 546 outdoor paupers. By the eighties the workhouse was overflowing; but to some the distance of the workhouse from the town still looked attractive as a means of discouraging pauperism.[5]

Almost every winter there was acute distress among the poor and families of casual workers. One night in the winter of 1886 there was a meeting of more than 300 unemployed in the Central Market, and many claimed that they were near starvation. A deputation appeared before the council, a private relief subscription was opened, and the surveyor was instructed to provide work at 2s. 6d. per day for fifty unemployed men on street cleaning. On the Board of Guardians there was constant bickering about whether the poor were better treated in the country or in Grimsby. A few years earlier a country guardian had commented on the general prevalence of distress, and the following discussion, typical of many, took place.[6]

Mr. Good: There is a tremendous amount of distress relieved by private charity. The board would be perfectly astounded if they knew how much.

Mr. R. Iles: I do not think the private charity in Grimsby is more astounding than the charity in the country.

Mr. Good: I think very much more. You have not the slightest idea of the amount.

Mr. R. Iles: You have not the slightest idea of the charity in the country.

Mr. Good: Nor do I wish to have any idea.

Mr. R. Iles: The farmers keep men employed when we can't afford it.

Mr. Good: Yes, and lower their wages to two shillings a day.

Perhaps the spirit of Gradgrind was equally alive on both sides of the borough boundary. But as a result of the phenomenal growth in the town, wage rates except at harvest time, were much higher than in the villages. Even in the sixties the flow of labour into the town was actually causing the wages of some country craftsmen to rise. The Grimsby bricklayers struck unsuccessfully in 1864 to get their daily wages raised from 4s. to 4s. 6d.; but even so, this was higher than building workers could earn in the country and in 1865 journeymen bricklayers and joiners in the Caistor area demanded an increase to bring them up to the Grimsby level. Their employers met at the *Talbot Inn* and agreed to an increase. And when the farm labourers in the Alford district were threatened with a reduction of wages from 3s. to 2s. 6d. per day some prepared for emigration while others set off for Grimsby to look for work on the docks. While country workers were struggling unsuccessfully to protect their meagre standard of living, and deserting the land in thousands, Grimsby wage-earners were usually able to strike successfully to improve their conditions. Dock labourers in 1871 demanded an increase from 3s. 6d. a day to 4s., and met at the Temperance Hall to plan a campaign for a general reduction of hours. Building trade employers tentatively agreed to a nine-hour day for their men. Shipsmiths and ship carpenters won a nine-hour day, and the latter, earning between 30s. and 33s. a week, struck for, and got, an increase of 6d. a day in 1873. A long strike of stonemasons, during which many left the town, brought their wages up to 32s. a week with an hour's reduction in work.[7]

Though wages were so much higher than in the country, the majority of the new inhabitants lived in an unhealthy environment. It would nevertheless be a mistake to see them as having exchanged a healthy country life for urban squalor. Reports of medical officers to the Union show that many villages could display conditions differing only from those in Grimsby in that there was no smell of decaying fish to add to that of pigs, cows and piles of nightsoil. But in Grimsby, up to the end of the century, there was little in its performance of which the local authority could be proud.[8]

After an outbreak of small-pox in 1871 the Local Government Board sent Dr. Home to inspect the town.

Taking the common occurrence of choked drains [he reported] full privies, huge accumulations of manure from pigsties and stables and offal from slaughter-houses, of the general filthiness of many courts and streets as the test, I can only say that I should never have guessed an inspector of nuisances existed in the borough.

Almost the only thing he found to praise was the good quality of the water supplied since 1862 by the Waterworks Co. But only 1,300 out of 4,053 houses had a piped water supply. There were still two public wells, at Red Hill and in South Saint Marygate. Most houses drew incredibly bad water from private wells contaminated by surface drainage. At Brown's Buildings he found cases of enteric fever. There were nine houses there all drawing stinking yellow water, containing maggots, from the same well. Over 3,000 houses had no water closets but box closets, overflowing and infrequently emptied by contractors appointed by the council. There were five main drains, none of which was of more than two feet in diameter taking not only surface water but also the overflow from cesspits and water closets. Four of them discharged into the open Clee drain which also contained decaying fish refuse. At the northern end of Victoria Street there were constant complaints about the smell of excrement from a sewage outfall lying on the muddy banks of the creek which had once been the entrance to the Old Dock. Everywhere, but especially in the most densely populated parts, he found pigs kept in back yards, sometimes as many as ten to a single house. He felt, he said, 'almost justified in saying they are protected in the borough, considering that the efforts of individuals whose children's health has suffered and whose comfort has been poisoned, have, hitherto, failed to have this disgusting nuisance removed'. The onset of the small-pox epidemic had been gradual and might have been controlled, but the council, as the local board of health, had entirely failed to make proper preparations.[9]

The only response of the council was to resolve to adopt the Public Health Act of 1872. In the previous decade population had grown from 11,067 to 20,244. The same rapid increase continued both in the borough and on the land east of the boundary adjacent to the fish dock. There was urgent need for reform, but it was not until 1874 that the council appointed a medical officer of health. Even then, the Local Government Board, a body surely schooled to administrative stoicism, expressed surprise that his salary was so small. Most councillors preferred to go forward as slowly as possible, and they were ably abetted by several of their salaried officers. Only a few, such as Henry Smethurst, warned them that a hot summer 'might bring them something more than they expected'. He was referring, surely disinterestedly, to the amount of fish refuse in the East Marsh drain. But professional opinion was against him. Joseph Maughan, the surveyor, gave the councillors the assurance they needed. Grimsby was comparatively well off and it was a mistake to regard it as badly drained.[10]

When Maughan had to be silent, the voice of William Grange was heard. When the inspector of nuisances appeared before the borough magistrates in 1875 to complain of fish houses in Albion Street, Grange, as clerk to the magistrates, told him it was no concern of theirs. He must report to the local board in writing. But another magistrate protested that this was useless. The board did not meet and the surveyor did not carry out his instructions. The inspector added that he had seen the surveyor two or three times in the street 'but you might as well talk to the man in the moon'. In the following year Dr. Keetley complained that building by-laws were repeatedly infringed with the connivance of the surveyor. He frequently got the local authority to pass plans which he falsely certified as complying with the by-laws. In defiance of the by-laws yards were left unpaved, and rooms were too small. Councillor Wenney, a smack-owner said he 'knew of houses where the basement floor was laid upon the ground, no joists being put between, and the water oozing up'. Another councillor knew of scores of houses built lower than the asphalt footway. But it was said that the surveyor would need a dozen assistants to see to such matters, and Grange, as town clerk, assured the council that houses in Hull were smaller and that Grimsby houses were 'vastly superior'.[11]

Both the town clerk and the surveyor seem to have connived at the improper adoption of new streets. There were complaints in 1876 that streets were often passed as flagged when they were not. Maughan admitted that streets had been adopted with footpaths asphalted or gravelled, but the town clerk saved him by observing that 'he adopted the exact words of the act of parliament, which really meant that the work was really done to the satisfaction of the board'. It must have been unusual for a town clerk, with a private conveyancing practice, to place so strained an interpretation on the meaning of an act, and it may be noted that council minutes recorded streets as flagged and kerbed, never as gravelled or asphalted. The surveyor too had his private practice, though an attempt had been made to force him to devote his whole time to his appointment under the new urban sanitary authority. There is no evidence that either of these officials was corrupt, but they do seem to have exposed themselves to considerable suspicion by loyally carrying out the often unexpressed wishes of the unenlightened majority of the councillors.[12]

This is not to say that officials failed entirely in their duty. The inspector listed scores of nuisances to which he wished to call the attention of the urban sanitary authority. At a house in Burgess Street a pigsty at a higher level soaked through a nine-inch wall into the rooms. In Holme Street there were three houses with an unpaved yard which could not be washed down and which was contaminated by leaking closet boxes. Access to eleven houses in King Edward Street was through pools of filth from a closet box leaking into a three-foot passage. The list was interminable; but whatever the council minutes recorded the Augean stable remained unswept.[13]

There was an epidemic of scarlatina in 1882-3 which caused 122 deaths. The Council had already agreed to share with the Clee-with-Weelsby local board the cost of new four-foot main drains, but this was too late to stop the epidemic. Shaken by this visitation, they then prohibited the carrying of fish offal through the town in carts and insisted that it must be carried in casks; but their insistence was so feeble that the carts continued to be used and the offal to drop on to the roads. The medical officer of health could do little apart from trying to educate the councillors through his quarterly reports. He warned them that too many wells were still in use and that the nuisance from smoke was growing. There was high infant mortality from diarrhoea. 'I attribute this in part', his report said, 'to the want of proper care and nursing. The infants are left in charge of elder children, their mothers being at work in fish houses and other places. Very many infant lives, I believe, are sacrificed to this practice.' Occasionally he was able to get something done. He had often warned the authority that epidemics of measles and whooping cough started in Orwell Street near piles of refuse on the property of the railway company. In the summer of 1886 he had the satisfaction of seeing this refuse from the pontoon taken out of the town. Even this satisfaction might have been denied him but for pressure from the Local Government Board.[14]

A Dr. Braxall from the Board had made an inspection in 1885 and warned them that cholera, as he said, was staring them in the face. The disease might at any time be brought in from the continent and they were not in any position to fight it, though local people were afraid of infection from Hamburg emigrants on their way to America, and from cargoes of imported furniture. He urged them to attend to drainage and water supply and to seek the powers of a port sanitary authority. To a certain extent they had carried out their duties with regard to water, but there were still too many wells, all potentially dangerous. Closet boxes were not emptied often enough, and though the old fever hospital had been deliberately burned with its beds and bedding as an additional precaution, the new iron hospital was totally unsuitable. He came again in 1887 and found little improvement. He noted that 10,000 emigrants had passed through in the previous year, and that the port sanitary authority would have to inspect all of them. Visiting the Emigrants' Home, he found them all huddled together, men, women and children, in one enormous building. And he observed that the medical officer of health had not always performed his duties in the spirit of the Public Health Act. The sewers were still not properly ventilated and for nearly half of every day were blocked by the tide.[15]

The corporation duly became a port sanitary authority, and continued to devote itself to the neglect of its duties. There was still no building inspector and therefore there was no means of ensuring that building plans passed by the council would be adhered to. Some urged that the appointment of an inspector might improve the health of the town. Instances were mentioned of houses with joists laid on the grass which grew up between the floorboards, and of new houses in the West Marsh where the tenants had to bale water from under the floors. Alderman Charlton thought that it would be extravagant to appoint a building inspector as the building of the town was almost complete and there would be little for him to do. Fortunately he was wrong. The town was about to expand its boundaries and take in an area which would force it to regard its responsibility for public health more seriously and also to emancipate itself from the Caistor Union.[16]

As long ago as 1855 land had been leased to the MS and LR to extend its line from Grimsby to Cleethorpes, though it was not until 1861 that the bill was promoted. At first the line ran through bleak open country, but by the seventies there was no building land left in the borough within reach of the docks, and houses were being built in the area of Clee-with-Weelsby parish known as New Clee. Over 2,000 people lived there in 1871, and over 11,000 in 1881. New Clee station was opened in 1875. Caistor Union had already expressed alarm about the unhealthy state of this new suburb. A rural guardian remarked that the powers of an urban sanitary authority were needed, and wondered why the parish vestry had not sought to join Grimsby or Cleethorpes. The Clee guardian said that they might eventually form their own local board and that they were afraid of the Grimsby rates on the one hand and of the high cost of a contemplated sea-wall at Cleethorpes on the other. The union medical officer reported that New Clee was the worst place in his district, and in 1878 the Clee-with-Weelsby local board was at last formed. Its bye-laws dealt interestingly with the spacing of bathing machines on the shore and the separation of men from women bathers; but its real problem was the slums of New Clee.[17]

Grimsby had a typhoid outbreak in 1887–8 and the medical officer of health urged that since there was 'an almost continuous prevalence of fever of one sort or another it is high time some serious inquiry into the general condition of drainage was made'. It was coming to be realised that the problems of the town were inseparable from those of its New Clee overspill. The Caistor guardians again expressed concern at the squalor and poverty of New Clee, and of the slums erected in defiance of the Public Health Act. Small-pox appeared and spread to both areas. The local board found it had to build its own isolation hospital as Grimsby refused to admit patients from houses outside the boundary. It was thought that visits of fishermen to brothels in New Clee were helping to spread the disease. When the Local Government Board sent Dr. Page to report on an outbreak of enteric fever, he found New Clee with a population of 17,000, about half that of Grimsby, nearly all dependent on the fishing trades. Most houses had piped water from Grimsby, but there was the same objectionable system of nightsoil collection and sanitary bye-laws were completely ignored. Infant mortality, rising to 162 per 1,000 births in 1887 as against 150 in Grimsby, was mainly from diarrhoea and scarlatina. Parts of New Clee had gained such a noisome reputation that in 1889 the owners of property in Charles Street petitioned to have the name altered 'as the street had obtained such a notoriety for immorality that the very name was sufficient to prevent respectable tenants taking houses. The alteration of name would raise the moral tone of the neighbourhood.'[18] It became Hope Street.

There were other incentives to seeking an amalgamation. One police force could serve both areas, and one councillor was an enthusiast for the scheme because it would keep clerical magistrates out of New Clee. There was the threat also of the new county council. The borough had been too small to be included in the original schedule of county boroughs, but with its population increased by half it would be able to escape almost entirely from the county. Alderman Smethurst said laconically that he had always objected to the county council and always would. As long ago as 1874 New Clee had been regarded so much as an extension of Grimsby that the first board school, Holme Hill, had been built there. It is worth noting that from the beginning

The County Borough

the school board, of which Smethurst* was now chairman had been strongly nonconformist. Sectarian feeling was influential and there were probably few voters willing to place themselves under a county council thought to be dominated by squires and parsons.[19] The council resolved to seek the annexation of Clee-with-Weelsby, the local board was quite prepared to acquiesce, and for the first time the borough extended its medieval boundaries. Councillors for the additional wards were elected in 1889. Application was now made to the Local Government Board to have Grimsby designated as a county borough, which it duly became on 1 April 1891; and before the end of the year the borough again had its own coroner and its separate quarter sessions.[20]

The problem of relations with the Caistor Union was solved at the same time. In spite of the relatively high standard of living in the town, there were many unemployed almost every winter and the pressure on the workhouse increased. It was said that the pawnshops were full of craftsmen's tools, and it was a common saying that when a cargo was to be unloaded in dock there were enough men seeking work to carry the ship itself bodily away. It seemed illogical that the poor law should still be administered by a board of farmers and landowners at Caistor. Yet it was feared that the rural guardians might simply seek to ease their burdens by getting rid of Grimsby and New Clee, and evade the Union Chargeability Act by driving the village poor into the town. This was not at all what Grimsby wanted. At a Local Government Board inquiry as to the need to extend the Caistor workhouse Grimsby representatives opposed any immediate alteration. They wanted to wait until the result was known of another appeal by the MS and LR against its rating valuation. Grimsby would lose nearly £10,000 if it was separated from the Union before the appeal. The Queen's Bench division duly decided that the rateable value of the Grimsby docks was £22,500 and not, as the MS and LR claimed, £566. The way was now clear and in 1889 the council petitioned for a separate Union, to consist of Grimsby and twenty-six adjacent parishes. The council was so afraid of finding itself presented with a Union consisting of the town only that it sent in a further petition 'that the Local Government Board will not be induced to alter their decision by any resolution that may be passed by the Caistor Board of Guardians who are evidently desirous

---

* He was elected on to the first school board as a Primitive Methodist. At this election there had been over 10,000 votes for eight nonconformist candidates, 3,532 for six Anglicans and 1,183 for two others.

of crippling the extent of the new union'. This catastrophe, however, was avoided. The new Union was formed with Grimsby as its centre, and in 1890 the gentleman jockey, J. M. Richardson of Healing, became the first chairman of its board of guardians. Paupers were still sent to Caistor, on terms agreed between the two Unions until the new workhouse was built on land bought from Lord Yarborough near the new cemetery on the Scartho boundary.[21]

A *Times* correspondent visited the town in 1892.

It is a flourishing working class town [he wrote] with a population of 53,000. Its staple industry is fishing, and since that is in a very prosperous condition the inhabitants earn good money and are for their class very well to do. The town, being new, is laid out for the most part with ample air space and presents an unusually clean external appearance.

The extent to which Grimsby had become the sort of town he described was politically significant. Ben Tillett had spoken at a mass meeting of the dockers at the Temperance Hall in 1890 to form a branch of the Dock, Wharf and General Labourers' Union. Both parties competed for the votes of the newly enfranchised working men. Some local Conservative leaders, and their newspaper, the *Grimsby Observer*, had long displayed working class sympathies and when Henry Josse,* the Liberal M.P., resigned in 1892, the Liberals felt that their best hope of holding the seat was to put up Henry Broadhurst, the Labour leader recently defeated at Sheffield. But perhaps he was not far enough to the left. At any rate Edward Heneage, the Liberal-Unionist, regained his former seat. Keir Hardie thought that the Liberals had wanted Broadhurst as a figure-head for Labour in the House of Commons, and *Reynold's News* believed that the voters had rejected him as a political impostor. No one was in a position to know. What was perfectly clear was that in the twenty years which had elapsed since the Ballot Act, though a few old men still talked nostalgically of bribery and election riots, Grimsby had at last become a truly political constituency.[22]

---

* Henri Josse was French by birth. He was managing clerk in a solicitor's office at Caen at the time of the 1848 revolution and became secretary of the Caen Democratic Association. He was imprisoned by Louis Napoleon, expelled from France in 1852, and subsequently refused to return when a political amnesty was declared. He entered the service of Hippolyte Worms, a coal exporter with branches at Cardiff and Newcastle. Josse came to Grimsby to open the coal trade as a result of negotiations with Edward Watkin of the MS and LR in 1856, lived at Barnoldby, became Worms' partner, a Lindsey J.P. and chairman of the Grimsby Liberal Association.

But other things had changed little. The *Times* had sent its correspondent because there was again a danger of cholera being brought from the continent in the emigrant ships. Like all previous visitors, he found the drainage very bad, with the sewage rising in the sewers when they were blocked by the tide for eight hours each day. Some parts of the town were undrained, and many house drains were 'mere channels of brick or tile loosely laid'. Pigsties, though perhaps fewer, constituted much the same nuisance as twenty years previously. Yet, on the whole, he thought the cholera scare was doing good. There was a foolish clamour for quarantine, encouraged by the press; but the people were aware that a real cholera epidemic could destroy the fish trade. A hospital ship had been provided to supplement the inadequate fever hospital, a committee was carrying out a house to house visitation, and extra medical inspection was being arranged for incoming vessels. Shortly after his visit the council at last decided to build a sewage-pumping station on land leased from the MS and LR. Water was taken from the fish dock for flushing the drains, though some felt that this water was so polluted as to make the drains a worse danger to health. William Grange gave his usual pontifical assurance: they had no power to take water elsewhere, unless they went to the Water Company, and James Alward aptly compared his fellow councillors to rats in a hole, unable to get at the river and trapped by the Water Company.[23]

By the time Grimsby became a county borough, its basic industry had altered out of all recognition. In conditions highly favourable to the owners and demoralising to fishermen, steam continued to replace sail at a rate which reflected the inflow of a large amount of capital into the industry. At the end of 1898 there were only 277 sailing smacks and liners left to compete ever less successfully with 340 trawlers, most of which were still under six years old. Within two years only 61 smacks were left and there were 471 trawlers. Except for skippers, mates and a few others, share-fishing was at an end and most of the crews were paid by wages. Formerly owners had wished to abolish or seriously to modify share-fishing and substitute wages, but by 1901 a majority were convinced that it would be in their interest to pay the crews under a system in which wages were supplemented by a percentage of the proceeds of the voyage. This, they maintained, would give the men an incentive to work better; but in the opinion of the men, under this poundage system, their earnings would fall and they would have no chance to share in the concealed profits of the industry which accrued to their employers. The owners, however, were determined to impose their own system, and formed themselves into the Grimsby Federated Owners Protection Society Ltd.[24]

At the beginning of July 1901 they refused to sign on crews except under their new terms and soon over 400 trawlers were tied up. 'To those in the trade', the Federation said, 'it has long been apparent that unless resolute steps are taken to reduce expenses in the working of the vessels the fishing trade of Grimsby, rapidly declining, will ere long cease to exist.' This was so manifestly untrue that from the beginning the public was hostile to the Federation. It was even hoped that the banks would put pressure on the owners to make them see reason, but nothing was heard from these immortals and the struggle continued, with increasing bitterness, until October.[25]

The men staunchly maintained that they were the victims of a conspiracy:

> The bugbear of the trade, the reason of the losses on the working of the vessels, is the bonus system. Vessels would pay well, and the dividends would be large but for the heavy directors' fees, the high salaries of officials, and the many trading bonuses which render it impossible to present an honest balance sheet. The men chiefly concerned in the (trawling) companies are also the men concerned in the ice companies, the coal syndicate, and the various stores and fitting shops. They are able to make the expenses of the vessels as heavy as they wish and secure their profits in other ways, and it would therefore be suicidal to go on the share system. Already the owners, although the vessels show practically speaking no profit at the end of the year, are making large incomes by directors' fees, by salaries, by commission on sales, and by their numerous bonuses.[26]

Fishing did not cease entirely. Smacks were not affected and enjoyed a brief revival of prosperity. Thomas Campbell, and Messrs. Hagerup and Doughty, got their vessels to sea, and but for a shortage of skippers more would have sailed. For most fishermen, however, the lock-out meant increasing hardship. They were willing to accept arbitration, but the Federation insisted that they must first go to sea on its terms. At first the dispute had been conducted peaceably, but destitution was fraying the tempers of the men, and, after an attempt by Smethurst's firm to bring in foreign crews and engineers from inland towns, rioting began on the fish dock and the offices of the Federation were smashed. Though the rioters were said to be irresponsible youths and fishing apprentices, violence injured the cause of the fishermen, and their leaders exhorted them to co-operate with the police. The next day the police charged a crowd of spectators. Detachments of the Sheffield and

Manchester police, and from the Lincolnshire Regiment were brought in, and the riot act was read in Riby Square.[27]

The men continued their resistance for another ten days. Then, following intervention by Lord Yarborough and Lord Heneage, they gave in. Their leaders congratulated them on having 'practically won a glorious victory'. In fact it was a defeat. They went back to sea on the terms offered by the Federation pending an award by an arbitrator, Sir Edward Fry, appointed by the Board of Trade. His award, issued at the end of the year, gave them a little more than the Federation had offered; but the reduction of wages, against which they had fought, was imposed on them, and any increase in their earnings would have to come to them from the poundage which it was expected that the accountancy of their employers would keep at a minimal figure. Freed of their labour troubles, the owners were soon able to add another hundred trawlers to their fleet and the sailing smacks dwindled to less than thirty. The town seemed to have achieved its ultimate destiny as the home of the steam trawler and the fishing millionaire.[28]

NOTES

1. CB, 1 June 1837; LRSM, 1 Dec. 1837.
2. Ibid., 19 Aug. 1836, 13 Jan. 1854.
3. G. Obs., 21 Oct. 1874; LAO, Caistor Union MB, 10 and 25 April 1855; G. Gaz., 3 Oct. 1856; G. Obs., 21 Oct. 1874, 7 Jan. and 6 Oct. 1875.
4. Ibid., 17 Feb. 1879; MB, 4 May 1874, 6 March 1876, 3 Aug. 1874.
5. MB, 3 Dec. 1874; G. Obs., 13 May 1874, 7 Feb. 1872.
6. Ibid., 24 Feb. 1886, 1 Jan. 1879.
7. LRSM, 6 May 1864, 29 Sept. 1865, 30 Oct. 1874; G. Obs., 29 Nov. and 20 Dec. 1871, 31 Jan. and 21 Feb. 1872, 4 June 1873, 21 and 28 April 1875.
8. LRSM, 12 Feb. 1864.
9. G. Obs., 10 Jan. 1872.
10. MB, 2 Sept. 1872; G. Obs., 8 July 1874.
11. Ibid., 31 March 1875, 5 April 1876.
12. Ibid., 18 Oct. 1876; MB, 2 Oct. and 16 Nov. 1876.
13. MB (Highways), 17 July 1876.
14. G. News, 6 March 1885; LBH, 16 Jan. 1886; MB(SA), May 1886; LBH, May 1885.
15. G. News, 6 March 1885; MB(SA), 1 Aug. 1884; G. Obs., 27 April 1887.
16. G. News, 2 Dec. 1887.
17. MB, 14 Sept. 1855, 4 Sept. 1861; G. Obs., 4 July 1875, 1 July 1874, 4 Aug. 1875.
18. MB(SA), April 1888; G. News, 16 March 1888; MB(SA), 22 June 1888; G. Obs., 6 Feb. and 23 Jan. 1889.
19. G News, 29 June 1888; LRSM, 22 May 1874, 24 May 1876.
20. G. News, 29 June 1888; MB, 22 Aug. and 7 June 1888; 29 Nov. 1889.
21. G. News, 27 April 1888; G. Obs., 3 and 10 March, 30 June 1886; MB, 28 May 1889, 9 Jan. 1890; G. Obs., 23 April 1890.

22. Ibid., 2 Nov. 1892, 22 Jan. 1890, 15 March 1893.
23. G. News, 6 Jan. 1893.
24. Jackson's *Grimsby Almanack* 1899; Alward, op. cit., 234, 250.
25. G. News, 2 and 5 July 1901.
26. Ibid., 5 July 1901.
27. Ibid., 12 and 26 July, 20 and 27 Sept. 1901; G. Obs., 26 Sept. 1901.
28. Ibid., 10 Oct. 1901; DNB (1912–21), 200–3.

Postscript: the Twentieth Century

To have those who were actors in the scene safely dead is the limiting and liberating condition of the trade of a local historian. In the present century he must speak with a different voice, and can never claim, as some writers of fiction do, that his narrative does not at any point refer to living persons or actual situations. Let us, then, try to see an actual situation as a visitor to the town might see it if he arrived for the first time in the 1930s.

He would be most likely to arrive by train, and as the line crossed the Freshney he would conclude, wrongly, that this was the stream which had made Grimsby a medieval port. If the purpose of his visit were historical research, it would take him to the town hall where he would find an archive collection in much the same condition as that in which Alfred Gibbons had seen it when he made his inspection for the Historical Manuscripts Commission in the 1890s. If time permitted, he would find that one or two of the documents seen by Gibbons were missing, and this, and the cutting off of all seals of any value would lead him to conclude, rightly this time, that it was only recently that the administration of the town had begun to be conducted with order and decency.

A lunch-time stroll round the town would show nothing of real antiquity except the lovely tower of the parish church, and yet in those days, and until past the middle of this century, near St. James's and along Bargate and Brighowgate, Grimsby looked much more like a small market town than a place which so aggressively prided itself on the enormous size of its fishing industry. Nothing whatever would be seen which suggested ships and the sea, and there was something symbolically right about this. A casual visitor would not be aware that this was only the historical residuum—what was left after the real direction of affairs had been removed from the historical centre of the town—and that more than a mile away, there was a second and larger town centre south of the docks spreading down Freeman Street from Riby Square. Those who made their living on the sea rarely moved more than a few hundred yards from this other centre. Their time on shore was too short. Those who served the industry in a professional or administrative manner either spent their working day in the old-world town, or returned through it to their residences at night, and the richest of all were out in the country, semi-squires farming and owning land, hunting with the Brocklesby or at any rate photographed at the hunt balls. But all of them, save for a very few, made their living, received their salaries or earned their dividends from fish. If there was a glut at the fish-meal factories the wind would remind them of this.

This outward movement, perhaps no more marked than in other provincial towns, almost halted the growth of the population in the twentieth century. It did grow from 77,000 in 1901 to 92,000 in 1931; but in the next thirty years there was an increase of little more than seven per cent. In the area round Grimsby, on the other hand, in Cleethorpes and the Grimsby Rural District, the population grew from 29,000 in 1911 to 40,000 in 1961. Those responsible for the administration of the town consistently claimed that Grimsby was the natural centre and almost the sole cause of the growth of this minor conurbation. It was recognised that the opening of the Great Dock at Immingham in 1912 was also a cause, but it was claimed that most of the Immingham labour came from Grimsby, and the frequency of tram services along the light railway connecting the two ports (until the cost of maintenance of the track made the trams uneconomic) would seem largely to have vindicated the claim until Immingham began to turn into a small town, though served by a parish council only, in the middle of the century.

None of this, however, would be immediately visible to our imaginary visitor. If he was a person of reasonable curiosity he would soon realise that what he was seeing in the old town was certainly not the fishing port, and if he went to look for it, he would probably never find it, since the nineteenth-century misgovernment of the town had left the inhabitants without a single yard of ground on which they could stand and look at the ships and the river, unless their business took them on to the docks and they could show a pass to the policeman at the entrance. A retired naval captain, making a social survey in 1936 (and clearly getting many shocks in the process) wrote:

Although the dock estate is not entirely bounded by a definite wall or fence, a boundary is formed by railways, streets of houses, timber yards, or where no such demarcation of limits exists, by walls and fencing. Where roads or pathways enter the dock estate, whether gates are placed there or not, dock police are stationed at these points and their duties are to scrutinise all who enter or leave.

Postscript: the Twentieth Century

This was one of the things of which the author, Captain F. A. Richardson, approved. He was concerned that those seamen who had preserved some innocence should not be preyed upon by touts and prostitutes, and he was not inclined to accept the police view that there were only about thirty of the latter. For the town, it was completely satisfactory to have so definite a boundary between itself and the area which directly or indirectly provided the livelihood of most of its people. But if the visitor wanted to see the river, he would have to go to Cleethorpes.

He might perhaps still be unfortunate and pick a day when the river was invisible. If the tide had gone out and there was heat-haze or a slight mist, nothing would be visible except mud and sand. It was this huge distance between the high and low-water marks which had made the construction of a port so difficult. When the newest of the fish-docks had been opened in 1934, like all the docks except the earliest, it was dug out of land which had been reclaimed from the river specifically for dock-construction. If the sea were visible, it would probably have the semi-Arctic look familiar to all lovers of the North Sea. In water not very different or so far away, 1,072 men had died in 216 fishing vessels in the first of the World Wars, and this had perhaps been about a fifth of those who before the war had worked in trawlers. Half had been lost in mine-sweepers, without which the Grand Fleet would never have left Scapa Flow, and the other half in fishing. The cenotaph which recorded these and other losses stood in a pleasant suburban spot so far away that no trawlerman of the thirties was likely to see it.

Proportionately, the fishermen had suffered more heavily than any other occupation group in the first war, accounting for just over half of the war deaths. Nearly all the rest were killed in France, and in the infantry. In an incomplete roll of honour produced in 1919 nearly 500 Grimsby men are shown as having been killed while serving in one or other of the fifteen battalions of the Lincolnshire Regiment. The heaviest losses were those of the 10th Lincolns, formed in 1914 and known as the 'Chums' battalion: 117 or more of them were killed, chiefly in the 1916 Somme offensive. The battalion had been formed round the nucleus of the OTC of the old municipal college, with the Hon. G. E. Heneage as its first commandant, and Major W. A. Vignoles, the borough electrical engineer, as its first adjutant—and subsequently lieutenant-colonel commanding. They trained in Brocklesby Park until the summer of 1915 and reached France in January 1916. On the Somme they came under such heavy fire that only a lieutenant and four men reached the German lines, where they remained for several days. The regiment was so depleted by its losses at Vimy Ridge, Passchendaele and the 1918 German offensive, as well as by the removal of men to be trained as officers, that in the last months of the war it had been used only for the training of American troops. There were heavy Grimsby losses too in the 5th Lincolns, a territorial battalion, which went to France with the first of the territorial divisions in 1915 and was decimated at the Hohenzollern Redoubt. But in a coda to a local history such as this final chapter it is not possible to do more than recount the losses of the first war, and to say that those of the second war were comparable with those of other towns of its size. The first is stressed here because it was as traumatic for Grimsby as it was for the whole generation which was involved, and in some measure for their successors. But it would also be unjust to fail to record that fortunes were made here too between 1914 and 1918, and that the jam made in Grimsby appears in the memoirs of many old soldiers, not always with a favourable mention.

In the 1920s the town had suffered from the housing shortage. Introducing the Grimsby Corporation Bill to the Commons committee in 1927 and speaking of Bradley Hollow on Laceby Road, the Rt. Hon. H. P. Macmillan, K.C., had said:

There is happening in this district what I am afraid is happening on the outskirts of many towns... A little community has been formed there, largely through the difficulty of getting sufficient housing accommodation in the town, or inability to pay for it, composed really of squatters. There are tents and vans and bungalows there... They have no sanitary provision of any sort whatever.

This, and similar conditions at Scartho, were among the main reasons which enabled the borough to obtain the first extension of its boundaries since 1889. Except for two private estates, the proprietors of which would not sell, there was no more building land left in the town. Mr. Macmillan gave the committee a review of the position and the history of the borough:

It has a community of a rather special character. It prides itself on being the largest fishing port in the world. No less than 700 steam trawlers have their base at Grimsby, and for every man afloat on a trawler something like four or five men are engaged on shore in the industries of curing and packing and so on.... There is one matter which is holding up further progress somewhat, that the Railway Company, in 1912, got the power to make a great fish dock at

Grimsby.... The dock has not yet been constructed and the disposal of sewage —as you can see at the present moment the whole sea-frontage is in the hands of the Railway Company as the dock owners—necessarily is affected by the arrangements made under that act.... There used to be a large number of box-closets, and these have been altogether entirely eliminated, and the sewerage defects generally have been made good.

The electricity undertaking, started in 1901, was the property of the corporation. By 1927 most of the obsolete plant had been replaced, electricity was being supplied to the Admiralty radio station at Waltham, and said Col. Vignoles in his evidence 'to the Post Office Beam Station at Tetney, which signals to Australia'. The supply of water and gas were still being undertaken by private companies, but the corporation had bought the tramways in 1925 and was about to start running its first trolley-buses. This picture of an enterprising and well-conducted corporation, and the fact that there was complete agreement with the neighbouring local authorities, resulted in an easy passage for the bill, and the boundary extension increased the area of the borough from 3,260 acres to almost 6,000. Little Coates was entirely absorbed except for a few acres which went to Great Coates, 124 acres were taken from Bradley, 403 acres from Weelsby, and 79 per cent of Scartho was also taken in.

There was room to expand, but no comparable increase of population. What happened here, as in so many other towns, was that many of those who could afford to move away from the centre provided themselves with mortgages and suburban houses, though a substantial middle class and a retired *rentier* population continued to live in large Victorian houses within ten minutes' walk of St. James's church. It was the movement into the new suburbs, however, which gave the town its new appearance. Even before the extension of 1927 there had been practically continuous building up to Scartho village, and in Little Coates the Gilbey estate had sold 740 acres to builders. By 1939 the corporation also had built 714 houses on the new Nunsthorpe estate, and in spite of the distance from the docks, a few fishermen were living there. By the sixties the council had built more than 5,000.

So much land was taken for building, and for recreation grounds and allotments, that after the second war the corporation made an emergency application under the Boundary Commission Act of 1945 on the grounds that the extent of war-damage and the shortage of land inside the boundary was likely to make rational development impossible. This time the aim was to annex Cleethorpes, Healing, Great

Coates, Bradley, Waltham, Weelsby, Humberstone and parts of Immingham and Stallingborough. The application was made in May 1946 and the reasons for it were summarised as follows:

> ... The proposed area is one of strong community of interest within itself, and particularly industrially and socially. Most of the inhabitants get their living from the ports of Grimsby and Immingham, and particularly but not exclusively from the fishing industry ... There is little community of interest with the remainder of Lincolnshire which is predominantly rural ... Cleethorpes, Immingham, Healing, Great Coates, Waltham and Humberstone are largely overspill development from Grimsby ... Cleethorpes is primarily a suburb of Grimsby, where most of the working population are employed. ...

All this was substantially true, but was not sufficient to move the Boundary Commission, and it was not until the sixth decade of the century that the town received another small addition to its area on the west and south sides, with the western boundary overlooking the church and the site of the former moated manor house at Great Coates. Inside its boundaries, however, the corporation was soon to be relieved of one of its embarrassments. For a hundred years it had been the trustee of the Freemen's lands and their clerk had been the town clerk. William Grange, himself a freeman and a solicitor in private practice, had seen no conflict between his duty to the corporation and his duty to the freemen, who feelingly described him as the best friend they ever had. His successor, the first full-time town clerk, had somehow contrived, if not to live at peace, at any rate to avoid war with the freemen, though there was a rumour of physical violence threatened or used against the town clerk. After the second war, the position finally became intolerable. The majority of the inhabitants tended to regard the freemen as people who received an entirely unmerited dividend from the corporation, and failed to see that in all respects but one the property of the freemen was exactly like that of any other ground landlord and that their title to it was as good. On their side the freemen, the majority of whom were certainly not affluent or endowed with administrative skills, tended to be chronically suspicious of the corporation and the two officers whom they had to share with that body. The corporation, quite apart from the difficulties in which the town clerk and the borough treasurer found themselves in dealing with the freemen, now realised that in a considerable area of the town it could not fulfil its planning functions unless it was able to sever its connection with the freemen, and in 1949 it obtained an act which finally ended the historic link with them. The position was summarised by counsel for the corporation in introducing the bill:

The three main objects of the bill are these. The first is to transfer the trusteeship of certain lands in Grimsby known as the Pastures from the corporation to the official trustee of charity lands . . . The corporation have no control over the disposition of the land. They have to obey the behests of a certain committee called the Pastures Committee, and owing to a difficulty which has arisen in connection with the redevelopment of the central portion of Grimsby it is necessary that the corporation should divest themselves of this trusteeship. . . . The principal reason, of course, is that in connection with land acquired compulsorily for the purpose of any of the statutory duties which they have to perform, and of which they are trustees, no trustee can buy his own trust property . . . The second object is to authorise this body known as the enrolled freemen to appoint a deputy clerk and a deputy treasurer . . . The town clerk and the borough treasurer are by statute the clerk and the treasurer to the enrolled freemen. Your lordships can see what difficulties arise when there is an entire conflict of interest between the corporation on the one hand and the freemen on the other . . . The third object of the bill is to discontinue the Freemen's Grammar Schools. . . . They oppose the first two objectives but they do not oppose the third . . . Parliament has in the past dealt by statute with the property of freemen in different towns where it existed. But before this arose—it was brought to a head by proceedings under the Town and Country Planning Act 1944—in the case of Grimsby, nothing comparable had arisen in any other place.

In spite of their inherited distrust of the corporation, the freemen expressed a passionate wish to have it continue as their trustee, but their love was unrequited and they were unable to keep their unique legal position which virtually exempted them from planning legislation. The act was passed, and the freemen's estate was soon eroded by compulsory purchase orders which resulted in the erection of towerblocks of flats surrounded by acres of empty ground and nowhere for children to play.

By the 1960s it was difficult to measure how far the town had freed itself from its dependence on fish. A visitor now would find it even harder to see the special character of the town, but inside a few days would probably come to the conclusion that without the trawlers and seine-netters Grimsby would soon be like Jarrow thirty years ago. Until the sixties the only weekly industrial report appearing in the *Grimsby Evening Telegraph* was on fishing, and other publications about industry in the area would be seen to contain a good deal of promotional rhetoric about the advantages of establishing industry on the south bank of the Humber, but little in the way of statistics. The visitor would, nevertheless, probably conclude that a very great amount of capital had been invested in heavy industry on sites extending westwards to East Halton, but that these industries were capital-intensive, employing comparatively small amounts of labour and producing a huge volume of traffic.

The character of fishermen would be seen to have altered since the thirties. Then, in the areas near the docks, Captain Richardson had found 182 residents per public house, and 2,300 per public house in the suburbs; and there would no longer be the fifteen cinemas which he had been inclined to regard as morally uplifting because they took men away from undesirable clubs. It would be impossible to find the 1,200 unemployed fishermen—more than a sixth of the labour force—whom Captain Richardson had counted, or the sub-standard housing near the docks. He had written:

Practically all the old type of property of the city . . . which includes examples of almost every unsatisfactory scheme of planning, are to be found in and about the areas to which the greatest proportion of the seafarers, particularly the fishermen, resort to and live in. In these areas are numbers of back-to-back type of houses, houses to which access is only gained by a narrow alley, double houses and other similar specimens . . . of bygone days. There are 300 houses hereabouts consisting of two rooms, one above the other, and a number of houses having a one-man fish-curing factory, if not part and parcel with the house, then very closely adjacent to it.

All this had gone. There were fewer fishermen on fewer and much bigger ships. The sexual morals of which he wrote are harder to evaluate. He thought fishermen were of less than average physique, gave little trouble to the police because policemen were bigger and stronger, and about 60 per cent were married 'or living in a married state'. There were no brothels, so unmarried fishermen could not live there as they had done in the last century. Many single men, when they were on shore, lived in lodgings for which they paid a retaining fee when they were away. Sometimes several men paid for the same room, occupying it in turn, and this was a satisfactory arrangement.

There is an element of house-pride among the women of the district, but this, unfortunately is by no means universal, and does not amount to a local characteristic.

It was less satisfactory when the landlady also acted as the lodgers' mistress, particularly when this was done in rotation for several lodgers.

Postscript: the Twentieth Century

This shocked him, but he was more worried by the conditions which he found in clubs. This is no place to pursue his worries further. He meant well, and perhaps we can cautiously conclude that since his time there has been a convergence between the moral standards of the trawlermen and those of the rest of the population, and that even in 1936 his survey found most men decent and reasonable, and everyone knew that at sea the majority could act with unselfish heroism if the occasion arose.

In 1881, in a population of about 40,000, 5,000 or more fishermen had caught rather less than 1,000,000 cwt. of fish. Seventy years later, in a population of more than 90,000, about 3,200 fishermen landed 3,970,000 cwt. of fish. This 1951 figure was the highest to date and has not since been exceeded. In addition over 1,000,000 cwt. were landed from foreign vessels, and this figure has tended to rise each year. Obviously since 1881 productivity, measured in terms of men at sea, has increased by a factor of four or more, and if this fact could properly be considered in isolation, we could safely conclude that the community has become very much less dependent on one staple industry. But the facts cannot be isolated so simply, nor, on the other hand, would it be safe to conclude that a larger population had come to depend on a smaller number of men in the distant storm-beaten line of ships. Perhaps the community was most dependent on fishing about the time when Captain Richardson made his social survey. Then the number of persons serving the industry on shore was larger, since all the trawlers were coal-burners and rather more than a ton of coal and half a ton of ice was needed to produce each ton of fish. The timber yards and a paper mill were the only large employers of labour not linked with fishing, and with the growth of Immingham the commercial docks had lost most of their importance.

By the middle of the century the situation had changed. In the Grimsby exchange area of the Ministry of Labour—an area larger than the town—there were 63,000 persons employed in June 1965, with 20,900 in manufacturing industries, including about 3,000 trawlermen. Not less than 12,000 persons, it may be assumed, were in jobs dependent on fishing. There were large food-processing and freezing plants in the town, and a huge chemical industry on the Humber bank, as well as some heavy engineering at Immingham. The situation was changed too, in that, except in the distributive and service trades, most people were working for anonymous corporations with head offices in London; and in trawling it had become almost impossible for a fisherman to become an owner. In the 1880s £1,000 would have set him up. Now, £250,000 would not go very far, though a few syndicates of skippers were contriving to own and operate small seine-netters.

Like practically every provincial town, Grimsby had lost its economic autonomy and seemed to be losing its identity. For at least fifty years most of the ablest students from the grammar and technical schools were more likely to make their career elsewhere than to settle in their native town. Those who remained often did so with a feeling of failure, and there was a sense in which all this was the end product of a long and peculiar history. In less than a lifetime in the nineteenth century Grimsby grew from little more than a village to a large port, and it grew at a time when the corruption which had been the soul of its old corporation was still a fragrant memory for many. It is not surprising that it was unable to produce good government until the present century, or that the minds of so many were taken up with the gambler's hope of sudden wealth from the fish trade.

Now no one could grow rich except by the expertise of those who have turned the handling of money into an art. Most such persons were unknown or unloved, and though very large fortunes had been made, none of this had ever been reflected in any public benefaction other than the kind which might produce a Lloyd George knighthood. There was certainly wealth and power, but no longer in the town itself. And as the new industries grew, they spread away from the town in the direction of the deep-water dock at Immingham. The great mud flats which had first attracted Scandinavian settlers to the mouth of the Humber were making the Royal Dock less attractive. The whole history of the town had been an exercise in defiance of geography, and there was no doubt that it would continue to be. The town would change, would suffer from its past and from its disadvantageous position, but it would continue and would probably flourish. Few things are as indestructible as an urban settlement.

TABLE I: POPULATION AND FISHING

	Population	Fish landed (excluding foreign landings) Tons	Number of vessels
1801	1,524		
1811	2,747		
1821	3,064		
1831	4,048		
1841	3,700		
1851	8,860		
1855		188	
1861	11,000	5,300	
1871	24,000	30,000	302
1881	42,000	49,000	607
1891	56,000	64,000	625 (but 861 registered)
1901	75,000	99,000	478
1911	77,000	190,000	575
1921	85,000	138,000	622
1931	92,000	181,000	545
1951	94,000	198,000	250
1961	96,000	150,000	240

From 1861 the population is given in thousands and the hundreds and units are omitted. From 1871 the population is that of the municipal borough *plus* that of the adjacent area of Clee-with-Weelsby, subsequently incorporated in the borough.

TABLE 2: APPRENTICES IMPRISONED

```
BM = Brixham     —  140 apprentices in 1887, 195 in 1898
GY = Grimsby     —1,041       ,,            ,,   432   ,,
H  = Hull        —  170       ,,            ,,    18   ,,
LT = Lowestoft   —   81       ,,            ,,     8   ,,
PH = Plymouth    —   21       ,,            ,,     2   ,,
R  = Ramsgate    —  129       ,,            ,,   143   ,,
SH = Scarborough—   21        ,,            ,,     1   ,,
```

Annual imprisonments for desertion as follows:

	BM	GY	H	LT	PH	R	SH
1883	0	139	7	0	0	1	0
1884	2	132	11	0	0	3	0
1885	1	114	23	1	0	1	0
1886	3	123	17	0	0	0	2
1887	10	130	17	0	0	6	2
1888	4	130	17	0	0	0	2
1889	1	123	15	1	0	0	2
1890	1	119	18	0	0	0	2
1891	0	108	15	1	0	0	3
1892	2	113	15	0	1	0	0
1893	1	73	17	0	0	0	0
1894	10	56	0	0	0	0	0
1895	1	48	0	0	0	1	0
1896	6	44	0	0	0	0	0
1897	1	21	0	0	0	1	0
1898	2	31	0	0	0	0	0
1899	2	31	0	0	0	1	0
1900	0	49	0	0	0	0	0
1901	1	53	0	0	0	0	0
1902	1	52	0	0	0	0	0

In 1902 there were 39 apprentices at Boston and 12 were imprisoned. After 1902 the Board of Trade ceased to have responsibility for fishery statistics, and the Ministry of Agriculture and Fisheries was not interested in fines and imprisonments.

TABLE 3: GRIMSBY SHIPPING, 1814–1960

(a) Total annual clearances of ships (excluding fishing vessels)

	Overseas	Coastal
1814	31	81
1824	237	129
1832	51	111
1844	41	54
1854	722	423
1864	1,675	497
1874	2,601	2,136

(b) Annual value of exports

1860	£1,666,000
1870	£15,976,000
1880	£7,389,000
1890	£8,318,000
1900	£11,061,000
1910	£20,112,000
1920	£13,146,000
1930	£10,250,000

(c) *The shift of trade to Immingham*

After 1912 much of the trade left the commercial docks for the new port, which, however, had its statistics included with those of Grimsby. The relative position of the two is shown by the following figures (tons) for total annual inward and outward traffic.

	Grimsby	Immingham
1956	1,965,000	4,684,000
1957	1,841,000	5,110,000
1958	1,533,000	4,179,000
1959	1,056,000	3,955,000
1960	1,041,000	4,935,000

Appendix I: Early Parliamentary History

The town archives contain the following early references to election of members of parliament.

Court Roll 13 Ric. II, Tuesday after Epiphany 1390 'Elleccio burgensium pro parliamento. Walterus de Sluthby et Ricardus Misen electi sunt ex tocius communitatis assensu ad essendum ad parliamentum domini regis tenendum die lune proximo post festum sancti hillarii proximum futurum apud Westmonasterium et dicti Walterus et Ricardus capient iter suum versus dictum parliamentum die mercurii proximo sequenti et datum est eis sufficientes warantas sub sigillo communitatis ex tocius communitatis assensu pro parliamento predicto et ad faciendum ulterius ibidem totum commodum seu emolumentum . . . que pro salvacione iuris ac libertatis ville predicte facere poterint. Tenor cuius waranti sequitur sub hac forma in gallico compositi. Copia cuiusdam waranti communitatis: A toutz iceux qui cestes lettres verrount ou ouiront maior baillifs et tout la commune de Grymesby salutz en dieu. Sachez nous avoir ordeigne et assigne et mise en nostre lieu nos bien amez et conburgez Walter de Sluthby et Richard de Misen ionctement et severalment nos especials attornez et generalz pur faire et assentir pur nous et nostre ville au parlement nostre siegnur le roi a tenir a Westmoustier le lundi prochin apres le feste de Seint Hillar' prochin avenir a ceo que illeoques ou leid de dieu par le commune assent de la roialme sera ordeigne et auxi de pursuer departe le roi nostre seignur et pur nous et nostre ville devaunt soun consaille en sa chauncellerie et en toutz autrez lieux ou nos avons affaire et apursuer devens toutz gentz. Donant et grantant as nos ditz attornez ionctement et severalment nostre plein et sufficeant poiar et especial maundement et general pur faire si nous esterons presentz en nos proprez persons pur le commune profite de nostre ville et dapropuitier ore et argent en nostre noum au quele somme que lur semble busoignable pur faire bone fyn et espleite de toutz chosez queux sount profitable a nous et a nostre ville. Eiantz ferme et estable queconque lez avauntditz nos attornez ou ascun deux facent ou face pur nous et en nostre noum en toutz busoignez pur le commune profite de nostre ville. En tesmoignance duquele chose a icestes nous avouns mise nostre commune seal. Doun a Grymesby le mardie proschin apres le tiphaine lan du regne nostre seignur le roi Richard second puis le conquest dengleterre treszime.'
(Election of burgesses for the parliament. Walter Sluthby and Richard Misen were elected by the whole commonalty to be at the parliament of the Lord King to be held the Monday after the feast of St. Hillary next at Westminster, and the said Walter and Richard shall set out for the said parliament on Wednesday next and to them has been given under the common seal sufficient warrant by the assent of the whole commonalty for the parliament aforesaid

Appendix

and for the further purpose of doing there whatsoever they may for the ease and profit and for the safeguarding of the right and liberty of the town aforesaid. The substance of this warrant follows written in the French tongue.

Copy of a certain warrant of the commonalty: To all who shall see or hear these letters the mayor, bailiffs and all the commons of Grimsby, in the name of God, greeting. Know that we have ordained, assigned and set in our place our well-loved fellow burgesses Walter Sluthby and Richard Misen as jointly and severally our special and general attorneys to act and to assent for us and our town at the parliament of our lord the King to be holden at Westminster the Monday next after the feast of St. Hillary in those things which there by God's help shall be ordained by the common assent of the realm, and also both for us and for our town to proceed before our lord the King in his Council and his Chancery and in all other places where we are concerned to proceed with all persons: giving and granting to our said attorneys jointly and severally our full and sufficient power and particular and general authority to act as if we were present in our own persons for the common profit of our town and to borrow gold and silver in our name to whatever amount seems necessary to them to bring to a satisfactory determination all matters profitable to us and to our town: holding good and established whatever our attornies aforesaid or either of them do or does for us in our name in all things needful for the common profit of our town. In testimony whereof to this we have set our common seal. Given at Grimsby the Monday after Epiphany (10 January 1390) in the 13th year of the reign of our lord the King Richard the Second after the Conquest.)

Court roll 25 Hen. VI, 31 Jan. 1447

'Hec sunt nomina presencium in communi aula placitorum coram Willelmo Est maiore ... qui eligerunt Willelmum Duffeld et Ricardum Duffeld burgenses parliamenti domini regis apud Cantebr''

(These are the names of the burgesses present in the common hall of pleas before William Est the mayor ... and they elected William Duffeld and Richard Duffeld to be burgesses of the Lord King's parliament at Cambridge.)

Court roll 33 Hen. VI, 1 July 1455

'Burgenses pro eleccione burgensium parliamenti domini regis.'

(Burgesses present for the election of burgesses of the Lord King's parliament.)

Maior	Est et Asseby
Ricardus Tomlynson	Edon et Asseby
J. Hall	Edon et Asseby
Roger Barbour	Langholme et Asseby
J. Langholme	Neuport et Grymesby
Willelmus Est	Grymesby et Langholm
J. Lek	,, ,,
J. Cok	Edon et Grymesby
Johannes Graynesby	Grymesby et Asseby
Ricardus Asseby	Grymesby et Langholm

Willelmus Chapman	Langholm et Grymesby
J. Shirref	Edon et Grymesby
Robertus Beverley	Langholm et Grymesby
Ricardus Hall	Edon et Langholm
Thomas Hopkynson	,, ,,
Robertus Miles	Edon et Grymesby
Thomas Bolyngton	,, ,,
Willelmus Wayte	,, ,,
J. Dovele	,, ,,
Roger Skendelby	Grymesby et Langholm
Willelmus Carlton	Edon et Grymesby
Henricus Cotes	,, ,,
Ricardus Bramley	Edon et Neuport
J. Mathewe	Edon et Grymesby
Thomas Beel	,, ,,
J. Bayous	,, ,,
Thomas Brughton	,, ,,
W. Edon	Yerburgh et Asseby
et Johannes Swanland	Edon et Asseby

It will be seen that the voters, beginning with the mayor (*maior*) are listed on the left. In the court book they are listed serially and the names of the persons for whom they voted are written above the name of each voter, usually in an abbreviated form, *Grymesby* and *Langholm* never being written in full and Edon sometimes represented by the capital 'E' only. The list is printed here because of the exceptionally early date of the poll.

Court roll 38 Hen. VI, 2 September 1460
'Burgenses parliamenti qui burgenses eligerunt Hugonem Edon et Robertum Peresson preter Johanne Cok et Brughton ad essendum ad parliamentum domini regis.'
(Burgesses of parliament: these burgesses elected Hugh Edon and Robert Peresson besides John Cok and Brughton to be at the Lord King's parliament.)
Cok and Brughton seem to have been elected to deputise if necessary.

Court roll 2 Edw. IV, 19 April 1463
A list of burgesses with apparently the record of a poll, but with the names of the persons for whom votes were cast incompletely recorded. One name was 'Saynton' and the others 'B' and 'E'.

Court Book I, f. 27 1483
'Electio burgensium viij die januarii anno regni regis Edwardi IV xxij pro burgensibus parliamenti domini regis tenti apud Westmonasterium coram Willelmo Glasyner maiore qui elegit Hugonem Bawforht et Edmundum Tawbot.'

Appendix

(Election of burgesses the 8th day of January in the 22nd year of the reign of King Edward IV for burgesses of the Lord King's parliament held at Westminster, in the presence of William Glasyner, mayor, who chose Hugh Bawforht and Edmund Tawbot.)

This is followed by a list of 25 burgesses with their votes shown by letters after their names. The letters are 'h g', 't', and 'h b'. One person is shown voting for Henry Grymesby, who would be 'h g', and another for H. Bawforht who is 'h b'. One vote was cast for a John Aunger.

Court Book I, f. 27v

'Pro Libertate Ricardi More . . . qui concederunt et affirmaverunt ad instanciam domini ducis glosistre et Thome Burght militis quod Ricardus More de Grymesby supradicto erit uterum burgensis sub ista condicione quod si predictus Ricardus More invenientur defectivus per inquisicionem xij burgensium de villa supradicta in suo juramento burgensis contra maiore suo. . . .'

This passage is left, as here given, incomplete, and appears to refer to the previous entry given above.

(For the liberty of Richard More . . . (names of mayor and burgesses) . . . At the instance of the lord Duke of Gloucester and of Sir Thomas Burgh they grant and affirm that Richard More, of the above Grimsby, shall be one of the two burgesses on condition that if the said Richard More shall by an inquisition of twelve be found defective in his oath to his mayor. . . .)

Court Book I, f. 49 1483

25 June 1 Edw. V. Hugh Edon and Thomas Broughton elected burgesses in parliament by the vote of the mayor and 21 others.

Court Book I, f. 28v

13 Jan. 1484. Hugh Bavforth and Stephen See elected for the parliament to be held at Westminster on the 23rd of January.

Court Book I, f. 30v

'Electio burgensium xxv die Octobris anno regni regis Henrici septimi primo (1485) pro parliamento predicti regis tento apud Westmonasterium septimo die Octobris proximo futuro viz . . .'

(Election, the 25th of October in the first year of the reign of King Henry VII, of burgesses for the parliament to be held at Westminster on the 7th day of October next viz . . .)

Then follows the vote of the mayor cast for John Saynton and Stephen See, and the votes of 29 other burgesses for Thomas Pormard, John Saynton, Henry Grymesby and John Aunger. Saynton is indicated by initials only.

Court Book I, f. 54

Poll as above for parliament summoned for 12 January 1489. John Moigne and Hugh Bawfoure appear to have been elected.

Appendix II: The Grammar School

The history of the now defunct Grimsby Grammar School was traced in the *Victoria County History* where A. F. Leach recorded the earliest mention of it in 1329. Since then it has been found that in 1241 Hailmer the clerk bore the title of rector of the schools of Grimsby. Leach was uncertain whether the school had existed continuously up to the time of its charter in 1547 and although the question remains undecided, on balance it seems likely that the school did exist continuously or with few intermissions. In a court roll of 1382 John de Waltham appears with the same title as rector of the grammar schools. In 1423 Walter Barker, described as 'scolemaystre', did fealty for a tenement in the town with lands in the fields, of the gift of Agnes Brigsley. James Seymour in 1442 was owed 8d. by Walter Laceby for his schooling and 2s. for *Victoria Gallorum* in the school, the meaning of which is not apparent. William Walker, shoemaker, in 1447 assaulted various scholars of the school of Grimsby with sticks and blows from his fists; and on a Sunday night in 1499 Thomas Thomson, master of the grammar school, made an affray on William Butler, master of physic, with a dagger, and was himself wounded in the arm. There is, however, no trace of any school endowment before 1547.*

* Nuncoton cartulary in Bodley MS (Top. Linc. d. 1.) (information supplied by Mrs. D. Owen). VCH, 480–2; CRG (10), 5 Ric. II, April 1382; CRG (22), 21 Hen. VI, 1 July; CRG, 15 Hen. VII, 28 Aug.

Index

Abbey, 239
  Farm, 109, 276
  Road, 19
Aberdeen, 26–7, 239
Admiralty, 50, 102, 103, 121, 129, 138, 223
  radio station, 295
Ague, 158
Ainslie, St., 74
Albert, Prince Consort, 214–15
Aldermen, 65, 106, 125, 153, 169, 172, 173, 174, 183, 187
Alehouses, 113
Alewives, 111
Alfred Terrace, 186
Altona, 268
Alvingham Priory, 4
Alward, G. L., 264
  George, 230
  James, 230, 254, 261, 264, 268, 271, 287
  Robert, 229
  William, 229
America, 180, 198, 205, 220, 222, 225
Amsterdam, 101–2
Ancholme, river, 3
Anderson, Sir Charles, 174n., 254
  Evelyn, M.P., 152
Angerstein, John Julius, 165
  Mr., 218
Anglo-French Steamship Company, 223, 237
Anson, Isaac, 242
Arbitration, 45, 58, 62, 73–4, 220, 224, 289
Archangel, 205, 223
Archery, 112–13
Argentille, 6
Aries, 270
Armine, Sir William, 144
Arrests, 66
Aske, John, 89
  Robert, 89
Assaults, 5, 14, 49, 57, 59, 61, 71–2, 76, 78–9
Assizes, 189, 193–6
Australia, 220, 223, 228
Ayscough, Ann, 94

Christopher, 25, 91, 102
Sir Christopher, 94, 99
Sir Edward, 129, 136, 141, 144–6
Francis, 94, 94n.
Sir Francis, 95
Richard, 94n.
Robert, 94
Sir William, 94

Babb, George (1), 153, 161, 163–6, 175, 182, 198n.
  George (2), 189, 197–8, 237
  Mary, 178
Bailiffs, 16, 24, 27, 31, 37–8, 45, 52–8, 60, 73, 102, 125, 188, 195
Balinger, 45, 48–9
Balne, 3
Baltic, 24, 180, 204, 222–3
Bank, 165
  Garfitt's, 178
  of England, 165
  Streath's, 203
Banks, Joseph, M.P., 150
Banners, 65
Bannister, Edward, J.P., 253, 255
Bargate, 1, 3, 80, 239
Bargates Farm, 109, 169
Barking, 228–9, 233
Barnardestone, Thomas, 59
Barnardiston, Sir Samuel, 144
  Sir Thomas (1), 136, 144–5
  Sir Thomas (2), 145–6
Bassingburn, Alan, le Aumener, 14
  Robert, 10, 12
Baxtergate, 5
Bayeux, Odo, Bishop of, 7, 8
Beaumont, John, Viscount, 60–1
Bellassis, Sir Henry, 134
Bellman, 84, 99, 175, 185, 189
Bellowe, John, M.P., 90–2
  Sylvester, 92, 95–6, 108
Bergen, 8, 137
Berneston, Thomas, 59
Bernie, 178

Bertie, Mr., 135
Berwick on Tweed, 21–2, 25, 28, 50, 100, 120, 124
Bethlehem St., 156n., 161
Beurere, Drogo de, 7
Beverley, 2, 11, 41, 45, 79, 80, 125, 152, 196, 270
Bird-nets, 109
Biscay, Bay of, 25
Blakeman, 36, 51, 75
Bloodaxe, Eric, 6
Blow, Elizabeth, 158
  William, 155–7
Blue Stone, 189
Blyth, 99
Board, Local Government, 278–80, 282, 284–5
Board of Guardians, Bethnell Green, 248, 257
  Beverley, 257
  Caistor, 249, 276–8, 284
  Grimsby, 286
  Holborn, 252
  St. George's, 258
  St. Pancras, 249
Board of Health, General, 217–18
  Local, 216–18, 237, 280–1
Board of Trade, 248–9, 258, 260–2, 266, 268, 271, 289
Bolingbroke, Henry, Viscount, 149
Bolle, Sir Charles, 127
  John, 133
Bombay, 225
Bones, 204–5
Booth, William, 127, 127n.
Bordeaux, 25
Borough, admission to, 112; see *Corporation*
  expulsion from 80, 111–12
Boston, 15, 126, 129, 158, 214
Boucherett, Ayscough, M.P., 165, 174–6, 187–8, 204
  Matthew, 151, 151n.
Boundary, 286
  extension, 285, 295–6
Bradley, 4, 13, 25, 54, 294–6
  Geoffrey, son of Ralf of, 13
  Ralf of, 10–11, 13
  wapentake, 17
Bransby, Charles, 145–50, 152
Bremen, 23, 204
Bribery, 150–1, 169, 171–6, 190–1, 193, 197–8, 202n., 212

Brick, 2, 3
  Company, 182
Bricklayers, 3, 115, 279
Bridge, foot, 238
  swing, 238
Bridlington, canons of, 32
Briggeho, 3n.
  William of, 13
Brighowgate, 3n., 25, 238
Brigsley, 14, 43
Brill, 48
Brittany, 25
Brixham, 228
Broadhurst, Henry, M.P., 286
Brothels, 80, 243–5, 251, 284
Brougham, Henry Peter, K.C., 196
Broxholme, Richard, 129
  Lt.-Col. William, M.P., 135–6
Bruges, 49
Brunswick, Duke of, 180
Building lots, 181–2, 216, 238–9
Bull Ring, 104, 115, 161, 185
Bullington, priory, 4
Bulls, 107
  baiting of, 105–6
Burgesses, 9–11, 16, 22, 39, 40, 53, 55, 58, 62–4, 108, 110
  disfranchised, 61, 103, 122n., 128, 148, 159, 190
  See *Freemen*
Burgh, Sir Thomas, 61, 307
Burgh-dike, Bourdyke, 2, 13, 75
Burial ground, 217
Burncreek, 1
Burringham, 33
Burton Stather, 268
Butchers, 98, 105, 115–16
Byng, John, Viscount Torrington, 155

Caistor, 10, 34, 158, 160–1, 213, 276–7, 279, 285–6; see *Board of Guardians, Workhouses*
  Union, 218, 276–8, 283–5
Calais, 25–6, 100
Calamy, Edmund, 133
Canonbig, 71–2
Capiter, Thomas, 157
Carterbrigge, 1, 3
Cartergate, 1, 76
Carts, 3, 14, 43, 64, 115, 162
Castle, 10
Catholic Emancipation, 200–2
Cattle, 105–6

impounding of, 187-9
market, 238
Cawthorpe (in Covenham), 31, 84
Cecil, Sir William, 95
Census, 178, 189, 212, 219
Chamberlain, Joseph, M.P., 261-2
Chamberlains, 3, 5, 25, 31, 33, 42-3, 61, 65, 100, 107, 109, 112, 142, 150, 162, 186-7
Chantry Farm, 152, 187
Lane, 83, 115
Rayner, 83, 92
Chaplin, Sir Francis, 144n.
John, M.P., 144, 147, 149
Sir Robert, M.P., 144n., 150
Charnel house, 83
Charter, 10-13, 16-17, 32, 34, 103, 144
of merchandise, 16-17, 25, 29, 33, 63-4
Chester, Ranulph, Earl of, 69
Chimneys, 3
Cholera, 216, 218, 282, 287
Churches, 7-9, 54
St. Andrew's, 267
St. James's, 1, 9, 51, 64n., 78, 80, 82-4, 91, 93, 109, 123, 125, 127, 130-1, 140, 179, 184, 198, 201, 209, 291
St. Mary's, 9, 51, 65, 69, 81-2, 84, 95, 109
Churchwardens, 82, 130, 162, 209, 242
Cinemas, 298
Cinque Ports, 42, 48
Clarke, N. G., K.C., 176, 195
Clayton, Christopher (1), 121, 152
Christopher (2), 141, 152, 160, 162, 170-1, 174
David, 152
family, 151-2
George, 141, 146-8, 150-1
Mr., 131, 140
Clee, 4, 7, 35-7, 44-5, 54, 62, 69-71, 92, 94, 107, 158, 162, 188-9, 195
New, 244, 283-5
with Weelsby, 282-5, 301
Cleethorpes, 75, 139-40, 155, 157, 182, 188-9, 208, 218, 283, 292-3, 295-6
Itterby and Thrunscoe in, 7, 70
Clinton, Edward, Lord, 103
Clock, 84, 105, 131
Cloth, 15
Coal, 37-8, 42, 99, 104, 112, 115, 139, 141-2, 223-4, 276-7
Coal, Salt and Tanning Company, 268
Coatsworth, William, M.P., 147, 150
Cobbett, William, M.P., 205-6

x

Cod, chests, 230
line fishing for, 228, 232
liner, 271-2
smacks, 230
Colchester, 38
Colepeper, Lord, 138
Cologne, 17, 22
Commission, Boundary, 295-6
Historical Manuscripts, 291
of array, 58
on Municipal Corporations, 190, 213
Sea Fisheries, 264
to survey town, 54
Commons, 105-6, 108, 111, 181, 186-90, 220
stint of, 106
Commons, House of, 73, 129, 133
Committee, 134-5, 174, 195
Select Committee, 250-1, 260, 262-4
Speaker, 58, 174, 195
Compass, 35-6
Constable, Robert, 56
Sir Robert, 35
Constables, 5, 114, 162, 208, 212; see also Police
Chief, 241-5, 250-1
special, 209
Constantinople, 180, 205, 223
Constitution, borough, 62
Contagious Diseases Act, 244
Convoys, 141, 180
Conyers, Christopher, 59
Copenhagen, 179, 225
Corn, 10, 15-16, 21, 25, 27, 37, 87, 99, 100, 105, 113, 116, 139, 204
Exchange, 237-8, 243
field, 4, 108, 149n.
enclosure in, 108
regulation of, 108
Corporation, 125-6, 128, 130, 134, 138, 141, 148, 153, 155, 159, 164-5, 169, 172, 175, 179, 182-3, 187-8, 193-4, 201-4, 206, 212, 215, 217, 220, 238, 243, 251, 294-7, 300; see also *Council*
Corrodiers, 70
Cotes, Great, 20, 44, 224, 296
Little, 13, 20, 59, 60, 75, 148, 155, 295
Milnewell Creek in, 20
Cotton, 225
Council, common, 64-5, 164, 169, 174, 174n., 187
county, 284
municipal, 212, 218, 224, 232, 237
County borough, 284, 287

Court, bailiffs', 56, 72
  borough, 10, 22, 24, 33-4, 52, 63, 66, 72, 75-7, 146, 148, 164, 183, 190, 194, 197-8, 213
  ecclesiastical, 77
  leet, 187
  mayor's, 176
  of Requests, 198
  papal, 71, 82
  piepowder, 66n.
  rolls, 28, 31, 44, 58, 65
  Templars', 14-15
Cricket, 185
Crimean War, 223
Cromer, 36
Cromwell, Oliver, 128-9
  Ralph, Lord, 59, 60
  Thomas, 91
Cuckstolpit, 5n.
Cumberworth, Sir Thomas, 59
Curtis (Curtays, Curteys), Anthony, 89
  Brian, 45
  Leonard, 88-9, 93
  Peter, 35
Customers, 50, 58
Customs, Grimsby borough, 9, 10, 15-17, 24, 32, 37, 64, 66
  Pontefract, 9, 10
  Scartho, 10n.
Customs, 7, 16, 152, 206
  Collector of, 121, 164
  Deputy Collectors, 43
  Deputy Comptroller, 148, 167
  Deputy Customer, 167
  Searchers, 103
  Sloop, 139

Danes, 6, 48, 50
Dantzig, 22-3, 28, 48
Darcy, Lady Sibyl, 58
  Sir Thomas, 53-4
Darrell, Marmaduke (1), 126
  Marmaduke (2), 149
Davis Strait, 178
Deansgate, 4, 115
Defoe, Daniel, 142
Demesne, 12
Denmark, 7, 180
Dissolution, Friars, Austin, 90
  Grey, 90
  Priory, St. Leonards, 90-1
  Templars, 14
  Wellow Abbey, 88, 90

Distraint, 17, 66
Docks, 6, 21, 44, 162-7, 169, 177, 199, 204, 206, 213-15, 219-20, 222, 236, 279, 293
  Fish, 229-32, 264, 287-8, 293
  Immingham, 292
  Junction, 224
  Old (Alexandra), 225-6, 293
  Royal, 215, 222-6, 230-1, 300
Dogger Bank, 177, 179, 229, 270
Dordrecht, 48
Doughty Road, 74
Drains, 280, 282, 287
Ducking stool, 5, 114-15, 130
Duel, 194
  judicial, 11
Duke of York's Gardens, 239
Dunghills, 2, 4, 115
Dunham, 33
Dutch Wars, 137-8

Earl Fauconberg, 178-9
East India Company, 144n., 152
East Marsh, 107, 110, 137, 181-2, 185, 187, 212, 238
  enclosure in, 108, 110
Edgehill, Battle of, 127-8
Edinburgh, 29
Edon, Hugh, 25, 29, 30, 41, 49, 50, 58, 60, 305-7
  John, 25, 33, 35, 48
  William, 27, 43, 49, 65, 306
Eels, 109
Egypt, 223
Elections, corporation, 64, 169-70, 173-174, 174n., 195, 198, 200
  municipal, 212
  of schoolmaster, 183
  parliamentary, 126-7, 129-30, 134-6, 144-7, 150-2, 158-60, 163, 169-76, 193, 197, 241, 304-7
  petitions, 150, 151n., 172-3, 176, 193, 195, 198-9
  polls, 60-1, 141, 151-2, 172, 193, 197-198, 200-3, 212, 305-7
Electricity, 241, 295
Elmeshale, William, 27-8, 32, 38, 41, 43, 77
Emigrants' Home, 225-6, 283
Emigration, 205, 225-6, 279, 282-3
Enclosure, 120, 188-91
  of East Marsh, 107, 110
  of West Marsh, 106, 108
Est, Simon, 41
  William, 33, 35, 55, 60, 305-6

Index

Evelyn, John, 129, 129n.
Exchequer, 10, 54-5, 71, 128
  acquittances, 55, 57, 134
  actions in, 110, 122
Excise, 199
Excommunication, 77
Exports, 223-5, 303

Fairs, 11, 66, 104
  sick folk at, 112
Famine, 16
Farms, engrossing of, 130
Faroes, 233
Fazakerley, J. N., M.P., 197-9
Federation, Grimsby Owners, 288-9
Fee-farm rent, 11-13, 21, 50, 52-7, 66, 73, 203-4
Felons, Associations for prosecution of, 190, 208-9
Ferry, 7, 8, 40, 111, 207; see also *Packet*
Filey, 32
Finch, The Rev. Martin, 136
Fire, Brigade, 240
  precautions against, 115
Fish, 16, 25, 28, 31-7, 64, 99, 104-5, 111, 140, 177
  guts, 115
  refuse, 279-80, 282
Fish-curing, 32-3, 231
Fish merchants, 232, 267
Fisheries, 36-7, 74
Fisherlads' Institute, 257, 259-60
Fishermen, 32, 163, 234-5, 241, 247, 260, 265-9, 288-9, 293, 295, 298
  casualties to, 256-67, 271-2
  Federation, 273
  Trade Union, 272
Fishing apprentices, 233-4, 247-73
  cruelty to, 256-8, 262
  desertion by, 252-8, 261, 273
  imprisonment of, 248, 250, 252-5, 260-1, 263, 302
  suicide of 259
Fishing industry, 6, 228-35, 247-73, 287-9, 291-4, 297-300
Fishing vessels, 35-6, 64, 140, 293
  steam, 229. See also *Smacks, Steam trawlers*
Fishmongers, 32, 98, 114
  London, 26, 34-5, 48
Fitzwilliam, Sir Thomas, M.P., 53
Fitties, 108, 110, 127
Flanders, 17, 21, 24

Fleeting, 229-30, 266-7, 269, 271, 273
Flemings, 16, 24
Floods, 51
Flottergate, 1, 2, 104
Forestalling, 34, 63, 87
Foxtail, 187
France, 25, 293-4
Fraunk, John, 14
  Philip, 14
  William, 14, 17
Frazer, William, 194-6
Freeholds, 57, 63, 158
Freeman St., 236-8, 291
  Market, 238, 244
Freemasons, 184, 207
Freemen, 144, 146-8, 158-9, 162-4, 170-2, 175-6, 181, 183-91, 193, 197-8, 202, 203n., 221, 232, 296-7; see also *Burgesses*
Freeport Wharf, 182
Frenchmen, 16, 25, 49
Freshney, river, 20-1, 52, 139-41, 167, 239, 291
Friargate, 76
Friars, Austin, 2, 21, 51, 77-9, 87-8, 91
  Grey, Franciscan, 2, 76-7, 87, 90-2
Fuller's earth, 121, 141-2

Gaimar, Geoffrey, 6
Gainsborough, 19, 61, 162, 204, 207, 213, 216, 268
Gallipoli, 177
Galway, 177
Games, 2, 24
  unlawful, 113, 131
Gaol, 2, 55, 72, 162, 208
  delivery, 56
  Hull, 261, 273
  Lincoln, 251-5, 258
Gas, 212, 295
  Company, 236-7, 277
Geese, 107
George, St., 161
Gerfalcons, 9, 15
Germans, 23-4, 220
Germany, 180
Ghent, 15
Gidley, John, 232, 234-5
Glasyner, William, 45, 62, 76, 307
Gloucester, Richard, Duke of, 61, 307
Glovers, 111
Godebarne, Robert, 22
  Walter, 22

Goldeburgh, 7
Goole, 207
Gothenburg, 207
Graham, 207
Grammar School, 92, 125, 155, 183-4, 232, 238, 297, 308
Granby Inn, 156n., 164, 181, 185, 190
Grange, William, 237, 261, 273, 281, 287, 296
Grant, John Peter, M.P., 193-7, 199
Grave-robbing, 210, 210n.
Gravelines, 15
Greece, 223
Grim, 6, 7, 46
Grimsby, arms of, 65
   Farm, 169
   King's farm of, 9, 11
   liberty, 12, 63, 73
   manor of, 2, 11-12, 69
   soke of, 4, 7, 9-14, 20
Grimsby Observer, 286
Grimsby Volunteer Infantry, 179-80
Gronow, Captain Rees Howell, M.P., 203
Grosseteste, Bishop Robert, 2
Grymesby, Edmund, 82
   Henry, 4, 62, 307
   John, 40, 62
   Simon, 40
   Sir William, 2, 9, 35, 62, 306
Guevara, John, 125
   Sir John, 124
   Francis, 124
Guilds, 2, 82-4
Gunpowder, 49
Guns and munitions, 46, 91, 99, 101, 109, 126

Halifax, Nova Scotia, 177
Halton, Francis, 127-8, 130
   Sir Roger, 127n.
Hamburg, 205, 222, 264, 282
Hardie, James Keir, M.P., 286
Hardy, James, 128
Harley, Robert, Earl of Oxford, 147
Harrington, Colonel, 127
   James, 126
Harris, Captain George, M.P., 202-3, 212-213
Harrison, Bransby, 185
   John, M.P., 163-4, 170, 172, 174
Hartlepool, 28, 39
Hastings, 42
Hastings, Bedell, 145

Hatcliffe, 43
Hatcliffe, John, 110
   William, 110
Havelock, 6, 7
   Stone, 191
Haven, 1, 2, 5-7, 15-16, 19-21, 29, 31-4, 37, 44, 51-2, 56, 64, 78, 80, 98-9, 102-4, 114, 120-1, 123, 131, 136-42, 161-7
   of St. Marybrigge, 51, 81
Haven Company, 164-7, 177, 197-8, 203, 206-7, 214, 222, 237
Haycroft, 107, 109, 185
Hedon, 42, 89, 102-3
   churchwardens of, 41
Heimskringla, 6
Heneage, Edward, M.P., subsequently Lord Heneage, 239, 261, 263, 286, 289
   G.B., 165
   George Fieschi, M.P., 201-2, 214, 217
   George, 93
   Sir George, 124
   John, 54, 101-2
   Lady Katherine, 116
   Sir Thomas, 90
   William, 93
Hermit, 1, 76, 81
Heron, Sir Robert, M.P., 195-6
Herrings, 14, 16 23-5, 28, 32-4, 38, 48, 64, 121
   curing of, 32-3
Hessle, 270
Hewson, Vice-Admiral George, 194
High Brigg, 121
High Steward, 102, 124, 127, 133, 136, 146, 149-50, 174, 187-8
   Deputy, 187-8
Hildyard, Christopher, 140
   family, 152
   Henry, 140
   Mr., 144
   William, 152-3, 160-1
Holderness, 7, 44, 87, 91
Holland, 25, 141-2, 179, 204
Holles, Freshville, 124
   Sir Freshville, 134, 149
   Gervase, 50, 77, 81, 95, 120, 122-9, 133-5, 162
   Sir Gervase, 92, 124
   Sir John, Earl of Clare, 125
Holme Bridge, 1, 74
   Hill, 239, 284
   manor, 70, 76, 86-7, 90, 92

Index

Home Office, 241, 253, 255
  Secretary, 254-5, 258, 260, 264
Horncliffe, John, 87
  Robert, 87, 89
Hospital, Fever, 282, 284
  Grimsby General, 239
  Leper, 61, 65, 80
  ship, 287
Hostages, 12
Hosts, 24, 32-3
House of Correction, 131, 186, 189
House of Industry, 186, 273
Houses, 2, 6, 7, 9, 116, 125, 213, 215-17, 281, 283, 298
  brick, 115
  decay of, 115
  shortage of, 294
  sub-letting of, 112
  timber-framed, 2, 80, 115
Howe, Admiral Lord, 179
Hull, 22-5, 38, 40-1, 48, 88-9, 103-4, 121-2, 142, 164, 167, 177, 206-7, 216, 228-31, 241, 254, 267, 269-70, 272
Humber, 19, 20, 36-7, 40, 44-5, 48, 217
  Conservancy, 224
  Grimsby Roads in, 123-4, 137, 141
  Street, 239
Humberstone, 69, 296
  Abbey, 4, 72
Hundred Rolls, 14-15, 17, 19
Hunting, 237
Huntingfield, William of, 12
Huttoft, 69

Ice, 230
  barques, 269
  Company, 266-8, 271, 273
  house, 231
  Norwegian, 231, 235
Iceland, 35-6, 38, 229, 271
Illuminations, 179, 181
Immingham, 296, 299, 303; see also *Docks*
Imports, 222-3; see also *Docks*
Indulgence, Declaration of, 136
Indulgences, 84
Industry, 297-9
Inspector of nuisances, 281
Interregnum, 130
Irby, 59
Irby, Sir Anthony, 123
Ireland, 8, 59
Irish, 219
Iron, 141-2

Jericho, 71
Jesuits, 95-6
Jews, 17n.
John, King, 11-12, 15, 51
Josse, Henry, M.P., 286, 286n.
Justices, 5, 34, 55, 58, 95; see also *Magistrates*

Kali, 8
Keetley, Robert, 218, 223, 229
  Dr. Thomas Bell, 236, 253, 267, 281
King, Col. Edward, M.P., 129-30, 133-5
Kingston, John (1), 93
  John (2), 124
Kinnard's Ferry, 19
Kirke, Lyon, 116n.
Knottingley, 2
Konigsberg, 222

Labourers, 112-13, 236
Laceby, 11, 13-14, 20, 69, 148
Lacy, Roger, de, 9
Lake, Sir Edward, 133, 136
Lathegarths, 62n., 70, 93
Law, wager of, 32, 45
Lead, 104
Leases, 162, 169, 178, 182
Leith, 28
Lepers, 81
Lesclusses, 24, 26
Lexington, Robert Sutton, Lord, 144
Lighting, 182-3, 209, 217; see also *Gas*
  electric, 241
  Siemen's electric arc, 241
Lilburne, John, 129
Lime, 141
Lincoln, 8, 13, 19, 25, 28, 126, 128, 161, 214
  Earl of, 14
Lincolnshire Regiment, 293-4
Linde, Sir Walter de la, 14, 20
Lindsey, 34
  Robert Bertie, 1st Earl of, 124, 127
  Robert Bertie, 3rd Earl of, 135
Little Field, 92, 107-8, 115, 185, 187
  Lane, 218
Lobsters, 228-9
Lock-out, 265, 288
Locomotives, 225
Loft, Lt.-Col. John Henry, M.P., 164, 174-6, 178, 191, 193-5, 204
  Street, 193, 217-18
London, 11, 15, 25, 34-5, 42-3, 148, 228-30
  grocer of, 109

316   Index

London—*contd.*
  merchants of, 104
  Recorder of, 53
Lords, House of, 129
Louis, Prince, of France, 12
Louth, 88, 120, 125, 127–8, 161, 175, 204, 206, 214
  Park, 88
Lübeck, 102
Ludborough, 34
Luxborough, Robert Knight, Lord, M.P., 152, 157
Lynn, 15, 23, 49

Mace, 5, 92, 145
Machinery, agricultural, 225
Magistrates, 232, 250, 253, 257, 273
  Bradley-Haverstoe, 244
  county, 254
  Essex, 249
Magnus Barefoot, son of, 8
Maintenance, 49, 58–9, 61–2
Malaria, 218; see also *Ague*
Malet, John, 14
Malt, 27, 37, 121
Malta, 204
Manchester, Edward Montagu, 2nd Earl of, 128
Mandamus, 190
Manfeld, Richard, 33, 35–6, 38–9, 42, 52, 60, 66n.
Manningtree, 228
Manor jury, 181
Margaret of Anjou, Queen, 62
Mariners, 57, 105, 163
  guild of, 51, 82
Market, 7, 66, 87, 94, 104–5, 140, 160, 185–6, 215, 217, 237–8; see also *Freeman Street*
  cross in, 2, 104, 104n., 116
  encroachments on, 104, 140n.
  New (later *Central*), 167, 182, 237, 240, 278
Market Rasen, 87, 255
Marshes, 1, 51, 99, 139
  regained from sea, 109
Mayor, 5, 13, 22, 24, 27, 40, 49, 52–3, 61–2, 64, 70, 92–5, 98–100, 103, 105–6, 123, 125, 127–8, 130, 144, 146–7, 176, 183, 198
  circuit of, 65
  Lieutenant of, 93
Medical Officer of Health, 280, 282–3

Mediterranean, 205, 223
Mellish, Joseph, M.P., 152, 161
  William, M.P., 165, 175–6
Memel, 177–8, 222
Mennonites, 225
Mercer, John, 27
Merchant Shipping Acts, 252, 260–1
Methodists, 155–8, 212
  Primitive, 234, 285n.
Miffin, Philip, 87, 89–91, 108
Militia, 137, 160
Mills, 3, 8, 11–12, 19, 20, 41, 51, 86, 98, 112, 123, 148, 205
  of Kaldehall, 69
Milncroft, 75
Milnebrigge, 3
Minesweepers, 293
Minstrel(s), Duke of Buckingham's, 117
  Earl of Northumberland's, 117
  Henry the, 62
Misen, Richard, 5, 45, 304–5
Miskenning, 10, 11
Missenden, Bernard, 61
  John, 61–2
  Robert, 61
Monds, Bernard, 250, 252, 254, 257
Monson, Sir John, 137
Moody Lane, 115
Moore, Arthur, M.P., 140–1, 144–152, 169
  James, 145n.
  William, 150
Mormons, 225
Mortemer, Ralf de, 7
Mortgages, 232–4, 267
Mott, Captain Andrew, 181, 196
Mudd, Harrison, J.P., 228, 233, 249, 254–5, 260, 264, 270, 273
Murdrum, 11
Music Hall, 245

National School, 198
Neatherd, 107
Nelson, John, 155–6
Netherlands, 24, 41
Neuport, John, 28, 49, 50, 52, 60–1, 306
Nevill, Geoffrey de, 11
  Hugh de, 14
  John, of Raby, 27
  Sir John, 40, 49, 50, 56–8, 60
  Sir Robert de, 13
New Holland, 208, 214, 221, 223
Newark, 127–9

Index

Newark, William, 146, 148
Newbiggin, 21, 217
Newby, Thomas, 191, 242
Newcastle, Thomas Pelham-Holles, Duke of, 152
Newcastle-on-Tyne, 28, 37-9, 49, 98-9, 101, 120, 139, 156, 276
Newgate, 176
Newsham Abbey, 4
Newstead-on-Ancholme Priory, 92
Newton, Roland, 59
Night walkers, 113
Nonconformists, 133, 136, 155, 234n.; see also *Methodists*
Normandy, 25
North, Dudley Long, M.P., 163-4, 170, 172, 174
Northumbria, 6
Norway, 8, 9, 12, 15, 21-2, 60, 121, 123, 152, 180, 223, 229, 271
Nottingham, 11, 19
Nuns' Farm, 107, 110, 127n., 128, 147, 149, 152, 157
Nunsthorpe, 295

Occupations, 15, 63, 152, 182, 190, 232; see *Fishing Apprentices, Fishermen*
Old (St. Mary's) churchyard, 81, 157, 216, 239
Old Market Place, 140n.
Oliver, The Rev. Dr. George, 184, 198, 201, 209
Ordinances, 62-3, 63n., 66, 185
Orford (Irford) Nunnery, 4
Orkney, 8
  Bishop-elect of, 13
Ormsby Priory, 2, 4, 116
Orwell, river, 23, 42
Osborne Street, 161
Outlawry, 34, 39, 43, 50, 66, 66n., 79
Over-fishing, 264-5, 270-1
Owenites, 212

Packet, 178, 207
  steam, 207
Painting, 122n,
  of the Prodigal Son, 116
Parish: see also *Churches*
  Clerk, 131
  registers, 158, 160
  St. Augustine, Wellow, 81
  St. James, 81
  St. Mary, 81

Park, 236, 239
  People's, 1, 236, 239
Parker, Alderman Samuel, 163-4, 169-73, 187
  William Colley, 217, 220, 242
Parliament, 42, 44; see also *Elections, parliamentary*
  Long, 126, 129
  Oxford, 129
  Short, 126n.
Pastures, 297
  Act, 220
  Committee, 221, 297
Pavement, 3, 183, 218
Pawlett, Lord William, 145-6, 149
Pelham: see also *Yarborough, Earls of; Anderson, Evelyn*
  Charles, 135-6
  Charles, M.P., 150
  Charles Anderson, 1st Baron Yarborough, 152, 161, 163
  Charles Anderson, 2nd Baron Yarborough, 176
  George, 135-6
  George Anderson, 188
  Sir William, 96
Penance, public, 84, 131
Pepys, Samuel, 134
Philips, Thomas, 127n., 128
Pickernell, Jonathan, 163-4, 166
Pigs, 106, 279-80, 287
Pilgrimage of Grace, 88-9
Pillar-boxes, 240
Pillory, 5, 114
Pinfold, 107
  Lane, 107
Piper Creek, 121, 139
Piracy, 13, 15, 23, 25, 45-6, 48-50, 57, 88, 101-3
Pitholme, 109-10
Plaskitt, Joshua, 174, 187, 197-8, 205-6
Plaster, 41
Players, Earl of Leicester's, 117
  of Stafford's, 117
  of Warwick's, 117
  of Worcester's, 117
  Grimsby, 117
  King's, 117
  Lord Mountjoy's, 117
  Smedley's, 184-5
  village, 117
Plays, 117, 184-5
Plymouth, 42

Pole, William Wellesley, 163, 170-4
Police, 212, 241-5, 266, 288-9, 298; see also *Constables*
Pontoon, 231
Poor Law, 186
  commissioner, 276
  settlements, 171, 182, 195
Population, 54, 66-7, 70, 158, 160, 178, 202, 212, 215, 219-20, 280, 284, 292, 301; see also *Census*
Pormort, George, 96
  Thomas, 96
Port, 177, 213, 222, 225, 293; see also, *Docks, Fishing Industry, Haven, Statistics*
  fishing, 228
Poundage, 287-9
Press Gang, 130, 138, 160
Prince Regent, 196, 200
Privateers, 179, 181
Prizes of war, 179-80, 223
Prussia, 21-2
Pryme, Abraham de la, 133, 139-40
Public health, 215-19, 279-84
Public houses, 243-4, 298
Purveyance, 100
Pye, John, 25, 27, 34, 45, 48
  Thomas, 33-4

Quarantine, 216-17, 287
Quartermen, 29, 32, 64, 105
Quayage, 20
Quebec, 177, 179, 223
Queen Caroline, 201
Queen's Head, 163, 171, 178, 199, 200
Quo Warranto, 144

Races, 124, 130, 185
Radley, Sir Henry, 126
Railway, 1, 6, 213-15
  East Lincolnshire, 214, 228
  Great Northern, 221, 228, 231
  Manchester, Sheffield and Lincolnshire, 214, 220-2, 224, 230-1, 235, 250, 264, 277, 283, 285, 287
Ranger, W., 216-17, 219
Ransom, 27, 45, 49, 50
Rates, church, 130, 136
  general district, 277
  highway, 217, 277
  poor, 173, 277
  valuation, 277, 285
Ratepayers, 218

Ravenserod, 7, 20-1, 44
Rayner the Deacon, 8
Recorder, 61, 124, 127-8, 130, 133-6, 145, 149
Recusants, 95
Reed, James, J.P., 224, 253, 261
Reeve, 10-11
Reform Bill, 202-3, 212
Rendel, James, 214, 217-18
Rennie, John, 166-7
Restoration, 129-31, 133, 137
Revenue cutters, 198, 202, 208-9
Revesby Abbey, 4
Revolution, 144
Riby, 69-71
  Gap, 127
  Square, 289, 291
Richardson, Captain F. A., 292-3, 298-9
  John Maunsell, M.P., 286
Rideford, Haket de, 10
Ridford, Sir Henry, of Irby, 58
Rifle Corps, 238
Riga, 205
Riots, 146, 156, 241, 288-9
River Head, 1, 19, 98
Roads, 161; see also *Pavement*
  repair of, 3, 4, 81, 161-2, 183, 217, 240
Rolphe, Major Edmund, 137
Roos, Lord, 50, 61
Ropery, 178, 212-13
Rossiter, Col. Sir Edward, M.P., 130, 130n.
Rostock, 177
Rotterdam, 141, 222, 225, 264
Routhe, Joan atte, 71
  William atte, 71
Russia, 223, 225-6
Rye Hill Leas, 187

St. Andrew, chapel of, 1
  hermitage of, 76
St. John a Bower House, 84
St. Leonard, Priory of, 1, 4, 11, 51, 54, 75, 79, 90-1, 152
St. Malo, 15
St. Mary's: see also *Churches*
  churchyard, 81; see also *Old Churchyard*
  cross, 3n., 81
St. Marygate, 25
  North, 5
St. Marykirklane, 5
St. Olaf, 8
St. Petersburg, 223

Index

Salmon, 25, 28–9, 35, 103, 229
Salt, 7, 23, 27, 29, 31–2, 36, 104, 121, 141–2
  Ings, 1, 109
  works, 7, 31, 110
Saltfleet, 27, 32, 45
Sanctuary, 74, 79, 80
  Lane, 2, 79
Sandwich, 13, 15, 42
Sanitary Authority, Port, 282–3
  Urban, 281–2
Saynton, John, 61, 306–7
Scarborough, 32, 42, 45, 48, 149, 164, 207, 230, 255
Scartho, 10n., 11–13, 75, 78, 286, 294–5
  rector of, 34
School Board, 285
Schools, grammar and technical, 300
  Holme Hill, 284
  Municipal College, 293
Scotales, 11
Scotland, 8, 21, 26–8, 62, 101, 103, 117, 123
Scots, 27–8, 39, 127
Scrope, Sir Adrian, 133–4
  Sir Gervase, 127
  Lord, 4
  St. Leger, 135
Seal, borough, 6, 7, 25, 145
See, del (*or* atte), Alexander, 4, 39
  Joan, 71
  John, 21
  Sir Martin, 4
  Peter, 4, 55
  Stephen, 307
Septennial Act, 150, 159, 196
Sergeant, bailiffs', 56
  common, 5, 51, 73, 79, 107, 183
  mayor's, 56, 65, 183
Sessions, Caistor, 55
  Lindsey, 276–7
  Quarter, 133, 186, 208, 276
Sewage disposal, 216, 219, 279–80, 287, 295
Share system, 265–8, 287–8
Sheep, 71, 75, 105–6
  stealers, 114
Sheffield, 213–14, 221, 288
Shelley, Sir John Villiers, M.P., 203
Sheriff, 9–12, 58
Shields, North, 39, 52
  South, 28
Ship, 20, 99, 121, 141
  cog, 51
  H.M.S. *Frederick*, 160
    Greenwich, 160

Princess Caroline, 157
Royal Sovereign, 194
Salamander, 160
impressment, 44–5
iron, 270
long, 13, 51
Money, 126, 129
names, 99–101, 121–2, 137, 139, 141–2, 177–81, 204–8, 222–5
Sea Ruter, 137
votive, 65–6
Shipbuilding, 44, 140, 229, 270
Shipwrights, 44, 234, 265, 279
Shireff (Sheryffe), John, 26, 43, 45, 60
  Thomas, 50
Shops, 2, 114
Simwhite Bridge, 1, 98, 115, 161, 161n.
Sixhills Priory, 4
Skins, 105
Skipwith, Edward, 95
  John, 31, 111
  Sir William, 58, 93
Skippers, 232–3, 247–8, 259–60, 263, 266, 268–9, 271–3, 287–8
Slates, 2
Smack-owners, 232–3, 248–51, 253, 259–262, 265–6, 273
  Association, 234–5, 248–51, 254–5, 258–259, 265–9
Smacks, 228–35, 247, 253, 256, 263–6, 268–73, 287–9
Small-pox, 215, 279–80, 284
Smethurst, Henry, J.P., 233–4, 244, 251, 255, 269, 280, 284–5, 288
  Henry, junior, 252, 269
Smith, Adam, 214
Smuggling, 43, 100–1, 207–8
Snaith, bridge at, 42
Somertymyng, 5, 21
South Sea Company, 145, 149–51
Spain, 15, 25
Spital, Garths, 53
  House, 76, 80
Spurn, 20, 157; see also *Ravenserod*
Stamford Mercury, 160, 190, 195, 204, 215, 240
Staple, 25, 43
Star Chamber, 48
Station, Bus, 238
  New Clee, 283
  Town, 228
Statistics, apprentices imprisoned, 302
  exports, 303

320 Index

Statistics—*contd.*
  fishing, 230, 232, 247, 264, 271, 299, 300
  shipping, 303
  trade, 222–6
  vital, 216, 218
Steam capstans, 268
  cutters, 266, 272–3
  engine, 213
  roller, 240
  trawlers, 253, 259, 269–73, 287–9
Stephenson, Robert, 215
Stocks, 5, 114
Stockfish, 35
Stockwith, 140
  East, 19
Stone Bridge, 1–4, 52, 98–9, 123
Stralsund, 22
Strikes, 220, 266–7, 269, 272, 279; see also *Lock-out*
Suburbs, 295
Suffolk, Charles Brandon, Duke of, 89
Sunderland, Robert Spencer, 2nd Earl of, 135
Surgeons, 113n.
Surveyor, 217–18, 240, 280–1
Sutcliffe, Matthew, Dean of Exeter, 94
  Solomon, 94, 110
Swallow, 4, 7, 10, 54, 70, 87, 92
Sweden, 220
Swinefleet, 41–2, 69, 75, 91
Swineherd, 107

Tailboys, family of, 4, 59, 60
  John, 59
  Lord, 50
  Robert, 59
  Walter, lord of Kyme, 59, 61
  Sir William, 60
Tanners, 111
Tattershall Castle, 103
Technology, College of, 1
Teetotallers, 233, 250
Telegraph, 240
Telephone, 240–1
Templars, 10, 14
Tennyson family, 152
  Charles, M.P., 196–201, 203, 214n.
  George, 153, 164–7, 170–1, 173–4, 174n., 175, 178, 182, 187–8, 193, 204
  Ralph, 160
Tetney, 32, 69, 136
Theatre, 185
  Royal, 240, 245

Thimolby, John, 95
  Sir John, 89
  Richard, 89, 93–5, 116
  Sir Richard, 93, 95
Thorganby, 70
  Hall, 127
Thorold, 164
  Richard, 188–9
Thornton Abbey, 4
  Abbot of, 91
  College, 92
Tiles, 2, 41, 141, 182
Tillett, Ben, M.P., 286
Timber, 3, 15, 41, 98, 115, 121, 123, 139, 141–2, 152, 204, 223
Times, The, 286–7
Tithes, 32, 69–70, 75, 83, 131, 182
Tolls, 7, 11, 15, 19, 20, 25, 31, 36–7, 42, 52, 64, 141–2, 162
Torksey, 19
Torret Hall, 155n.
Town Clerk, 2, 95, 128, 148, 151–2, 160–1, 174–5, 183, 189, 194–6, 237, 281, 296–7
Town Crier, 219, 219n., 236; see also *Bellman.*
Town Hall, 2, 51, 65, 162, 179, 209, 214, 216, 237
  new, 238, 244
Trade, 10, 15, 19–29; see also *Docks, Statistics, Exports*
Trades' Union Congress, 271
Trafalgar, 194
Trained bands, 123
Tramway, 295
  Company, 239–40
  Immingham, 292
Transportation, 155, 199, 208, 209n.
Trawl, beam, 228
  Fishermen's Society, 267, 272
Treadmill, 186
Treasure, 114
Treasury, 170, 206, 224
Trent, river, 19
Trinidad, 205
Trinity House, Hull, 121–3, 207
Tugs, 269
Turgot, Bishop of St. Andrew's, 8
Turnpike, 161–2, 206
Turves, 41, 99, 104, 107
Twelvemen, 106, 153, 158; see also *Council*
Typhoid, 284

Index

Tyrwhitt, Sir Philip, 134, 134n.
  Sir Robert, 93
  Tristram, 95
  William, 54

Unemployment, 213, 271-2, 278, 285, 298
Upper Sands End, 155n.
Utterby, John, 70
  Robert, 71
  William, 71

Vaccination, 215
Vaughan, Sergeant John, 176, 194-5, 197
Venereal disease, 250-1, 255
Vicar, 221, 221n.
Vicarage, 133
Victoria, Queen, 215
Victoria Street (formerly Loft Street), 19, 104, 237, 280
Vienna, 180
Vignoles, Lt.-Col. W. A., 293, 295
Vyner, Robert, M.P., 150, 151n.
  Thomas, M.P., 145-7

Waith, 43
Wake, Baldwin, 13
Waltham, 43, 158, 196
  toll bar, 206
Watch, 55, 114
  committee, 241-3, 245
Water supply, 182, 217-18, 280, 282, 284, 295
Waterloo, 181, 204
Watkin, Sir Edward William, M.P., 224, 255, 286n.
  A. M., M.P., 255
Waterworks Company, 237, 280, 287
Weapons, 116, 126
Weavers, 5
Weelsby, 1, 70, 75, 148, 209, 295-6; see also *Clee*
Weights and measures, 52, 102
Well, 13; see also *Water Supply*
Wellow Abbey, 1, 4, 8, 15, 19, 32, 41, 54, 69-75, 78, 86-8, 90-1, 172
  abbot of, 8, 37, 51, 72, 77, 83, 86-7, 90
  Milne bank, 110
  parish of St. Augustine of, 51, 72, 81
  with Weelsby, parish of, 162
Wellowgate, 5, 21, 86, 159, 172
Wellowstokelane, 74

Wells, Lord, 4, 59
  Richard, Lord, 61
Wesley, the Rev. Charles, 157
  John, 151, 155-8
Weslyd, Cyriack, 148
  family, 136, 136n., 138
  Philips, 128
  William, 128
West country, 41-2
West Haven, 2-4, 21, 51, 98
West Marsh, 162, 224, 236, 238-9
  enclosure of, 106, 108
  leases, 106, 169, 186-7, 206, 283
  mortgage of, 141
Westmorland, Earls of, 4, 50, 52-4, 58, 60, 80
Whaling, 178-9, 181
Whitby, 39, 48, 101, 163-4, 178, 208, 223, 268
White Friars, 124-5
Whitgift, John, Archbishop of Canterbury, 86, 90
  Robert, abbot of Wellow, 90
Wild fowl, 109
Willoughby, Lord, 4, 59
  of Eresby, Peregrine Bertie, Lord, 124
  of Parham, Francis, Lord, 129
  Sir Robert, 34
Windmill, 14, 108
Windows, glass, 116n.
Wine, 15, 23, 25, 27, 38
Wintringham, John, 224, 237, 239, 249
Wintringham Road, 74
Witham, river, 19
Woad, 27
Wold Newton, 161, 209n.
Women, 57
Wood, 42
Wood, Charles, M.P., 202
  Robert, 163, 170-4
Woodstock, Edmund of, Earl of Kent, 52, 54
Wool, 17, 24-5, 43, 142
Workhouse, 233, 248-9, 252, 255, 258, 273n., 278, 285
  Caistor Union, 249, 276, 285
  Grimsby Union, 286
  Hull and Sculcoates Union, 237
Worksop Priory, 4
World Wars, 293-4
Worms, Hippolyte, 223, 286n.
Worsley, Charles Anderson Pelham, Lord, 213-14, 220

Wray, Sir Christopher (1), 126–7, 129–130
  Sir Christopher (2), 135, 138
  William, 129–30, 133
Wulfoo, 74

Yarborough, Earls of, 163–76, 186–7, 190–1, 193, 196, 198–204, 214–17, 221–3, 237, 259, 277, 289; see also *Pelham, Worsley*
  Hotel, 221, 241
Yarmouth, 24, 255, 272, 288
York, 6, 13, 33, 38
  James, Duke of, 133

Zeeland, 24, 43

GRIMSBY AND MEDIEVAL LINCOLNSHIRE

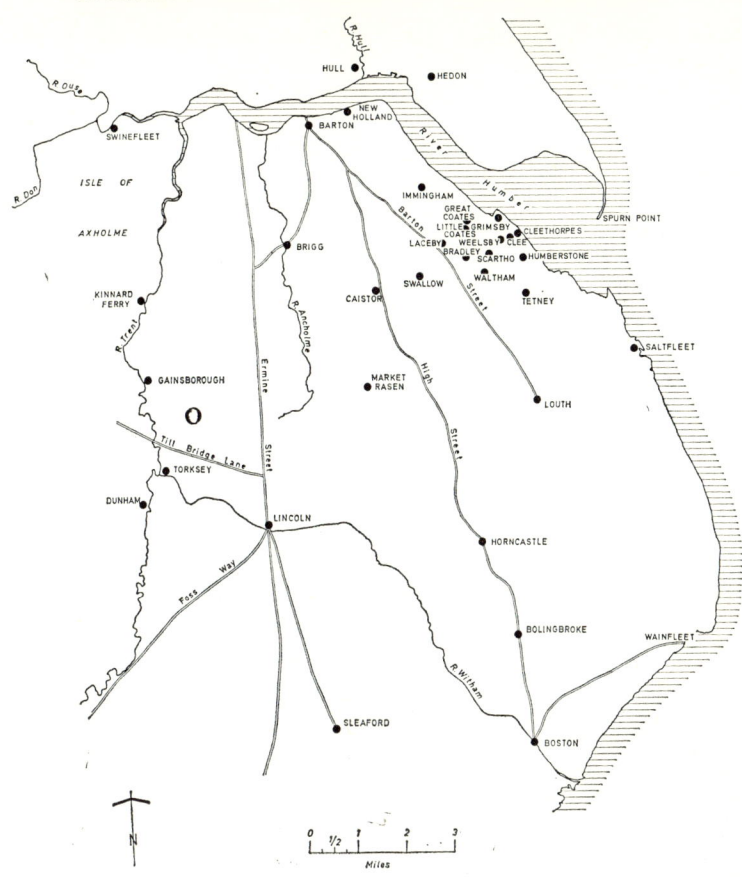

MEDIEVAL GRIMSBY

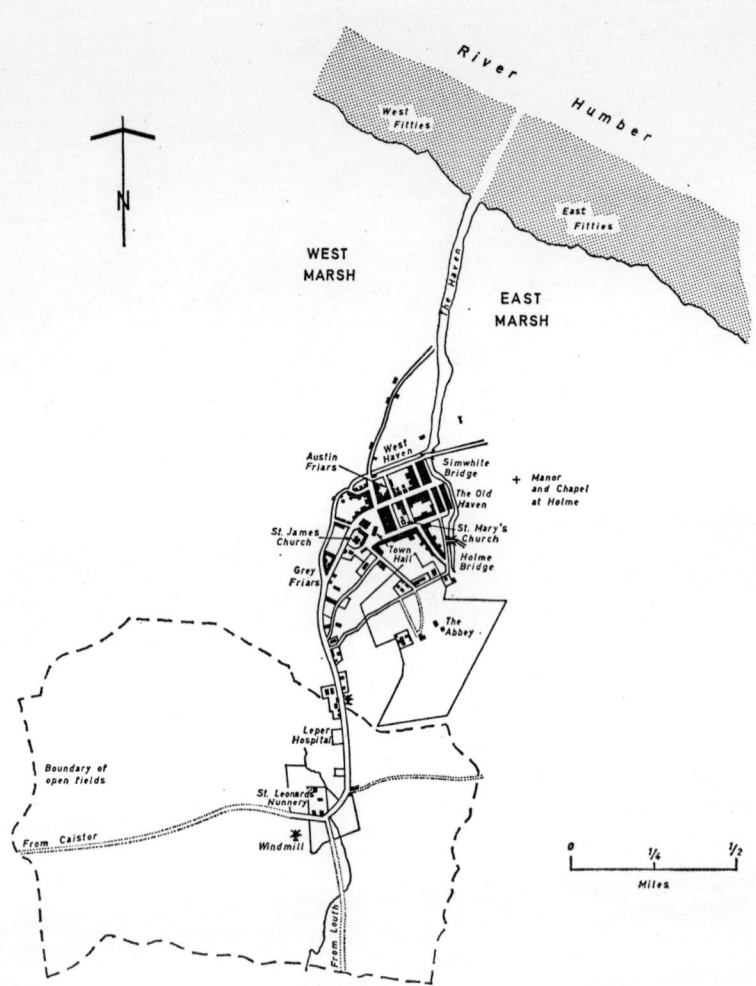

GRIMSBY IN 1625

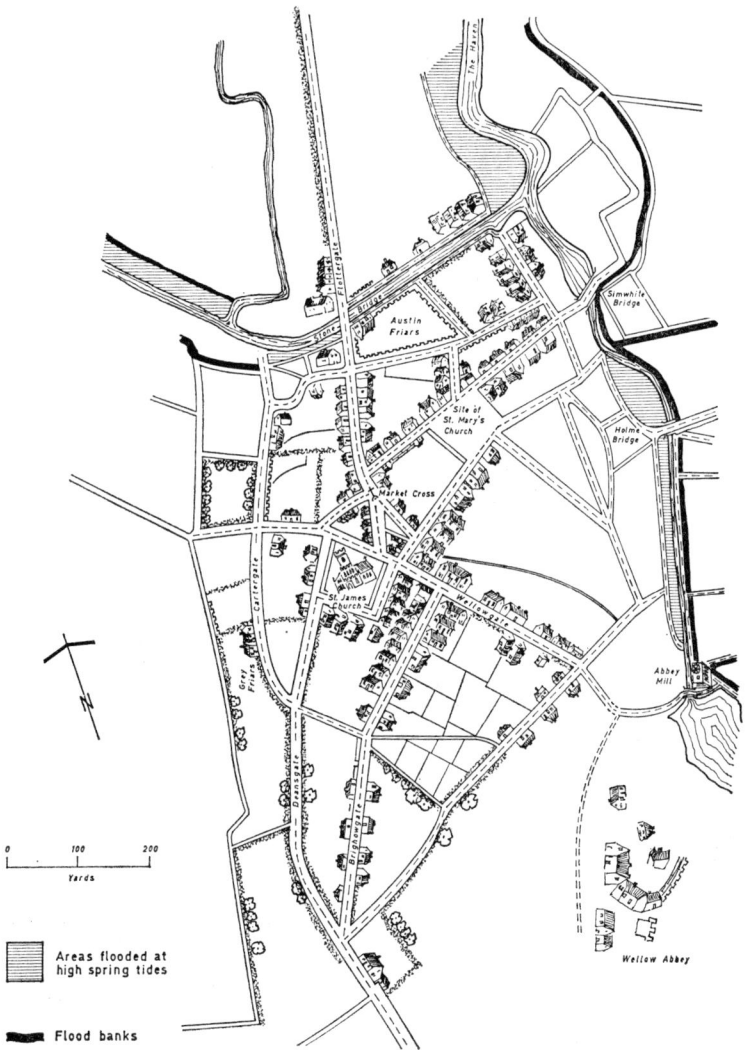

GRIMSBY IN 1840

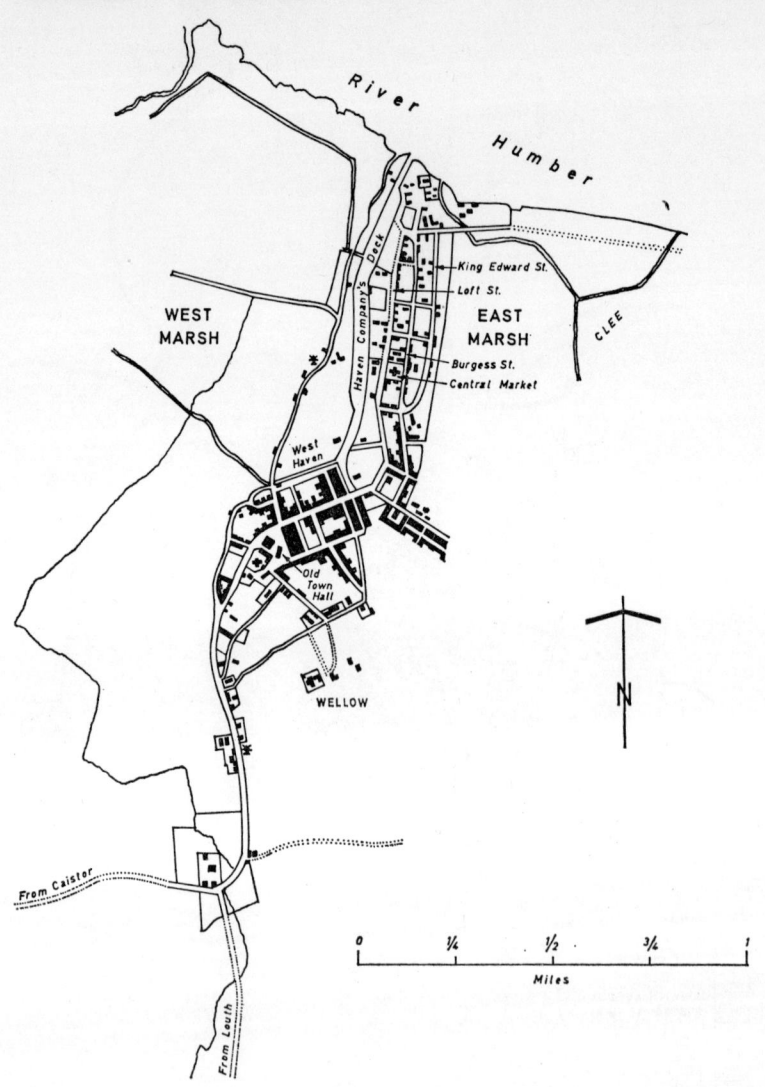

THE GROWTH OF GRIMSBY
(1960 boundaries superimposed on map of <u>circa</u> 1840)

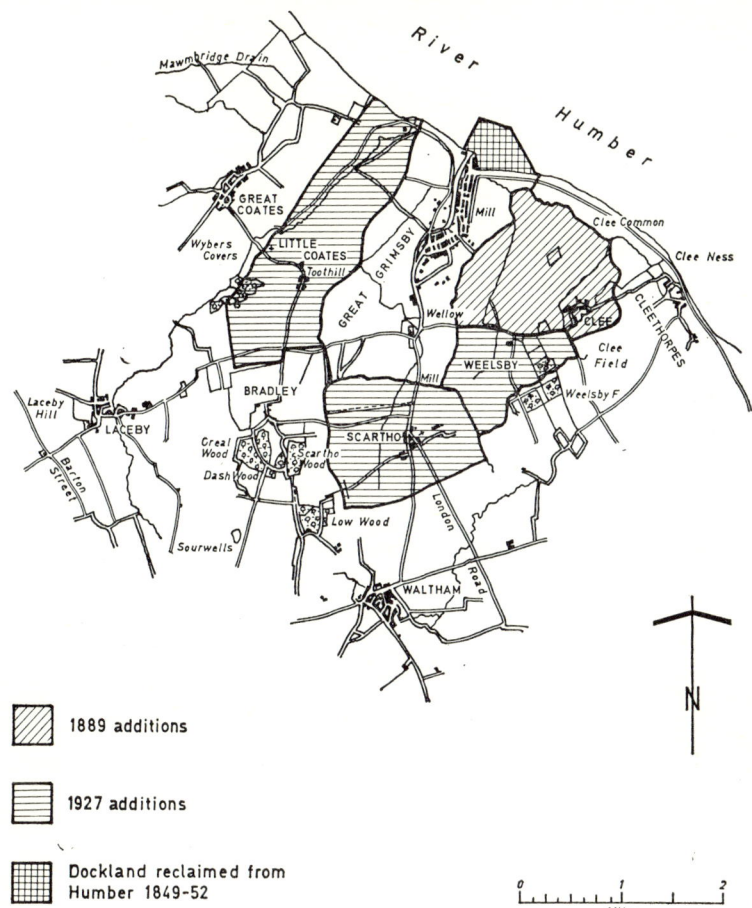

GRIMSBY AND THE DOCKS 1960

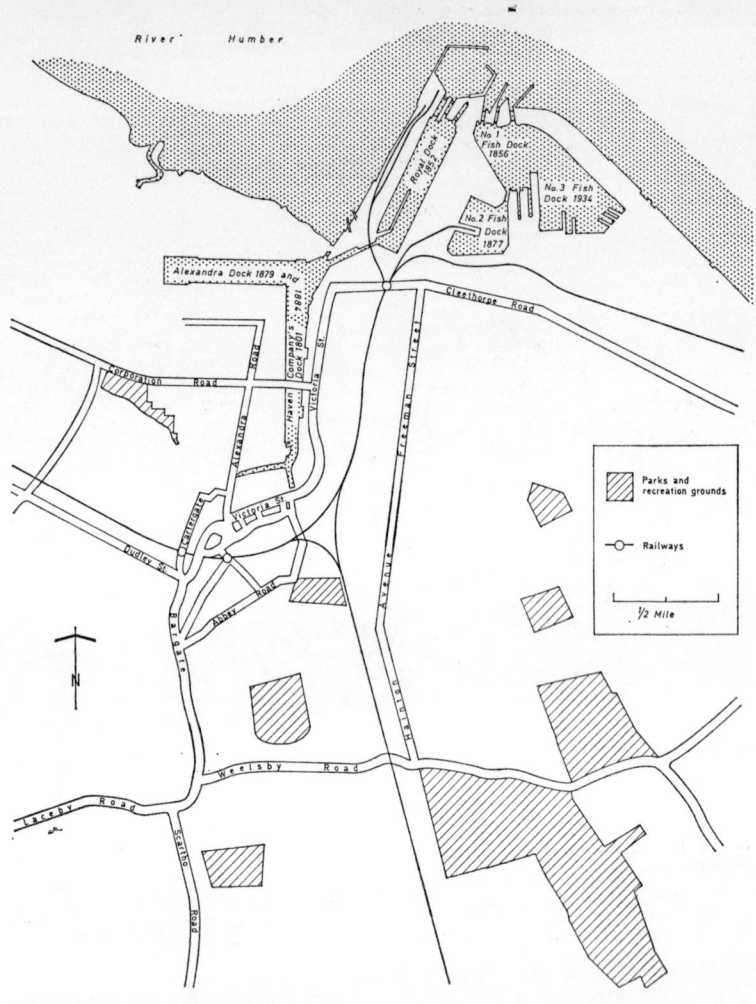